E. Herbert-Caesari

from a drawing by Victor Caesari

E. HERBERT-CAESARI

[Diplomé, La Regia Accademia di Santa Cecilia, Rome]

THE
VOICE OF THE MIND

Foreword by
NOEL BONAVIA-HUNT, M.A.

&

Introductory Lesson by
BENIAMINO GIGLI

LONDON
ROBERT HALE LIMITED

BOSTON
CRESCENDO PUBLISHING COMPANY

© E. Herbert-Caesari 1951 and 1963

First edition 1951
Second edition 1963
Reprinted 1971

ISBN 0 7091 2549 6

Robert Hale & Company
63 Old Brompton Road,
London, S.W.7

SBN 87597 048 6

Library of Congress Card Number 70 123575

Crescendo Publishing Company
48-50 Melrose Street,
Boston, Mass., 02116, U.S.A.

Printed in Great Britain
by Lowe & Brydone (Printers) Ltd., London

*With commingling love and admiration I dedicate
this work to my daughter*

ALMA

*coloratura soprano, who through her superb voice
of moving beauty, her technique, skill and artistry,
is become a rare embodiment of the true Bel Canto
and a lustrous vindication of the one and only
School*

A man cannot bury his meanings so deep in his book but time and like-minded men will not find them.

Emerson

It is simplicity that emerges with all its charm, as the final seal upon art. Whoever hopes to attain this quickly will never achieve it, one cannot begin at the end. One must have studied much, even immensely, to reach this goal, and it is not easy.

Chopin

The human voice remains the most moving, the most plastic, the most beautiful instrument that exists. Only the modern world seems to have forgotten that it is an instrument and that the singer, to achieve perfection, must fashion his or her instrument before attempting to play on it. This the average singer, even the average good singer, notoriously fails to do.

Francis Toye

So many students are unwilling to submit to the toil and drudgery which are as necessary as ever if really solid results are to be achieved. A fatal self-satisfaction seems to be one of the commonest failings of the average singer.

Luisa Tetrazzini

There is a far too prevalent tendency to shirk the real hard (technical) work which must be accomplished before lasting success can be attained. No matter how naturally talented any individual vocalist may be, he or she cannot possibly produce the best results as a singer unless the particular organs have been subjected to a proper and sufficiently long course of training.

Enrico Caruso

Impresarios, Directors of Opera Houses, orchestral conductors, and composers are really worried about the dearth of good voices, and already envisage the possibility that soon some of the best Italian operas will no longer be performed, for lack of good singers. There is a real crisis as regards voices, and things are getting worse every year. If no solution is found we shall have to say farewell to Verdi, Donizetti, and Bellini. The open competitions now being held are for the express purpose of discovering new talent—young singers whose vocal cords have not been ruined by bad teachers,

Extract from the Milan daily
Il Corriere della Sera
February 16, 1937

CONTENTS

ILLUSTRATIONS

Frontispiece   E. HERBERT-CAESARI
BENIAMINO GIGLI   *facing page* 19

DIAGRAMS
by Anthony Caesari

The diagrams illustrating the direction and height of the sound-beams of the different vowels, varying in relation to pitch, may be considered as closely approximate to the actual sensations experienced by the singer whose production is physiologically and acoustically correct. They apply proportionately to every category and calibre of voice; the student, therefore, may consider them to correspond to his or her particular voice, taking into account the slight variations thereof peculiar to the individual voice.

N.B.—As the term "Sound-column", which we used in *The Science and Sensations of Vocal Tone*, is now referable merely to sounds energized in a cavity or resonator, it is no longer appropriate as expressing the character and function of the vocal sound-wave train, or *main stream* of the vibration, proceeding from the larynx upwards. We have chosen, therefore, the term SOUND-BEAM as best expressing this particular phenomenon, since a beam is essentially directional in function and subject to focusing effects.

FOREWORD

FROM CHILDHOOD it has been my lot to listen to musical sounds, sounds from pianos, sounds from organs, sounds from violins, sounds from orchestras, sounds from throats. In my adolescent days I heard some really good singing, and my father was a severe critic of vocal tone. He had his own ideas, too, of how voices should be produced and I can realize how near he was to the truth as I recall many of his theories. But today! Whatever would he have said about the vocalists that scream and wobble all around us, vying with each other to get their voices across the ether and the atmosphere? My father used to insist on "natural and effortless beauty of tone" produced by methods in harmony with Nature's laws and resulting from a correct technique. He did not set up as a teacher—he was far too preoccupied in other spheres of activity; but he could detect the slightest flaw in vocal production. From him I learned *something* of this art, but what is of greater importance, I inherited from him my keen interest in beautiful sounds.

If the human voice is the grandest of all musical instruments, it is indubitably the worst treated today. How often on hearing a singer and his instrumental accompanist have I prayed for vocal silence! The accompanist is too often far the greater artist and his instrument far finer in musical quality than that plied by the singer. Moreover, the accompanist's personality is so much more attractive, setting the example of restrained humility that the singer would do well to emulate. If only the latter could be prevailed upon to use his organ in like mood and manner, he might rise to nobler emotions and cease to irritate the listener with that terrible self-conscious emotionalism. When in addition to this straining of sentiment he defiles the air with a succession of sounds that insult every law of Nature, one begins to wish that Nature had not endowed human beings with the vocal organism. Sing naturally, sing correctly, sing humbly—this is the message I would hand to every manipulator of voice.

But who can teach the art of singing? Fate has brought me into close touch with many preceptors each of whom has hugged the notion that *he* alone holds the secret of vocal technique. And, of course, he *may* be the fortunate possessor of that secret. A man who fondly imagines that he has the golden key is not necessarily a vain boaster or a charlatan. Most of these folk have an inkling of the truth, and their mistake is to suppose that they know all the truth. On analysis I have found that upon a very small substratum of truth they have in varying ways built an accretion of fallacies, some imported, some self-evolved, which completely vitiate the whole system. The lurid light of cold scientific law disintegrates such false systems into a collection of ill-fitting units incapable of forming a logical whole. And were there no science to play the part of critic, the pupils themselves would amply justify the condemnation which these methods merit. The acid test that a tree is known by its fruits applies with as much cogency to vocal systems as it does to personal character.

Having over a number of years subjected the phenomena of vocal technique to a close and critical examination, and linked them up with allied sound systems, I am not surprised at the lamentable failure of present-day methods of voice training. Nature's insulted law is vindicating itself in the studio and the concert room. And it need not be so. For the art of singing is not lost, as the chapters of this book abundantly testify.

I well remember the day when I first made the personal acquaintance of the author. Imagine the feeling of relief and joy which I experienced as he unfolded to me the main theme of his teaching method and enunciated with a clarity of exposition that made me envy his pupils those principles of vocal technique which are embodied in his earlier book * and still further elaborated in the present volume. His system I found to be truer to scientific laws than that of any other in the field of my acquaintance. And he was getting results. Strange this anticipation by the old Italian School of the subsequent findings of physical science! I attribute it to a wise, not to say uncanny, combination of intuition and common sense. The thread of truth has been handed on through generations of teachers and singers till at length it has been woven into a texture which we now call the Italian method. Yet Italy— like all other countries—has her charlatans, and the criterion of results has to be applied there as elsewhere. For this reason it is

---

* *The Science and Sensations of Vocal Tone* (Dent, 1936, 1950).

very necessary to refer to the *old* School when speaking of the Italian method, and the author of this book stands in line with that old School. That School will come into its own again, thanks to this book and to the justification which modern science has been able to give it. Those of my fellow-countrymen who ardently desire to assist the revival of the vocal art in full swing are recommended to read this book and digest its contents. In it they will find treasures both old and new. They will realize, long before many pages have been turned, that the road to perfection is steep and difficult, and cannot be rushed. And the author is only too well aware of this fact: he is, therefore, deeply concerned with the student's point of view and the need for encouragement along the thorny path of progress. He takes the reader by the hand and helps him at every successive step towards the desired goal. Thus gradually the wings of freedom are formed till at length the student becomes the accomplished artist able to ply his instrument with a joyous independence and a supreme self-assurance. The goal of all true art is naturalness: every singer is asked to be true to his best self and to treat his vocal organs with due respect. He must not try to run before he has learned to walk and he must be sure that Nature sanctions every effort. This is very ordinary common sense, and the author's pages exhibit the philosophy of common sense in every line. Yet this alone would not suffice: instruction, experience and enlightenment must go hand in hand, and the student must work out his own salvation with patience and perseverance. With a good master at his side this work is transformed into an inexpressible joy, hope is wedded to enthusiasm, and the acquisition of new, strange powers is vividly felt. Those who make the great adventure offered to them by the author of this book will assuredly experience all this and more, and they will materially contribute their quota to the new school of British technique which we hope will not too far hence be reared in this country on the stable foundation of Nature's laws.

NOEL BONAVIA-HUNT

B

Ad Alma Cesari,
con la più viva simpatia
e ammirazione artistica
Biavietti
1946

INTRODUCTORY LESSON
By Beniamino Gigli
(With authorized comments in italics by the author)

ALL THE CELEBRATED singers of the past, other than Italian, such as Sims Reeves, Charles Santley, Emma Albani, Marcella Sembrich, Nellie Melba, Victor Maurel, Marcel Journet, Dinh Gilly, and others, not only were well acquainted with the Italian language but knew from experience that the so-called Italian vowels A, E, I, O, U (or rather, the five vowels as conceived and pronounced by the Italians) constitute the *true basis* of voice and song, that is, of the Bel Canto. They all knew that in order to sing well a sound knowledge of Italian is indispensable— that is, a knowledge of the language as spoken by the Italians themselves, a language that knows no other vowel sounds than the above-mentioned (and of course modifications thereof), that has no nasal, no guttural, and no harsh sounds whatever. The Italian talks with these five vowels both in their purest form, and with slight modifications thereof for the purposes of greater expression and accentuation, according to circumstances. Furthermore, the Italian's conception of these five vowels in relation to his own spoken language demands imperatively that they be produced on a clear and flowing basis. A good Italian singer—a product of the real School, one and only, *speaks* as he sings for the very reason that basically he expresses himself mainly with the aforesaid five pure fluid vowels, which for convenience sake are called Italian, or classic, but which as a matter of fact are found in practically every language of civilized and uncivilized peoples, although not always, or shall we say rarely, if at all, under the same purity of form and colour and accentuation as known to the Italian.

I also share the view that *good singing must be based on the five vowels*, a, e, i, o, u, in their purest form, and modifications thereof.

[*Gigli means of course five pure monophthongal sounds (i.e., single vowel sounds). For instance:* AH, *as in* father; EH, *as in* Mary, there,

19

or that in May *(the first sound, and not the* i*)*; EE, *as in* feel; OH, *as in* police, polite, *or that in* rose *(the first sound, and not the* u*)*; OO, *as in* pool. *Inversely the diphthongal form abounds in English, such as* AHi, EHi, OHu *(I say go)*. *Only very rarely are the two sounds written in English as in the case is* flow, yellow, *etc. The general practice is for two sounds to be embedded in one letter. Take the phrase,* I gave him a useful rope: *We find* AHi gEHiv him EHi iOOsful rOHOOp. *There are no such double sounds implied in one written vowel in the Italian language; they write out every spoken vowel sound, and speak every written vowel, with very few exceptions.*]

Now as regards the formation of these vowels in relation to singing I must bring into sharp focus a highly important factor, viz.: the absolute necessity for *mentally* conceiving beforehand the vowel sound and its colour or timbre, whether in pure or modified form, that one wishes, or is about, to produce. In other words, *every vowel sound must be mentally shaped and mentally given the requisite colour*, according to circumstances, *before* being physically produced on a natural and spontaneous basis, fluid and untrammelled. Certain methods aim at a heavily emphasized vowel production solely on a physical basis and without any *mental* shaping and colouring beforehand. Which can only lead to grossly exaggerated forms with consequent stiffening, in degree, of the parts engaged in such production; the tonal product suffers accordingly. Any exaggeratedly emphasized vowel sound constricts the throat; and assuredly no tone issuing from a clamped adjustment and setting, however slight the constriction, can ever be spontaneous, harmonious, and expressive, let alone beautiful.

Inversely, the very fact of *mentally* conceiving, and *mentally shaping* and colouring *each vowel sound* to be sung (in pure or modified form according to what one has to express) *before* producing it, induces simple and spontaneous (natural) movements of the parts concerned. *This is what I have always done myself, and this is what I advise every singer to do.* And if he or she is not used to this mental work of preparation, not having been taught it, I would sincerely advise him to start right away to cultivate this vitally important habit. It merely demands concentrated vigilance over a certain period of time. With patient and persevering practice the thinking and doing merge as one, a flash split-second action.

[*Antonio Cotogni, admittedly Italy's greatest baritone of all time, and brilliant exponent of the old School, gave the author the following advice in* 1907 *when a student in Rome—advice which is correlated to and confirms Gigli's own statements, and practice, on this very subject: "Remember that* always *you must* mentally *shape each vowel and impart to it the right colour, timbre, and expression before* actually *producing it." And when, somewhat astounded and very much impressed (not having heard of such a thing before) I almost demurred: "What, always, and every vowel sound?" Cotogni answered, "Yes, every vowel and always, for as long as you are a singer and sing; the habit is soon acquired, and such thinking before doing becomes really quite an easy matter." Verily such thinking is "the shape of things to come" (tonal things). We have always stressed this point with excellent results to pupils, adding, "Think more and do less."*]

When one has to pass from one vowel to another on the same note, or an interval, it is necessary, imperative even, to avoid any sudden or brusque change of the internal shaping and tonal setting. As far as the high notes are concerned I can say that the passing from one vowel to another (or, say, consecutively to all the vowels one after the other) on the same pitch, for example, is barely felt; in other words, the difference of position of the focused tone in the resonance cavity between one vowel and the next is so slight as to be barely noticeable.

[*This bears out what we explained on this point on p.* 51 *(and pp.* 79–81 *of the parent work:* The Science and Sensations of Vocal Tone), *viz., that, when production is correct, the sound-beams of AH, AW, OH, OO, when sung on the same high pitch, are so close together as to be almost touching, and that, consequently, the passing from one vowel to the next is barely felt, if at all, by the singer himself. When, however, we go from one of the above four vowels to EH or EE, then some difference of position is felt, in degree, relatively great or small according to the individual. Indeed, there can be no hard and fast rule on this delicate point because voices, like faces and bodies and minds, while based on one universal model or mould, each have slight, and often marked, variations of detail of form and expression; consequently the actual shape of the mouth-pharynx and head cavities will vary ever so slightly from individual to individual (a point to be reckoned with). Each individual, therefore, is something of a law unto himself in this respect. When Gigli speaks of little or no movement from vowel to vowel, on high notes, he means specifically an oil-smooth action of tongue and palate and pharynx while they are co-operating in the internal shaping that we identify as vowels, as soon as the tonal stream pours into the various shapes (vowels) and out again into space. The difference in the shaping from vowel to vowel is of course slight, and each shape, or each vowel, must merge, or melt, so to speak, into the next with perfect smoothness.*

Gigli is anxious to stress the fact that the merging of one vowel into the other should be so smooth in action as to preclude any brusque or rough movement internally where the change of shape for each vowel in the mouth-pharynx cavity is so slight that the mere thought of making the gliding change is sufficient to produce the required physical effect. This, after all, is the key to legato *singing. There must be no deliberate physical attempt to do this shaping of the various vowels, because the singer will invariably overdo and over-emphasize the actual adjustment of the parts. After all, speech and singing is thinking aloud; in speech, no one sets about deliberately shaping lips, tongue and palate, because they adjust themselves automatically as a result of thousands of generations of humans "thinking aloud" to one another. Undoubtedly the vowels subconsciously are shaped a split-second before the physical utterance. In singing, however, where we have pitches rising well above those of speech, and where we have a vocal mechanism to deal with, the mental formation of the vowels before their physical utterance must be deliberate and well planned, whereupon the physical parts adjust themselves automatically in strict compliance thereto. The shaping thought is invariably accurate, and therefore also the physical adjustment, provided the singer knows exactly the sound of, and what shape, his tonal product (vowel) should be on every pitch. And this is a question of training; it was one of the pillars of the old School.]*

The vowels EE and EH, OH and OO, are narrow sounds, in degree, on the low and lower medium notes. But once we are on the high pitches they must be given ample space for development, just as if they were of the same "aperture" as the AH vowel. Which space-providing for purposes of tonal amplification is made primarily with the *mind* and the *will* of the singer (cervella e volontà).

[Here again Gigli stresses the mental factor; he means here that the singer should mentally anticipate and mentally gauge and provide for the exact internal space for appropriate resonant development (amplification) of the vowelled tone, and will the whole to happen. To create space in this way the singer must get MENTALLY BEHIND and ABOVE the tonal focus—particularly on all notes from E♭, fourth space, upwards. The physical reaction within the mouth-pharynx is immediate

and adequate. Also to think "back of the vertical" is definitely space-creating. Gigli invariably stresses the combination of "brain and will" (cervello e volontà) when discussing technique.] (See Chapter XII.)

It is all a question of thought and will exercised and developed for some considerable time by the singer, first during his studies and then on the operatic stage or concert platform.

The EE vowel, in particular, is a very much narrower sound than AH when produced on low and lower medium notes; consequently it neither has nor can it be given the same amplification as the latter on these low pitches.

[*The physical reason for the feeling of narrower vowel sound is that the tongue, in order to produce the EE vowel, rises close to the arc of the palate while the soft palate descends in degree, thus leaving only a very narrow aperture between the tongue surface and palatal arc. And the lower the pitch the closer the approximation and consequently the narrower the tonal feeling of EE, the sound having a mere slit of an aperture in which to develop and leave the mouth. Hence the sensation on the low notes of tonal compression-cum-narrowness of space and position.*]

Inversely, when sung on a high or head note the EE vowel can, and should, be given the same space for tonal amplification as AH.

[*As the pitch rises the mouth-pharynx cavity should be shaped gradually towards an oval internally in a vertical direction; in which case the tongue will not, and cannot, arch so much nor the soft palate descend so much, thus leaving a greater space (or aperture between tongue surface and roof of mouth) for the tone to develop and soar into the head cavities, and then rebound into the mouth and out to an admiring world. Gigli, at this juncture, in order to illustrate his ideas, sang some phrases of operatic arias. The tone was beautiful, continuous and fluid; the passing from vowel to vowel, word to word, was made without any noticeable or, say, barely appreciable change of internal shaping, particularly on the high notes. And then for further demonstration, he went just from vowel to vowel on the same pitch, then up the scale, and finally in intervals. All consonants, moreover, were clear cut and so naturally prepared and released without a trace of exaggeration (and certainly no "mouthing", as the constant forward-production method induces) that the tonal stream suffered no appreciable "cuts" therefrom, giving the impression that he speaks as he sings—as in fact he does. But everyone knows that Gigli's diction is perfect, effortless, oil-smooth.*]

You see, the passing from one vowel to the next is made above all MENTALLY, and without any direct, willed physical effort in this sense. I do not dwell on the physical, but primarily on the mental shaping and on the gliding-merging of vowel to vowel internally. When the thinking is correctly based, the physical part reacts and adjusts itself accordingly, with equal accuracy. My singing I *create in my mind* first of all. *It must be so.* After all, everything in the world is a product of thought, human and divine; everything made by man is the result of thought, a mental concept. And SHAPE plays a highly important part.

[*Gigli again sang some well-known phrases: it was a joy to listen to him, and to watch, as the lovely tones issued from that throat of throats. I found myself muttering "What a singing machine the man is". As he attacked the syllable Vi of "Viva" in the Brindisi of* Cavalleria Rusticana, *how he opened his mouth, after releasing the V consonant, to permit the amplification and emergence of that sparkling ee vowel of his! In fact, it was shaped and open practically as much as if he were producing the AH vowel. (As I listened and watched it occurred to me what a grand object lesson this would be for so many students, singers, and teachers who ignorantly or misguidedly cultivate the habit of keeping the mouth with just a slot-like opening when singing the ee vowel on the upper medium and high pitches.) Then he produced a series of high G's and A's on the AH vowel, modifying the vowelled tone from dark to openish timbre. Be it noted that these openISH high G's and A's which he purposely produced for demonstration purposes, may seem to the un-tutored, or not too finely trained, ear to be too "open", when in fact they have just sufficient tonal (vowel) modification or rounding to avoid blatancy. These openISH tones, when they are not pushed to extremes, as is easily possible, can be very effective, and are what the old School called "chiaro-scuro", meaning an openish vowel-tone with just sufficient vowel modification or rounding to avoid blatancy. The great Antonio Cotogni explained to me, in 1907, the subtle significance of "chiaro-scuro" (light-dark) in vocal tone. It conveys the idea of a clean, bright tone with a darkish rim round it, and vice versa, a darkish tone with a bright rim. It means a beautifully balanced tonal colouring of light and shade. The good singer is able to produce at will nuances of either type. Gigli often produces these tones, and at times opens them out more than most singers could without becoming blatant; and he will do this on the AH, OH and EH vowels right up to high G sharp, and occasionally A natural, in opera and in concerts. But the tones are so balanced as to avoid blatancy or vulgarity. The line of demarcation is extremely subtle. Listening to his special demonstration on these lines one noticed that the vowelled tones were given that small curving, or modification, which spelt, as Gigli puts it: "The exact measure" (la giusta misura). Not all tenors can, or should, produce tones as "open" as Gigli's for they may not have his qualities of subtle pliability and fast, accurate adaptability of the mobile parts within the mouth-pharynx cavity. And, moreover, not many tenors, if any, have Gigli's MIND.]*

For my part, I would not teach or recommend all tenors to produce certain of these openish tones. Every singer, whatever his category of voice, male or female, is in a sense a law unto himself in this respect because, in view of individual variations in structure and in the actual quality and degree of pliability and adaptability of the mobile parts concerned in the internal shaping, not all voices, indeed few do, lend themselves so readily to certain tonal nuances. Consequently, every singer must experiment on his own voice, preferably with the aid of a really knowledgeable teacher (alas, so few today), as to how much, or how little, he can "open" an AH, or OH, or EH vowel on an upper medium pitch, or on certain head notes, without degenerating into tonal blatancy, in which vulgarity is just round the corner. This is absolutely an individual matter and can only be solved individually. There must be no slavish imitation of anybody at any time. Then again, the employment of these openish tones must be governed by and depend on the psychological moment, what emotion has to be expressed, and what the singer has to portray with may be only just one note. Here again the vowel and its colouring (modification) is the basis of and KEY to the situation, as in fact it is to every vocal situation. Let the student bear this highly important factor constantly in mind. A correctly balanced vocal mechanism teaches the singer himself to a fine point how much the tone may or may not be "opened", and just how much it should be "gathered up" (raccolto), or closed (rounded) to avoid blatancy.

[The openish or chiaro-scuro tone is one produced with a vowel such as AH, AW, OH or EH that has had, so to speak, the "corner" curved or rounded off just sufficiently to smooth over the tonal "point" or pointed-ness; mechanically it means a very slight rounding of the pharyngeal cavity (internal mouth); but the singer, to obtain this slight curving or rounding, merely THINKS of the exact amount of the vowel modification he wishes to have, and of the timbre or "colour" the modification

gives to the tone. To this mental shaping we get an exact physical reaction: the mobile parts of the mouth-pharynx adjust themselves accordingly. The singer must never attempt the actual physical curving, however slight, because inevitably he will overdo it. For instance, to round off slightly the open AH, as in father, all the singer has to do is THINK of the already modified AH vowel sound to be found in words such as song, sorry, promise. *Although written with O, the sound is a modified AH that we distinguish as AH^2 in this and in the parent work; which sound also has its characteristic shape.*]

When the vocal mechanism is correct and the singer really knows *what* to do, the *how* and *why*, there should be no difficulty in producing a high note with any vowel.

As regards breathing in relation to singing, I would point out that when production is not correct there can be no balanced breathing, no adequate, no accurate dosage or control of the outgoing breath to sustain the position of the tone itself; in which case the singer has to fall back on great muscular effort.

The basis of the breath "tank" is the diaphragm; and the exact dosage of the outgoing breath to produce, sustain and feed a given tone according to the singer's thought and will (pensiero e volontà) depends firstly (basically) on the proper action of the diaphragm, and secondly (and highly important auxiliary) on that of the lower or "floating" ribs. When a vowelled tone is not well positioned or placed, be it *f* or *p*, when it is not correctly sustained by the breath (appoggiato) and "tuned in", it gives a "hanging" impression (a ciondolone), a tonal flatness and slackness that assuredly lácks character and "telling" qualities; it will have little or no expression and "complexion". With such tones, particularly in *mezzavoce* singing, the breath escapes together with the tonal stream, diluting and weakening it. As a result the full phrase cannot be completed properly for lack of breath, much having been lost in this way without benefiting the tone. Every tone must be well positioned, sustained (appoggiato) and tuned in. And the thought and will of the singer contribute positively and in no small measure to this tonal positioning and sustaining. Without a balanced positioning-sustaining no tone can possibly have or be given colour, accent, and expression; consequently it will be more or less "dead". Inversely, every tone produced must be given a colourful life in exact degree (in giusta misura) according to circumstances.

Come and stand in front of me. See how I take breath. Put your hands here. Feel how during inspiration my diaphragm is lowered (thus pushing out the abdominal wall) and how lateral rib expansion completes the act. Feel again how the abdominal wall has now somewhat sunk inwards (as a result of the sideways expansion of the lower ribs), and how *flexible* all is. Note particularly that there is no rigidity or hardness at all in this region, but just a flexible firmness with "give" in it. And note well, furthermore, that AS SOON AS I COMMENCE TO SING I FORGET ALL ABOUT THE DIAPHRAGM AND RIBS, *all about the breathing machinery and its action*, and sing on the air accumulated right underneath the larynx.

[*At this juncture Gigli touched his chest just below the larynx. He forcibly stressed, by repetition, the above words (which are verbatim) about forgetting his breathing machinery after he has taken in breath and starts to sing. And teachers, students, and singers are well advised to bear this in mind. Knowing the importance of the breathing factor, and aware of the generally accepted erroneous ideas on the subject, Gigli again said to me: "Feel here again as I take breath, here in the pit of the stomach where the action of the diaphragm can be felt, and note how as I complete the inspiratory act and commence to sing there is no hardening or stiffening of the abdominal wall and behind it." Thereupon, as he took breath and started to sing, I placed the palm of my hands on his lower ribs, left and right, and pressed my thumbs firmly into that part of the abdominal wall which lies just under and between the lower or "floating" ribs. The whole was firm, but supple and resilient to palm touch and thumb pressure with an elastic "give" in the parts; there was no trace of rigidity or hardening anywhere. Incidentally, as a matter of additional interest, I would state that I have similarly "laid hands" on the breathing machinery in action of a number of world-famous singers. The tale, in every case, is exactly as told above by Gigli. It could not be otherwise. And this refers to the male singers, because women do not inbreathe exactly like the men do, as is explained in a later chapter, although there are a very few exceptions.*]

Finally, I just want to say a few words in regard to the "Nota Tenuta" (marked *Ten*). It has an inherent duration value that is neither too long nor too short. If held too long it rapidly degenerates into vulgarity; if too short it will fail of true expression. Either way it will fall short of æsthetic and artistic values. Certain singers erroneously believe they are securing a fine effect by holding a note for a longer time than its exact measure (giusta misura). Aesthetic law and that governing expression cannot be disregarded with impunity. For the right expression and telling effect on the audience the note should be held for an exact time value which is regulated with fine precision by an artistic-æsthetic sense that may be innate in a singer (who thus feels it instinctively), or acquired by long experience.

BENIAMINO GIGLI

London: December, 1946

CHAPTER I

PROSPECT AND PERSPECTIVE

WELL MAY THE STUDENT of singing, as he stands bewildered amidst the chaos of conflicting vocal systems, ask himself if there exists anywhere an ultimate goal to reach. It is a fact that everywhere the student, to whom this questioning is perhaps one of the deepest concerns of his life, is seeking and demanding an answer to it. If there were no ultimate truth, no reality in vocal technique, if there were no reward for the earnest seeker, this uncertainty would be without meaning. But the very fact that there is such a universal questioning bears witness to the existence of that which is sought.

With a melancholy self-confession of failure so many students of singing, after years and perhaps a lifetime of striving, reach the conclusion that the phenomenon of vocal mechanics is something that partakes of the incomprehensible, something beyond the common grasp. Baffled by the supposed mystery, their minds can frame only a dim and delusive image of the whole.

Even as he who gazes at the sun unassisted by instruments wrought by science from natural elements can receive no true impression of it, seeing but little of its shape and nothing of its detail, so the student deprived of the assistance of elements furnished by a combination of science and empiricism cannot readily conceive a true picture of vocal mechanism with its detailed phenomena.

If a thing is Real, existent, it is THERE for the seeking, and unalterably so, even if no thought were given to it and no attempt made to discover it. Vocal mechanism is a Reality, and embedded therein are the laws of physiology and acoustics. Whether or not the phenomena of vocal mechanics can be made intelligible to a student will depend firstly on the exactness of the knowledge imparted to him, secondly on the form of its presentation and exposition, thirdly on his understanding, his powers of deduction, of apprehension.

The reality of vocal mechanism can be reached only through its particular laws. It is not incomprehensible; it does not lie beyond the sphere of sense nor beyond the grasp of anyone seeking the truth.

Behind the features of correct vocal tone in the form perceived by the listener lie the mechanical phenomena of which it is a pure, concrete manifestation. And behind the phenomena lies Reality: the sum total of vocal mechanics, the long-sought goal of vocal aspiration.

The knowledge of vocal mechanics such as we possess is derived from and built primarily upon natural elements. CORRECT SENSATIONS OF VOCAL TONE, interpreted in their proper light, will be found to REFLECT WITH EXTRAORDINARY FIDELITY THE MECHANICAL ADJUSTMENTS OBTAINING WITHIN THE VIBRATOR AND RESONATOR SYSTEMS. An accurate knowledge of the working of *both* systems is indispensable. Only in the light of the extended vision accruing therefrom will the student be able to examine in detail what before he could not discern in outline, for true sensations of vocal tone are the exponents, the externalization of such physiologic-acoustic laws that appertain to the creation and production of voice.

With the aid of knowledge, seeking sharpens our vision as we strive to peer through the phenomena of the sensations into the reality that lies behind them. According to individual capacity there are degrees in the horizon of vision as well as degress in the horizon of purpose.

A certain type of mind is readily stirred to anger by new ideas, or, shall we say, a novel form of presentation of fundamental truths. Hostility narrows and shutters receptivity. Unless we are sure of our ground it is never profitable to live exclusively within the fixed boundaries of our own ideas, however good they may seem to us, for none of us can afford to reject ideas and expositions that appear to be destructive of the barriers behind which we feel, or pretend to feel, comfortably secure. Change of attitude is a rare virtue, for it requires moral courage to face those stern things called facts.*

* "We are incredibly heedless in the formation of our beliefs, but find our-selves filled with an illicit passion for them when anyone proposes to rob us of their companionship. It is obviously not the ideas themselves that are dear to us, but our self-esteem which is threatened. . . . We like to continue to believe what we have been accustomed to accept as true . . ." Professor James Harvey Robinson (*The Mind in the Making*).

In certain respects it is misleading to say that we learn from experience. If experience is based on false premises, as is too often the case today in the teaching of singing, what really useful experience can a student acquire except of the bitterest from which only a rude awakening can emancipate him and set his feet on the right road. The capacity to learn from experience, bitter or otherwise, seemingly is a rare gift. Bitter experience is useful when it is salutary, when it shocks the individual out of a fool's paradise, when it acts as a lodestar. It is remarkable how even intelligent people will hold tenaciously, aye stubbornly, to wrong ideas imparted to them by a teacher the weight of whose knowledge and authority is an unknown quantity and merely suggested by rhetorical jingle. Even in the face of constructive experience a certain type of mind will reach false conclusions. The prevalence, and seeming prosperity, of the fallacies abounding in the modern world of song indicate clearly how little students challenge the overture of ideas introduced often with the trumpetings of incompetence.

If we desire a scientific approach to vocal mechanics we cannot rest content to base conclusions on experience alone, even if of the right kind; we must also be informed and guided by theory, because theory is a necessary instrument of thought for disentangling the apparently complex nature of the phenomena.

If a fallacy is accepted without challenge or question by a student it eventually crystallizes into a belief. And by dint of exercising this fallacy not only will the belief become more deeply rooted in his mind but he will theorize about it and enthusiastically glorify it. He will attempt to forge a number of such beliefs into a semblance of reality, suffusing it with false intelligibility. False theories accrue from false, and from wrongly expounded laws. What then is the value of such "knowledge" even if based on practical experience?

How can the student bridge the gap between understanding and reality? By means of the theoretical "link" which makes the crossing possible. Theories are not laws although closely related to them. Science explains laws by means of theories, or rather the erecting of theoretical models. Consequently, the student should not be satisfied with a mere nodding acquaintance with the particular laws governing vocal mechanism but should strive to gain a scientific insight into their meaning and working, and so attain an intelligent grasp of the organic whole. Then, and then only, will he be in a position to expound these laws to himself as well as to others, with benefit to himself, his fellow students, and the art as a whole.

Every effort should he devote to the discovery of the laws in question in order to render vocal nature intelligible primarily to himself. By vocal nature we mean the degree of mechanical completeness, fitness, and efficiency inherent in the vocal organs in general, and in his own in particular. Very rarely is this degree so high as to border on, let alone touch, the hundred per cent. mark.*

The average voice reveals a fairly high degree of mechanical incompleteness; but that is precisely where the teacher's art steps in. Through mental and muscular re-education the mechanism can be developed, completed, and restored to its rightful heritage, and to such a high degree of efficiency that it is indistinguishable from that of a completely natural voice.

What the student requires is not a profound erudition in either physiology or acoustics but a practical working knowledge of such aspects of the particular laws as apply to his art.

We believe that, like a natural law, a complete "school" of vocal mechanics is something which lies hidden in reality until discovered by the seeker. By the same token it is not unreasonable to assume that all inventions or discoveries always actually existed, were THERE for the seeking thousands of years ago, aye, since the world took shape. The laws were *there* from the beginning, *there* for the seeking. In the past they formed part of the imponderable. Today, discovery has vested them with intelligibility. The once inconceivable and incomprehensible we now take for granted.

Pure vocal mechanism IS, not was, not will be. Its immutable laws await, in eternal vigil, *individual* discovery and externalization.

Without craftsmanship there can be no true art even though intelligence and imagination are present in high degree, for they can never fill the gap of imperfect technique. Only a sound technique can give the singer mastery of the means of expression; only when a vocal tone is of accurate form and pattern can he pour into it such expression and emotional colouring as will complete its content.

* In Italy the author has heard several *completely* natural voices in which all tones, with all vowels, were models of mechanical perfection from the lowest to the highest pitch. In these exceptional cases Nature had *completed* the mechanism (see footnote, p. 49).

If with the aid of proven concepts the student is able to discover for himself the laws governing vocal mechanics and make them his own, so to speak, he will order his experience accordingly. Gradually these laws will be to him both revealing and predicting: revealing the "nature" or degree of mechanical fitness existing *de facto* in his own vocal organs, and predicting how the failings of vocal-mechanical incompleteness will ultimately conform to and express these laws with adequacy. Such individual discovery of the laws will satisfy the student's intellectual desire in this direction. Practical application then enters upon a comparatively easy stage, and experience gradually advances and consolidates the frontiers of his knowledge until intelligibility finally leads to reality: vocal reality.

The habit of detailed thought and enquiry does not come easily; it entails tireless energy and perseverance; ultimately it becomes second nature. Our every action in life is habit-forming. Are we not all of us "walking bundles of habits"? The infant repeats the old, old story of trial and error until the details of his daily life are handed over to the "effortless custody of automatism". In like manner must the details of vocal mechanism be so conducted as finally to hand them over (almost entirely) to such effortless custody. (We say "almost", because a certain degree of conscious control *is* necessary.) Rational study and experiment are the means to this end. The student would be wise to remember that a wealth of experience lies in trial and error, and in a chain of failures.

The *mind* that has helped in no small measure to drill and mould the vocal parts into a balanced whole *must* retain a certain degree of conscious control, and not be relegated, once a certain degree of automatism has been acquired, to the inferior state of sleeping partner as far as the mechanical action is concerned. The degree of conscious control contemplated is an impulse to act, create, produce, direct, perform, and accomplish; a control of the processes of selection, of shaping and launching the appropriate vowelled tone, and then maintaining it. A control, therefore, of the means and ways of tonal production.

Complete automatism of the mechanical whole is one of the delusions with which so many students and singers are badly infected: it carries a danger signal that none can afford to ignore. No matter how well schooled and good his mechanism may be, no matter how "natural" and automatically accurate, no singer

C

can afford to sit back and expect it to function perfectly every time and all the time. The very nature of the vocal instrument is such that it is subject to almost every variation in bodily equilibrium to which the nervous system and mental states bring no small contribution.* Muscles, nerves, and brain suffer from fatigue. Mind and metabolism are not always in a state of perfect equilibrium: moodiness, discontent, worries, anger, physical excesses and disturbances, atmospheric conditions, all play their part singly and in combined form in unbalancing the system; so surreptitiously do they creep in at times that only the vocal organs seem to register the lack of equilibrium in some way or other. For instance, some or all of the sixty-odd muscles within the larynx itself may be affected by sluggishness of action; this alone is sufficient, of course, to upset the niceties of tonal colouring and balance. At other times the vocal cords themselves feel stiff and seem to resist some or all attempts to produce the subtler qualities of vocal tone. Your fine automatism breaks down at some vital point and fails to respond to the normal demands made upon it in the usual expectant mood.

Because the mechanical parts have to be assembled with every breath he takes when singing, and reassembled with every change of pitch and vowel and word, all of which includes an exact poising of the breath pressure that varies according to circumstances, can any singer feel absolutely certain that every adjustment will be made with unfailing accuracy? We think not, because never can he be sure that his subconscious dictates (automatism) to the vocal machinery will be obeyed to the letter.

To rely wholly on automatism also invites trouble of a deferred nature, such as the acquisition of faults and bad technical habits that infect mind and mechanism by imperceptible degrees. And their insinuation is so extraordinarily subtle that it may well escape the vigilance of the keenest mind.

The ideal combination is therefore quasi-automatism plus an indispensable minimum of conscious control over mechanical adjustment and production. With the vocal mechanism thus under control it is a simple matter to attune the mental vibrations of interpretative thought to the purely physical ones produced by the instrument: in short, to wed mind to matter.

* The larynx is an ancillary organ of mind, even as is the solar plexus.

There is one exception: Once the breathing apparatus has been properly drilled as a separate unit and has acquired the *habit* of accurate performance, it may safely be handed over to automatism. No other part of the vocal whole can be given such apparent freedom of action. However, this applies purely to the *muscular action* of the breathing machinery, and *not* to the actual output of breath nor to the degree of its pressure. As explained in Chapter XV, the singer should *not* make his demands *directly* upon the breathing apparatus.*

This work, like the parent work (*The Science and Sensations of Vocal Tone*), is both analysis and synthesis. A microscope placed at the gaze of the student, it strips vocal tone of its seeming mysteries and lays bare its mechanical components in order the better to assemble them again into a working whole.

As in the case of the parent work, which has, in writing, the full and unreserved acceptance and commendation of world-famous singers such as Luisa Tetrazzini, Beniamino Gigli, Dinh Gilly, Tito Schipa, Giovanni Inghilleri, Joseph Hislop, and others, every phase, aspect and detail of vocal technique elaborated in the ensuing chapters has been subjected to the most exacting and searching tests extending over many years; the exposition, therefore, can be accepted by students with the utmost confidence.

"I may say to my critics: Try the experiments; investigate with care and patience as I have done. If, having examined, you discover imposture or delusion, proclaim it and say how it was done. But, if you find it to be a fact, avow it fearlessly, as 'by the everlasting law of honour you are bound to do'." (Sir William Crookes)

In every field man investigates, theorizes, delves into the apparently imponderable, seeking, inventing, discovering, and handling natural phenomena and material agents, producing brilliant results without fully comprehending all the laws governing them. It is by results, by the final product that we are able to determine and understand sufficiently for our purpose the working of a particular law. "By their fruits ye shall know them."

The processes of imaginative thought carry us from the sphere of intelligibility into that of reality because imagination is the condition of all true living and doing; it is the fundamental creative force ever reaching out towards reality.

---

* Hence Gigli's dictum, p. 27, para. 1.

CHAPTER II

KNOWLEDGE AND PATIENCE

THAT LIFE IS NOT EASY is the common experience of all. If it were, all initiative would freeze. As it is, initiative requires a stimulus that only knowledge can provide, as Shakespeare says:

Ignorance is the curse of God,
Knowledge the wing wherewith we fly to heaven.

So knowledge is power, and the pinion of achievement.

The mere accumulation or memorizing of facts does not constitute Knowledge in the true and living sense of the word. The facts herein offered to the student should be considered as energizers of thought; in other words, they should be made the base for his own thinking. Facts are the seeds to be planted and cultivated until flowerage and fruition. Facts are food for thought.

Plato wrote that "Knowledge is an activity of the soul". Therefore, to think is to live. To live is to do, and to advance in the doing.

A fact imparted is not a stopping place but a milestone marking a stage in personal development along the endless path of endeavour; it is a harbinger of light in the blaze of which dark concepts slink out to inescapable oblivion.

Facts are too precious to be allowed to wither in a miasma of inertia. They are not ornaments to be immobilized on the shelf of mind, but generators of hot scintillæ that ignite the fires of achievement.

But was there ever achievement without that calm and persevering endurance we call Patience, holding the skies? Ask any great painter, sculptor, singer, violinist, pianist, astronomer or gardener, what sustained their efforts during years of hard study and disappointing experiment. With one voice their answer will be: Patience, the cementing influence in the building process.

Patience is the prongless spur. It is the essence of that thing we call Success. But the patience we mean is militant, and excludes the frailer kinds that acquiesce in afflicting evils or reduce man to bovine stupidity. Patience must not be the master of man, as it is of ox and ass, but he must be the master of it. There must be nothing inertly passive about patience, for its constructive qualities are calmly dynamic.

When presented with fact upon fact and detail upon detail, the student may show impatience, for he wants to gather more than he can hold, and bite off more than he can chew. The process of assimilation is necessarily slow, so his must be a patient impatience, the *festina lente*, hasten slowly, of the old Roman sage. For unbridled impatience robs thought of its clarity and work of its finish. Rabelais said, "He who has patience may achieve anything," and Rodin, the sculptor, "Slowness is beauty." Does not slowness connote enduring patience?

Patience is flowing harmony; impatience, strident discord.

The numerous facts presented in this volume—most of which have been corroborated by Science, constitute for the discerning student a working base of many platforms, and a prime mover toward achievement.

The various phases of vocal technique have been elaborated in unusually minute detail, for "the highest attainable knowledge of any object is reached only when we have exhausted all available standpoints from which it may thus be examined, and have moulded and compacted into one synthetized whole the various aspects which the object has presented to our view when regarded from these different standpoints".*

* *The Anatomy of Truth* (Hugh Capron, F.R.A.S., F.L.S., F.R.G.S.).

CHAPTER III

THE DECLINE OF SINGING

THE REAL CAUSES

THERE IS ONE THING in the world of song that is much misunderstood and subject to the most extraordinary discussions and even heated contention, and that is vocal technique. At no time in vocal history as today has there been so much confusion, so many divergent views and conflicting opinions as to the fundamental principles, cause and effect, of vocal mechanism. Where such a truly natural thing is concerned it seems incredible in our so-called enlightened age that there should be this lack of unity in thought and action.

Beauty is said to be a matter of opinion. But is it? We rather believe that Beauty is of a fixed quality, a reality existing behind appearances, an unassailable citadel, a combination of pleasing qualities, a definite standard of grace and excellence. Beauty is fitness. When line is given its true function, there Beauty lies. When form, colour, expression combine to perfection, when this all manifests life, harmony, movement, intelligence, we have Beauty at her best.*

No mere personal opinion, impression, or reaction can negative the existence of such attributes in a truly beautiful object. The opinion we form is merely our reaction to the contemplation of a particular object; but if we lack instinctive or cultivated appreciation of form, colour, and function, our angle of view must

* Many hold the view that Beauty is a relative term, meaning that everyone is privileged to decide for himself what is beautiful. Well might one say that Virtue is a relative term, or Truth, or the principle of mathematics. And because this unreasoned opinion is in general so carelessly accepted by the majority, culture of the arts is heading slowly and surely for a chaos of ugliness, a retrogression to the first feeble attempts of primitive man. Witness the slant today in terms of surrealist daubs, sculptured monstrosities, and architectural atrocities. Is it the deliberate cult of ugliness? Or incapacity? Obviously, the latter induces the former.

necessarily be warped in degree even though we are unaware of the obliquity. Neither a distorted view nor the contemplation of one facet only can disprove the reality behind an appearance.

There seem to be no two opinions where a lovely flower or a glorious sunset are concerned, no question among the masses as to the opaline beauty of voices that with heart-gripping quality soared to the summit of world appreciation. Why? Because appreciation is untrammelled by prejudice. The universal reaction to the contemplation of beautiful flowers and sunsets is one, the appreciation is one; equally, universal appreciation of and reaction to certain qualities of vocal tone are one. When related to a given object, Beauty is either there or not there, and the reaction to it of only one person out of a hundred may be correct; the other ninety-nine are beauty-blind. It can never really be one of personal "opinion" even though the individual likes to think it is, for a mere opinion may not be a correct reaction; often it is not.

If we now approach the question of beauty in vocal tone and that of the technique producing it, we are confronted at once with a skein of tangled opinions, and too often personal opinions at that, built solely on ignorance and bombast. And the reason? The gradual decline of singing, essentially a mechanical decline, in every country, which began over a hundred years ago and now fast approaching its nadir, is having the effect of destroying gradually the faculty of appreciation of the beautiful in vocal tone. Everywhere the public ear is no longer being educated as formerly by a legion of fine singers in one uninterrupted stream; in fact it is fast deteriorating and now accepts and applauds almost any tone or series of mere sounds provided they be loud, yes, loud and cheap. The few fine singers of the old guard still in harness and a sprinkling of young singers that are emerging because of their exceptional vocal means, their talent and dogged industry, can do very little to stem the tide of aural deterioration.

There is an ideal beauty in vocal tone which all cannot expect to attain, but which all could at least strive to attain. But the striving must be properly directed. Through training, or instinct, or an admixture of both, we may all learn to analyse and appreciate ideal vocal tone. The appreciation of beauty in vocal tone is latent in the human mind; it can therefore be cultivated.

What is the cause of the present low standard of singing in every land, what the cause of the aural deterioration, and what the cause of the mechanical decline? One answer covers all: Vocal technique is made and considered today more or less a personal thing. By this we mean that there are a thousand and one personal methods, personal opinions and fads as to what constitutes vocal mechanism and production. Most of them are destructively nonsensical, for the personal theories have no foundation in fact. It is only fair to add that most of those teaching false methods were themselves taught that two and two make five, a thing they blindly accepted, knowing no better. Whether an idea, pernicious as it may be, is deliberately taught or allowed, for lack of correction, to develop in a student, the same harmful result will accrue.

The real causes of the decline of singing are seldom adduced although the fact of decadence has been bemoaned during the last hundred years. The decline today is so very grave that a frankly revealed analysis of the causes is imperative.

Undoubtedly, the very first cause was the fact of the ever-increasing competition in every field of endeavour. The struggle for existence and the preoccupation of choosing a trade or profession became gradually more acute; and with the rising tide of population came the many new inventions that quickened the tempo of living. Life in consequence became more strenuous, more exacting, and human relations less tolerant. All the trades and professions gradually became overcrowded until finally the supply exceeded the demand. Consequently, many square pegs were forced unprofitably into round holes. So many individuals possessing little innate tendency or instinctive ability were thus readily induced to enter the profession either as singer or teacher, or both. The impatience of these desultory students stricken with the money-making fever was such as to curtail all thought of long and serious study, which before and in the beginning of the nineteenth century often extended to ten years, and up to the 'nineties still kept at five, six, or seven years, in Italy. It is easy to imagine how limited was the knowledge assimilated by these misfits who first brought mediocrity into being, and subsequently swelled its ranks in ever-increasing measure. (Mediocrity did not exist (in Italy) a century ago, for the adequate reason that there were no jobs, no money for second-rate singers, no pupils for second-rate teachers.) With the gradual swelling of its ranks mediocrity, unfortunately, was soon to find a ready market with the aid of mediocre-minded impresarios who were content to form second and, ultimately, third-rate opera companies and run seasons of opera, and travel with them from place to place in Italy, and abroad, giving performances at smaller and less important theatres and, incidentally, developing a second- and third-rate aural appreciation among a new type of audience with little money to spend. Mind you, the first elements of mediocrity we are here contemplating as second-rate, and living, say, eighty or ninety years ago, were much better equipped than many singers today who have made name and fortune. At least the first mediocrity in some cases possessed a no mean sum of technical knowledge; but because this was not complete they were not at that time considered first-class.

These comparatively speaking second-raters gradually withdrew from active service and devoted their remaining energies to teaching. Their first pupils took away with them, after a more or less shortened period of study, less knowledge than they themselves possessed. With few exceptions, this is invariably the case when study is not prolonged. Although not too well equipped, these pupils sallied forth as singers to lower the standard of the first mediocrity and, incidentally, to lower still further public appreciation of vocal values, of vocal beauty and correctness. As teachers in their turn, these singers ultimately turned out pupils who carried away still less knowledge. And thus deterioration grew apace. As generation succeeded generation, the first pupils of the first mediocrity turned out pupils whose pupils and pupils' pupils acquired less and less knowledge until it reached the stage when, to fill in the obvious gaps, the many personal fads, theories and fallacies of production were duly hatched, and handed down to the present generation. Students had (and still have) to be given something to "chew" for their money; so why not something mysterious, or outlandish, some wonderful "secret", some panacea for all vocal defects? The ever-widening chasm of ignorance had to be bridged somehow, anyhow. Thus were the many erroneous ideas grafted on to a limited knowledge of vocal technique, of the real *School* of singing which was a school of thought, of accumulated proven experience, a school of *facts* that produced the highest results. What then was the prime motive behind all this pretence, this humbug? The ever-increasing struggle for existence, to make some sort of a living, to make money. In face of this burning money question conscience was often shelved, and the art itself was considered by so many solely as a means to an end. "As soon as any art is pursued with a view to money," wrote Samuel Butler, "then farewell in ninety-nine cases out of a hundred to all hope of genuine good work." To this great truism we would add that if the singer, or teacher, puts his art above everything with a view to perfecting it, the money will come in practically an unending stream, provided of course the individual possesses the requisite mental and material elements of success. But the moment a singer or teacher places the money factor first in thought and action (and this is what Samuel Butler meant) his art will never receive in the first place that careful and devoted cultivation which aspires to perfection. This was the shortsighted policy that informed the aforementioned mediocrity, singers and teachers, in no inconsiderable number, and unfortunately is still the main driving force today which, with few exceptions, propels the would-be exponents of this art of arts.

The fact remains that today the great mass of students in every country is discouraged by the tedium of indifferent teaching, by the conflicting opinions on production, by the scant knowledge acquired, by the poor progress made, by the ruined voices.

Another army of motley elements arose to swell the ranks and so advance the process of decline: professional men of all sorts entered the teaching fraternity, such as doctors of medicine, orchestral conductors, composers, pianists, organists, coaches, etc. If they had had proper training no criticism could be levelled at them, but in the majority of cases their "teaching" was based on the scantiest knowledge picked up haphazard.

Again, certain medical investigators of vocal phenomena misguidedly chose as subjects singers whose technique was far from perfect; too often it was a singer with a "name", under the assumption that "fame" is synonymous with correct production. It should be, but today it is not always the case; so many are puffed up artificially by influence and propaganda. As a result, these wellmeaning men were often led to draw wrong conclusions which, subsequently incorporated in the books they wrote on singing, did, and are still doing, incalculable harm. The meaner minds, in support of pet theories of their own concoction, are for ever quoting the inaccurate data.

Without the aid of exact, correct sensations of vocal tone the problem of technique can never be solved by physiologist, teacher, student or singer; inversely, with their aid the functioning of the vocal parts can be brought under intelligent control.

It is unquestionably true that ignorance and charlatanism are mainly responsible for the muddy stream of ideas that has polluted a natural function, a natural mechanism governed by certain known laws.

There is no cavilling, no heated discussion among mechanical, electrical, aeronautical and civil engineers all over the world as to the laws or fundamental principles governing their respective fields. There is no quibbling as to the laws governing the fundamental design and construction of musical instruments; and none to speak of as regards the playing technique thereof. Why then should there be in regard to vocal mechanism and production? The ignorance of the many *personal* theories, methods and fads holds the answer.

The decline was furthermore accelerated by a galaxy of books on singing purporting to possess the key to technical achievement, with a few short cuts to success obligingly thrown in. Few gave enlightenment; some were uncompromising, other steered a middle, non-commital course, filling page after page with idle verbiage. In this connection a world-famous singer once told me that he "could lecture on singing for a whole week, non-stop, and say nothing". Unfortunately, few students mentally challenge the many inconsequent statements made by pen and lip; for the greater part everything is blindly accepted as sacrosanct, until disillusion casts its first shadow.

However correct they may be, oral explanations of such a subtle subject as vocal mechanism and production are susceptible of distortion and misinterpretation in the course of decades and centuries of individuals, not of one but of many different nationalities. Unless there is complete loving devotion and understanding in a given direction, the human mind will inevitably indulge in both subtraction and amplification. Here, therefore, is another source of vocal decline.

Yet another fateful cause of decline resides in the *tessitura* of certain modern and ultra-modern operas written with little or no knowledge of the capabilities of the human voice, no love for it, and with a magnificent disregard for its delicacy and beauty. They are voice killers. Even when production is correct, the strain imposed destroys first the bloom of a fine voice and then the power of balanced adjustment through gradual exhaustion of the laryngeal muscles, and of the vocal cords in particular. The final stage sees the once proud possessor going to swell the ranks of international wobblers.

The present generation has to face the hard facts of the decline. The insinuation that perhaps the singers of the past were no better than, and possibly not even as good as the present ones, is unveiled sophistry adducing fable for fact. There is still a goodly number of individuals able to remember and to compare the immediate past with the present, having witnessed part of the decline, gradual but only too obvious. The decline is mainly in the *mechanical* field.

Seeing that every voice in the world, irrespective of nationality, is moulded upon the same model or design, and that every voice has the same mechanism that functions in accordance with laws of a fixed and unalterable nature, any intrusion with "personal" methods, fads, and baseless theories that run counter to these laws (as they nearly always do) interfere with and derange the system. There is no such thing as a strictly individual mechanism or a national mechanism. Vocal mechanism is no more Italian than English, or American, or German. Strict obedience to the laws is what matters.

One cannot profitably graft on to a natural process productive of what is known as a good school of singing (the foundation of which is ninety per cent. good mechanics) an excrescence of personal fads and personal guesswork concerning such contributing factors as the breathing machinery, the tongue, the soft palate, the laryngeal action, and so forth. The slightest maladjustment of one factor upsets the balance of the whole. It results in inefficiency.

Most voices today are bludgeoned, distorted, cramped, forced, and in general fearfully ill-treated in varying degree, until Nature calls a halt in no uncertain terms. Is it any wonder that the decline of singing is so serious?

CHAPTER IV

THAT PERNICIOUS FORWARD PRODUCTION METHOD

EXCELLING IN ODD CONCEITS, the human mind is prone to scout with dogmatic fervour any idea that runs counter to its pet tenets. Not for the opinionated, that prefers effortless thinking, but for the open-minded teacher, student, and singer do we expose the falsity of this method.

The so-called "forward production" method is largely responsible for the general low standard of singing, technically speaking, and for the ruin of innumerable voices. Its history is inglorious. It is invariably wedded to that obsession: Diaphragmatic drive. The nefarious marriage has wrought untold harm.

Now what is this thing that has been so widely accepted and so little challenged? With an air of finality we hear on every hand: "His, or her, voice was 'well forward'," or "was not forward enough." Many critics repeat these phrases as a matter of course. It is supposed to express good production, or the lack of it. Teachers, students and singers imbued with the method enthuse about the idea of "the well-forward tone". But, we are at liberty to ask, on what basis of *fact*, on what scientific platform do these votaries stand? Can they adduce physiological and acoustical facts in support of their method?

Whence came this constant forward production idea, this *mania?* We would point out that many of the old adages are not only incomplete but positively misleading, and more liable to be misunderstood than apprehended. With the gradual decline of singing they were pounced upon as "keys" to the old School by legions of incompetent self-appointed "teachers" that found it profitable to invade the vocal Klondyke. Therefrom they extracted what they conceived to be the essence, the arcana of the old School technique for long buried in frozen folds. Ideas frequently suffer distortion from faulty language or misleading words.

Our considered opinion is that the forward production idea

originated from a misinterpretation of the old adage: "Cantare a fior' di labbra", that unequivocally suggests that one should "sing on the edge of the lips". As a figure of speech it is decorative rather than instructive. It is positively misleading because it embraces only a small part of the truth, and we all know how dangerous a little knowledge can be.

Let us examine dispassionately how such a quarter-truth was, unwittingly perhaps, used for spawning a pernicious method of voice production that has taken such a hold on so many would-be exponents of the art. To the casual observer, at close quarters, ignorant of true vocal technique, a good singer sometimes may give the impression of producing his tones, or some of them, right on the lips; and the better the production, invariably coupled to good diction, the stronger seemingly the impression. Of course, all tones come out of the mouth past the lips which are much used for certain consonants. Now this lip movement, for forming the consonants and then springing apart for shaping the ensuing vowel, is most noticeable up to D natural, fourth line, in all voices, because all tones (all vowels) are tuned into the mouth-pharynx cavity no higher than the arc of the palate. They are all, therefore, more or less on a "speaking" basis. Hence the "forward" impression. On the other hand, the foci or points of impingement of the various sound-beams,* particularly of the upper medium and high notes, are far removed from the lips, teeth, and hard palate—as will be explained later. Even though these notes actually are focused far from the lips-palate combination they may still give the impression (to the gullible eye and untutored ear) that they are being produced "well forward"; the eye is fascinated mainly by the lip movement helping the formation and release of the consonants, and with its impressions overawes the ear. But the trained ear knows better. And so, perhaps, arose the mischief. This deceptive impression of "forwardness", hoodwinking the brain, sowed the seed of error and ultimately blossomed into the

* In the parent work, *The Science and Sensations of Vocal Tone*, we used the term "sound-column" merely to follow the traditional expression employed by the old School, viz.: *colonna sonora*. In this work, however, we shall use instead the term "sound-beam", since the word "column" has been appropriated by physicists to express a cubical volume of air at resonance, whereas in our description of the vocal mechanism we are referring to a longitudinal train of sound-waves. (See *N.B.*, p. 11.)

"Forward" method. It is indeed most unfortunate that a method of voice production, a bad one, should have been evolved, and subsequently extolled, from a pretty saying plus a surface impression.

The main concern of the singer are the tonal foci or points of impingement as they reflect, and are the final expression of, vibrator-resonator adjustment. From the mechanical standpoint, the singer's art consists in creating, with the aid of vowels, sound-beams of varying diameters and heights that exactly satisfy the acoustical requirements of the different pitches. After allowing these sound-beams to follow their *natural* trend or direction in relation to pitch and vowel, and after coupling the *top* (focus) of the tonal streams, as they occur, into the appropriate resonator, the singer's mechanical job is finished, and all he has to do then is to infuse feeling, expression, and accent into the focal points (or platforms)—the mental and physical vibrations combining to form one vibrating unit. Of course, all this takes place almost simultaneously.

The real mouth of the singer is not the lip-aperture, as so many conceive it to be, but the internal cavity, of which the back half, or pharynx, is the most important, because consisting of mobile, adjustable parts. The front half is of a bony, fixed nature, and not so spacious as the back half which is also the gateway to the head cavities.

A referendum among teachers, students and singers all over the world would reveal that a very high percentage employ and are taught the forward production (monofocal) method, generally coupled to diaphragmatic drive. Now, in face of two contemporaneous facts, (1) the serious decline of singing, (2) the employment of the forward production method by a vast majority, is it not reasonable to assume that (1) gave birth to (2); and that, as (2) became more and more widely adopted, it accelerated (1) to a high degree? It is symptomatic, not mere coincidence.

What is this method, and why is it pernicious? The forward production is monofocal, that is, it inculcates the principle that all tones, irrespective of pitch and vowel, should be placed (or shall we say "driven") "well forward" on the hard palate, preferably "just over the upper teeth". An extension of this method requires all tones to be placed "in the mask", and "just between the eyes on the bridge of the nose". This "dans la masque" business is an offshoot of the so-called French school whose tonal products are so often tainted by a horrid nasality. Is it not again significant that of the French singers like Maurel, Journet, Dinh Gilly, and others who won international fame, not one employed this "mask" stunt? And not even the Pole, Jean de Reske, who, it is said, used to teach it together with the diaphragmatic drive.*

However, the monofocal principle of forward production is concerned mainly with the hard palate and demands therefore that all vowelled tones be concentrated, or, say, compressed within a relatively restricted area. So far as they govern vocal tone, the laws of physics and acoustics are blissfully ignored by this method which obviously is unaware of the fact that high pitches mean tall, narrow sound-beams that cannot possibly be compressed forward against the hard palate, the cavity having insufficient height.

The forward thrust of upper medium and high notes causes too much vibrator in length and vertical thickness to be engaged, thus producing sound-beams that are much too short and broad for such pitches; consequently the tone can never soar into the head cavities where the high pitches belong. The diaphragmatic drive is employed precisely to *boost* up the frequency of the vocal cords, but is rarely successful. And this is why most forward production merchants constantly sing flat, just under the pitch practically all the time. The men produce *tubed* tone (the Italians call it "tubato") and the women hooting tone. Forward production constricts the throat, inducing rigidity of the parts in varying degree, especially when coupled to diaphragmatic thrust; as a result, the tone hardens, thickens and loses any quality it might have if properly produced.

If this forward monofocal production represented the whole truth it would be a very simple matter for anyone with a voice to sing correctly from the technical standpoint. If concentration of all tones, irrespective of pitch and vowel, on the hard palate or on the nose bridge, is the right method of voice placing or production, then teachers of vocal technique have no call for existence; a coach or somebody playing the piano is all that a student would require, or a short pamphlet.

* Jean de Reske studied, as a tenor, for five years with Antonio Cotogni, the greatest Italian baritone of all time, who assuredly did not teach him this "mask" stuff, nor the diaphragmatic thrust, nor the murderous fad "coup de glotte". Cotogni himself told the author, when a student in Rome, that Jean was "*not* a tenor". His very words were, "*Non* è un tenore."

According to the champions of that other "secret" of production, an individual with a voice and a "beautifully developed" diaphragm has merely to fill up with air, exert high pressure with it against the vocal cords, and his work is done! Oh, sweet simplicity. A certain individual who should have known better wrote: "Look after the diaphragm and the voice will look after itself"! Coming from such an "authoritative" source, all comments on this paternal, albeit asinine, advice to students are superfluous; sometimes silence is not only golden but also charitable.

It is incredible that so many otherwise intelligent people should accept blindly this diaphragm-cum-forward-thrust folly as "technique"—and that is what they call it. Its structure, like its credentials, are threadbare. Vocal technique and singing include very much more than that. Did singers study from seven to ten years in the past, with probably a one-hour lesson every day, just to learn how, with the assistance of a donkeyish diaphragm, to place or swing all tones "well forward" on to one spot, and a limited spot at that? No intelligent person would believe it.

At this juncture the student is possibly desirous of being informed how and why this constant forward production method is pernicious, particularly if dissatisfied with his progress and secretly in doubt about the genuineness of the "method" on which his training is based. If in spite of everything he feels the necessity of clinging to the method, we would ask him to ponder seriously over the following:

As soon as a singer starts to produce tone, inexorably he comes up against physical laws and physiological processes that *must* be followed if good results are to accrue. In Chapter VII is explained how for the production of every tone, every pitch, the vocal cords, or vibrator, have correctly to be adjusted in length, thickness (vertical depth), and tension; which adjustments vary according to the pitch, because to every pitch corresponds an exact number of vibrations per second (frequency). The higher the pitch the greater the frequency.

Such adjustments attain automatically to perfection on every pitch, with all vowels, in the *completely* natural voice.* From the

---

* A completely natural voice is one that, without training, is able to enunciate and sustain with perfect ease and freedom all vowelled tones on all pitches in its particular compass; in other words, a voice that has no mechanical defects or difficulties, no matter the pitch or the vowel on that pitch, a voice in which

mechanical standpoint the majority of voices are not completely natural, for Nature rarely completes the work, and the actual functioning is often erratic and leaves much to be desired. (Indeed, is she not also very remiss with faces, bodies, eyes, hearts, etc.?) To remedy the mechanical shortcomings the teacher's art steps into the breach, but should do so only on natural lines. And "natural" includes physics and physiology. He can complete the work by developing the mechanism and regulating its functioning only by strict obedience to the relevant laws. If the naturalness of a voice, mechanically speaking, has an efficiency of, say, fifty, sixty, seventy, or eighty per cent., it means that the vibrator mechanism is undeveloped and not functioning correctly for the remaining fifty, forty, thirty, or twenty per cent. Therefore, the incompleted portion, so to speak, of the mechanism and its functioning must be carefully coaxed, moulded, drilled, developed, and tuned to a hundred per cent. mechanical efficiency. It boils down to muscular education.

Every vibrator (vocal cords) adjustment plus resonator adjustment produces a sound-beam which is the main stream of vowelled tone. This tonal stream or beam must find lodgment and be coupled (tuned in) within well-defined resonating zones in order to reveal and develop to the maximum its physical properties. An important point is that the sound-beam must be *allowed* to follow its natural trend or direction; therefore, it must not be "placed" or thrust on one spot in a resonating zone not its own.

If any sound-beam is not allowed, or encouraged, by the singer to follow its natural trend, and instead is forced into another direction not acoustically, not rightfully its own, there is tonal distortion in degree. For it is only by correct vowel shaping, which varies slightly in relation to pitch, that a *natural* direction can obtain for the resultant sound-beam. Such internal shaping of the mouth-pharynx cavity for the purposes of appropriate vowelled tone, not only assists vibrator adjustment but goes a long way to securing correct direction of the beam itself. A correct vowel shape in relation to pitch confers freedom and looseness to the throat. (See Chapter XIII.)

exact vibrator-resonator adjustments obtain automatically at any and every pitch within its compass. It means practically flawless production. In Italy the author has heard several such completely natural voices, and, moreover, had the opportunity of subjecting some to minute analysis. (See footnotes, pp. 201, 348.)

Often we hear of teachers insisting on "a nice forward AH". Error number one that has bred many other errors. THERE IS NO SUCH THING AS A FORWARD AH, because the *natural* direction for the sound-beam of the AH vowel, well shaped and produced, is more or less vertical on the low and lower medium pitches, while on the upper medium (from E♭, fourth space, upwards) and high pitches it inclines backwards in varying degree and increases in height. Any attempt, therefore, to incline or curve it forward to the region of the hard palate or nose bridge, whether on low or high pitches, as required by the forward production method, must result in vowel distortion. And distortion means bad, unintelligible vocal tone.*

As far as the five classic vowels are concerned—AH, OH, OO, EH, EE, constituting the basic vowel sounds of all languages, to which we add a sixth, namely, AW, we find that (as fully explained both in this and in the parent work) while on the lower and low pitches some certainly point forward with their sound-beams, as do OO, OH, AW in varying degree, on the higher and high pitches, however, not one beam of any of the aforesaid six vowels do so *naturally*. Indeed they are all far removed from the region of the hard palate and nose bridge seeing that as the pitch rises, all beams of all vowels (including the short English vowels) soar gradually higher to couple in to the head resonating zones located back of the Vertical (see Chapter XII), and therefore far from being "frontal". (See Diagram I, p. 57.)

There is a physical-acoustical reason why sound-beams of high pitches couple into the head cavities and in slightly different directions. Our scientist collaborator will substantiate this in his Scientific Supplement that closes the present chapter.

The well-trained singer *allows* the beams to take their *natural* direction; his every adjustment has this end in view.

The high-placed foci of head notes, irrespective of the vowel employed, are nothing but the TOP of the respective sound-beams. They are clear-cut sensations of tone that reflect exactly the dimensions (length and thickness) and tension of the vibrator (vocal cords) employed for the particular pitch. The higher the

---

* The vowelled tone is distorted because for a given pitch the particular resonator *must* be of a certain shape. But offer to the sound-beam a shaping inappropriate to the pitch, and you throw it off its *natural* course, and, by so doing, upset and distort the vibrator adjustment itself.

pitch the smaller the tonal focus (or *top* of the beam) because less cord is engaged, while the tension increases proportionately. And the smaller the effective length of vibrator used, the narrower becomes the sound-beam; consequently, the narrower the beam the smaller the focus. All this is fully explained in Chapter VIII.

What happens if the singer deliberately places or concentrates a high note, *all* his high notes, "well forward" somewhere on the hard palate, or nose bridge, in obedience to the forward production method? The immediate, baneful, result is sixfold: (1) too much vibrating element (excess in length and thickness of vocal cords) is engaged in every case, the excess departing very considerably from the actual or *exact* effective cord lengths and thicknesses acoustically pertinent to the different pitches, thereby violating acoustic laws and contravening physiological processes; (2) the resultant sound-beams broaden and shorten to excess as a result of the undue lengthening and thickening of the cords, as per (1) above, and, moreover, are warped by the fact of being curved forward into an unnatural resonating zone—that is to say "unnatural" as far as the high pitches are concerned; (3) the spreading of the foci (focal points) as a direct result of the increase in diameter of the sound-beams, out of all acoustical proportion to pitch, as per (2) above; (4) the resultant tone is rendered heavy, ugly, unmanageable; (5) distortion not only of the sound-beams but also of the vowel shapes and tones themselves, making enunciation more or less unintelligible; (6) an exaggerated increase in breath pressure becomes necessary in order to sustain the excessive "load" to which the cords and the entire larynx with its sixty muscles are thus subjected; and the greater the breath pressure the more the cords are inclined to thicken, and the more they thicken the greater must be the breath pressure to boost up the frequency and sustain the weight of the production. It is a most vicious circle that strains the vocal organs and induces a state of rigidity of the parts. Is it any wonder that so many sing flat? And have a wobble?

It was precisely for supporting the tonal load as per (3), (4), (6) above that the brutal diaphragmatic thrust was evolved, and glorified.

Nature obligingly permits the violation of her own laws, for a time, then repents and rebels. The distressing wobble is the hallmark of her revenge.

Be it noted that it is a physico-acoustical impossibility to concentrate a high or head note forward on the hard palate, the nose bridge, "over the eyes", and employ for its production a small vibrator (as is acoustically correct); it cannot be done, for *the very act of placing or thrusting a high note "well forward" induces and engages too big and heavy a vibrator for that pitch.*

Be it also noted that it is a physico-acoustical impossibility to secure, and focus, a high-pitched note well up in the head cavities by employing a long, thick, and "heavy" vibrator. It cannot be done, for such a high note accrues, or rather should accrue, only from a small and light vibrator generating a "tall", thin beam. Inversely, a long, thick vibrator generates only a short and broad beam which cannot soar sufficiently.*

The majority of singers indulge in a reckless waste of vocal capital; to sing on capital signifies the habitual employment of too much cord in length and thickness. Ultimately it spells vocal bankruptcy. The singer should sing on interest, which means on resonance.

If physical laws require, as we know they do, the sound-beams to follow certain directions, why manhandle Nature and force the tonal streams into other channels that in certain cases are diametrically opposed to the *natural* trend? It does not make sense.

Misleading as it is, the appeal that the constant forward production method has for so many is to be accounted for by the fact that it is easy to grasp and apply, although entailing an excessive labour that taxes the vocal organs to the utmost. Furthermore, the

* There are actually two vibrating mechanisms at the disposal of the human singer. The first is the laryngeal, with its vocal cord mechanism; the second is the *soft palate*. The true function of the latter has only quite recently been discovered by N. Bonavia-Hunt, who has conducted exhaustive experiments proving that the soft palate is set in vibration by the energized sound-beam when this is correctly focused on to it. Nature has supplied man with this valuable auxiliary vibrator—a gift not to be neglected and despised. The principal function of the vibrating palate is to energize the air columns situated above it in the head cavities (a vibrational relay, therefore); but it also helps to stabilize the sound-beam by cancelling out undesirable frequencies (such as inharmonic overtones), and the nett result of the process is the maximum of purity as well as of volume. When, therefore, the voice is *correctly produced*, the soft palate is given its proper function as intended by Nature.

N.B.—The singer, however, must *not* concentrate on, nor attempt to control, the working of the soft palate; his business is solely to create, feel, and manipulate the sound-beam which, upsoaring, is felt by him to pierce straight through the soft palate, as shown in the various diagrams.

average student and singer simply loves to feel and hear a "big" sound rattling inside his mouth, whatever the pitch and vowel; and the more forward it is the better he likes it because convinced that all is well. Especially on high notes the feeling of "big" tone gives what he calls "satisfaction", and the bigger the better, he thinks. The majority fall into the trap.*

This disordered dream must give way to reality. The reverse is the truth, for *the higher the pitch*, irrespective of vowel, *the smaller must be the sensation of concentrated tone or focus and the higher its position in the head resonators*. Tall, narrow sound-beams of high notes mean resonance in abundance; they connote compactness, strength and carrying power. (See Chapter XVII.)

To conclude, we can confidently assert that not one great singer of international fame (and we have known intimately many of both sexes and of different nationalities) employed, or employs, the constant forward production method. Surely that is no mere coincidence. But more eloquent still, for some people perhaps, is scientific fact that will come as a welcome addendum.

A SCIENTIFIC SUPPLEMENT
by NOEL BONAVIA-HUNT, M.A.

All sounds must be started by some form of originator. The originator is, of course, energy, and something has to be energized. When that something is energized (i.e. set in motion) the result is the disturbance of the elastic medium known as "air". This disturbance is maintained by continued supply of pressure or energy as required. Now it is not possible to disturb one mass of air particles without disturbing another and another and another. Thus we find we have set in motion a *train* of waves, vibrating to

* The feeling of big, "meaty" and "rich" tone on all pitches appeals mainly to the vanity of certain singers, and in many cases enhances that feeling of self-importance from which we all suffer. It is the singer's most dangerous snare; so beware then of this so-called "richness". Its champions ignore the fact that real tonal richness does not accrue from heaviness of production. Tonal overloading (through engaging too much cord in depth, in relation to pitch) upsets the orderly sequence of harmonics that spells good quality, bringing into undue prominence the higher dissonant overtones all in a bunch and so producing that hardness of tone which is the inevitable consequence of forcing Nature's beautiful mechanism. (Why thrust the tone forward when it *has* to leave the mouth in any case? See diagrams, pp. 174, 234.)

and fro. The air so set in motion may be either free or enclosed, and there may be varying degrees of freedom or of enclosure. We can speak of the free air of the prairie, or of the sea, or of the street, or of the concert hall. The "freedom" is comparative in each of these instances. Again, there is the enclosed or the confined air of the room, the corridor, the cupboard, the tunnel, the tube, the vessel, the horn, the box, the sea-shell. All are comparative instances of confinement. Sound waves are propagated in air space, and the larger the space the more rapidly are these waves damped, that is, each successive wave is weaker than its immediate predecessor; and at length they are absorbed. If, however, the waves come in contact with the enclosed or confined column of air, this air column is set in motion and produces a *separate* set of sound waves in that enclosure, and this separate sound is added to or superimposed on the original wave train. Since an air column of this nature is capable of producing sound in itself by sympathetic attraction from outside, it is called a "resonator". We have here a picture of one set of waves being coupled to another set of waves, and the result of the combination of the two sets of waves is a third set of waves, which increases the complexity of the note or sound.

Mr. Herbert-Caesari condemns what is known as the "forward" method of voice production in singing, because it advocates a *single* coupling of the vocal mechanism to the resonant air columns associated with the mouth. Moreover, it definitely and arbitrarily selects what this coupling shall be, irrespective of frequency, intensity, and quality. The starting apparatus here is represented by the vocal cords charged with pressure air from the lungs. The sound waves are produced immediately above the cords and vary in frequency, intensity and quality according to the shaping, tension, and vibrating frequency of the cords. Now this original sound is immature and embryonic by itself. It requires considerable reinforcement. Furthermore, it has to be propagated in outer space. Possibly, the idea at the back of the minds of those who advocate the "forward focus" is the apparent necessity of throwing the voice into the mouth so as to encourage radiation in outer space. If so, *the method defeats its own ends;* for the law of reflection ordains that the sound thus "placed" will suffer attenuation through friction and diffraction before it has a chance to start its radiating career.

According to Mr. Herbert-Caesari, the singer must select and call into service the correct resonator for each and every note produced by the vocal mechanism, and *then*, after making the proper coupling, he can send the finished product forth to an admiring world. It should be fairly obvious, even to the non-technical observer, that it is not possible to couple up to any of the various resonators at will if the voice is deliberately directed on to one single—even if it be a central—spot or focus. There is nothing in the vocal apparatus corresponding to a central common ante-chamber leading to various resonant chambers or cavities. The latter are better conceived as so many rooms entered by doorways from a common corridor of irregular shape. The doorways (that is, points of accessibility) have to be first detected and then engaged, as required. One is almost reminded of the technique of ancient swordsmanship and the delicate thrusts of the rapier picking out this or that spot on the adversary's body.

Mr. Herbert-Caesari calls attention to another point. He insists that for each note (i.e. frequency) produced, the vocal cords must be adjusted to the correct tension, thickness, and length, and that this triple condition of the cord has to be coupled to the correct resonator at the correct point of junction. A high note, for instance, requires a small, compact portion of the cord to be set in vibration, and the sound thus produced is coupled to a suitable resonator in the head, which is situated high up and is therefore only engaged by directing the vibrating air stream more or less vertically on to a small focus.

This is a most interesting theory which would appear to receive corroboration when we realize that the higher the frequency the smaller should be the *effective* capacity of the air column coupled in resonance. The epithet "effective" is important in this connection, as the actual cubic content of the resonant chamber need not necessarily be small. The effective capacity can be modified by means of introducing outside air to the resonator or to the vibrant stream. It might be thought that the head cavities would be too large to act as suitable resonators for the higher notes. This is not so, for two reasons. First, these particular cavities possess narrow orifices and comparatively non-yielding bony walls which not only establish a higher formant than the other resonant chambers (e.g. pharynx, mouth, chest), but help to reflect the sound back to the mouth. Secondly, the mouth and nose introduce outside air to the vibrating air column as it makes its longitudinal travel up and down between larynx and head, and thus tunes it to the resonator selected as most suitable for it. This is known as an "induced draught", and the particular function of the nose and mouth just described is not as sufficiently recognized as it should be. If the note is focused on the hard palate (i.e. the alveolar arch of the mouth), it has to be tuned to the mouth resonance which varies with each vowel sound formed. It is quite impossible to effect this tuning adjustment unless the pitch of the note is quite low.

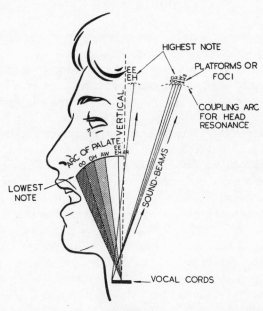

DIAGRAM I

N.B.—*We would ask the student to note (1) how on the high notes the four sound-beams of AH, AW, OH, OO incline backwards with respect to the vertical; (2) how they closely approximate, leaving little space between each other; (3) the space separating the AH–OO group and the EH–EE; (4) the angle of inclination of the EH and EE with respect to the vertical.*

CHAPTER V

THAT "COVERING" BUSINESS

or

THE BUD AND THE ROSE

A STRANGE SUB-TITLE: nevertheless, in a peculiar way it analogizes the difference between bad and good adjustment of the vocal organs and subsequent production.

Widely used in English-speaking countries, the term "to cover", as applied to vocal tone, has no parallel in foreign lands where the art of singing is cultivated, except in Germany where, possibly, it originated (*decken*). Thus we hear, and read, such phrases as: "The tone was well covered", or "not covered enough", or "too covered". From our point of view this term is quite meaningless and misleading. It conveys little or nothing of value to the student, who nevertheless glibly rolls it on his tongue, his eye the while expressing incomprehension. It means well, but is a lamentable failure from the practical standpoint. (See p. 229.)

Be it noted that we are storming the fastnesses of erroneous thought and procedure in vocal technique in this and other chapters solely in the interest of the divine art.

Let us linger a moment on the edge of this misnomer: the student is told to "cover" the tone. What does it mean, what is the implication? What does it convey to the student searching for *facts*, particularly as no adequate explanation is forthcoming? As a matter of fact not one in a hundred taught to "cover" could offer us even a sensible explanation. The dictionary says that verb means: to hide, to clothe, to extend over, to brood or sit on, to conceal something, etc. It is clear that not one of these fit the case, not even indirectly. It is true that where voice production is concerned we are obliged sometimes to employ and even coin words that may be inadequate to express a function, or a sensation of tone. This is admissible only when it is impossible to find the right one because non-existent. This, however, is not the case with "cover". A vocal tone cannot be covered, not even by a stretch of the imagination. It is a curious fact that we always hear and read of covering the *tone*, with never a mention of the vowel. To be intelligible and have meaning, tone should include vowel; but too often in the modern singer we find that it does not. Witness the appalling diction of the majority of singers. If we substitute mere tone for vowels, if we deprive the human voice of clean-cut vowels, the whole art of singing fails of its purpose; if we also deprive it of consonants, as so many singers do, we may as well pull down the vocal shutters and retire. On the other hand, vowel must and does include tone, whatever the individual quality.

Such a doltish, ambiguous term as "to cover" was coined from misunderstanding, or ignorance. And because of the present chaos in teaching, every endeavour should be made to eliminate misnomers from vocal terminology, and choose words that are representative wholly or partly of a function or a tonal sensation. At the very least, let the chosen term be an approximation. There is no approach in the term "cover". A student wants facts, not fiction.

To break away from an old habit is perhaps difficult, and irksome, for the human mind loves a groove. So we will form a new one. We will speak of vowelled-tone, drop that inept term "cover", and use instead: to modify, or round off, or darken the vowel. The first two have at least the merit of expressing a function, a movement. The Italians have always used, and still use, the phrases: "scurire la voce" (to darken the voice), or "colorire (arrotondare) il suono" (to colour the tone). But by voice and tone they invariably mean vowel. You darken or colour the tone by rounding off (arrotondare) the vowel.

Now the mere *thought* of modifying or rounding off the vowel reacts on the mouth-pharynx cavity that immediately and automatically assumes a rounder shape. To illustrate: to modify or round off the open AH in *father*, it is sufficient to *think* of the modified AH sound in words like *song, promise;* whereupon the mouth-pharynx adjusts itself automatically in strict accordance with the *mental* shaping. The singer has no actual physical shaping to do; and let him not attempt it, for he will merely succeed in overdoing it. The student must bear in mind that this shaping is essentially internal (mainly the pharynx). And once this internal shaping has been effected, the lip shaping (lip-aperture) will look after itself automatically as a direct result thereof. Sometimes, however, what is considered a nicely shaped lip-aperture leads the inexperienced to assume that the internal shaping is good. Due to their mobility, the lips can be shaped to apertures that often are no true index to the internal shaping; consequently we can see an enchanting lip-aperture and hear ungrateful effects because proceeding from an incorrect internal shaping (mouth-pharynx cavity). Many ill-advised teachers tell their pupils to smile and show a dozen teeth or so in an effort to be "natural"!

Let us take the AH vowel, as in *father*: we can modify, round off, darken, or colour it (four terms expressing one and the same thing) by mentally shaping it so as to approximate the AW vowel (as in *paw*) in varying degree according to the amount of colour, or expression, we wish to introduce. Note that we say "approximate" because, for obvious reasons, the AH vowel must not be modified, rounded off, darkened or coloured to the extent of transforming it into AW. The more AH is rounded or darkened, the more closely will it approximate to the AW vowel. There are several slight modifications or nuances of AH before the AW is reached, and the first of these, as stated above, is the modified AH sound in words like *song, God, promise, solemn*. Likewise we can modify or round off the AW by darkening its colour gradually towards OH, as in *police, polite* (of which both O's are monophthongs, that is, a single vowel sound). We find the same OH sound in words like *rose, pole* (which, however, are diphthongs, that is, two vowel sounds written and pronounced in one syllable), the *oh* sound being followed by a short *u* sound, as in *put*. The AW may approximate, but must never merge into OH. However close the approximation, the modified vowel must retain its basic, characteristic qualities. Again we can so modify, round off, darken or colour the OH to finally approximate very closely to the OO vowel, as in *pool*, in both shape and timbre. But it must not lose its basic quality, its identity, by degenerating into OO—unless the singer wishes to mix the two vowel colours deliberately for some purpose. But that is another matter. *Vowels and their intervening nuances are to the singer what paints are to the artist.*

Also the EE vowel, as in *feel*, and the EH vowel, as in *Mary, there* (both of which are monophthongs), or the EH sound in *maid* (the first sound of this diphthong which is followed by a short *i*, as in *pin, chin*), can and should be somewhat modified or darkened to meet the exigencies of pitch and expression, as explained in later chapters. The EH can be gradually modified (1) by a narrowing or telescoping action so as to make it approach the *i* sound, as in *pin* (which actually is composed of two sounds: a narrow *eh* sound, as in *pet*, and a tiny *ee* sound sitting, as it were, right on top of it); or (2) by *thinking* of a "domed" internal shaping of the mouth-pharynx cavity, the feeling being that of an inverted U; or (3) again by *thinking* of an *ir* (as in bird) sound and internal shape. This is particularly important on the high notes. Of course, the higher the pitch the greater the tendency for the vowels to mix or merge one into the other in appropriate percentages.

Whatever his prepossessions on the subject, the reader should honestly ask himself whether the word "cover" is a proper conveyance for the aforementioned shapings or movements within the mouth-pharynx cavity, which take place automatically as a result of the singer *thinking* the vowel modifications. Viewed in the proper light, and without bias, the term is clearly uninforming and inadequate. To the great number of pupils that has passed through our hands and had received previously certain training, and to the legion of disillusioned students and singers that came to us for audition-advice, this wretched "covering" business had meant little or nothing; only very occasionally one perhaps had an inkling, a shadowy approach to the mechanical principle involved; otherwise they were all completely mystified, for no concrete explanation had been given them. Interrogation elicited either vague replies or downright evasions. Only the term itself was well embedded, and repeated parrot-like.

We do not suggest that the term means nothing to every student, singer and teacher.

When a singer makes an adjustment that produces well-balanced tone it does not matter what label he gives it in his own mind: he can say to himself that he is "tarring" or "whitewashing" the tone.* No harm is done, so long as he keeps the funny term to himself and does not pass it on to others as representative of a technical process.

Terms are employed to explain and possibly reflect the means

* On a pupil's copy of *The Messiah* we saw the words "Black snore" written over a high note by one of his former teachers to indicate head-voice "covering"! This student, who had already made a name for himself in the concert world, confessed that he had never understood the import of this term.

whereby ends are secured. We should avoid the use, therefore, of inane words. If a student is told to "cover" the tone and given a definite explanation of the principle involved, well and good as far as that student and that teacher are concerned, although personally we would still object to the term itself because its intrinsic meaning is nil. But if, as in the majority of cases, no adequate explanation accompanies the order, or advice, to "cover", what is the student to do? All attempts on his part to analyse the term must be abortive because its etymology affords not even the faintest clue to the technical procedure involved. From the technical standpoint the term is barren. To be told, and not taught, to do a thing is a pretty hopeless business. So he looks wise, pretends he has understood, and meantime is told to keep on trying because the head notes are bound to come "in time" by covering them! So he goes on covering with ardour and insistence, still pretending to himself and secretly considering it all just another vocal conundrum that will, perhaps, be solved one day.

If, on the other hand, the student was told, and taught how, to modify or round off the vowel, at least he would have something to go by, to work on, even if no further explanation were forthcoming; he could attempt adjustment with some possibility of success, for a not inconsiderable amount of informative juice could be squeezed out of the terms themselves. A simple appeal to the dictionary in the case of the verb "to modify" would reveal that it means "to change slightly in form". That alone conveys something substantial for a working basis. But "to cover" is lost in the mists of query when applied to vocal tone.

Again, the unenlightened use of "covering" tends to cause the student to close or cramp his throat, thereby bottling in and smothering the tone. This in turn reacts adversely on the vibrator mechanism, for, as explained particularly in Chapter XIII, the slightest distortion of the mouth-pharynx cavity unbalances in equal degree the mechanism of the cords.

Distortion of the resonators signifies a cramped, clamped shaping that is analogous to the closed bud, within the tight folds of which lie hidden the inherent beauty of colour and formation of the rose complete and replete with splendour. An inherently beautiful tone can be so cramped and crushed as a result of wrong internal shaping within the mouth-pharynx that it is unrecognizable as such. But release it, knock off its shackles, open it out and shape it to full bloom, and we obtain a perfect picture of form, colour, and "perfume".

If past experience had only envisaged a tightly-closed rosebud, the beauteous possibilities of the rose, when open to its fullest establishment, could never even be imagined. Knowing only the bud, we could never imagine even such potentiality of form, colour, and odour. A babe that knows only of the rosebud can never imagine a rose in full bloom; and from the standpoint of vocal technique so many students and singers (through no fault of their own) are babes, because their minds and voices have been fed on pappy oddities and enigmatic phraseology.

Even as a rosebud is a cramped, compressed thing without the rose's true ultimate shape, colour, and perfume, and therefore complexion and expression, so the tonal product of this baneful "covering" business is, in the main, a headless, cramped thing so little like what it could be if it were not smothered in the folds of constriction.

The normally open rose represents the ideal vowel formation and colouring. The painter first *sees* form and colour before physically applying the latter within the former; like the sculptor, he gives shape to his imagination. After all, vocal tone is nothing but *shaped* vibration. Physical science defines a liquid as "that which has definite size but no definite shape until it takes the shape of a containing vessel". In vocal science we can say that vocal tone is a vibrational "fluid" that has no definite shape until it takes that of the mouth-pharynx while pouring into, through, and out of it. And as it comes out of it into an admiring world it still retains its intrinsic qualities of form and colour. Even as molten metal is poured into a mould of preconceived utility, so the vibrations produced basically by the cord mechanism flow into the mouth-pharynx mould of preconceived and preadjusted shape in order to produce a shaped vibration called a vowel.

What would happen if we wrote and spoke with the same confusion of vowel and consonant as is encountered in the majority of singers today; conversation and correspondence would be more or less at a standstill. What we know of "covering" is that it is a no-method that produces confusion because it is itself a product of confused thought.

Too open a rose, as in overbloom, analogizes the too open or blatant tone. Blatant tone is due to too much cord in length being engaged for a particular pitch, that produces too broad a sound-beam; and these two errors or excesses are due to a wrong shaping of the mouth-pharynx cavity, an error that in turn is the outcome of wrong *mental* shaping.

Modern "methods" remind us of the spurious sovereign: surface shine in abundance and empty promise of purchase. They are sponsored in the main by individuals with an ear not attuned to what constitutes *ideal* vocal tone that should obtain on all pitches with all vowels. Because of the lack of proper training and from the absence, more than ever today, of suitable standards for comparison, these votaries fail to appreciate the characteristic form and quality of vocal tone accruing from *correct* mechanical adjustments on the entire vocal compass; they fail, moreover, to realize that *every vowel at every pitch has a distinct individuality all its own*, particularly on the upper medium and high notes. (See p. 70 (footnote) and p. 318.)

CHAPTER VI

HOW LEARNING TO SING BY IMITATION
MAY BE UNPROFITABLE

INASMUCH as so many precepts and principles of the teacher's art have been lost or forgotten, recourse to teaching by imitation seems in the main to be the usual and only medium of expression, supplemented at times by casual remarks of doubtful utility.

Let us examine dispassionately this method of teaching by imitation. Criticism, to be useful, should be constructive to the extent of offering a measure of compensation for demolition.

Actual vocal examples can be illuminating, or destructively misleading. We can cultivate an "ear" by listening to good vocal tone produced by eminent singers in the theatre or concert hall, or even to carefully selected gramophone records. But when we have thus cultivated an "ear" for good tone, what have we actually learned? Have we gained positive knowledge of the *causes* underlying the effects we have learned to appreciate? To this you, as a student, may retort by asserting that you have imitated or have tried to imitate these tonal effects and by so doing have been able to produce your own voice in a better way. We grant this possibility. The idea is good, but inchoate. What we wish to stress is: Has any actual *knowledge of cause* been acquired by such imitative process, have any basic facts, physiological and acoustical, been deduced from these vocal effects? We think that every attempt to reproduce an effect without possessing some knowledge of cause must come within the domain of blind experimentation. The student cannot afford to speculate in guesswork procedure.

What does teaching by imitation offer us? Does the imitative method inculcate substantial elements? In the first place the singer must be himself, and not a more or less poor imitation of somebody else, whoever that may be. It is a mistake to suppose that a pupil can usefully attempt the imitation of the tonal quality (if any) of a teacher's vocal demonstrations, even supposing they are good technically speaking. Provided adequate explanations are forthcoming he can, however, endeavour to apply the mechanical principles involved in such demonstrations and thereby improve his own individual quality.

If a singer, particularly a great singer, is in his prime, he will not settle down to systematic teaching. Even should he retire before the signs of vocal wear are apparent (they rarely do) and take up teaching, he might possibly attempt to start the pupil where he (the artist) left off, impatiently expecting him to put into immediate practice the sum total of vast experience.

Teaching is an art in itself and requires a special turn of mind. Even as some brilliant mathematicians are incompetent as teachers because unable to communicate their ideas in comprehensible form, so in very many cases is the great singer a failure when it comes to explaining to an untutored mind his sensations of vocal tone and the technicalities on which they are based. It is one thing to know and another to impart with clarity.

Every pupil is a mind that requires a somewhat separate treatment, and if individual peculiarities are to be met successfully explanations must be varicoloured. The teacher, moreover, must be able correctly to diagnose the individual mental and physical traits and vocal defects, and adduce appropriate remedial explanations easy of comprehension, otherwise total or partial failure will result.

What if the retired singer turns to teaching with a badly worn voice? Are we to believe that the pupil is able to acquire real technical knowledge merely by imitating frayed tone floating, maybe, now on the crest now in the trough of a vocal wave popularly known as "wobble"? Are we to believe that a male student is able successfully and profitably to imitate the tones produced by a female teacher for demonstration purposes? Reason cannot subscribe to such an obvious absurdity. If, however, she confined her teaching to technical aspects, vocally illustrating some of them, then she could be as successful with male as she may have been with female students.

Supplemented by adequate explanations, a woman teacher could profitably demonstrate vocally the mental and physical aspects of such technicalities as the attack of the tone, laryngopharyngeal adjustment, vowel formation and modification in relation to pitch, the formation and release of consonants, *messa di voce*, *legato* singing, and so on.

Again, as regards the accepted practice of teaching by imitation, it is preposterous to think of a young, fresh voice imitating slavishly the decrepit tone of natural or acquired old age with its frayed edges, bald patches, and sagging propensities.

What can a soprano really learn by attempting to imitate the tones of a male voice even supposing they are well produced and not of the worn variety? Vocal demonstrations can be constructive only when accompanied by adequate explanations of the technicalities on which they are based. It is only under such considerations that the male teacher can successfully train a female voice, and the female teacher a male voice.

All this comes under the assumption that the teacher is able at least to produce his or her voice correctly. How many can? On the other hand, what must be the net results of the imitative method of teaching when vocal demonstration issues from a badly adjusted medium (as is so often the case), when the vocal examples are poor or downright bad, when the product is *basically* wrong?

Again, under the assumption that the vocal examples are the product of a sound technique, we do not of course exclude the possibility (particularly when nature has been technically lavish) of a voice being produced well solely, more or less, as a result of imitation, or of a successful career being made on this basis. Thus, quite oblivious perhaps to his technical prowess he is content that the voice "just happens". Should he get off his vocal line, however, he is lost unless he can go to a good teacher for readjustment. Defects, sometimes the outcome of tonal exaggerations or of mannerisms, creep into production, imperceptibly develop and accumulate to the point where the singer finds himself confronted with some note or notes completely out of gear. This calls a halt for introspection and overhaul. Lacking, however, that indispensable knowledge of cause and effect, having, in other words, no technical grounding, he is quite unable to diagnose the trouble, let alone apply the remedy.

The technically untutored ear often condemns certain vocal tones. However, it is one thing to recognize a bad effect and quite another to diagnose correctly the *cause* of the error and select and apply the proper corrective.

We are aware that teaching by imitation, interspersed perhaps with some explanation or other, is the procedure adopted by most teachers all over the world. The almost universal adoption of such a method, however, affords no guarantee of its excellence. To our thinking it is one of many symptoms of the present grave decline in both teaching and performance. Imitation may have something to commend it; but at best it is only a means to the end, a very limited means, and offers nothing basic or substantial from the technical standpoint. And without technique where are we?

When a pupil produces tone that is woolly, or guttural, or throaty, etc., a well produced vocal example, even if rather worn or weak, may possibly be able to show up and illustrate first the defect and then the correct form. Vocal examples of this kind and to this end are genuinely useful and constructive; but they constitute merely a small part of the actual teaching of the physio-acoustical processes, cause and effect, responsible for vocal tone of ideal form and quality, for the art of teaching is *based* on technical considerations, its true office being the inculcation of knowledge, of facts, of working principles that admit of no blind groping and guesswork.

After all, it is not unreasonable to suggest that pupils go to teachers in order to get facts, not rhetoric; they want to come away after a course of study feeling that they have acquired at least a working knowledge of vocal technique, a knowledge built into brain and voice. Does not the acquisition of a sound technique spell vocal independence for the pupil and make for ultimate mastery and success?

Summing up, we must labour the point that to train successfully all categories of voices, male and female, a complete technical knowledge is essential, for it is the *sole* basis on which a teacher can diagnose faults, bring into bold relief the cause of a defect and supply the corrective. By technical knowledge we mean only such physiological facts as relate to acoustical laws, and only such acoustical facts as relate to physiological laws, as far as they govern vocal tone; it also includes such aerodynamic phenomena as are associated with the vocal mechanism.

CHAPTER VII

THE PROCESS OF GRADUAL ELIMINATION OF THE VIBRATOR MASS

Part I

IN ANY ATTEMPT to demolish a theory that has long enjoyed unchallenged acceptance in some quarters, there must be put forward an adequate constructive alternative. The conventional term "register" as applied to the human voice is not merely a misnomer but definitely misleading. Not only does it fail to offer a clear conception of what it purports to stand for, but reveals no detail of mechanical procedure or process.

When a number of physiologists invaded the field of vocal mechanics the term "register" was invested with importance in an attempt to explain and possibly to displace the old but harmless, even if incomplete, terms: "head voice" and "chest voice". At the time, one only, Sir Morell Mackenzie, the renowned throat specialist, came very close to the truth by stating (still employing, however, the term "register") that "every note is a register unto itself".

The introduction and acceptance of the new term and the theory it stood for did incalculable harm because it was instrumental in provoking that cleavage of thought which is the chief disintegrating element responsible for the decline of singing. This is no mere coincidence, but a traceable fact. After over a century of investigation physiologists are still nonplussed as to the exact behaviour of the vocal cords and of the laryngeal unit with its sixty-odd muscles, particularly where the mechanism producing an ascending scale from the normally lowest to the normally highest note is concerned. However, in the scientific world the acoustician and aerodynamical expert are advancing the frontiers of vocal knowledge today more than the physiologists who have enjoyed a long innings without actually adding much of value to vocal lore. The latter have reached this impasse because so many of their "findings" are totally at variance with well-defined sensations of vocal tone experienced by all singers whose production is correct, physio-logically and acoustically. This is no diatribe belittling the work of well-meaning men. Unfortunately, however, and particularly from the beginning of·the twentieth century as medical science advanced rapidly, many physiologists worked in collaboration with singers and teachers whose knowledge of vocal mechanics was incomplete, or patchy, or perhaps a product of personal theories, or pet tenets and fads spiced with plausible rhetoric; consequently, they were misled. Many of the books they published were harmful.

Students of singing read, and are told, that "a register is a series of tones produced by the same unchanging mechanism". Is this the case where the violin, clarinet, cornet, harp, piano, saxophone, etc. are concerned? Much depends of course on the meaning attached to the word "mechanism". Now, where vocal tone is concerned, how can a series of tones be produced by the same "unchanging" mechanism when: (1) each tone has its own pitch, i.e. an exact number of vibrations per second (the number varying according to the pitch) which should be produced by a mathe-matically exact length, thickness, and tension of vocal cord, and good only for that one pitch; (2) each note thus produced gives rise to and has its own sound-beam of an exact size in height and diameter; (3) each note thus produced with physiological and acoustical exactness has its own peculiar and characteristic quality-colour;* (4) every tone of the vocal scale is produced by a slightly

* There are three basic timbres peculiar to and distinguishing the three groups of notes classed under Chest, Medium, Head. We call them "Group Timbres". To differentiate them, we suggest that the Head timbre is light blue, the Medium a darker hue, and the Chest a dark blue. Each timbre acquires its idiosyncracy, distinguishing it and making it readily recognizable, from the shape and location of the resonating cavities serving it.

To illustrate: the Head voice, that includes the series of notes as from F sharp, fifth line, upwards, has a distinctive Group timbre all its own, that even the layman is able to recognize. Superimposed on this timbre there is (1) the individual and characteristic pattern or shape of *each* note of said series, which accrues from the particular mechanical adjustment of the vibrator-resonator systems for each pitch, and distinguishing it in slight degree from its neighbour above and below; and (2) the *personal* quality or tonal "complexion" dis-tinguishing the singer's voice from all other voices—even as features and expression distinguish a face from all others.

Again, to illustrate: a high A, *well* produced by a tenor (by all tenors, irrespective of nationality), whatever the calibre of his voice from light to different laryngo-pharyngeal adjustment as the scale is ascended from the lowest to the highest pitch. No "unchanging" mechanism within or without the larynx can possibly accomplish this and express vocal fitness and balance. When a tone is perfectly produced, none of the above mechanical factors are applicable to any other tone above or below that tone. Luisa Tetrazzini wrote: "If you ensure that each individual note is right, the problem of the 'registers' need not trouble you."

From the vocal standpoint, pitch is the product of a vibrator having an exact length, an exact thickness, and an exact tension, varying for every pitch, which, when set in motion, vibrates an exact number of times per second (frequency). Also the frequency varies for every pitch. If, as in the case of a tuning fork, the vibrator is man-made with precision to give a certain pitch, its numerical vibration per second is exact and unalterable; if man-adjusted with precision, as in the case of the laryngeal vibrator

dramatic, reveals a truly characteristic Head-voice *timbre*, a characteristic "ring", and a pattern or shape peculiar to it alone which are due respectively to the exactness of the adjustment of resonator and vibrator. And so every note of the tenor voice is of the above threefold characteristic: Group timbre, individual shaping, personal quality enfolded within the well-produced tone. All notes of a Group have naturally a close family likeness.

Also, the medium series of notes from F natural, fifth line, to F natural, first space, have their collective Group timbre on which (1) and (2) are superimposed as above. And the same thing applies to the notes below this last mentioned F, which form the series known as "Chest". Be it noted, however, that all the chest notes and the first few of the medium from F, first space, upwards, are not markedly characteristic as regards (1) above. Only the highly-trained ear is able to detect the extremely slight note-to-note variations.

The above considerations apply to all categories of voice, male and female.

It is a lamentable fact that for the greater part teachers, while able to recognize Group timbres and appreciate the singer's personal quality, are not sufficiently instructed in the art of recognizing (1) above, actually *the* greatest asset of a master because it connotes exact knowledge of both cause and effect; in other words, of correct mechanical adjustment for every pitch and with every vowel as revealed in balanced tonal product. It also connotes recognition of faulty adjustment, however slight it may be, and exact knowledge of the corrective to be applied. This is teaching polished to the finest of fine arts. Hearing becomes so sensitive under such analytical work that it practically amounts to *vision*, clear-cut vision of the varying mechanical adjustments. We have developed the fine art of "seeing" through hearing (even as, with eyes closed, we can "see" through touch). We often wonder what most teachers listen for, what tonal models they have in mind and ear. In bad production, (1) above is rigidly uniform and therefore monotonous. (See (T), pp. 317-8.)

(vocal cords), its numerical vibration per second can, and should be equally exact, although not necessarily unalterable. The tuning fork, normally unalterable, can have its pitch lowered by the application of a piece of cobbler's wax, and raised by slightly filing the tip of the prongs (an example of "elimination").

Once it has been properly adjusted for a given pitch with a certain vowel, the vocal vibrator is not unalterable, because an *excess* breath pressure will inevitably increase to excess the vertical thickness of cord employed, thereby lowering the pitch in degree. One excess causing another excess. And this is the main reason why so many singers are *flat* most of the time.

Copper wire is coiled round the low strings of the piano in order to lower their pitch. If a vibrator, apart from being thickened, is also lengthened, even in slight degree, the pitch will fall. We have therefore two pitch-lowering factors, to which a third can be added, viz. that of lowered tension of the cords. Conversely, if the vibrator is made both lighter (thinner) and shorter concurrently with an appropriate increase in tension, we get three pitch-raising factors. This acoustical law applies to all vibrators, including the vocal cords. In ordinary man-made vibrators the shortening process alone is sufficient to raise the pitch, and the lengthening to lower it, as in the case of the violin string, the tension and thickness of which remains unaltered in the process. The filing of the prongs of a tuning fork not only shortens but lightens it, thereby raising its pitch, while the increase in mass resulting from an application of wax is sufficient in itself to lower the pitch of the fork; the factors of tension and length do not arise in this particular instance.

Where the vocal vibrator is concerned the question is not so simple, for a complicated system of muscles, governed by a mental factor, actuates it. Which actuation is mainly subconscious or automatic.

If the vocal cords are correctly adjusted for a given pitch and the note is produced *forte* (a maximum compatible with vibrator and tonal balance) we have three main factors to deal with: length, thickness, and tension of vibrator. Now in every vocal vibrator adjustment for a given pitch, the factor of length is, or should be, absolutely unalterable because length varies with the pitch, and to every pitch corresponds an *exact* length. It should be, must be unalterable, therefore, because the slightest increase in length of the vibrator will decrease the pitch in corresponding degree. Not even under the impulse of a *crescendo* must it lengthen (as it may well do if the vowelled tone is "opened" too much in relation to the pitch); if it does, even in slight degree, the pitch falls. From the vocal standpoint, therefore, length of vibrator in relation to pitch should be unalterable. Vocal nature is adamant on this point and has allowed no margin for manœuvre in this respect. For a given pitch, she objects to the slightest increase or decrease in the vibrator length. Knowing this, we can say categorically that length is pitch. While establishing this factor, however, she correlates the factors of thickness and tension which must obtain in balanced proportions in relation to pitch. She yields some points in regard to the matter of vibrator thickness in depth; for instance, if the pitch has been established, by length, first on a *piano* basis, the subsequent *crescendo* to *forte* engages a gradually increasing amount of vocal cord vertically in depth—the length remaining unaltered during the process. On reaching what we call a normal *forte* we envisage a vibrator that has been given first its exact length and then its maximum permissible vertical thickness. From this point she has conceded an additional margin, over and above the normal *f*, for purposes of a maximum *crescendo* we call *ff*. But should the *crescendo* overstep this final maximum permissible margin, even in slightest degree, the pitch will fall unless an extra dose of lung pressure is forthcoming—a brutal measure to be shunned by the true artist. Even so, the forced breath pressure may not succeed in boosting up the frequency; on the contrary, it will very likely thicken the cords still further, which will flatten the tone still more.

Acoustic law determined this maximum line of demarcation; obedience to the law expects that it will not be surpassed. If the singer is wise, only on exceptional occasions will he exceed the normal *f* and draw upon the reserve of vibrator thickness. With practice and experience he will eventually get the feeling. Through his sensations of tone, culminating particularly in the focal points, he will be able ultimately so to regulate the *crescendo* development of the vibrator in depth that the aforesaid maximum limitation will never be exceeded. *By concentrating on the focal points* the singer's mind will gradually acquire the *feel* of balanced development from minimum to maximum, and so, indirectly, control the output of the vibrator itself.

Let us compare normal *f* in singing to a glass normally full to the brim, and the extra allowance of maximum development to the small extra amount of water that can be added without overflowing—provided it be carefully done. As drop after drop is added, the surface appears to bulge slightly and even overlap the rim of the glass; and yet it does not overflow. There comes a stage, however, when *one drop more* causes an overflow, no matter how carefully the last drop is added. Or if several drops are added rudely, the whole of the extra allowance above the normal overflows. And so with the voice: even one extra degree of development in depth over and above the line of extra maximum allowance is sufficient to upset the whole laryngo-pharyngeal adjustment for the particular pitch and vitiate the quality of the tonal product.

The third factor is breath pressure and its concomitant: resistance. Even though possessing a manœuvrable margin, it also has a definite permissible maximum beyond which it must not be exercised. If exercised to excess, even in slight degree, it will unduly increase the vibrator thickness in depth. This aspect has been fully dealt with in the ensuing chapters.

From the above, the student can deduce the fact that Nature has *not* made the three main factors—length, vertical thickness, and tension-pressure—foolproof. On the other hand, she has endowed man with a measure of intelligent discernment which obviously she expects to be used.

The laryngeal vibrator is adjustable in length, thickness, and tension *at the will of the singer*.* The fact that *to every pitch in the vocal scale corresponds a truly individual vibrator adjustment* (individual because no two pitches, however close together, are produced by exactly the same vibrator length, thickness, and tension) is sufficient to expose and dispose of the fallacy that "a series of tones" are produced by "the same unchanging mechanism".

It is true that the difference between the laryngeal adjustment for one note and that, say, for its immediate neighbour above or below, is extremely slight. On the low and lower medium notes the difference is almost imperceptible, while on the upper medium and high notes the difference from note to note is still slight (mechanically speaking) but definitely perceptible, through tonal

* Here the acoustician and expert teacher disagree with certain physiologists who, voiceless as they generally are, dogmatically assert that "the singer has no conscious control whatever over his vocal cords". (See our "Terminal adjustment" countercheck on p. 92 (footnote).)

sensations, to the singer himself who makes the adjustment (if he has had the proper training), and to the listener on account of the different quality-colours that distinguish particularly the high notes one from the other. But if the difference is slight, sometimes very slight, between one note and the next, say, a semitone or a whole tone, the sensation is marked for the singer particularly when there is an interval of a third, fourth, or fifth, etc.; consequently, the custodians of the vocal registers theory, born and bred as it was apparently in ignorance of vocal-acoustical law, are skating unconsciously on thin ice.

Unfortunately, "a series of tones" can be produced by the "same unchanging mechanism". Too often today do we hear well-intentioned but misguided singers apply this pseudo-technique. And what is the outcome? A fearful straining of the entire vocal apparatus, a more or less forced production, a monotonous tonal product often flat and with little or no variety in shape and colour; and, ultimately—the universal wobble. The brutal procedure is invariably to boost, with forced breath pressure, a thick and long cord adjustment of a low note to produce a higher note that acoustically and physiologically (mechanically) demands a much smaller vibrator.

Apart from the physical harm it does (preventing or obstructing that natural process of gradual elimination of the vibrator mass, i.e. length and thickness of cord, as the scale is ascended, a process that is *the main key to correct production*, as explained below), the register theory has always created and still creates the confusing impression that the voice is made up of several disparate links instead of being formed of one perfectly graduated piece of vibrating, resonant material.

Part II

Certain scientific facts known in the last century were considered somehow to be unrelated to the human vibrator. For instance, the fact that a vibrator must be short and thin (of small, light mass) in order to produce a high pitch, and conversely, of comparatively much greater mass in length and thickness to produce a low pitch, seems to have left investigators unmoved and uninterested from the vocal standpoint. And still today it leaves a few of the older physiologists equally unmoved in spite of the scientifically confirmed facts now at our disposal on this and many other aspects of vocal technique. Is it any wonder how a century ago the fallacious theory of vocal "registers" came into being? There is no excuse, however, for the modern champions of this old fallacy.

Between the two extremes, representing the normally highest and the normally lowest note of the human voice, there are many graduations in vibrator mass; in other words, different effective lengths, and thicknesses (in depth) of vocal cord are engaged to satisfy the different conditions of pitch. On an ascending scale the cords gradually shorten and get gradually thinner; and, conversely, on a descending scale they gradually lengthen and thicken in depth. Until the normally highest pitch is reached on an ascending scale, every successive note is produced by a gradually *decreased* vibrator mass, and, on descending again until the normally lowest pitch is reached, every successive note is produced by a gradually increased vibrator mass. A beautifully simple mechanism.

With few exceptions, as will be explained later, the graduations of decrease in the vibrating element as the scale is ascended are practically uniform; in other words, the shortening-thinning process occurs with "measured step". As the scale is descended, the graduations of increase in vibrator mass are similarly regular.

This graduated reducing or eliminating of the vibrator mass as the scale is ascended and its gradual accretion as the scale is descended, is a natural process or mechanism operating in strict accord with acoustical law. While this process is inherent in the human voice, not all voices are endowed with a *completely* natural (or finished) mechanism; indeed, few are. Consequently the mechanical or rather the muscular lapses in this sense must be made good by rational re-education of the parts concerned. We repeat that the majority of untrained voices are mechanically incomplete or, say, undeveloped, and from percentages of "naturalness", ranging approximately from forty-five to seventy-five or eighty per cent., have to be brought into line up to the possible optimum of complete mechanical efficiency or complete naturalness of one hundred per cent. by the teacher's art.*

* By "mechanically incomplete" is meant a voice that does not function to perfection from the lowest to the highest pitch on the principle of gradual elimination of the vibrator mass as the pitch rises, whatever the vowel employed. A "completely natural" voice is one that does. (See footnote, p. 49.)

Anent the exceptions in the graduations referred to above we must point to a phenomenon, little known, by the way, occurring at more or less fixed points or notes of the scale. And all categories of voices have their characteristic notes in this sense. It is simply the fact of an *extra* shortening and thinning of the vocal cords at these points, as is explained hereunder. Because the phenomenon is simple, and because the sensation to the singer is so slight, it has been overlooked and neglected; and yet it is a factor of paramount importance in vocal technique. The student will realize this as he reads on.

Now, by way of example, let us take the soprano voice and, with the aid of the miniature searchlight of knowledge at our disposal, follow its mechanical processes on an ascending scale.

For the purpose of measuring the graduations representing the note-by-note shortening process of the cords chromatically on an ascending scale, we propose to divide one inch into sixty-four parts or grades. As the length of cord in sopranos is generally about half an inch (it is slightly more in the bigger calibres) and assuming her compass to be thirty-two notes (semitones) from B♭, below middle C, to F, five semitones above high C, we are dividing this half-inch vibrator into thirty-two equal degrees or grades, one for each semitone. Consequently, each step in the shortening process will be represented by 1/64th of an inch, the entire length of half an inch vibrator being thus divided into 32/64ths.

Obviously, in view of the mysterious X still unexplained in vocal mechanics, this scale measurement cannot apply to men's voices nor to certain of the bigger calibres of female voices, as in the former the cords vary in length from three-quarters to (very occasionally) one inch, and in the latter anything from the normal half to three-quarters of an inch, especially in the big dramatic soprano or mezzo-soprano. In both cases the compass is about two octaves, or twenty-five semitones, or a little over, sometimes. However, the illustration will serve the purpose of forming a mental picture of the working of the wonderful laryngeal vibrator mechanism, and as such, can be proportionately related to the individual category of voice possessed by the student reading this work.

As soon as our soprano commences to ascend the scale her vocal cords immediately begin to shorten by regular graduations of 1/64th of an inch per semitone.

N.B.—Be it noted that each shortening is accompanied by a

degree of thinning of the vibrator mass thereby gradually lightening it in compliance with the acoustical law governing pitch. The student will also bear in mind that the shortening and thinning processes are invariably accompanied by a gradually increasing tension (connoting proportionate resistance) of the cords, that is also measurable in regular degrees or graduations. He should also note that the gradual "loss" or elimination of the vibrator mass as the scale is ascended finds ample compensation in an ever-increasing resonance. We cannot stress sufficiently the importance of these factors of acoustical law.*

With these premises in view let us now accompany our soprano note by note up the chromatic scale, on the AH vowel. As she makes her note-by-note excursion from low B♭ through the six pitches—B♮, C, C♯, D, D♯, E (first line)—her cords will shorten by six graduations of 1/64th of an inch each: a total, therefore, of 6/64ths.

We now come to the phenomenon mentioned above: From this E♮ to F, first space, our soprano's cords (if so far her mechanism is correct) will not be content with the regular 1/64th shortening. They demand an *extra*, further shortening but only very little. Which *extra* shortening is of course accompanied by an *extra* thinning of the cords that, summed up, signifies an extra lightening of the vibrator mass (We can almost "hear" the student thinking, as he reads this: "How is this done?" The answer is the "lift-up", as explained in Chapter XVI.)

Now the immediate result of all this is that the resonance increases proportionately. In other words, the sound-beam that had by very small degrees increased in height, enjoys an *extra* increase as on the said F♮. This very slightly taller sound-beam on F enables the voice to couple or tune in to the exact resonating point within Zone N.1, i.e. the mouth-pharynx cavity (see Chapter XI). Consequently, no "break" occurs from this E to F♮, the "bridging" being perfectly executed by the above described processes.

---

* The cord-shortening process is achieved by what we could well call a forward-creeping muscular grip moving pincer-like horizontally along the adducted cords, with a "braking" process progressively *stilling* portion after portion of the vibrant cords. For an ascending interval the forward-moving grip adjusts itself accordingly. On a descending scale, or interval, a reversing (releasing) action takes place. It reminds one of the action of a "zip"-fastener, closing and opening. (See p. 81.)

The aforesaid seven notes, B♭ to E♮, reflect the so-called chest quality.

As our soprano proceeds upwards note by note from F through the six pitches—F♯, G, G♯, A, A♯, B (third line), her cords will again shorten by a further 6/64ths. Here again we meet the phenomenon of minute *extra* shortening of the vibrator; therefore, provided her mechanism is so far correct, from this B♮ to C♮, third space, her cords will not be content with the regular 1/64th shortening; they demand a further shortening (minute, if you will), as in the case above from E to F. Which extra shortening is accompanied, of course, by an extra thinning of the cords, and therefore a general lightening of the vibrator mass. It is well to remember that also the thinning process is effected by regular graduations and synchronizes with the shortening process. The net result is a slight extra increase in resonance; in other words, a slight extra increase in height of the sound-beam of C which is thus enabled to tune or couple in its correct focal point within the mouth-pharynx resonator. (See para. 4 and footnote, p. 127.)

We must remind the student that also the tension of the cords increases by regular degrees, the tensioning process synchronizing with the shortening and thinning processes. The vocal cord mechanism operates, therefore, under three simultaneous processes, viz. shortening, thinning, and tensioning with "pari passu" graduations as the scale is ascended; the effect of the three processes in operation is a gradually increased lightening of the vibrator as the scale is ascended.

As our soprano continues to ascend, taking in her stride first the two notes C♯, D, fourth line, which are tuned in to Zone 1 (mouth-pharynx), and then E♭, E♮, F♮ (fifth line) which are tuned in to the Intermediate zone (located just above the arc of the palate), her cords will again have shortened by another 5/64ths. In Chapter XI we have designated this Intermediate zone as the threshold of Zone 2. We will not dwell here on the sensations the resultant sound-beams give to the singer as regards their gradually increasing height, their inclination with respect to the vertical, their gradually decreasing diameter, as this has been elaborated in Chapter X, and elsewhere.

When passing from F♮ to F♯ fifth line, we again encounter the same phenomenon of the *extra* shortening of the cords. This time, the "extra" is more pronounced and quite noticeable to the singer.

If, as we assume it to be, her mechanism is correctly adjusted on
F♮, it will demand (peremptorily, this time) an extra shortening
of the cords in order to bridge it over to the F♯, which is *the entry
note* to the true head resonating zone (Zone 2). This extra shortening, attended by an extra thinning and therefore general lightening
of the vibrator (plus an appropriate increase in tension), effects just
that extra increase in height of the sound-beam (resonance) that
will permit it to couple (or tune) into the head resonator.

From this F♯ to high C there are seven notes, and each will
demand the regular 1/64th shortening. All sopranos, whatever

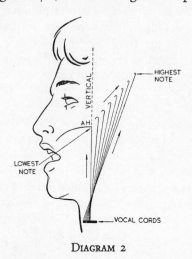

DIAGRAM 2

their calibre, as well as the mezzos and contraltos, enter the true
head resonating zone at F♯, fifth line; that is to say they *should*, and
will do so when their mechanism is correct either naturally or as a
result of study.

Again, due to the mysterious X in vocal mechanics, the shortening process seems to incline towards a certain irregularity as soon
as the true head resonator is reached, for the movements of the
sound-beams are quite marked. In fact, the increase in height and
the direction taken with respect to the vertical are much more
perceptible than before. And this phenomenon of the sensations
of tone applies to all voices, male and female, as soon as the
"head voice" is reached. Chapter X deals with this point more
thoroughly.

At high C♯ the Super-head resonating zone commences. This, by the way, is also a little known fact. As our soprano goes from high C to C♯, once again we are confronted with the same phenomenon of an *extra* shortening of the cords in order to effect the "bridging" and consequent entry to the Super-head zone. (See Diagram 9, p. 152.)

Having reached high C, our soprano's cords will now be shortened to the extent that only a minute (pinhead) effective length remains for producing the next five notes in the Super-head resonating zone. In fact, on reaching this high C, after ascending all the way from her lowest note, her cords will have shortened not only by the normal 26/64ths of an inch, but a little more besides, corresponding to the miniature total of the three *extra* shortenings abovementioned. According to our hypothetical scale of measurement, therefore, she has an effective length of vibrator left to her that is slightly less than 5/64ths wherewith to produce her super-high notes; the other 26/64ths being now *inert or motionless*, or, as we prefer to say, "eliminated", that is, *eliminated from active participation in the vibrational field*. This minute effective length of vibrator available to our soprano merely consists of the *extreme anterior end* of the adducted cords because, as stated before (footnote, p. 78), the stilling or eliminating process of the cords executes a back-to-front horizontal movement.*

It is indeed wonderful how such a minute effective length of vibrator is able to produce a series of notes of such high frequency and carrying power while being still further shortened during the process! (See p. 226, minute focal point of E in alt.)

This extraordinary capacity of a half-inch long cord to produce well over thirty notes has been regarded as an inexplicable phenomenon by teachers and physiologists alike. We are, however, able to throw some light on this "miracle of Nature" with the help of our scientific collaborator, Mr. N. Bonavia-Hunt. He says that he has been able to produce notes from treble G to the

* On p. 1194 of the *British Medical Journal*, December 10, 1938, we read: "Pressman's film (1938) which was shown this year to the Royal Society of Medicine, showed clearly that . . . on the high notes the *anterior part* of the cords vibrates." This is indeed a gratifying pointer from the scientific field as it substantiates in 1938 what the author had already published in 1936 in *The Science and Sensations of Vocal Tone* (Dent, p. 176), and, moreover, what has been known to him for thirty years through analysis of correct sensations of vocal tone.

F

top A of the piano (twenty-seven notes) by means of an organ reed pipe fitted with a *very* thin vibrator made of *aluminium* and only five-eighths of an inch in length. The top A (3,480 vibrations per second) was sounded by a vibrating length of one-sixteenth of an inch only. A vibrator formed of lighter material still, if sufficiently stiff, would be capable of producing a further octave of notes with ease. The resonator employed for the production of all the twenty-seven notes abovementioned consisted of an inverted conical tube of appropriate length and internal capacity to accommodate *all* the notes. The applied wind pressure was unchanged. The vibrator was graduated in length by means of the usual tuning spring drawn along the surface of the vibrator tongue.

If so unadaptable a mechanism is able to produce more than two octaves of notes in this upper region of the musical scale, it does not require an abnormal degree of credulousness on our part to believe that a highly elastic, adaptable, variable mechanism (in which mass, weight, tension, pressure and vibrating length can be adjusted in an almost endless permutation of conditions) should be capable of producing at least two and a half octaves of musical sound, and very exceptionally three octaves (see footnote, p. 102).

Just as a reminder we would add that the extra shortening of the cords occurring at the four above-mentioned points is invariably accompanied by an extra "lift-up" of the tone, a factor of great importance. (See Chapter XVI.)

We believe that the above illustration of the vocal-mechanical processes obtaining on an ascending scale, together with the scientific confirmation relevant thereto, are sufficient to bring into disrepute the vocal registers theory that is still accepted by so many.

A consideration which serves to temper our censure of the founders and champions of the vocal registers fallacy is the fact of the as yet, even today, little known vocal-acoustic law governing vocal mechanism, viz.: The lower the pitch the more the primary element (vibrator mass) and the less of secondary element (resonance); and conversely, the higher the pitch the less there is of primary element and the more of resonance. This is because the mechanical principle exacts:

(a) that the lower the note, the thicker and longer must be the vocal cords, with a comparatively low tension;

(b) that the higher the note, the thinner and shorter must be the vocal cords, with a comparatively high tension.

Even though the great teachers of the remote and immediate past, and the very few still with us, sensed and applied empirically the principle involved, securing brilliant results, physiological investigation was conspicuous for its sightless eyes and unhearing ears.

The results on resonance of this law operating within the laryngeal mechanism can be summed up in the fact that the longer and thicker the cords (or the greater the vibrator mass) the shorter and broader the sound-beam, and vice versa, the shorter and thinner the cords (or the smaller the vibrator mass) the taller and narrower the sound-beam. A very simple law indeed. So simple that it is today almost entirely ignored, but violated by the majority.

Consequently, as our soprano ascends the scale from the lowest to the highest note, her laryngeal mechanism, when graduated as above, produces a sound-beam that gradually increases in height and decreases in diameter. This phenomenon, as fully explained in Chapter X, occurs in all voices, male and female, when production is correct.

If, when ascending the scale from the lowest note the singer's cords do not, either naturally on their own, or as a result of thought-aided adjustments gradually shorten and decrease in bulk, as described above, the particular "bridging" points we mentioned will be reached with too big a vibrator. What happens? Production become relatively laboured and "sticky", and the note itself is inclined to be flat on account of a slightly lowered frequency due to the vibrator not being of the exact size in relation to the pitch. And because the note is "out of gear" the tone gives the impression of being lugged or pushed up. It can occur in all voices, and actually on any note. Again, particularly in the contralto and mezzo voices, at the "bridging" point E to F (first space), or one, two, or three notes higher up, Nature asserts herself and, against the singer's will and non-comprehension, abruptly "eliminates" from the vibrating length some if not all the superfluous vibrator mass which the singer has brutally dragged into the fray. Which elimination consists of a shortening and thinning of the cords in a sudden spasmodic attempt to retrieve laryngeal equilibrium in relation to the particular pitch. This brusque mechanical movement within the larynx jerks the note by jogging the sound-beam with a split-second interruption. The impression on the ear is that of a "break". Hence the term oft used and little understood.

The process of gradual elimination of the vibrator mass is exemplified on a large scale by the harp, in which the lowest note is produced by the longest, thickest, and loosest string, and the highest by a short, thin, and appropriately stretched string; every successive note between these extremes being produced by a gradually shorter, thinner, and tighter (more tensioned) string.

Again to illustrate: In reed instruments such as the oboe, clarinet, saxophone, the player shortens the length of the vibrating reed as the pitch rises by tightening and reducing the lip-aperture. On low pitches the lips are loose ("loose embouchure") and on high pitches the lips and reed are small and tight ("small embouchure"). The small and tight lip-aperture coincides with the small effective length of reed remaining with which to produce the high notes. And the higher the note the smaller must be the effective length of reed.

If we whistle up the scale from the lowest note, we gradually tighten the lips and reduce their aperture in order to produce the higher pitches. The violinist, to produce a higher note, slides his finger up the string in order to shorten its effective length. Here again, the higher the note the shorter must be the effective length of string. The same mechanical-acoustical law governs one and all.

In short, "elimination" means that as the pitch rises so the vibrator "grows small by degrees, and beautifully less";* it means a gradual shedding of the load.†

* The author was an intimate friend of the late Dinh Gilly, the eminent French baritone, who passed on in 1940, in London. Many were the hours spent together discussing vocal technique. Seated at the piano, a favourite demonstration of his was to attack a high B♭ *p* and then make a gradual *crescendo* to *f*. Still clear in memory is the knowing grin that afterwards broke on his expressive face as he pressed the tip of his right thumb against the tip of the little finger. As he thus held aloft his right hand to emphasize the *smallness* of the tonal focus of the high B♭, which as a sensation he had experienced, we would nod to one another in silent accord—the silence of attuned thought and understanding. *He* knew all about true vocal technique.

† The object of the above detailed exposition is to give the student a clear, informative picture of the wonderful laryngeal mechanism at his disposal. The more he understands the working of the vocal cords the better he will treat his vocal instrument as a whole. It is all the more important as the singer cannot see or touch his instrument—at least, not the motor part of it.

The average singer knows little or nothing about his instrument, what it

The student at this juncture will be asking himself what mental-physical assistance is available to the singer as regards the eliminating processes described above. In the ensuing chapters he will find all the information he requires.

Lord Kelvin wrote: "I often say that if you can measure that of which you speak, and can express it by a number, you know something of your subject; but if you cannot measure it, your knowledge is meagre and unsatisfactory."

PHYSICAL NOTES
by NOEL BONAVIA-HUNT, M.A.

There are certain elementary physical laws that govern the pitch variation of musical notes. They are: (1) the higher the note, the quicker the vibration; (2) the quicker the vibration, the smaller and lighter the vibrator; (3) the smaller and lighter the vibrator, the smaller the energy required to set it in motion.

The subject becomes more complicated when we have to deal with the question of resonators, and, while it is one of paramount importance, we are not concerned with it in this present stage of our enquiry.

Mr. Herbert-Caesari deals with the laryngeal mechanism and its adjustment to suit varying pitch-frequencies during singing. Scientifically, this adjustment is known by the familiar name of "tuning".

Now, whatever may be this or that man's pet theory as to the

looks like, how it works, how it should be played on. The "technique" he is taught, too often is based on false premises. After perhaps two or three years of desultory study he sallies forth to conquer the world. His instrument, in most cases, mechanically incompleted by Nature and possibly defective, cannot possibly be completely fashioned in such a short time. How then can he learn to play on it properly?

Unlike the singer, the violinist or pianist (or any instrumentalist) is able to see and handle his instrument which comes to him a finished product in every detail, and ready to play on; moreover, he knows more or less how it is made, how it functions, and is taught a well established technique. Whereupon he devotes from five to ten years of unremitting study in order to master it. But what extra study would he have to make if his instrument came to him in an unfinished state, with bits and pieces that required laborious fitting? He would be handicapped at the outset, as are most singers in that their instrument is also not in a finished state, and can only be brought to mechanical completeness through rational study.

actual origin of the human voice, one fact remains unchallenged and irrefutable, viz., that the vocal cords vibrate only during phonation. They are wide open when we breathe, and when we whisper. They come together (almost) as soon as we start trying to make a sound. They come together, separate, come together again, separate again, and continue this cycle of operations so long as we produce a musical note. In short, the vocal cords vibrate at a regular frequency. The more rapidly they vibrate, the higher the pitch of the note produced. Thus our first law is well illustrated.

Secondly, it must be remembered that the higher the pitch of the note, the shorter is the length of the sound wave formed in the air. The sound wave is formed immediately on the front surface of the vibrator. While, however, the *length* of the wave is short, its *amplitude* varies according to the intensity or power of the note. Power is produced by pressure, and *not* by increasing the size of the vibrator. The idea of using an ounce of material when a gramme will suffice is abhorrent to Nature: it equally offends our sense of proportion.* Therefore, since the singer has a certain muscular control of his cords, and can use as much or as little of them as he deems desirable for the work in hand, Nature would expect him to make wise and profitable use of this power of selection as he sings up and down the musical scale.

Thirdly, the driving force is due to pressure from the lungs. But this particular aspect of the matter cannot be dealt with here. Suffice it to point out that the larger the mass of material to be driven, the bigger the inertia, and the more obstinate the resistance to pressure: therefore, the greater the work to be done. *Surely it is the height of unwisdom to overwork oneself by attempting to move a larger mass than is necessary*, with the increased pressure and strain involved, *when a smaller mass and a smaller pressure will ensure a greater efficiency.*

* Sir Isaac Newton wrote in *Principia:* "Nature does nothing in vain; and more is in vain when less will serve." (Author's note.)

CHAPTER VIII

THE RELATION OF VIBRATOR TO RESONATOR

CERTAIN INVESTIGATORS of our time have stressed the importance of the resonator almost to the exclusion of the vibrator
(vocal cords) whose function is relegated to an ignominious
and negligible quantity; the main trend of their argument, adduced without any true backing, is that the vocal cords are of
minor importance and that the resonating cavities above the
larynx constitute the prime function of voice.

In the various fields of human endeavour the first theorem is the
search for *cause* with a view to its possible control. To attempt to
control effect without some knowledge of cause is a most irrational
procedure. A defect manifested in the effect rarely can be remedied
without knowledge of cause. To diagnose the error in an effect is to
know the error in cause. To know cause is to control cause; to control cause is to control effect. The control of both cause and effect
is the sum total of vocal aspiration from the mechanical standpoint.

Man is endowed with a most wonderful laryngeal mechanism
to which is coupled a highly sensitive adjustable resonating system.
On p. 92 we explained how a certain degree of conscious control
of the vocal cords, or rather of their *terminal adjustment,* is possible
through the "feel" and visualization of certain tonal sensations
accruing from correct laryngeal adjustments appropriate to the
variations in pitch; and by adjustments we mean varying effective
length, thickness and tension of the cords.

A few physiologists—voiceless, we assume—have stated dogmatically in writing that the singer "has no sensations in his
larynx" and that he "cannot exercise any conscious control of the
vocal cords". Inaccurate and misleading, such mischievous statements only aggravate the existing vocal chaos; that they trip so
lightly from the medical mind is a matter of grave concern. False
concepts are quite numerous enough as it is.

The relation of the vibrator to the resonator (mouth-pharynx
and head cavities) is extremely intimate and hypersensitive; the
one is useless without the other, even as is the violin body without

the string, the pianoforte soundboard without the wire, the reflector of a motor headlamp without the bulb; and conversely. The slightest error in the one generates error in the other.

Actually, every vibrator adjustment includes an appropriate resonator adjustment. And the vowel is the chief factor whereby this dual adjustment, this coupling system, is secured. The better the vowel shape in relation to pitch, the better the adjustment of the cord mechanism (see Chapter XIII), because correct vowel shaping is the *key* to its exact adjustment.

The varying sound-beams (that is, varying in diameter and height according to the pitch) incited by the laryngeal tone find lodgment in the resonating cavities of the mouth-pharynx and head at *exact* points of impingement provided they are assisted and *allowed* to follow their natural trend, their natural direction.

Every laryngeal tone has a split-second precedence over its resonant reinforcement in the pharynx-mouth and head cavities; in fact, it generates a sound-beam that, reflecting shapes and colours we call vowels, converges to a focal point on some part of the particular resonator, the height and location of which point will naturally vary according to the pitch and to the vowel employed. Every pitch has a sound-beam peculiar to it as regards height, diameter and location. As fully explained in Chapter X, the sound-beams accruing from the varying laryngeal adjustments to secure the different pitches are of different height and diameter; the tall and narrow beams of high pitches tune in to the upper cavities (head), and the short and broad beams of low pitches to the mouth-pharynx cavity.

On the low and lower medium notes, for which the vocal cords are of comparatively little tension and the adjustable parts of the resonators but slightly stretched, the foci, or focal points, which are merely the TOP of the sound-beams, are, in the singer's sensation, spread and undefined—even as the circle of light from the sun, passing through a magnifying glass is spread and undefined before being brought to a sharp, burning focus. As a result, there is no feeling of tonal concentration on the low pitches, as in fact there is on the high pitches; this is also due to the comparatively low frequency (vibrations per second). But as the pitch rises, particularly from D♮, fourth line, upwards, and provided the vibrator adjustments are correctly made on the principle of gradual elimination of the vibrator mass, so do the focal points get gradually firmer and smaller, more compressed and concentrated, still retaining, however, their flexibility. They get smaller and firmer because the sound-beam gradually narrows and the frequency increases as the pitch rises, whatever the vowel employed. And the sound-beam narrows gradually because the cords shorten as the pitch rises; simultaneously with their gradual shortening, the frequency increases.

It is particularly from D, fourth line, upwards, that the TOP of the sound-beam, as it goes from pitch to pitch on an ascending scale, and gets gradually smaller and firmer, constitutes a series of "steps" or "platforms" up the domed resonating shaft. *The higher the pitch, the smaller and firmer the platform*, therefore.

N.B.—Focus, focal point, platform, point of impingement, focal "feel", all mean one and the same thing. We prefer *platform* because, in the singer's sensation, the point of impingement of the *top* of the sound-beam, particularly of high notes, constitutes a flexibly firm *step* on which he does his work.

Those who sing on the breath-pressure or diaphragmatic-thrust method (and they are legion today) will never succeed in securing *exact* laryngeal adjustments, and consequently never *exact* adjustments of the resonating cavities (particularly the mouth-pharynx) for the different vowels and pitches, for the coupling between vibrator and resonator demands much too subtle an adjustment to permit of any slapdash, blind and brutal onslaught; tones and sounds of all sorts are produced by unbalanced coupling, but, in our view, it is not singing.

We invariably stress the importance of visualizing tonal sensations. Just what are these sensations that the singer should visualize? It amounts to seeing with the mind's eye, through the sense of touch, the *platform* (focus) of every note, particularly from E♭ upwards (fourth space), which platform is linear because it is merely the *top* of the sound-beam; that is, it is linear in the singer's sensation. Consequently, as the pitch rises, as in an ascending scale, so the linear sensation of tonal "feel" or touch of the impinging sound-beam gradually gets smaller because the beam itself gets gradually narrower. Therefore, the higher the pitch, the shorter or smaller the platform.*

* One of the most important laws of psychology is that if we *concentrate* upon an idea long enough and intensely enough, to the exclusion of all else for the time being, it will in time assume a concrete form. How much more so is this the case where vocal vibrations are concerned.

A highly interesting phenomenon is the fact that these linear sensations of vocal tone (irrespective of the vowel used) which can be felt and visualized within the resonating system, reflect *exactly* the dimensional adjustments of the vocal cords, in length and thickness, varying according to the pitch and the varying degrees of their tension-resistance. For instance: if for a high A the adjustment of the vocal cords were, say, length 2; thickness 1; tension 6 (corresponding to a real laryngeal formula), the corresponding *platform* in the head resonating zone would, as a sensation, be dimensionally of the same size, the same consistency, the same degree of tension-resistance: no more, no less. Therefore:

We postulate the mechanical-acoustical principle that the small, compact platform or focus of a high note (irrespective of the vowel used) firmly impressed on to its *exact* spot or locus within the right resonating zone, *reflects* and endorses *exactly* the length, thickness and tension-resistance of vocal cord employed to secure that particular pitch. And it applies to all pitches.

To this phenomenon is intimately related another one of equal interest, viz.: *The effective length of vocal cord engaged for a certain pitch equals the effective diameter of the sound-beam upsoaring therefrom.*

Consequently, irrespective of the vowel employed, length of vibrator (which must include appropriate thinning of the mass, and adequate tension) is *exactly* reflected by the diameter of the sound-beam produced by it. For instance: the diameter of the sound-beam of a high note produced by a small vibrator is equally small, and that of a low note produced by a relatively big vibrator is equally big.

It stands to reason that a minute length of vibrator (engaged for a high note) can but give rise to an equally minute tonal stream, or sound-beam, for only a thin stream can issue from a tiny slit or aperture (glottis) offered by the aforementioned minute length. Inversely, the bigger the aperture, as on low notes, the bigger the tonal stream.

It is primarily by such sensations of tone that we are able efficiently to control the varying adjustments of the vibrator and resonators in an ascending or descending scale, an aria or a song. It is positive control over cause and effect. But control, in the true sense, can be efficient only when the tonal sensations accrue from really correct adjustments. (Also erroneous cause and effect can come under some sort of control; but we are not interested in the ways of vocal error.)

So highly sensitive is the coupling system between vibrator and resonator that the slightest alteration in the size and location of a platform (or focus) within its own particular resonator, disturbs in corresponding degree the equipoise of the vibrator adjustment. If by excessive breath pressure, for instance, the platform were increased beyond its definite permissible maximum (expressed in maximum tonal development, or *crescendo*, compatible with vibrator-resonator balance for the particular pitch) the immediate effect is a correspondingly (undue) increase in the thickness, and more often than not also in the length, of the vocal cords; which excess imposes a new adjustment of the vocal cords that is un-suited for the particular pitch. This, of course, throws the original setting out of gear, even if only slightly as in certain cases. The second immediate effect is the lowering of the focus from its original and balanced position within the resonating zone (and there are no two or more positions but one only, within the particular resonator for the coupling or focusing of a certain note with a certain vowel). Now this lowering of the focus is due to the creation of a broader and shorter sound-beam by the unduly thickened, and possibly unduly lengthened, cord. And it stands to reason that the shorter sound-beam (even if only a fraction too short) cannot possibly couple in to and contact the same spot occupied before. So the new out-of-gear vibrator adjustment (producing a low-pitched vortex tone) is forced to maintain some semblance of the pitch (that in the meantime is slightly "under" or flat on account of the shortened beam and lowered frequency) by the rude persuasion of an unduly increased breath pressure, perilously near to indiscriminate *blast*. Having erred in this way, the singer feels obliged to apply this extra breath pressure in order to sustain the extra load, the excessive tonal "weight" of the position, and also to force up the sagging pitch. Because they have been told that the voice works more or less automatically, most singers know little or nothing of deliberately thought out vibrator-resonator adjustment as we understand it. And because so very few voices are mechanically perfect, even those who have had what is called "training", most singers are inclined to tonal flatness, some more than others; their ear tells them nothing, but subconsciously aware that all is not well somewhere, they exert still more breath pressure without really knowing why, and secretly hope for the best.

Now all this imposes a severe strain on the vocal organs as a whole, and on the cords in particular.

In the case of an upper medium or high note positioned well within the appropriate resonating zone, the singer when making a *crescendo* feels he is applying the breath pressure directly to the platform or focal point; obviously, this is impossible, for the actual pressure is exerted solely against the adducted cords. But because the *top* of the sound-beam (platform) exactly reflects what goes on down below inside the larynx, and because the singer's mind is mainly impressed by the feeling of platform, the actual vibrator and its reflection, the platform, are seemingly one and the same thing. Hence, on the high pitches, the sensation of exerting breath pressure directly against the platform high in the head cavities above the arc of the palate. Which ever way you look at it, singing is mainly a mental process.

N.B.—The parrot-cry of the day is that "there can be no conscious control of the vocal cords". This is one way of evading something about which a cloud of ignorance has gradually formed. In all such discussions on the conscious and subconscious control of the laryngeal muscles, the central point of the question is generally overlooked. We challenge anyone to prove that there is no conscious control of what we call the TERMINAL ADJUSTMENT of the vocal cords. But as it is a *sensation* of vocal tone, it is either misunderstood or not considered of sufficient importance by certain writers and teachers to whom the very thought of "control of the vocal cords" is anathema and therefore taboo; to such as these it is beyond the pale of possibility. However, we would point out that the principle of terminal adjustment is of paramount importance in true vocal technique. As a proof of our contention we will press into service an analogy illustrating the point: If, for instance, we wish to pick up a pencil, or any object, from the table, a complicated operation from brain to fingertips ensues: the several groups of muscles in shoulder, arm, wrist, and hand concerned in the movement, function almost exclusively in the subconscious state. In other words, we can say that ninety-five per cent. of the action is unfelt and not consciously controlled. But nobody in reason will say that *the pressure exercised at the fingertips* and the *feel* of the ultimate grip, however slight it may be, are not consciously under our control nor within our field of sensation. Nor can it be denied that we are able consciously to regulate at will and control the degree of pressure, the ultimate grip (*terminal* grip) to be applied by the fingertips with extraordinary exactitude. Even as the pressure of an artist's fingertips on pencil or brush, and again the pressure of pencil and brush to paper and canvas can consciously be regulated and controlled to a nicety, so can the "terminal adjustment" of the vocal cords be consciously regulated and controlled. It is a question of nicely balanced sensation, a sensation that can be

PHYSICAL ADDENDUM
by Noel Bonavia-Hunt, M.A.

Only a human being can adjust both the larynx note and the resonating cavities simultaneously when producing voice: it is a great and wonderful privilege.

There are at least *nine* different resonators in the human head, and these must not be confounded with other reinforcing systems such as the sympathetic diaphragms with which the human body abounds. All of these auxiliary systems are brought into play during the singing of a song at some time or another. If it were not for the sympathetic assistance of cartilaginous and bony diaphragms in various parts of the body it would be impossible for any of us to produce low notes of any reasonable volume and intensity.

Another point that should be noticed is the important fact that *unless the note is so placed that it can be reflected back from the point of incidence* to the correct portion of the mouth, it has little chance of being propagated from the mouth to outer space with the desired intensity and carrying power. *Reflection plays a very important part in voice production*, and it would seem that Mr. Herbert-Caesari's exposition of "focal point" technique can be quite adequately explained from the scientific standpoint by reference to the laws of reflection and diffraction.* He is insistent on the rule that the higher the note produced the smaller and more concentrated the

"shaped" and controlled consciously. What indeed could an artist do without a conscious control of the *feel* and *touch* of his creative points of pencil and brush, the *terminals* of his mental and physical actions? Similarly the singer has conscious control of the vocal cords as far as their "terminal" adjustment is concerned. (Both in this and in the parent work, we call this terminal adjustment: Platform.) This is no figment of the imagination. Every student can be taught this control, and even the so-called dull one is able to grasp and apply the principle to advantage. If this is something new for most students, singers, and teachers, they will find it worth while entertaining, instead of summarily dismissing it as nonsensical or impracticable. We need not refer to works of certain medical men (often quoted by the parrot-minded) who dabble in vocal sidelines, in order to learn that no *individual* muscle in the laryngeal group concurring in the adduction and general adjustment of the vocal cords can consciously be controlled: this we all know. But only ignorance will deny that there can be conscious control of the *terminal adjustment* of the vocal cords at all pitches and with all vowels. (See footnote, p. 183.)

* See Diagram 12, p. 174.

focal point, and that this focal point is situated at a greater distance from the vocal cords and further up in the head. There is nothing actually corresponding to the action of a lens focusing light rays on to a spot in space, though the analogy is of service in teaching: it is, however, well known that sound waves can be directed towards a given spot through a suitably shaped conduit, and a good instance of this is Jessop's high note beam diffuser, also the old-fashioned speaking-tube of ante-telephone days. Now, the vibrating air column at the higher audio-frequencies is *narrow and beam-like;* it can therefore be directed to a small area for reflection purposes. One may regard the passage between the larynx and the head cavities as a kind of corridor from which the mouth and nose are outlets to the atmosphere. The object of "focusing" the air column, or sound-beam, in the corridor to cavities and dia-phragms in the upper part of the head is to divert it from the mouth and nose, and to establish a point of reflection appropriate to each wave-length. But what is not generally known in scientific circles (and less still in vocal circles) is the fact that the soft palate is a highly important vibrator which Nature has provided for the singer's use. A certain method advocates, and certain singers practise, the deliberate raising of the soft palate in order to make it rest against the pharyngeal wall when producing notes of all pitches. They do this presumably in order to shut the air inside the mouth and pharyngeal spaces from communication with the air in the upper cavities of the head (the main idea behind this method appears to be to secure "big" volume, and "meaty" tone on every pitch by the fact of concentration in the mouth-pharynx cavity). If by "air" is meant the air particles in these various chambers, then the shut-off is effectually accomplished; but if by "air" is meant the *vibrant* air set in motion by the vocal cords and amplified by the throat resonators and other parts of the human frame vibrating in sympathy, then there is no effective separation of the upper and lower head cavities and spaces. And for this reason: the soft palate cannot really be held motionless against the pharyngeal wall during the singing of a note: it either vibrates in tune or out of tune with the laryngeal note. Some palates are naturally less mobile than others and their owners are handicapped in this respect.

We can now see why Mr. Herbert-Caesari makes such a point of correct focal adjustment, why he urges the student to find the right "platform", why each note must have its appropriate "focal point of impingement": for it is only by employing these accurate adjustments that the vibrating palate can be made to execute the correct number of vibrations per second in due relation to the frequency of the vocal cords and the note produced by them. No living person can deliberately and consciously control the vibration of his palate, he can only do so indirectly, and in singing he can make his voice the controlling genius—a fact as wonderful as it is little realized. Now the vibrant palate sets in motion the air particles in the cavities above it, so that a most beautiful, soft adjective tone at the required pitch is superimposed on the laryngeal-cum-pharyngeal tone provided the coupling of the two vibrating systems is "at resonance". The substantive note is laryngeal in origin, and the palatal note is adjectival only, being "launched" by what Mr. Herbert-Caesari calls the "sound-beam" or substantive wave-form. It is clear therefore that any theory which attributes the genesis of vocal tone to the vibrant air in the head cavities instead of to the vocal cords owes its origin to a grave misapprehension. Sound cannot be energized apart from the vocal cord motion, the source of all vocal tone.

To sum up, we have various points of reflection from the pharyngeal wall, the hard palate, the soft palate, the teeth, and the tongue: we have various resonating cavities or chambers: we have various soundboards setting up notes of their own: we have two vibrating mechanisms, cordal and palatal. And we have a natural horn for directing the output towards the listener.

It is interesting to note that if a singer happens to engage a resonating cavity or diaphragm in his head whose natural frequency is actually the same as the note he is producing, the amplitude of the vibrations thus caused may be so intense as to bring on a fit of giddiness. This is especially likely to occur when producing high notes at high intensity; but the sensation is only temporary and is not experienced after due practice.*

* In fact, a well-produced high note that is being "drilled" at high intensity may even cause a temporary blackout. I have seen students, particularly sopranos and tenors, and of strong constitution, actually totter and grope for something to hold on to during or immediately after production. After a few experiences of the kind the phenomenon goes, never to return. (Author's note.)

CHAPTER IX

PRESSURE AND RESISTANCE

MOST TEACHERS and singers are quite convinced that the higher the note the greater must be the breath pressure. So let us examine this acceptance in the light of physiologic-acoustic facts. Whatever the note, high or low, pitch can be independent of breath pressure that surpasses an indispensable minimum; this is not obvious at first sight. Inversely, for a *crescendo* or *f* singing, the breath pressure must be increased accordingly; this is obvious to all.

If the mass of the vocal cords is gradually eliminated as the pitch rises so that on the high notes only a small piece of cord is engaged (a very small piece indeed on the highest note) there is plainly no need for the singer to exert extraordinary breath pressure to set in motion such a tiny vibrator.

Assuming an ascending scale of two octaves, sung rather slowly, we can state categorically that, with a good production on the principle of gradual elimination of the vibrating element, there is absolutely no need to increase the breath pressure as the pitch rises: it can be kept *constant* all the way up the scale to the highest note. This is no theory but an actual possibility easy of verification. However, while thus keeping the breath pressure constant as the pitch rises (by employing an indispensable minimum of breath for each note) the singer must seek and maintain a gradually increasing tension-resistance of the gradually diminishing vibrator, which is *exactly* reflected by the gradually diminishing focus. Nobody in reason is suggesting that a song should be sung with a "constant" breath pressure: that would be extremely monotonous. We adduce the possibility of the scale merely to illustrate our thesis.

We can fill our lungs with air, but if the *will* to sing be lacking the vocal cords will not move, and the air stream will pass through the glottis (i.e. the space between the open cords), without encountering any organized resistance. Where there is insufficient resistance there can be no useful work for the pressure.

Pressure and resistance are the antagonistic forces actuating all mechanical procedure, the moving spirit of action: antagonistic but mutually indispensable. To illustrate: Walking and running are both a matter of foot pressure against a more or less resisting surface; the propeller and wings of an aeroplane exert pressure on the air that offers resistance, and flight is the result; the pressing violin bow seeks and meets the resistance of the stretched string. Writing, drawing and painting are all based on pressure and resistance. The wind-resisting sail propels the yacht. Key pressure turns the resisting lock. Wood offers resistance to the pressure of the invading screw. The inflated motor tyre presses against the resisting road surface. And so forth. Inversely, if a surface is soft and yielding, such as thick mud or sand, or a hard surface is thickly smeared with grease, walking, running, and driving a car is considerably slowed, or rendered impossible, because the resistance to pressure is negligible or nil and the "restoring force" is absent.

In the vocal cord mechanism, resistance cannot be really effective unless there be effective tension. Air pressure, plus *will*, induces tension and resistance, resistance being dependent on tension. The singer must *seek and will in* the exact degree of tension-resistance as it increases from note to note on an ascending scale. And this does *not* mean forcing through direct muscular action. All muscular action within the vocal machinery must be *indirect*, and definitely a reaction to thought.

Whence comes the force of the air from the lungs? First of all, air has weight and therefore exerts pressure *per se*, albeit in relatively small degree. The pressure exerted by the air in an ordinary room is due mainly to the charge of its molecules as they "bombard" everything therein that is solid: furniture, walls, etc. Such air pressure, however, is insufficient for the purposes of phonation: it needs compressing, for compression holds the promise of force and work. By force we mean here energy—not strain or brute effort. Compression of the air is nothing but the crowding of the molecules more closely together than they are normally: Force is something intangible and cannot be measured directly; it can only be measured indirectly by what it does, by its effect.

When we complain of "forced" tone we mean an *excess* of applied force, an excess over the indispensable amount, an excess that spells strain. In this connection the champions of the much-

G

lionized diaphragmatic drive consider their output of forced blast a well-ordered and calculated component! They even call it "breath control". Actually it is disorderly, uncontrolled conduct.

As no appreciable amount of that incalculable element known as mind is splashed over a singer's diaphragmatic muscle, as there are no brains in his belly, and as finally there is no real live point of expenditure within the breathing muscles proper whereby the output of breath can be really controlled, there can be no measurement of the actual output of force or breath pressure for a given note with any real approach to accuracy. Hence sheer direct muscular action is pretty blind. It has no subtlety. *Only* from the *point of expenditure*, which is also the point of tension-resistance, viz. the adducted vocal cords, and only from the vibratory sensations given off by this point or source is the brain-cum-mind, or mental "I", able to calculate with exactness the degree of pressure, breath pressure, to be applied to the resisting vibrator (adducted vocal cords) for a given note, a given effect. Which degree determines the output of breath. (We would remind the student that particularly on the upper medium and high notes, from E♭, fourth space, upwards, the TOP of the sound-beam, which we call platform or focus, accurately reflects the varying degrees of pressure-resistance actually obtaining within the laryngeal chamber.) (See Chapter XV.)

This "I", that seemingly is more ethereal when we are asleep, has memory and a subconscious calculating compartment. By dint of calculating on the basis of the memory and visualization of the vibratory sensations it is possible for the singer, for the "I" in him, to pre-calculate, to predetermine, to sense before and while producing the tone exactly how much breath, how much pressure, should be applied to secure both the initial and the subsequent effect or effects that he has in view.

There is no other process of calculation available to the singer as far as the output of breath and pressure is concerned. There is no pre-calculating, no pre-sensing "compartment" within the breathing machinery itself—in spite of its deification by certain flamboyant methods.*

---

* Pre-calculation of the kind in different spheres of activity seemingly is related to motion. Thought, philosophy avers, consists of detecting differences. And it is by the continual exercise of such detecting that the "I" in us is able ultimately to develop this prescience to a fine point of efficiency. To illustrate:

Let us revert again to the subject of compression: If we take an efficient bicycle or motor tyre pump we can readily pull out the handle, with its small piston-head ringed with leather, to its full length without encountering any appreciable resistance; as we let go the handle it readily drops into place again. If we now pump without attaching the nozzle of the rubber tubing to the tyre valve, or otherwise stop up its aperture, we can feel and hear the outrush of air; here again there is no appreciable resistance at any given point. But if we tightly stop up the nozzle with one finger and hold or stand the pump vertically with the handle drawn up to the maximum, the latter will not now fall to the bottom of the cylinder again; it cannot, because the passive resistance of the air in the now closed tube holds it up. By pressing hard on the handle we can force it downwards, and the more we press the more resistance we encounter. By so doing we are actually compressing or crowding the molecules gradually more closely together. If, when sufficient compression has thus been secured, we take our hand off the pump, the handle will bounce upwards; or, if without releasing the handle, we work or bounce it up and down several times in quick succession we feel that the compressed air inside the pump has a positive *spring* in it—as much as if the piston were pressing against a real metal spring. Physical science knows this as the "spring of air", since air is elastic. The more we compress

Imagine a road barely wide enough to permit three cars abreast. Two cars, one fifty yards behind the other, are travelling in the same direction at a good speed, while a third is approaching at a high speed from the opposite direction. The driver of the car behind the first suddenly decides to pass and "cut in". Assuming him to be an experienced driver he is able to pre-calculate, or sense: (1) the speed of his own car (without looking at the speedometer); (2) the speed of the car in front; (3) the speed of the oncoming car; (4) the exact distance to be covered before all three cars meet; (5) the space and time available for the final cutting-in; (6) the acceleration, if any, that the driver of the oncoming car may make, or is making unconsciously maybe, or positively in a spirit of devilry; (7) the possibility of acceleration by the car in front in a spirit of competition stimulated by the peremptory tooting from behind. Consequently, the cutting-in driver has practically seven calculations to make, and at a given moment almost simultaneously with split-second decision, with nothing to go by but motion and varying degrees thereof. Motion is therefore the incentive to instinctive calculation. And it is the sensations inspired by motion that form the background of all such calculation. The squirrel pre-calculates his leap from branch to branch, the rook his alighting on a thin, swaying branch, the pilot landing his plane. There are many other examples pointing to instinctive calculation or pre-calculation that is born of motion and the practice of motion.

the air within the pump in this way, the more the pressure on the surface of the piston-head increases. Compressed air exerts pressure on the weakest or most movable part in order to find an outlet: it therefore exercises force.

The laryngeal mechanism cannot work itself: work must be put into it by the force applied; which force is supplied by the pressure resulting from molecular compression of the air we draw in. The mere fact of inspiration does not imply or induce compression, except in negligible degree. But the very fact of the desire, the *will* to sing, induces first the compression of the air (in adequate degree immediately underneath the larynx) and then the adduction of the vocal cords. The will to sing causes the thus compressed air to exert pressure against the adducted cords, thereby setting them in motion, and the tone is launched.

For his pressure "fuel", the good singer relies and draws upon the small mass of compressed air situate immediately underneath the vibrator, as stated above, and not upon the brutal thrust of general compression of the full lung capacity. He looks upon the zone of the small mass of compressed air in the light of a primary feed system that is replenished by the main supply system, or lungs, as occasion demands. The principle is very similar to the fuel supply system in a motor car: the small carburettor feeds the engine by releasing the exact amount of fuel required for every engine speed, and in turn is replenished by the main fuel tank; an engine fed directly from the main tank could not even start, as it would choke. Likewise the laryngeal mechanism subjected to forced feeding by a blind, brutal diaphragmatic drive audibly reveals the strain. Unfortunately this reckless muscular action is all too prevalent today.

According to the degree of "airtightness" of the vocal cords, when adducted, of different singers, so will the amount of pressure-breath necessary to produce the same note vary from individual to individual. So many singers' vocal cords lack the right degree of adduction; this is due mainly to a certain muscular slackness, that in most cases can be remedied by appropriate exercises. When the cords do not approximate with sufficient closeness to prevent air leakage while tone is being produced, we get an attenuated, impoverished product. In cases of pronounced air loss the tone is woolly and inert, with no "bite", no line, no sparkle, no carrying power. And because it also lacks authority it will be unconvincing.

Merely to increase the breath pressure is no remedy. Muscular re-education through appropriate exercises is the only remedy, and gradually the optimum resistance of the cords will be secured thereby. With well-adducted cords no air passes through them as tone is produced. What breath is taken by the singer must come out of course; but only in the form of heat and energy does it escape through well-adducted cords as tone is being produced.

CHAPTER X

SOUND-BEAMS

or

THE ACOUSTICAL ASPECT OF SINGING

Part I

A CERTAIN ACQUAINTANCE with the purely acoustical aspect of singing is absolutely necessary to the student if valuable lessons are to be drawn from the experience of practice. A modicum of scientific knowledge, such as it is, enables him to analyse more accurately his sensations of vocal tone; without it, reliance upon uninstructed practice and observation can be misleading.

Few singers seem alive to the fact that as soon as they adjust the vocal organs for the production of tone they come up against acoustic law—in so far as it applies to vocal mechanism. It is not sufficiently appreciated that to sing well, from the mechanical standpoint, certain acoustical principles *must* be applied. A strict, not a slipshod, obedience to the law is an indispensable condition; in this case, to know is to obey.

It is clearly apparent that as far as the singing voice is concerned Nature has endowed man with a mechanism that, in a sense, functions according to laws that are peculiar to it, and it alone. Mechanically and acoustically the larynx is in some respects a law unto itself. For instance, what man-made musical instrument is able to produce from two to two and a half octaves, and even more, with a vibrator only half an inch in length—as in most sopranos? * What instrument other than the human voice produces a sound-beam ever-increasing in height and decreasing in width as the pitch rises? What man-made instrument is as small,

* This is the normal cord length in all the female categories; occasionally we find the heavier calibres of sopranos, and the mezzos and contraltos, with slightly longer (and thicker) cords. In men, the normal length is ¾ inch; exceptionally up to 1 inch—like Caruso. Mozart stated that he heard in Parma, Italy in 1770, a young singer, Lucrezia Ajugari, with a range from G below middle C, to C in alt, which "she gave purely". It is the most highly pitched voice referred to in musical history, the compass being almost 3½ octaves.

compact, so adjustable and efficient, and such a begetter of tonal beauty and power as is the human voice? What else can produce such a variety of tone colours?

Science has not yet succeeded in probing the mystery of certain aerodynamical and acoustical properties that are peculiarly individual to the vocal machine, properties that, however, were instinctively utilized long ago by empiricism.

The expert in aerodynamics and the acoustician have infinitely greater possibility than has the physiologist of finding the solution. During the last few years much progress has been made by the former in this direction. On the other hand, the thoroughly competent teacher is familiar with the factual aspects of these distinctive and characteristic vocal laws, and has learned to interpret and obey them.

It is not sufficient for us to know that certain phenomena exist and occur, that certain well-defined sensations are felt during the act of singing, with correct production; it is our duty to inquire what these sensations are, whence they come, how they are produced, and why the singer experiences them. What? Whence? How? Why? We can theorize about the uncorroborated phenomena, but it will not alter the fact of their being.

In the chapter above on "The Relation of Vibrator to Resonator", we have gone into the question of the intimate relationship between the cord mechanism and the resonating system; consequently, our present discussion embracing the highly important factor of the sound-beams will extend the vista of this relationship in no small measure.

The salient features of the sound-beam are (1) effective diameter, (2) height, (3) direction. These vary according to the pitch and vowel, i.e. (1) and (2) relate to pitch, and (3) to vowel,—the variations coinciding with the change in length, thickness, and tension of the vocal cords as the pitch rises.

Sound-beams accruing from adjustments *accurately* made in relation to pitch and vowel are the embodiment of the acoustical laws peculiar to the vocal instrument. They externalize these laws.

We are not concerned here with the warped sound-beams responsible for the heterogeneous sounds produced as a result of partial or general maladjustment of the vocal organs with which our ears are regaled today, but solely with beams that are acoustically accurate.

From the ideal standpoint, the singer should only produce tone that, at least, is mechanically and acoustically correct within his particular compass, even if quality of tone in the highest sense is lacking. Not all voices are of supernal quality.

We said that the relation between vibrator and sound-beam (which naturally includes the resonator) is a highly intimate one. This relation is mathematical; therefore it is binding. It is mathematical in the sense that for a given pitch the vocal cords should be of a certain length, thickness, and tension—the exactness of the three factors amounting to a real formula: *Laryngeal formula*. This in turn creates a sound-beam which, for the said given pitch, will be of definite diameter and height, the exactness of the two factors amounting to a real formula: *Resonance formula*. Now each formula is perfectly correlated to the other, and together they combine to produce what in scientific language is called a "coupled system". A coupled system has been defined as "a system formed of two separate systems, neither of which can perform its own free vibrations without interference from the other". But a better definition still is: "A vibratory system which is the net result of two separate vibratory systems acting on each other" (Bonavia-Hunt). The definition is worth memorizing.

In the vocal instrument the two systems are represented (1) by the eddies or vortices (or rotating cores of air) issuing up from the vibrant vocal cords, and (2) by the longitudinal vibrations of the column of air above them. Upset the one in the smallest degree and you automatically upset the other in equal degree. Which reciprocity is of the highest sensitivity. Inseparably interwoven, the two adjective systems cannot be pulled out of alignment without seriously distorting the substantive system as a whole. It reminds one of a pair of scales: the slightest movement of one pan is registered exactly by the other pan.

The process of formation of a sound-beam is briefly as follows: The vocal cords are set in vibratory motion by the air coming from the lungs; they act as reeds and also produce eddy currents or vortices, one eddy at each complete to-and-fro motion of the cords. Thus the vibrating cords create air-waves within the ventricles immediately above them, which in turn establish sound-waves passing through the false cord edges and upward.* For instance, to produce middle C the cords vibrate 261 times in one

* See appendix, p. 362.

second, and high C 1,044 times (New Philharmonic Pitch). In one second, therefore, 261 vortices in the first case, and 1,044 in the second, are launched into the cavity above. The smaller the cord length, as on the high note, the smaller the eddies. The vibrating vocal cords at the same time set in vibration the stagnant air just above them in the throat. By this means is established a vibrating sound-beam that, in turn, is reinforced by the sympathetic vibration of the air in the resonant cavities (mouth, pharynx, nose and head). The beam is now complete. This is a simple picture of the aforesaid two separate systems forming the *coupled* system in vocal tone.

We now wish to stress an important matter from the standpoint of the singer himself, i.e.: The tonal sensations consist, for him, chiefly of the sound-beam (the *main* tonal stream) stretching upwards to find its *natural* point of impingement on a given reflector surface according to the pitch-cum-vowel; and from E♭ (fourth space) upwards the major sensation is precisely the TOP of the beam; and the higher the pitch the more intense and marked the sensation aroused by just the top of the beam; the mind clamps on to it exclusively, apparently ignoring the rest of the beam, even though sensing its existence and its angle with respect to the vertical. Inversely, the listener hears only tonal "globes" (vowels), never the sound-beam and its focal point. An audience perceives the finished product only, and not the processes of manufacture. The singer's main concern is the formation of the vowel in relation to pitch, and the creation of sound-beams.

The student will understand, therefore, that as soon as he produces vocal tone he is, as far as he himself is concerned, erecting a sound-beam with the aid of the vowel.

Unless he is very observant and analytical, a beginner cannot be expected to have immediately a clear perception of the sound-beams, the variations they undergo in height and diameter, their different points of impingement, and the direction they take according to the pitch and to the vowel employed. Experience has first to be gained in this work of intimate observation, of analysis of vocal tone. Women seem to be more acute observers in this respect than men—at least at the outset. On the other hand, the experienced singer, or student, wise in the ways of true vocal technique, is singularly alive to every subtle change occurring

naturally, or *willed* by him, from note to note. To such, the
sensations of tone he creates are clear-cut and full of meaning.

We would stress the fact that the mind is ever prone greatly to
exaggerate all sensations of tone and of tonal touch, and will do so
until the singer brings them into the right perspective. The student
is advised to remember this, and to be on his guard. Note how the
mind exaggerates most sensations, particularly in the head: a tiny
crack, chip, or hole in a tooth, or the space left after an extraction,
are felt to be many times their actual size when investigated by the
tip of the tongue. When a vowel is modified it is merely the result
of a *very slight* rounding of the mouth-pharynx cavity; the
untrained mind will magnify the degree of rounding to an extraordinary extent, with the result that the student, if he attempts
a deliberate physical rounding of the parts, will be certain to
overdo things and cause tonal distortion. No one, certainly not
the teacher nor the singer himself, knows or can know, how much
the soft palate, the pharynx generally, and the tongue move when
forming a vowel or when modifying (or rounding) it. Only the
singer's mind knows, subconsciously, the exact amount; and so he
has only to *think in* the vowel shape, or vowel modification-cum-
sound he wants to produce, and the parts will obey the mental
message by adjusting themselves automatically without any direct
physical action on the singer's part.* This *thinking in* of the vowel
and of its modifications is of paramount importance; and the
reaction to this mental shaping (and apprehension of the vowel
sound relative thereto) is merely a very slight curving of the
mouth-pharynx cavity, particularly the pharynx part. In other
words, a vowel-rounding thought produces automatically a
minute curve.

* When we say "mentally shape" or "think in" your vowels, we do not
mean that the singer has to abandon physique altogether. To this mental
shaping there must be added the *bracing* influence of mind and nerves in order to
actuate the appropriate muscles and sustain their action. This bracing of the *will*-
cum-nerves is absolutely necessary. One must always *will* to sing, *will* the
muscles to function (and not force them by brutal breath pressure). Man has
been possessed of speech for many thousands of generations; consequently his
vowels are shaped subconsciously, automatically, and pitch is limited. But the
art of singing is a comparatively "recent" acquisition, is based on a complicated
mechanism, and covers a wide range of notes; consequently, all vowels must be
mentally shaped with deliberation, whereupon the parts concerned react to the
thinking.

We now postulate that:

(1) the effective diameter of a sound-beam equals the effective length of vocal cord employed to produce a given note; consequently—

(2) the lower the note, the greater the effective diameter of the relative sound-beam because the lower the pitch the greater the effective length of vocal cord engaged;

(3) the higher the note, the smaller the effective diameter of the relative sound-beam, because the higher the pitch the smaller the effective length of vocal cord engaged.

Therefore:

(4) the higher the pitch, the narrower the sound-beam and, vice versa, the lower the pitch the broader the sound-beam.*

To every pitch corresponds, acoustically speaking, a sound-beam of definite height and diameter, a height and diameter varying according to the pitch. The *exact* height and diameter of a beam is determined by the *correct* effective length and thickness (in depth) of vocal cord engaged—the effective lengths and thicknesses varying according to pitch. We therefore stress the following:

(*a*) a sound-beam will be short and broad when a long and thick cord is employed;

(*b*) a sound-beam will be tall and narrow when a short and thin cord is employed.

Consequently, to take the extreme pitches:

(*c*) if the normally lowest note is produced, as acoustic law demands, with the longest effective length and maximum effective thickness, in depth, of cord having relatively low tension and sufficient firmness, we get the shortest and broadest sound-beam; and

(*d*) if the normally highest note is produced, as acoustic law demands, with the shortest effective length and minimum effective thickness, in depth, of cord having adequately high tension and flexible firmness, we get the tallest and narrowest sound-beam.

---

* We wish to make it clear, in view of possible criticism from scientific quarters, that by "effective diameter", as applied to the sound-beam, is meant the R.M.S. cross-section of the columnar wave-form taken as a whole from its inception at the cords to the point of extension above. The irregularity of the beam is assumed.

If, theoretically, to the pitch of high A♭ corresponds a sound-beam of, say, 2 in diameter and 7 in height, how unreasonable it is to suppose that one can produce a good and well-balanced tone on this pitch with a sound-beam of, say, 5 in diameter and 4 in height, or 3 in diameter and 6 in height, resulting from mechanical adjustments which are hopelessly incorrect as far as that pitch is concerned. And yet that is what the majority of singers are doing in this technically unenlightened age, and, adding insult to injury, boost up the frequency with forced breath pressure. But they don't always succeed in this: hence the reason why so many singers are flat on certain notes, if not most of them. The next symptom to appear is the wobble.

A woman, generally, is less likely to err on the side of brutality of production (unless she has been "traviata" by bad teaching) than is man, who seemingly loves to indulge in the "rough stuff" The average woman is endowed with a greater instinctive delicacy of touch than man. But in the case of the really great artist, whether composer, singer, poet, painter, sculptor, and so forth, we invariably find a strong feminine quality in their mental make-up, revealing the masculine hand with the feminine touch. Is it not precisely the feminine quality inherent in the typical tenor voice of fine quality that renders it so eminently, so universally, attractive? The big, all-male blustering dramatic tenor can astound, but not captivate. Your hard-boiled, matter-of-fact businessman, or politician, has no trace of femininity; of that he boasts, little recking his loss. Vice versa, the great female artist invariably reveals masculine traits. Again, witness the rugged exterior and inward delicacy of Michelangelo; the athletic build of Leonardo da Vinci with the finely chiselled face and delicate hands that could draw the finest line and bend a horseshoe; the slight quasi-feminine build and features of Raffaello, possessed withal of masculine mastery. Just to adduce three out of the many possible outstanding examples of creative genius possessed of marked feminine traits; and this applies equally to the great composer.

The physical *base* of all sound-beams is the horizontally adducted cords offering vibratory resistance to air pressure from the lungs, whether they are engaged in their entire length for the production of the lowest note, or the merest tip (front end of cords) for the production of the highest note. And the key to the establishment of this base, which in turn is responsible for the erection of sound-beams that are exactly proportionate to pitch (in height and diameter), whatever the vowel employed, lies (1) in the correct adjustment of the cord mechanism on every pitch, which in turn lies (2) in the principle and process of gradual elimination of the vibrator mass as the scale is ascended from the lowest to the highest note, which in turn is governed (3) by correct vowel formation and modification in relation to pitch. The next thing of vital importance for the singer himself is accurate knowledge of the behaviour of the sound-beams proper, i.e. the different directions taken by the beam on the lowest note, according to the vowel used, and the subsequent directions followed as the pitch rises to the highest note. Which directions of the beam are intimately linked to and are absolutely dependent upon the correct shaping of the mouth-pharynx cavity (vowel formation) in relation to the pitch, whether low, medium, or high. (The whole question of beam direction has been explained thoroughly in the parent work, *The Science and Sensations of Vocal Tone*.)

If, when you are about to produce a *high* note, you unknowingly, or deliberately, form a full size, open-toned vowel (in its pure form, as spoken, without modification) you cannot possibly create a tall and narrow sound-beam—such as acoustically appertains to the said high pitch, for the simple reason that such a broad, open vowel induces the employment of a considerable length, and thickness, of cord out of all proportion to the particular pitch. With a big section of cord it is an acoustical impossibility to produce a tall, narrow sound-beam, such as a high pitch demands. If, on the other hand, we mentally form and then produce a tone based on the *thought* of a rounded (or modified) vowel, we create an appropriately tall and narrow beam, because such thinking reacts on the cord mechanism, reducing the length (and thickness) of cord to be employed. Only a small piece of cord can produce a *narrow* beam; only a small piece of cord can produce a *tall* beam; and only a tall and narrow beam can reflect a well-balanced *rounded* tone on high pitches. The mental-physical preparation to produce a tall and narrow beam requires, furthermore, anticipation of the height and direction the sound-beam, or tone, will and should take *naturally*. The very *thought* of the direction the beam should take naturally, frees and opens the throat, without there being any necessity for the singer to deliberately (physically) do so.

Part II

THE IMPORTANCE OF A DIMINISHING ARTICULATION

We now approach a highly important factor, i.e. that of the relationship between sound-beam and consonant. The importance of a diminishing articulation as the pitch rises is not sufficiently realized by singers.

Our first postulate is that the actual preparation of the consonants, i.e. the movement of lips, tongue and soft palate must be

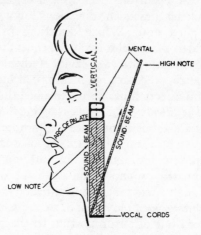

DIAGRAM 3

decreased gradually from about E♭, fourth space, or F upwards. All consonants must be made gradually smaller, lighter, crisper and more flexibly compact as the pitch rises from said points towards and on the high notes. It is logical that if we have gradually to reduce the amount of effective vibrator as the pitch rises, thus creating a sound-beam gradually decreasing in diameter, we must also bring into line the consonants themselves by simultaneously reducing gradually their articulated preparation in order the better to make them "fit", so to speak, the particular beam, whatever its diameter.

If the formation, or preparation, of the consonant is not reduced in "size" on the high notes, if, in other words, too much tongue contacts the palate, as for certain consonants, or the lips sloppily compressed, as for other consonants, the oversize preparation, or consonant, will weigh or slam down on the ensuing adjustment, thickening and lengthening the cord mechanism out of all proportion to the pitch. The slamming or thumping of a "weighty" consonant is damaging in every sense, for most assuredly there can be no delicate adjustment in either the vibrator or the resonator systems. There must never be a coarse or rough impact of a consonant.

The "size" of the consonant must be such as will exactly accommodate itself on *top* of the particular beam, so to speak (see diagram, p. 110); it must be neither too small, and be "engulfed" by the beam (and be inaudible in consequence), nor too big and so "overlap" the top of the beam, weighing down and deranging the mechanism.

It may well seem strange to be advised to form and place the consonant on "the top" of the sound-beam, particularly when, in the case of high notes, the top of the beam tunes in to points high up in the head cavity. The student will ask how is it possible to form and release the consonant high up in the head right above the palate and therefore far from the consonant-forming lips, tongue and soft palate. The answer is: One cannot, and does not. So let us look into the matter. There are three factors to be considered: (1) the vibrating mechanism of the vocal cords in the larynx; (2) the vowel, which is nothing but the shape given the mouth-pharynx cavity, into which the vibrations pour, accommodating themselves therein as they progress upwards from the vibrator; (3) the consonant formed by lips, tongue and soft palate, separately or in combined form, with movements of the jaw.

Structurally, the sequence of the three factors is:

3 ↑ consonant: lips, tongue, soft palate.

2 | vowel-shaping: mouth-pharynx.

1 | vibrator mechanism: the base of vocal tone.

The vowel-shaping within the mouth-pharynx cavity must be considered in the light of a mould into which, surging upwards from the laryngeal motor, the tonal stream pours—even as molten metal is poured into a mould. One cannot imagine a metalworker pouring the white-hot fluid indiscriminately on to the floor in order to cast a wheel, a crankshaft, a piston, an axle, a gear, or anything that demands shape and a function. The liquid must have a mould, a shape in which to settle. Similarly, the tonal "fluid" must find a well-prepared shape (mouth-pharynx) into which it can readily flow and accommodate itself, otherwise the tonal product (vowel) will be nondescript and unintelligible.

Now, the consonant, which is nothing but a slight movement of lips, or of tongue and palate, combined with an appropriate jaw movement, must be *mentally* prepared and released *on top* of the vowel shaping. This relation must be maintained because, no matter where the preparation of the consonant is located, it is always physically above the vibrating mechanism in the larynx. And the mere fact of always *mentally* forming and releasing all consonants on top of or above the vowel shaping (or, say, in the case of the higher and high notes, on the top of the sound-beam itself) is a very considerable help towards maintaining the balance of the laryngo-pharyngeal adjustments. It must also be remembered that consonants, in the main, are temporary interruptors of the tonal stream.

On the low and lower-medium pitches it is comparatively easy to grasp and apply the principle of the consonant being formed on top of the vowel, inasmuch as the vowels are felt, as a sensation of tone, in the mouth-pharynx cavity; inversely, the tall and narrow sound-beams of high notes impinge on the higher focal points in the head cavity, and the singer not only has no sensation any more of vowel in the mouth-pharynx but of no tone at all. As far as he is concerned, the vowel is now merely *sensed* to be within the high focus, which he could consider in the light of a miniature vowel. Of course it is more difficult to imagine the consonant being formed and released so high up and so far removed from their actual points of preparation. But if we get the habit of *mentally* forming and releasing all consonants *on the top* of the sound-beams, i.e. their points of impingement, or focuses, we shall keep the laryngeal mechanism light and undisturbed—a very important thing. (See pp. 271–5 for special exercises.)

Be it noted in this connection that the singer, on the upper medium, and high notes in particular, does not feel the whole of the sound-beam *but only the top of it* as it impinges against various points in the head cavity. The top of the beam and the focus are one and the same thing. (We also call it platform.)

We would now ask the student to carefully study the following diagrams. They exemplify the "reduction" in the formation of the labial consonants B and P. We shall also include M, although not a true consonant nor an interruptor of the tone, being a mixture of lip compression and nasal "buzz": the cords vibrate and the sound passes out through the nose—

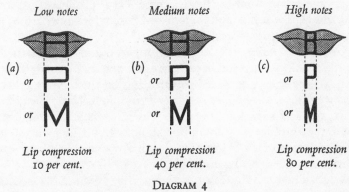

DIAGRAM 4

Note how, theoretically, on the normally lowest notes at (*a*) the lip formation for B is so much greater than for the normally highest notes at (*c*); note also the amount of lips used and the "size" of the B in the first case, and how small the amount of lips used and how the "size" of the B is reduced in the second case. Note, furthermore, the amount of lips used and the size of the B for the medium notes at (*b*), and compare with the other two. Actually, it is a question of degrees of compression: if the low note requires 1 of compression, spread over a relatively big lip area, the high note will require, say, 9 of compression distributed over a very much reduced lip area. The gradual reduction of the lip compression area from the lowest to the highest note coincides, theoretically, with the ever-narrowing beam as the pitch rises; in other words, a theoretical reduction of the consonant. The high compression of a small lip area spells compactness. The same diagrams are applicable equally to P and M, from the standpoint of labial compression. To form and "pronounce" B P or M on *high* notes correctly, *only the central part* of the lips should be compressed lightly, but firmly, compactly, and with a light, crisp, quick release. Be the pitch high or low, the P must be tighter than the B; an insufficiently tight P will invariably be heard as B, and a bad one at that.

H

Except when it is hard, as in *can*, *come*, and is then practically a K, the soft C, as in *cedar*, *century*, is practically an S. So we will analyse the soft C and S together, considering them as one. For this sibilant the tip of the tongue curls up lightly towards the front upper teeth. Never must the tip slide on to and protrude over the top of the lower front teeth, otherwise TH is produced instead. And this is how soft C and S are lisped.* Z, which is a hard S, is much less frequently lisped.

For the preparation of D, the anterior part of the tongue is used, the tip resting against the hard palate just above the upper front teeth. As the scale is ascended towards and on the high notes, *the amount of tongue used must be gradually decreased* until only the point of the tip, so to speak, is engaged. It is important to remember that as the employable amount of tongue is gradually reduced, so the preparation of the D must acquire an ever-increasing firmness. (And this applies to all consonants.)

We shall take the F and V together as they are both made with the bottom lip touching the edge of the upper front teeth. The only difference between them is in the degree of compression or, say, contact of lip and teeth; it is greater for the F. In fact, if for F this contact is not sufficiently firm, the slack preparation so loosens the consonant that it actually becomes a V. The contact of lip to teeth must, therefore, be firmer for F than for V. As the high pitches are reached, the area of contact between lip and teeth must be gradually reduced so that, on the highest notes, only a miniature F and V are formed—thus fitting or matching the very narrow beams of the high pitches. Too often one hears V instead of F. Given good vowels but poor consonants, we get meaningless sounds that convey nothing to the listener. What then do we get when both vowels and consonants are bad?

For G, when it is hard, as in *garden*, *garnish*, a considerable part of the tongue, especially the back half, contacts the soft palate on the low notes; they spring apart for the formation and production of the vowelled tone; this separation of tongue from palate must take place smoothly and rapidly, however, without jerking. As the scale is ascended *the contact area of tongue and palate must be*

---

* Quite a number of singers are inclined to inject a slight lisp into the S when singing. It must be eliminated (by not allowing the tip of the tongue to touch the top of the lower teeth) as it mars the purity of the S, and detracts from its forceful sibilance.

gradually reduced so that on the high notes less tongue touches less palate until finally, on the highest notes, only a very minimum of both is used to produce a miniature G, so to speak, light, crisp, yet firm. When the G is soft, as in *gem, genius*, only the front half of the tongue contacts the hard palate. The preparation of J is exactly that of soft G.

The preparation of K is similar to that of the hard C, as in *came;* it is close to that of the hard G, as in *gone*, only the latter engages more tongue. The contact of tongue and soft palate is firmer for K and hard C than for hard G. This closer, firmer contact for the K gives the feeling that it is not so deeply engaged throatwards as the hard G seems to be. If, therefore, the K is not light, high and firm in preparation (contact) and is allowed to slacken ever so little, it easily degenerates into hard G, and a bad one at that. The same process of diminishing articulation applies also to the K as the high notes are being approached, so that on the highest notes only a very small but firm K is produced to comfortably accommodate itself, as it were, on the top of the narrow sound-beam. And this is achieved by gradually reducing the area of contact between tongue and soft palate as the pitch rises.

For L, *the end portion only* of the tongue contacts the hard palate; the point of contact must not be too far back, as this stiffens the tongue muscles, the ideal point being just back of the upper teeth. If it touches the teeth, or, conversely, is too far back, a heavy L is the result—for too much tongue is thereby engaged. And too much tongue for L means an unwieldy, sluggish consonant. The student can easily find the exact location for this and for every consonant: it merely requires a little experimentation. As the pitch rises the L must be made gradually smaller; consequently, the contact area of tongue and palate must be gradually reduced until on the high and highest notes only *the mere tip* of the tongue is employed. The miniature *l* thus produced will be light, firm and "perky". This is important and requires watching, because singers are inclined to engage too much tongue for L, particularly on the high pitches—and in fact too much everything, thereby weighing down on the vibrator mechanism and stiffening the parts. To make way for the ensuing vowel, the contacted parts must separate and the mouth spring open with an oil-smooth action. (See p. 267.)

M is a "buzzer" consonant; it is not really a consonant within the ordinary meaning of the term, nor does it interrupt the tone like the true consonants such as P, B, K, G do. It is formed by closing the lips and setting the cords in motion. The resultant sound is not a vowel: it is a buzz. However, it can be made to faintly resemble an OO vowel sound. As the mouth is closed the vibrations cannot escape through the lips and have no other alternative to that of soaring into the nasal cavities to come out of the nose itself. It is called humming, although one could call it "emming". If while emming we pinch the nostrils, the sound will cease completely because the vibrations, having no outlet, rebound from the head cavity and, reverting to the source, damp the vibrating cords. (In like manner, if you effectively plug up the exhaust pipe of an automobile the engine will stop.) As this so-called consonant engages the vocal cords it is more than ever important gradually to reduce its "size", *tonal* size, as the higher and highest notes are reached, because otherwise too much cord would be engaged on the high pitches, with dire results.* If therefore M is the first letter of a word to be sung on a high note, it is of the utmost importance to make a miniature *m*, or, in other words, an extremely small buzz, a tiny buzzing-point (a mere thread of tonal stream), which is tantamount to engaging a very small piece of cord. Actually, this buzz is a sound-beam, or rather the top of the beam; therefore for a high note it is felt high up in the head cavities. And the very *thought* of a high and small *m*-buzz is sufficient to induce, through reaction, the correct vibrator adjustment—and by correct we mean a small, effective length of cord exactly corresponding to the particular high pitch. Conversely, if on a high note a big, "meaty" M is formed, it means that a big, and therefore an acoustically inappropriate, piece of cord in both length and depth has been engaged and set in motion, with the result that the subsequent vowel tone will issue on the heavily laden wings of a broad and short beam. We will not dilate on this point as the student is well aware by now that, in obedience to vocal-acoustic law, high pitches demand tall and narrow sound-beams.

---

* Except on the lowest notes we definitely condemn humming (glorified today into a method) because (1) it is of no practical value whatever, and (2) is very tiring if use is prolonged, particularly on the upper medium and high pitches, impeding as it does correct adjustments of the laryngeal mechanism. It is *not* an aid to tonal "placing". It may be helpful on the low notes to acquire the *feel* of the vibrating cords.

N is also a "buzzer" consonant. Unlike the M, the mouth is slightly open for its formation, but the vibrations are effectually blocked out from the front part of the mouth by reason of the fact that for N the tongue, in arching, not only touches the palate but also the left and right walls of the internal mouth, thus erecting an airtight shutter dividing this space into two. Consequently, the laryngeal vibrations soar into the nasal cavities and out through the nose—just as they do for M. To check this, we have only to pinch the nostrils, whereupon the tonal flow stops, as is the case with M. Whereas for M the tongue lies loosely at ease, for the N it is slightly pulled back with the tip lying snug against the palate just back of the upper front teeth. As the N engages the cords, the same considerations adduced above for M apply equally to N as regards the gradual reduction in "size" of buzz as the pitch rises. Therefore a high note demands a small *n*—a small, compact buzz, impinging high up in the head cavity like that of *m*. And the higher the pitch the smaller and firmer the buzz.

P is formed by a meeting of the lips: the preparation is the same as for B which, however, is looser than the P, i.e. requires less lip pressure and therefore uses, so to speak, more lip surface. In fact, to form P, which is an interruptor of the tone, the lips must be more compressed than they are for B, and, moreover, the muscular compression seemingly converges towards the centre of the lips to engage particularly the two middle parts. Again the process of reduction applies as the pitch rises towards and on the high notes which demand absolutely a miniature *p*. And this means employing more particularly the smallest possible *centre* portion of the compressed lips. The feeling is similar to pressing the tips of the little fingers together (see diagrams, p. 113).

The Q, phonetically, is a *k* followed by short *i* and *oo*, the latter carrying the accent. In practically every word in the English language beginning with *q*, a *u* follows, as in *quite, quiet, quick, quote, quack, quest*, so it partakes of *kw*. When so used, the *w* part of it is a short *u* sound as in *put*, and as we glide rapidly over it to the rest of the words, as above—*ite, iet, ick, ote, ack, est*—there is a very faint suspicion of an aspirate, practically imperceptible. For the rest, the *k* part of the Q consonant is subject to the same diminishing process as explained above for K; consequently, on high notes there must be a tiny, firm, compact *q*.

R, as a letter of the alphabet, is pronounced AH. If it is the first letter of a word such as *ring*, or in the middle, as in *furrow*, it is inclined to be slightly guttural (with something of the *ir* sound as in *bird*), as it is made at the back part of the throat, while the tip of the tongue is slightly raised without, however, touching the palate. When uttered with a pure English accent it is only very faintly guttural, if at all; but in certain regions of the United States it is made very guttural—a thing to be avoided in singing. Although in speech the R is not "rolled" by the average Englishman, when singing in English it is sometimes advisable to do so for purposes of emphasis and effect. The Italian rolls every R: this is done with the mere tip of the tongue. As the breath is made to move rapidly over the tongue surface, so the tip is *willed* to vibrate rapidly and freely.

The actual mouth formation or, say, lip aperture, for T is similar to that for S (dealt with above); but whereas for the latter the tongue lies naturally at ease, thus affording space between its surface and the arc of the palate for the breath to pass through with a sibilant sound, for the T the tip of the tongue is pressed firmly but lightly against the hard palate just above the front upper teeth. If T is not crisply formed, if in other words the tongue tip is not firmly pressed against the palate, we get a loose formation; in which case not T, but a mongrel D will be produced and heard. Again, the same diminishing process applies as the pitch rises, and high notes demand a small, light, compact *t*.

V is, as stated above, a labio-dental, or lip-tooth, formation, and closely related to F. Which latter, however, is a tighter and more compact consonant than the former. The difference between them is in the degree of compression, the F giving the impression of being more "pointed", more centred, as it were. Also the V must be gradually reduced in "size" as the pitch rises towards and on the high notes; which reduction is secured by employing gradually less lower lip until, on the high notes, only the middle part, nicely compressed against the front upper teeth (the cutting edges), is engaged, thus producing what we call a miniature *v*.

W is actually more a vowel than consonant: is it not called a "double U"? The W part of words like *we, when, what, white*, is given the function of consonant but is really a short *u* (as in *put*) made by pursing of the lips and released with a tiny, imperceptible aspirate followed by the ensuing vowel. Conversely, in the word *few*, the *w* is a pure, classic long *oo* sound, as in *pool;* it is made up of *f*, a short *i* (as in *bit*)—although written *e* in the word—and the long, classic *oo* sound, which is stressed. Again, for example, in the word *flow* the *w* is an *oo* sound, preceded by *oh;* in the word *flowing*, the *w* functions more like a consonant and in a quasi-aspirated form as mentioned above, whereas in *entwine* the *w* is a short *u* sound (as in *put*). There are of course a great number of other examples which the student can profitably analyse for himself.

All double consonants such as *tr, pl, gl, bl*, etc. are equally subject to the said diminishing process as the pitch rises.

The X is merely a combination of K and S: in such words as *ox, wax, exit, axiom*, etc. it is pronounced *ks*. As both these have been examined, no further explanation is necessary.

Y is a "voiced consonant", but actually is a vowel. In Italian it is called a Greek I (*ee*). In words such as *young, enjoy, yacht, yard, yawn*, the *y* is merely a short *i* sound, as in *pit*.*

Z is a sibilant, like S, only somewhat harder. Like all the other consonants, its articulation must be gradually reduced as the pitch rises. High notes demand a small, firm *z*. The same principle applies all along the line.

The student is well advised to make a particular study of the formation of the consonants on the above lines; and until such time as they have attained, through constant practice, that state of perfection which passes into automatism, or quasi-automatism, he must be careful deliberately to introduce the required degree of tightness, of compactness in their preparation. Failing this, they become inaudible, and the actual words unintelligible.

Especially will he bear in mind that the formation of:

B, if insufficiently tight, becomes a nonentity;

C, „ „ „ degenerates into a hybrid G (He *gan gome* soon);

D, „ „ „ becomes a nonentity;

F, „ „ „ degenerates into a hybrid V (He is *vond* of her);

---

* Y is not a consonant, but mainly a short *i* vowel, as in *pit*, with a slight consonantal urge, particularly when placed at the beginning of a word as in *yacht, yelp, yeoman*. When in the middle, as in *payment, maypole, olympiad*, and at the end, as in *boy, say, employ*, it is a short *i* vowel sound. In the noun *prophecy*, it is a short *i* sound as in *pit;* but in the verb to *prophesy*, it is a diphthong consisting of an *ah* sound and short *i*, as above. Again, in *spying* it represents one sound only, viz. *ah*.

G, if insufficiently tight, becomes a nonentity;

K, „   „   „   degenerates into a hybrid G (He is so *ghind*);

L, „   „   „   becomes a nonentity;

P, „   „   „   degenerates into a hybrid B (*Blease* do this);

T, „   „   „   degenerates into a hybrid D (The *depid* water);

V, „   „   „   becomes a nonentity.

When consonants are small, light and compact, as they must be on the high notes, they are perfectly audible and form a fitting crown to the underlying sound-beams reflecting the various vowels.

Another important point to remember is that their release, as, for instance, when the tongue comes away from the palate, must be made without jerking, without roughness of any kind, in order not to upset the delicate sound-beams, and through them the equally delicate laryngeal adjustments from which they accrue. The separation of the consonant-forming parts—lips, tongue, palate, lowering of jaw—must be oil-smooth and speedy in action, never dilatory. (See last paragraph, p. 266.)

CHAPTER XI

THE RESONATING ZONES OF
THE DIFFERENT CATEGORIES OF VOICE

Part I

WE KNOW that every note is produced basically by a vibrator adjustment peculiar, in length, thickness and tension, to that pitch only. We also know that the tonal product of every pitch-cum-adjustment has its own individual characteristics, its own distinguishing quality particularly on the upper medium and high notes. To be able to reveal these characteristics and qualities these notes must be separated into well-defined groups that separately couple or tune in to a given resonating zone. The perfect vocal scale is a concatenation of a number of groups of notes of varying and distinctive tonal quality. Each series of notes forming a group must be tuned in to the resonator, or resonating zone peculiar to the group.

A note, belonging to a certain series, naturally (acoustically) related to a given resonating zone cannot efficiently be produced by "placing" or forcing it into another resonator not its own. The human voice unfortunately lends itself to certain abuses of the kind and continues to function, after a fashion; but the tone never can be good because physiologically and acoustically unbalanced. Whereas a high note can abusively be produced in the mouth-pharynx cavity (the wrong resonating zone) with dire tonal results, a low note cannot possibly be forced, let alone "placed", into the head resonator for the simple reason that its sound-beam is too short, and no amount of breath-pressure pumping will lengthen it; rather will it be shortened thereby.

If a wrong resonating zone is engaged for a particular pitch, the vibrator adjustment peculiar to that pitch will be partly or wholly upset. On the other hand, an incorrect vibrator setting cannot possibly give rise to a tone, a sound-beam, that will *naturally* seek out, enter, and tune in to its own rightful resonating zone, to its exact point of impingement. Hence the importance of securing correct vibrator adjustments (through correct vowel shaping) for every pitch, for they and they alone produce sound-beams of appropriate height and diameter ready for accurate tuning.

Whereas sound-beams are live, movable and manœuvrable things, the resonating zones are fixed as far as their respective locations are concerned.

The first zone of resonation is located in the mouth-pharynx cavity whose roof consists of the arc of the palate. The other zones are in the head above the palate. Within each zone a given series of notes find their exact reinforcement. Which reinforcement obtains only when the sound-beam of appropriate size relative to each note of the series is allowed to take or is given the correct direction in order to tune in at its exact point of impingement within the particular zone.

Correctness of beam direction is governed by the pitch, and the vowel being properly shaped in relation to pitch; consequently a note well tuned in to its own resonating zone satisfies the conditions of the "coupled system" on which the human voice is based.

We could say that each resonating zone not only accommodates a given series of notes but also imparts to them a distinctive quality-colour which distinguishes them from those of the other zones; and while every note of a series belonging to a particular zone is tonally an individual, it reveals the quality-colour characteristic of the zone. For instance, there is no mistaking the characteristic quality of a pure head note nor that of a chest note, so-called, as there is no mistaking the difference between the quality of a tenor's high G and that of A♭, or A♮ and B even though belonging as they do to the same head resonating zone; and the same could be said of a soprano's high notes from G to C. Apart from zonal characteristics, every head note has its own "personality".

When a note is properly tuned in to its natural resonator it reveals properties of harmony, balance, mastery and authority. To the singer the sensation is one of satisfying mental-nervous accomplishment with a minimum of physique, a maximum of mind, and a sum total of buoyant energy. To the listener the issuing tone gives the impression of disembodiedness; no machinery, no physique, but just detached, disembodied, floating tone.*

And so let us examine the different categories:

THE SOPRANO VOICE

In this category there is a range of calibres from very light to dramatic. The very light soprano is a smaller and much less vital voice than the true coloratura. Perhaps "pretty", but rarely is it able to express much emotion because as an organ it lacks both mechanical and tonal depth. Neither has it the penetrating quality of the coloratura which, of course, is a better and more intense voice altogether.

The light soprano, even as the coloratura and indeed all calibres, should be allowed to remain true to type and not subjected to a forced-blast fabrication in a misguided attempt to increase the natural calibre. Neither gracefully nor convincingly can their forced growth make them assume a bigger calibre than nature intended. Forced growth accomplishes one thing: the certain ruin of the voice involved.

Voices are peculiar things, enigmas almost, for one never can tell whether or not they will develop to an unexpected degree under the impulse of well-ordered exercise. Both the very light soprano and the coloratura, however, are so unmistakably characteristic that it is possible to foresee their maximum development within their own calibre; under normal work there can be no question of their encroaching into the next calibre. If we take the range of lyric sopranos from light to "spinto" (i.e. bordering on the dramatic) it is possible to assert that every adolescent voice unspoilt by certain "training" is more or less an unknown quantity as far as its future development is concerned. And this applies to all young and unspoilt voices of all categories.

Sometimes a young voice will denote by its smallness the light calibre, while potentially it may well belong to a heavier calibre. No teacher, whatever his experience, his knowledge, his fame, is able conscientiously to forecast the possibilities of ultimate development. Voices spring many surprises during a well planned period of study, and even after many years of professional work. This is

* If, with closed eyes, we listen to the tones of a great violinist we hear no horsehair being drawn over sheep-gut, no wood, no material medium, but just pure, isolated, disembodied tone floating across the auditorium,

particularly the case when the singer has carefully nursed the output during probation and growth. If a teacher thinks fit to indulge
in prognostications of the sort he should exercise a wise restraint
on his optimism, otherwise he may render himself liable to
charges of wishful thinking, or of charlatanism.*

Some voices mature more rapidly than others under the benefi-
cent warmth of appropriate exercise; others have the initial
advantage of a greater natural development without having undergone systematic work.

The coloratura comes within the range of light calibres. A
small voice but complete, compact, pliable, intensely vital,
penetrating, and insinuatingly attractive. It is really in a category
all its own. After it comes a range of light sopranos of varying
calibre whereupon we enter the field of the lyric of which there
are a number of calibres from light lyric to *lirico spinto*. As we
leave the *spinto* class we enter that of the dramatic.

The real dramatic soprano seemingly is a rare voice today. A
number of lyric sopranos of the bigger calibres endeavour to
become "dramatic" by the simple process of shouting. But the
tone is spurious, and no voice can withstand the forced march for
long; the prelude to the crash is a magnificent wobble. The fake
dramatic is a poor impersonation of the real; it manifests a false
optimism born of a false perspective.

The resonating zones are identical as regards location and
number not only in all soprano voices but in all women's voices
regardless of category and calibre.

We will now watch our model soprano as she progresses up the
scale and observe how she engages the different resonating zones.
And as we ascend the scale with her we propose to enlighten the
student as to the *modus operandi* of tuning in the several groups of
notes to their respective zones of resonation.

Starting from middle C or B♭ below it she will employ, say,

* It is well known that Enrico Caruso's voice was quite small in his early
twenties. He himself often related how his fellow students used to "poke fun"
(*Pigliare in giro*) at his voice on this account. Nobody, not even his teacher,
Vergine, with whom he studied several years, foreshadowed the future development of his voice to the outstanding status of *lirico spinto* to which it finally
attained. The epithet of "the cracking tenor" (*il tenore dalle stecche*) stuck to him
for the first few years of his career, as he invariably "cracked" on his high notes.
Nobody foretold its potentiality, nobody prognosticated, until after the event,
that his voice would carry him, and he his voice, to the top of the world of song.

the vowel AH, as in *father, padre*. This AH is pure and therefore open*ish*—not blatantly open; to distinguish its shape, sound and colour we call it AH¹. This vowel, like all vowels and modifications thereof, is the result of appropriate shaping of the mouth-pharynx cavity into and through which the vocal vibrations pour.

Keeping this AH shape and sound in mind and voice our soprano sings semitone by semitone up to E♮, first line. Up to and including this pitch all notes are designated as chest notes, or chest voice. The reason for this old terminology is that although the sound-beam of AH soars vertically to impinge against the arc of the palate, the major sensation for the singer herself is that more tone is felt in the region of the larynx or just above it. This phenomenon is due to the fact that the greater part of the vibrator mass is employed on all notes from the lowest to the said E♮, and the singer's mind is apt to be attracted more to the fundamental rumble rather than to the actual resonance which, in fact, is not impressive as the sound-beam has but a "vapour" touch as it impinges against the arc of the palate. It is only as she approaches C, third space, that the sound-beam begins to make itself felt and appreciated.

From E onwards our soprano takes leave of the chest voice, and to bridge over to the next note—F, first space—she "lifts up" the tone and rounds off the vowel very slightly. (See Chapter XVI on the Lift-up principle). The two movements are simultaneous. But remember, they are *mental* concepts followed by appropriate physical reaction.

By "rounding off" the vowel we mean a degree of modification of the basic shape in order to approach the modified AH sound in such words as *loft, fog, cough, not, sorry*, which we distinguish as AH².* Note that we say 'approach' the shape and sound of AH²: this is because the F needs very little lift-up and very little vowel modification to effect the 'bridging' from the E. Which slight modification we could call AH¹ᐟ² (as in *mine*, the AH sound of which is not so open as that in *father*, and not so rounded as that in *not*). The slight rounding process imparts a slightly darker hue to the tone. It is sufficient for the singer to *think* in the vowel shape and sound he requires; he has nothing deliberately physical to do in this respect for the reaction to the thought is immediate and

* The parent work, *The Science and Sensations of Vocal Tone* (Dent), deals in detail with vowel modification.

appropriate within the mouth-pharynx cavity and the laryngeal mechanism. (See Chapter XIII.)

Keeping this AH$^{1\frac{1}{2}}$ shape and sound-colour in mind and voice, our soprano continues chromatically up the scale to C♮, third space, the sound-beam soaring vertically all the time. As the pitch rises so the frequency increases, and she will readily feel, as she reaches this C, the contact of the top of the sound-beam with the arc of the palate. Which contact we call focus, or focal point, or platform. At this stage she no longer has any sensation of fundamental rumble within the laryngeal region.

Now, all notes from the lowest up to and including this C are located within and tune in to the mouth-pharynx cavity which we designate as Resonating Zone N.1. (See Diagram 9, p. 152.) We must point out that up to this note the sound-beam does not noticeably get narrower as the pitch rises from the lowest note; so our singer need not dwell on this aspect of the upward journey.

As regards Resonating Zone N.1. constituted by the mouth-pharynx cavity, the student is aware that the back part of this cavity, the pharynx, with its soft palate, tongue and gullet, is a pliable and adjustable network, giving shape to the vowels, whereas the front part, the mouth, with the hard palate, is a fixed bony structure, unpliable in the upper part and adjustable only by the fact of opening the lips wider whereupon the tongue may or may not descend or rise somewhat to co-operate in the different vowel formations.

In this connection it is vitally important to remember that the correct adjustment, or shaping, of the back part of Zone N.1 (the pharynx) affects favourably, from the standpoint of resonation, the front part (the mouth), even as its maladjustment, however slight it may be, adversely affects it as far as resonation is concerned. Furthermore, if the lips are deliberately protruded beyond the normal in a misguided effort to bring the tone "well forward" (the inane parrot-cry of modern methods), the zone of resonation is unduly extended horizontally, causing posterior distortion in degree. (There is a normal protrusion of lips, varying in degree, as we sing AW, OH and OO on the first octave and a little more, but the lips must never protrude for AH.) Indiscriminate lip protrusion is, in men's voices, one of the causes of sombre or booming tone varying in degree according to the reaction of the individual voice; in women's voices it is the main cause of hooting or "tubed" tone. The correlation between front and back part of the mouth-pharynx resonating zone is hypersensitive; the issuing tone inevitably reveals the slightest maladjustment.

The eight-note excursion—F to C—is accompanied by a delicately graduated modification or rounding-off of the vowel from AH$^{1\frac{1}{2}}$ to AH^2. It is all very subtle and requires an exquisite *mental* touch—similar to the delicate tinting of the artist's brush. However, the normally well produced voice will practically make the graduations on its own.

At C$\sharp$ (third space) our soprano is on the threshold of the Intermediate Resonating Zone. (See Diagram 9, p. 152.) Note that we say "threshold" because actually C$\sharp$ and D$\natural$ (fourth line) resonate mainly in the mouth-pharynx cavity, for, in light sopranos especially, the "head" of the vowelled tone pierces the arc of the palate slightly on these two pitches, while the "body" of the vowel remains in said cavity. The bridging from C$\natural$ to C$\sharp$ is effected by a slight extra lift-up and a very slight rounding of the vowel, simultaneously, so as to produce definitely AH^2.

In passing we must add that occasionally in some sopranos this natural bridging may occur from B$\natural$ to C. Students should be careful, therefore, to be guided by their tonal sensation in this respect.* (See p. 79.)

Keeping the AH^2 shape and sound-colour in mind and voice, our soprano continues up the scale semitone by semitone to F$\natural$, fifth line. Which five notes (from C$\sharp$) tune in with the top of the rising sound-beam to the Intermediate Resonating Zone, situate just above the arc of the palate (see Diagram 9, p. 152). As soon as she enters at C$\sharp$ the threshold of the Intermediate and travels up to said F$\natural$, her mind commences to register a threefold sensation of resonance. In fact, she feels that the sound-beam (1) *increases* in height; (2) *decreases* in diameter; (3) inclines somewhat backwards with respect to the vertical. This threefold movement of

---

* A word of warning here to all sopranos, irrespective of calibre, is imperative: In most cases sopranos fail to effect from C to C$\sharp$, third space, the slight *extra* lift-up of the tone that is so very necessary at this point. If the vibrator is not lightened at this point of entry to the Intermediate zone the singer will ultimately find herself in possession of a pulsing, flickering, or even wobbly note. In certain respects it is a delicate juncture in all female voices. So many sopranos, even of the light and coloratura calibres, develop a "knock" on this C$\sharp$ precisely because they habitually produce it with slightly too much cord, particularly in depth.

the beam within the so-called Intermediate Resonating Zone is slight on C♯ and D♮, but is marked from E♭ upwards. And the higher the pitch the more marked the triple movement of the beam (remember that our soprano is still employing the AH vowel).

Having reached F♮, fifth line, the highest note to be tuned in to the Intermediate, our soprano will have to effect another "bridging" in order correctly to produce F♯, *the entry note to the real head resonating zone (Zone N.2) or head voice.* The bridging consists of a slight *extra* lift-up and the simultaneous rounding of the vowel with AH³, a darker tone than AH² and closely approximating the AW sound, without however invading it. (There is no word with which to represent this darker tone.)

Keeping the AH³ shape and sound-colour in mind and voice, our soprano continues to climb, note by note, to high C. From F♯, therefore, she has seven notes to tune in to the head resonating zone (see Diagram 9, p. 152), and each note should be given a slightly darker tint by thinking not merely of the AW shape and sound but also towards OH and even OO, introducing tints thereof. (See Diagram 2, p. 80.)

The note-by-note modifications of the vowel shape are extremely slight, and the parts concerned will effect them if assisted with a finely tuned thought.

To secure well-rounded high notes, therefore, our singer will introduce, by *thinking* and *willing in* small tints of OH. But if the OH-tint is found insufficient to counteract the tendency (present in most voices) to spread or open the vowelled tone on these high notes, then a percentage of OO, as in *pool*, or of U, as in *pull*, definitely assists the rounding or "closing" of the tone. We call this the OO-thought or OO-nip; actually it is a minute curve. In the studio we tell the student to "think OO, or U", or, "sing towards OH-OO". These added small percentages of either OH or OO, or both, will not absorb the basic shape and quality of the AH vowel, in spite of its own modifications to which the OH and OO tints are added. But the singer must keep in mind and voice the basic vowel, and not overdo the modifications. When the modifications are slight and the added tints of OH and OO small, there is no distortion of the AH vowel.*

If our soprano can, or wishes, to go higher than top C, she will

---

* On no account must the lips be used for introducing these percentages of *oo* or *u* which need only to be *thought-in* at the height of the focus.

have to enter and tune in to Resonating Zone N.3, the final one, the "loft" of the soprano resonating system. We call this the *super-head voice* on account of the extraordinarily high sensation of location in the back upper part of the head. The sound-beam seems to reach the crown of the head. (See Diagram 9, p. 152.)

She will have to employ the usual "bridging" process when going from C to C♯, the entry note to the super-head resonation. So here once more she requires to make a slight *extra* lift-up which includes the simultaneous introduction of a goodly percentage of OH or OO, or both. The *mere thought* of a minute *oo*-curve or *oo*-hook is sufficient to achieve the end; indeed, these goodly tints need only to be *thought in;* the mechanical reaction is immediate and certain.

Possessing sufficient compass, our soprano can tune four or five notes in to the super-head zone from high C upwards. Few voices can produce a super-high F with good tone; indeed, from E♮ in alt tonal quality commences rapidly to fade in most voices, to leave a species of whistle. When a tone is deprived of quality, when it loses its complexion, its "personality", it cannot possibly *mean* anything. In the majority of cases such notes are just a stunt to impress a certain type of listener.

We explained in Chapter XVI the principle of the lift-up from note to note as the pitch rises. Now the *extra* lift-up of the tone at certain fixed points in the vocal scale, as mentioned above, is absolutely necessary in order to tune the tone (actually the top of the sound-beam) into the appropriate resonating zone. It is an established fact that *at these points* in the scale, the vocal cords demand a slight extra shortening and thinning; the shortening process is assisted by a slight rounding of the vowel, and the thinning process by the lift-up. The immediate result is a correspondingly slight extra increase in height of the sound-beam at each of these points thus enabling it to be perfectly tuned in. The student will now understand why so many singers are inclined to be flat at these particular points, for without the extra lift-up the beam will be just too short for accurate tuning.

As the scale is ascended from the lowest to the highest pitch there is a gradual note-to-note increase in the tension of the vocal cords. Although tension comes in more or less automatically, it is a good plan to deliberately seek and *will it in*. So many singers induce tension by sheer breath pressure. The better plan is to engage mind, nerves and *will*, whereupon the muscles respond to the call.

We now refer our soprano readers to "Concluding Remarks", (p. 153) as they are applicable to all categories and calibres of voice. She is also advised to read the sections on all the other categories, for she may well gather a few extra threads of knowledge that profitably can be woven into her own technical fabric.

THE MEZZO-SOPRANO VOICE

This category of voice has exactly the same resonating zones as the soprano (with the exception of the super-head); consequently, no useful purpose would be served by accompanying the mezzo up the scale with a running commentary. With slight variations the mechanical procedure for securing a well-graduated scale as outlined above for the soprano is applicable to the mezzo.

The mezzo will commence her scale, say, on low G employing the AH vowel. At E♮, first line, her so-called chest voice ends. As a tonal sensation the notes from this G to E seem to be resonating mainly in the lower part of the mouth-pharynx cavity (although the top of the sound column actually is contacting the arc of the palate, albeit with merely a "vapour" touch that is almost imperceptible to her). This low*ish* feeling is due to the fact that the mind is more impressed by, and fastens upon, the sub-laryngeal vibrations, which set up sympathetic vibrations in the trachea and thorax, obtaining on the low notes by reason of the relatively large vibrator mass employed for the production of the low pitches. In fact, the sub-laryngeal rumble is more prominent in the heavier categories of voice, male and female. Hence the old term "chest voice" or "chest tone". But as the pitch rises and the vibrator mass gradually diminishes as a result of the process we call elimination, the vibrations below the larynx cease because the resonance (sound-beam) gradually increases in height, comes more into its own and, by increasing its tonal touch with firmer points of impingement against the arc of the palate (due to the increasing frequency), impresses the singer's mind with its significance.

We said that at E♮ her chest voice ceases (or rather should cease normally, because for an *occasional* effect she can produce the next two notes with "chest" tone without doing any harm). She must bridge over to the next note—F♮, first space—by means of the lift-up and slight vowel modification (simultaneously), as explained above for the soprano. Whereupon a new timbre comes into the voice to paint and characterize the new series of notes, eight in all, from F to C, third space. Therefore from low G to this C the tone will have gradually and almost imperceptibly modified towards AH² (the sound in *song, promise*).

She will now bridge over to C♯, third space, the first note to enter the threshold of the Intermediate Resonating Zone, as does the soprano; she effects the bridging by a tonal lift-up and the simultaneous rounding of the vowel to produce AH². With this colour she sings C♯, D (which tune in to the threshold of the Intermediate Zone); then D♯, E and F♮, all three tuning in to the Intermediate Resonating Zone. As she sings these five notes the AH² colour gradually modifies, rounding off towards AH³ (a darker hue than AH², and approaching the AW sound). As stated above in the soprano section, the last three notes (D♯, E, F♮) tune right into the Intermediate Zone situate above the palate, but qualitatively they are not strictly head tones, for the real head resonating zone only begins at F♯ (fifth line). The notes tuned in to the Intermediate have a characteristic timbre all their own; it is neither mouth-pharynx nor head-voice quality, although approaching the latter.

Naturally, the mezzo's voice is of darker tinge than the soprano's; consequently all her vowel modifications will produce a darker timbre. Care should be taken never to overload the colouring.

From F♮, fifth line, she will bridge over to F♯, the entry note to the real head resonating zone (N.2). (See Diagram 9, p. 152.) This, as usual, includes the tonal lift-up and the rounding (darkening) of the vowel to AH³, as explained above for the soprano.

She sings the seven notes, F♯—C, in the head zone which colours them all with a peculiarly characteristic timbre. When well tuned in there is no mistaking their eminently attractive quality.

As our mezzo ascends from the F♯, keeping the AH³ shape and sound in mind and voice, she can gradually introduce small percentages of OH and/or OO (or U as in *put*) just like the soprano does. This not only "closes" the tone but beautifies it.

The mezzo is advised to read the soprano section first and then the contralto's after re-reading her own. Finally she should read "Concluding Remarks".

THE CONTRALTO VOICE

This category of voice has exactly the same zones of resonation and the same tonal points of entry therein as the soprano and the mezzo. Also the mechanical procedure for securing a well-graduated scale is identical; the tonal product is of course darker by nature than that of the other two categories, and this is due to a greater depth of vocal cords and to specific variations in the shape of the resonators.

Contraltos, like basses and sometimes baritones, are prone to overloading the tone on the low pitches, and carry on the process up to C, third space, and even higher (if the voice doesn't before this register a protest in some form or other). This often accounts for the monotony which characterizes their tones. The contralto is a fine timbre, but it must be properly handled and not rendered stodgy as it so often is; it can easily become boring and un-interesting. And so can the bass.

So many are seemingly not content to employ a definite vowel shape and colour, but a no-vowel mumble-jumble sound as non-descript as it is unintelligible. Under the mistaken idea that they are thereby producing "rich contralto tone", they persevere until at a certain pitch, sometimes about G♯, second line, or higher, the tone will suddenly jump out of its heavy mantle and present a thin and absurdly light and colourless ghost of itself by contrast. What happens is that the vocal cords, tired of the hard labour to which they have been subjected by such pomposity of thought, take the law into their own hands, ignore the singer's effort, and attenuate the effective vibrator mass to an excessive degree in one desperate spasmodic adjustment of some kind, any kind. The tonal body thereupon receives a bad jolt. This is also the direct cause of the proverbial "break" in the contralto voice which often occurs at G, second line, G♯, or even A. Because she makes a practice of engaging too much cord in depth in relation to pitch on a whole series of notes, producing heavy-laden tones that she considers "rich", she is dragging up her chest voice, so to speak, right beyond its normal finishing point—E♮, first line. Not having properly eliminated the vibrator mass her voice is unable to effect the necessary bridging from E to F; consequently the G, or what-ever the note the "break" occurs on, is produced with too much cord in length and thickness. The vibrating mechanism, unable to withstand the unnatural load (being in the wrong "gear") suddenly snaps into an excessively thin cord adjustment, and sometimes with an audible cut or break in the up-soaring sound-beam. A "break" reveals technical ignorance, or a vulgar streak.

It is not necessary to accompany our contralto up the scale in detail as the general basis of scale graduation laid down above for the soprano and mezzo applies; and she is well advised to read the sections carefully. At the three bridging points, E♮ to F, first space; C to C♯, third space; F to F♯, fifth line, she must avoid overdoing the vowel-rounding process. At these points the vowel modifications produce a slightly darker and richer quality; consequently, the contralto by reason of her natural tonal fullness has no need to add to the load of colour artificially, as it were, by digging into the tone. Why attempt to paint the lily?

She can avoid these pitfalls by commencing her scale on the lowest note with no more colour than AH$^{1\frac{1}{2}}$ (the AH sound in *eye*, *mine*, which is not quite so open as the AH in *father*), and she will find that, by reason of her natural darkness of tone, on reaching the first bridging point (E–F, first line, first space) her voice will readily produce AH^2 (as in *song*). Keeping this AH^2 shape and colour in mind and voice, she now climbs to the second bridging-point (C–C♯) and right on to the third (F–F♯) which she bridges over with AH^3 (a darker edition than AH^2 and approximating the AW sound without, however, touching it). If she merely *thinks in* the tonal colours and modifications, and avoids all physical attempts at shaping and colouring, the parts concerned and her voice will respond to her ordered *thinking*.

The contralto should bear in mind the brighter tones of the well-balanced mezzo and adjust her vowel colours accordingly, instead of trying to emulate the drone of the big bass viol as so many contralti are taught to do by certain masters.

At the three bridging points she will remember to make a little *extra* lift-up and *avoid* excessive rounding of the vowel. The bigger the voice the more easily are mistakes made in this and every sense. (And this goes for every category of voice.) She must be her own judge as to the percentages of OH and/or OO to be introduced for tuning in the series of head tones from F♯, fifth line, upwards. Again we must ask her not to paint the colours too thick.

Finally, our contralto should read "Concluding Remarks" at the end of Part II.

Recapitulation.—The resonating zones of the Soprano, Mezzo and Contralto voices, and the series of notes to be tuned therein, are:

ZONE 1: the mouth-pharynx cavity; from lowest note to C♮, third space.

INTERMEDIATE ZONE: the threshold of Zone 2, mainly above and basically on a level with the palate; from C♯, third space, to F♮, fifth line.

ZONE 2: the head cavity above the palate, and a continuation of the Intermediate; from F♯, fifth line, to high C♮.

ZONE 3: the super-head cavity above Zone 2; from high C♯ to F in alt, or higher.

Part II

THE TENOR VOICE

This category of voice, irrespective of calibre, has, basically, two resonating zones: the mouth-pharynx cavity, and the head cavity above the palate. Which latter includes the Intermediate zone of resonation; so we advise the tenor student to study the whole of Part I above. The mechanical procedure necessary for tuning in to these zones the different series of notes comprising the vocal scale apply equally to his category of voice. He should also read "Concluding Remarks" hereunder.

Let us now accompany the tenor up the scale from the normally lowest note:

Starting from middle C on the AH^1 vowel (as in *father*) it is plain sailing to C, third space. This first octave tunes in to Zone 1 (the mouth-pharynx cavity). The resultant sound-beam soars more or less vertically upwards to impinge against the arc of the palate. The points of impingement of the beam are barely perceptible to the singer on this first octave; especially on the lower notes they have merely a vapour touch. As a sensation, the beam *seems* to be contacting more or less the same spot on the palatal arc until said C is reached, viz. the middle of the arc. This lack of substantial contact of the beam is due mainly to the relative low frequencies of this first octave.

As he reaches C or C♯, third space, the *extremely light* vowel rounding which comes in naturally on the way up from the lowest note will reveal, say, an AH$^{1\frac{1}{2}}$ colour (as in *mine*).

In order to produce that brilliant quality typical of the tenor voice on D♮, fourth line, he should lift up and pull back (slightly) the tone as he passes from C♯ to D.

Keeping basically in mind and voice the AH¹ᵇ shape and sound, he continues his climb to F♮, fifth line. The four notes D to F tune in to the above-described Intermediate Zone, the location of which is exactly that in women's voices. Mind you, the D♮ resonates mainly in the mouth-pharynx cavity (Zone 1) but the *head* of the tone tunes in to the Intermediate (and by "head" we mean here the top of the sound-beam). As he ascends from D to F the vowel should be gradually modified (in very small degrees) so that on F♮ he will be producing the AH² sound-colour (as in *song, long, pod*). During the transit the singer will note the *triple* movement of the sound-beam (which becomes marked as from E♭ upwards). In fact, it (1) increases in height; (2) decreases in diameter; (3) inclines back of the vertical, all very gradually. And as from this E♭, fourth space, upwards, the sensation of vowel in the mouth-pharynx cavity commences to dissipate, to give place to the simple sensation of the rising sound-beam, the singer's mind is gradually more impressed by and attracted to the TOP of the beam itself and is therefore able clearly to note the aforesaid triple movement. And the higher the pitch past this F the more marked becomes the triple movement. The singer should observe and gradually acquire the mental vision of the *top* of the beam, which we call focus or platform.

Many tenors are inclined to make the central D♮, fourth line, too heavy, with the result that they carry on with an inappropriate thickness of vibrator up to and beyond F, fifth line, with poor tonal results. He can obviate all trouble of the kind by *assisting* the elimination of the vibrator mass, viz. by a *slight* tonal lift-up (and pull back), after which he can, if he wants to assist the mechanism, slightly round off the vowel towards AH². We know that this dual simultaneous movement, which is mainly mental, has a two-fold reaction on the vibrator: (1) the lift-up assists the thinning of the cords, and (2) the vowel rounding assists the cord-shortening process—A KEY THAT UNLOCKS THE DOOR OF TECH-NIQUE, the Open Sesame to the tonal treasure-bags that the whole world of students is seeking, and so often never finds.

He must now bridge over from F to F♯, producing the latter with AH³, a colour darker than AH² in *song*, and approximating AW, without touching it. With a simultaneous lift-up (a slight *extra* one) he will readily tune in to his true head resonating zone, that we call Zone 2. The lift-up includes naturally a pull-back movement (mentally conceived, by the way); this loosens the throat, opens it appropriately to permit the sound-beam to follow its natural angle with respect to the vertical.

As F♯ is a half-way note in certain respects we shall examine it later a little more closely. Meantime let us proceed. With this F♯ tuned in nicely with AH³ he will sing the successive six notes up to high C, *keeping in mind and voice* this shape and sound-colour. Most voices at this stage will require a definite tone-closing discipline because of the tendency to open out the tone as the pitch rises, a tendency due to incompleted muscular development, and training. And an open tone on high notes means bad, blatant tone, because too much cord in length is engaged thereby.

To obviate this possibility our tenor must introduce small but gradually increasing percentages of OH and/or OO (or U as in *put*) into or on top of AH³ (which latter must be retained basically) on the way up from F♯ to high C. These percentages must be *thought in*, not physically made by the singer, because he would be sure to overdo things. It is sufficient to *think* of a miniature *oo* sound (as in *pool*) or of a miniature *u* (as in *put*, *full*) and the parts concerned react immediately to the thought. The result is a mixed tone well compacted with AH, OH and OO colours. Remember that on these high pitches the lips do *not* participate at all in the formation of OO or U: the pharynx does most of the shaping in every case. It is generally a matter of pleasant surprise how gracefully the mechanism responds to such thinking. There are of course exceptions where some voices are refractory.

The average listener hears the basic vowel sound, and not the added vowel colourings which merely tint and beautify the basic vowel.

As he ascends from the F♯, fifth line, to the highest note, our tenor will observe how marked is the sensation of the afore-mentioned triple movement of the sound-beam. As the pitch rises and the beam soars, so the tonal platform becomes smaller by degrees and more "pointed"; due to the high frequency it not only feels to be *leaning* (appoggio) against a hard-domed surface but also "drilling" into it.

As explained fully in Chapter XXII, also the tenor voice possesses the additional mechanism called "pharyngeal" operating effectively from F♮, fifth line, to high C (and even higher) and which he can put to excellent and oft-times exquisite use, particularly on the head tones from high G upwards.

We said above that we considered F♯, fifth line, a half-way note because sometimes for special effects it can be sung with AH² instead of AH³. If with AH², without the "extra" lift-up, the tone will tune partly in the true head Zone 2 and partly in the Intermediate: a split-tone, therefore, partaking more of the Intermediate Zone's characteristic open brightness. One must be careful, however, not to overdo this openish tone because particularly on this note it is easy to cross the border into blatancy. Each singer must work out for himself how far he can open a certain note without making it blatant. Some voices can open their tones more than others without spoiling the quality.

The tenor should in most cases sing this F♯ with nicely openish tone whether with AH² or AH³ because it can be made very effective and telling in this way. Inversely, for mezzavoce effects, the AH³ should be given a decided tint of *oo* (as in *pool*) or of *u* (as in *pull*); which u-tint is placed, so to speak, like a tiny cap or hood on top of the AH³. This mixed tone clips right into the head resonating zone. If, with this mixed tone, the note is attacked first *p*, then developed into a *crescendo*, the u-tint or cap must be released and the tone opened out *f* into AH³, AH²⁺ or AH² (never AH¹). To open out in this way, *part* of the tone must come out of the head resonating zone to engage the Intermediate. And so we get the split-tone again. We call it "split" because the tone is tuned simultaneously into two different resonating zones, each of which imparts to the tone its own characteristic colour.

The F♮, fifth line, on the other hand, is, by virtue of its pitch and timbre, typical of and peculiar to the Intermediate Zone (even as E♮ and E♭ are). It should be sung in most cases with openish AH² tone and occasionally the darker hues of AH²⁺ and AH³ (which after all are only degrees of rounding-darkening towards the AW sound). (See Diagram 5, hereunder.) Care must be taken, however, never to make a blatantly open tone on this pitch; it is easy to do so. That is why we insist on that nicely balanced tonal product we call open*ish*, that is, nicely open but delicately rounded.*

* So many teachers are averse—needlessly so—to letting tenors produce F and F♯ (fifth line) and baritones E♭ and E♮ (fourth space) with open*ish* tone; as a result, these categories have recourse to that insensate "covering" and succeed in bottling up their tones on these pitches. To cover is to cramp; of that there is

For *mezzavoce* effects, this F can be given a sort of head voice colouring by a slight *oh*-tint, or *u*-tint, placed like a tiny cap on top of AH³—as explained above for F♯. But F♮ can never really be tuned in to the head resonating zone. In vain attempts to do so, many tenors darken to excess the tone; and as this excessive tonal darkening is invariably accompanied by the employment of too much cord in depth, the sound-beam will thereupon *decrease* in height, and consequently will be too short to be tuned in to the head; sometimes on this account it cannot even tune in to the

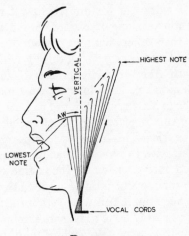

DIAGRAM 5

Intermediate, and so drops into the mouth-pharynx cavity with disastrous results. That blind, pseudo-technique called "covering" is also vainly employed with the same idea in mind.

So many singers apparently have difficulty in divorcing the thought of rounded vowel tone from heaviness and darkness of tone which, when excessive in relation to pitch, spells excess of cord employment in depth. Tone rounding (darkening) does not,

not the slightest doubt. Their scare is of course blatant tone. But there is a very marked difference between blatantly open tone and what we call openish tone, i.e. a tone just sufficiently rounded off. Is it not symptomatic that all the finest tenors and baritones, past and present, produced, where needed, these openish tones? Witness the records of Caruso, Gigli, Pertile, Schipa, Mattia Battistini, Titta Ruffo, De Luca, Stracciari, Dinh Gilly, and many others. Who are right— these, or those teachers?

and need not, necessarily induce or involve heaviness of mechanism and of production, for we can quite well have a rounded tone with a small, light, thin vibrator. It must be remembered that all tonal rounding is merely a question of rounding the pharynx; but this should not, and need not, so disturb the cord adjustment as to engage more cord in depth. One *can* rest a round object on a level surface without pressing on the latter downwards. And so it is with the rounded vowel-shape-cum-tone.

To ensure accurate tuning in to the head resonating zone the series of notes acoustically appertaining to it, it is an excellent plan to approximate the F♯ to the tonal sensation of G♮ (and *not* that of F♮); the G♮ to G♯ rather than to F♯; the G♯ to the A♮, and so on until the highest note is produced. Such thinking is of considerable physical assistance to the vibrator: it assists elimination of the vibrator mass, induces correct laryngeal adjustment and a dead-on-pitch tuning in of the relative sound-beam.

Recapitulation.—The resonating zones of the tenor, irrespective of calibre, and the series of notes to be tuned therein are:

ZONE 1: the mouth-pharynx cavity; from lowest note to D♮, fourth line, inclusive.

INTERMEDIATE ZONE: mainly above and basically on a level with the palate; from E♭, fourth space, to F♮, fifth line.

ZONE 2: the head cavity above the palate, and a continuation of the Intermediate; from F♯, fifth line, to high C.

THE BARITONE VOICE

Like all other voices, male and female, the baritone has two main resonating cavities: the mouth-pharynx, whose ceiling is the arc of the palate, and the spacious, domed head cavity above the palate. Each of these cavities is, in the baritone, divisible into two zones of resonation into which tune definite series of notes forming the scale. We shall comment on these zones as we accompany the baritone up the scale.

Before reading on, we advise the baritone student to peruse this chapter carefully from the beginning, and also the "Concluding Remarks", as several aspects of the general analysis are applicable to his own category.

We said above that the mouth-pharynx cavity was divisible into two zones of resonation. This "partitioning", however, is applicable to the baritone, basso cantante, and bass voices (and to no other category) for accommodating and colouring certain of their tones in the scale, as explained hereunder.

Normally, the baritone's lowest note is A (or A♭). As he slowly ascends the scale on AH it is plain sailing for the first octave. The AH[1] (as in *father*) will, or should, gradually, almost imperceptibly round off (or darken) so that on reaching A♮, second space, the tonal quality approximates AH[2], as in *sorry, long, song*. The resultant sound-beam of this first octave soars upwards more or less vertically to impinge against the arc of the palate. On the lower notes of this first octave the beam gives the sensation merely of a "vapour touch" against the palate; but after passing the half-way mark the point of impingement really begins to be felt. The reason for the misty and undefined sensation aroused by the feathery or vapour touch of the sound-beam on the lower notes is firstly the low frequency, and secondly that the singer's mind is mainly impressed by the more substantial fundamental rumble obtaining in the region of the larynx together with a measure of sub-laryngeal resonance. As the pitch rises the low-seated rumble gets beautifully less, to disappear entirely. By way of compensation for this feeble impingement of the beam, the singer can feel his mouth-pharynx cavity full of vowel. And this applies to all vowel sounds.

On approaching A♮, second space, however, he begins to feel there is something doing on the arc of the palate for the vibrations of the main stream of the tone (or sound-beam) are now making their presence felt thereon. This is also due to the now much-increased frequency, upon which the mind fastens with interest.

From this central A♮, second space, our baritone has to bridge over to the next note—B♭, third line—for it is here that a physiologic-acoustic "change" occurs, viz. a slight extra shortening of the cords. The bridging is effected as usual by a slight extra lift-up of the tone and concurrent rounding or darkening of the vowel (also slight) in order to produce on the B♭ a definite AH[2] colour.

At this point we must call a halt for some important explanatory remarks. We mentioned above the "partitioning" of the mouth-pharynx cavity. This is effected by our imaginary vertical (see Chapter XII) which, descending through the cavity, divides it into two zones: the mouth zone in front of the vertical, and the pharynx zone back of the vertical. Now, the exponents of the old

School distinguished this *front* half of the bisected cavity by the name of VUOTO, which means "Empty". We shall refer to it as the Vuoto Resonating Zone, or simply Vuoto Zone. It is an apt and most expressive term, as the first three notes (B♭, B♮, C) tuned in to them accurately give to the singer himself (and also to the listener) the sensation of completely disembodied tone of floating rotundity and apparently divorced from all physique; indeed, a sensation of complete isolation and suspension of the tone. There is not even the feeling of platform or of appoggio; no

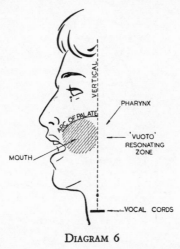

DIAGRAM 6

point of impingement and no feeling of sound-beam, but just a ball of tone.

The Vuoto Resonating Zone and the rich, round, characteristic quality of the tones issuing from it are peculiar to the baritone, the *basso cantante* * and the bass. There is something about such tones that partake of classic dignity and masterful authority.

The shape of the Vuoto Zone is essentially round. And to secure this internal rotundity the cavity must be shaped to an O. In this shaping the pliable, adjustable pharynx participates in no small degree, even though the particular O-shaping of the Vuoto is felt to be in the mouth part of the cavity in front of the vertical. (See Diagram 6.)

* The *basso cantante*, singing bass, is an enlarged baritone with a bass tinge running through its entire compass.

N.B.—We must again stress the fact (in all voices) that the singer's lips will of themselves automatically assume the right shape or aperture *indirectly* as a result of the internal shaping, *if he allows them to.* He should never deliberately shape his lips in a conscientious attempt to "improve matters", for he is sure to overdo it and cause distortion, in degree, of the ultimate mouth-pharynx shaping. Distortion is well-nigh complete when deliberate lip protrusion ignores internal vowel-shaping; it is reflected in hooting tone, which the Italians call *voce tubata* (tubed voice). And

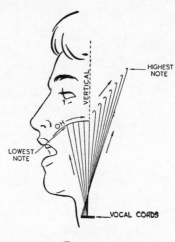

DIAGRAM 7

this is particularly true of the high notes. After the first octave or little more active lip participation in the shaping of AW, OH, OO commences gradually to dwindle until, on the high notes, it becomes nil or apparently so, whatever the vowel employed, as their activity in this sense is reduced practically to a minimum. Remember that we are talking of vowels, not consonants.

We said above that the Vuoto is essentially a round zone of resonation and that the roundness is given by forming the O vowel, a *single* sound as in *polite, police* or in Italian words such as *sonata, potente.* So, for our purpose, when we say O, or O vowel, we mean a monophthong—not a diphthong as in *pole, joke* in which the O is followed by a short *u.* Into this O Vuoto Zone the baritone tunes five notes: B♭, B♮, C, C♯, D♮ (fourth line). Due to the O formation, this resonating zone automatically imparts an O-tinge to AH², AH³, and AW when these are sung partly into it. (See Diagram 7, p. 142.) In regard to the OH vowel, it is sufficient to *think in*, and *will in* its shape and colour. We could quite well call the Vuoto an O-resonator. There can be no true Vuoto Zone without this O-tinge.

If the student will now glance also at Diagram 1 and note the approximate direction of the sound-beam of OH, on the lowest note, he will the more readily understand how the degree of O-tinting can be regulated at will by the singer. The process is quite simple: it is merely a question of curving the *top* of the sound-beam of AH or AW along the arc of the palate towards and into the OH vowel zone (located between the OH and OO in Diagram 1). In other words, mentally shape the OH sound and then sing AH or AW partly into that O-shape. Naturally, the AH becomes very rounded.

To form and engage the Vuoto Zone, say from A♮ to B♭, third line, our baritone must deliberately make the lift-up (with a pull-back, up-and-over mental curving) quickly, *think in* the O-shape and sing into it the AH or AW. The student must bear in mind that the physical reaction to every mental shaping is immediate, exactly reflecting the mind picture.

This B♭, B♮ and C♮ can be more heavily tinted with O than can C♯ or D♮. The reason for this is that when the AW and OH vowels are sung normally up the scale from the lowest note the relative sound-beam of both point forward into the mouth zone in front of the vertical to commence with, and gradually swing back along the arc of the palate to point more or less vertically upwards as C♯ and D♮ are reached. Consequently, on these last two pitches there is less AW and OH zones available in the mouth cavity in front of the vertical than there was before, for their shaping and direction of their beams tends to be upright preparatory to inclining back of the vertical as the pitch rises from E♭ upwards. The singer must respect the natural behaviour of the different sound-beams; he cannot afford to take liberties with the *natural* trend of any sound-beam.

While B♭, B♮ and C♮ can be pure Vuoto tones, arousing a sensation of complete tonal detachment, the C♯ and D♮ give the feeling of being "tacked on" again against the arc of the palate, the sound-beam pointing vertically upwards; as a result, they can be given only a limited percentage of curving into the O-zone. Any attempt to produce the C♯ and D with a biggish percentage of O or Vuoto similar to that given to B♭, B♮ and C♮ must result in tonal heaviness and distortion.

When produced in the Vuoto Zone the OH and OO vowels are in their element, so to speak. But to give them the buoyancy and feeling of complete detachment peculiar to and characteristic of the Vuoto Zone their tuning-in must be assisted by the aforementioned deliberate lift-up pull-back-and-over; which mental curve finds immediate mechanical reaction.

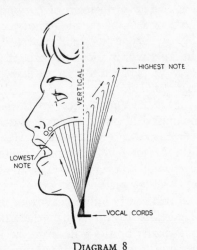

DIAGRAM 8

By the same token the EH (a monophthong, as in *Mary*, *there*), while not taking on any O-tinge when sung into the Vuoto, is nevertheless strongly influenced by the fact of the rounded O-cavity, accommodating itself therein by assuming a domed shape; for the singer, the sensation is that the EH has been shaped like a horseshoe, or an inverted U, and then detached and suspended in the Vuoto Zone. Once the singer acquires the feel of the Vuoto the rest is easy. The EE can also be sung into the Vuoto provided it is sufficiently rounded by introducing a percentage of French *u*, or German *ü*, as in *müde*. Like the EH, it cannot take on any O-tint but it can acquire the tonal buoyancy of the Vuoto. While we generally advise the EH and EE vowels to be sung with a straight upsoaring beam for about the first octave, they can both be given a quasi-horizontal direction (which, however, is not suitable for certain voices) and consequently tuned in to the Vuoto on B♭, B♮, C♮, and given only a tinge of Vuoto quality on C♯ and D♮ because on the last two pitches the relative sound-beams are practically upright.

The baritone need not engage the Vuoto Zone unless he wants to, but can continue up the scale in the ordinary way with gradual modifications of the AH up to D♮, fourth line, and "by-pass" the Vuoto position. In other words on the principle of the Academic Scale (see the parent work *The Science and Sensations of Vocal Tone*). In which case he will sing technically more like a big tenor although under the bright, openish tone one detects a baritonal substratum on the whole compass; and the bigger the voice the more marked this substratum. Light baritones have a "tenory" tinge, particularly on the higher pitches; big baritones can and should occasionally produce "tenory" tones when the mood and expression demand them and in fast-moving arias, as, for instance, "Largo al factotum".*

Having pointed to the existence and function of the Vuoto Resonating Zone we will now continue our excursion. Forgetting the Vuoto for the moment we return to the A♮, second space, and from there bridge over to B♭ with a lift-up pull-back and vowel-rounding movement, *mentally* performed, to produce the latter note with AH². Holding this shape-cum-sound in mind and voice, he will sing up to D♮, fourth line. On the way up, the tone should gradually darken (round off) towards AH³ which approaches the AW sound without actually touching it. (In a song, of course, this D♮ can be sung with AH².) The next two notes (E♭, E♮, fourth space) are produced with AH³; but as they tune in with the beam just back of the vertical, the singer should be careful not to allow

---

* The baritone voice, as we know it today, was unclassified as such in and before Rossini's time; it was called *tenore forte*, or *tenore corto*, strong, or short tenor. In fact, the rôle of Figaro was scored by Rossini for such *tenore forte*. The then baritone sang technically and acoustically like a tenor; the Vuoto zone was as yet undiscovered, and the dark baritonal substratum not employed. The principal tenor rôles were written for and sung exclusively by light tenors, called *tenore di grazia*, who, by the way, all employed the "Pharyngeal" mechanism (see Chapter XXII). Giorgio Roncone, it is said, was the first to discover the idiosyncrasies of the baritone voice, about 1830; he named and launched the new category, becoming himself one of the greatest baritones of the time. (From the Greek *barutonos: barus*, heavy; *tonos*, tone.)

the tone to open out backwards towards AH[1] which is too open and white for these pitches. They can, however, also be produced with a nicely turned and deepish timbre of AH[2]. These same two notes, together with F♮, fifth line, tune in to the Intermediate Zone, just above the arc of the palate. In the majority of cases E♭ and E♮ are sung with openish AH[2] or AH[3] timbre, but the F♮ never, because it demands capping or doming with a small percentage of OH every time it is sung. This O-cap imparts a nicely balanced dark timbre to the F♮; it can also be produced effectively with an OO-cap, or U-cap (as in *pull*). For colouring certain notes or phrases, and for *mezzavoce* effects, also the E♭ and E♮ can and should be O- or U-capped. To put this O- or U-cap on the AH[3] the singer must make the lift-up pull-back with the AH[3] in mind and voice, and then rapidly *think in* the O- or U-cap. We repeat that all the movements and shapings are performed primarily in the mental realm to find immediate response in the physical.

To engage the true head zone on F♯, fifth line, our baritone must lift-up from the F♮ and *think in* a greater percentage of OO- or U-cap *after* pulling back from the F position. And so on to G and A♭—the normally highest note of the baritone. The extraordinary part of it is that although more OO or U is introduced on these head notes, the tonal focus gets smaller and smaller the higher the pitch. Moreover, the basic AH[3] timbre is still retained in sufficient proportions for clarity of diction. The *thought* of this O- or OO- or U-cap produces a minute curving within the resonating zone (hence the term "cap", or "u-hook", which we also use), and, what is of vital importance too, this minute extra adjustment in the mouth-pharynx zone reacts on the vibrating mechanism in the larynx and assists the cord-shortening process in exact degree. (See Chapter XIII.)

When E♭, E♮ and F♮ are sung with dark, domed tone into the Intermediate resonating zone they certainly manifest a head-voice quality. But only the baritone and bass can and should employ such round, darkened tone in the Intermediate. Tenors and sopranos must never attempt it: they will court mechanical trouble if they do, apart from producing bad tone. Dark tone and heavy tone in the wrong place is voice-killing. (See footnote, p. 54.)

Be it noted that in the baritone voice the high F♯, G, G♯ and A♭ are the true or pure head tones; they tune in to the same resonating zone as do the same notes in the tenor voice (and in fact all voices, male and female). And the higher the note above this F♯, the more the baritone tends to take on a tenor quality; this is particularly true where the light baritone is concerned. Put side by side an equally well produced high A♭ by a big baritone and a dramatic tenor—there will be little to choose between them, technically speaking; the tenor's note, however, will have more "top" on it, more sparkle.

Only in the case of the baritone and bass categories, for simplicity's sake, we can consider as general head resonator the vaulted cavity situate above the arc of the palate. Consequently, not one of the six tones (E♭ to A♭) correctly produced and tuned in to this resonator is felt by the singer in his mouth-pharynx below the arc of the palate. This is particularly true when he "domes" and darkens the three notes E♭–F. These six tones give rise to no sensation whatever *below* the level of the palatal arc; below this level all physique, all physical and mechanical action is seemingly non-existent. This is one of the most remarkable phenomena associated with true vocal technique; it is inherent in all correctly produced head tones by all voices. If any tone from E♭, fourth space, upwards is felt in the mouth-pharynx cavity, production is wrong. This applies to all voices. Will the student please bear this in mind.

The only exception is the E♭ and E♮ (fourth space) sung with openish "split-tone", for the description of which see the Soprano Section, above.

The split-tone on E♭ and E♮ with AH³ can be unmixed, or given a tinge of OH (o-cap). It can also be produced with the AW vowel (which we could call AH⁴, seeing that it is a much modified AH albeit with a characteristic timbre of its own). On these two pitches the split-tone is invariably openish when sung with AH³, AW, OH or EH. By openish we do *not* mean a "slap open" or even slightly blatant tone, nor does it include even the slightest tendency to blatancy. But we mean a nicely turned tone with the "corner" rounded off just sufficiently to avoid any unpleasant tonal tendency.*

* There is a tendency in all baritones to open out particularly the E♭ and E♮ (fourth space) to a point of blatancy, and this because, as is correct, these notes tune in behind the vertical; even so, the vowels must be sufficiently rounded in order to curl over the sharp tonal corners. There must be no blatantly open "cockney" *aw*, or *oh*, or *eh*.

Whenever the AH³, AW, OH and EH vowels are sung on E♭ and E♮, there is always a strong tendency, in spite of the natural rotundity of the first three, for the tone to open out much too much; it is so easy to do so with this openish split-tone on these two particular pitches. This tendency is due to the peculiar resonant coupling of the split-tone which demands a delicately balanced shaping. For it is clear that if the upper portion of the globular tone, coupled as it is to the lower part of the head-voice cavity (the floor of which is the palatal arc), is not held there by the singer keeping in mind and voice the appropriate shape-cum-sound, it will open out and come down into the mouth-pharynx cavity. A split-tone has two-thirds of its being above the palate in the head cavity, and one-third below the palate in the mouth-pharynx cavity. The net result of the above described tonal opening-falling is a tone resonating entirely in the mouth-pharynx cavity which on the pitches E♭ and E♮ cannot be other than "slap open" and blatant, unless of course subjected to a closed-throat, bottled-in, "covering" process which unfortunately reflects "smothered hope". (See Chapter V.)

To prevent, therefore, such tonal opening and subsequent falling, the AH, AW and OH vowels should be well rounded on their own, or darkened with an *oo-* or *u*-cap which will "lock" the originally conceived shape-cum-sound. The EH should be darkened with a dome shape like an inverted U—keeping in mind also an IR sound (as in *bird*). Such mental concepts are the only keys to the solution of the problem. Mind you, the *u*-cap or *u*-hook which mentally is placed on top of the AH, AW or OH, should be smallish but with a firm little "nip" in it, so to speak.

No graduation below AH² must ever be sung on E♭ and E♮, split-tone or not, as the tone would simply be blatant, bordering on vulgarity.

There is another way whereby excessive tonal opening can be prevented on these same two pitches, and that is by holding the AH³ closely towards AW, the AW towards OH, and the OH towards OO. Just the *thought* is sufficient.

And now let us return to the Vuoto Zone for a few final remarks. The excursion in the Vuoto area from B♭ to D is accompanied by the very gradual modification of the vowel from AH² to AH³. As the baritone lifts up and rounds off the tone from

A♮ to B♭, B♭ to B♮, B♮ to C, he adds varying percentages of O to the basic AH tone. The amount of O-colour added for each note is not fixed, of course. For instance, in a song or aria he could introduce more O-colour on the C than on the B♭, although it is not advisable as it is so easy to overdo the Vuoto colouring. Actually the O-colouring in the Vuoto area can and should be beautifully graded from B♭ to D♮, in that the O-influence of the Vuoto becomes gradually less from note to note until at D♮ little Vuoto is noticeable.

As already explained above, only the first three notes of the Vuoto series—B♭, B♮ and C—when well produced in the Vuoto Zone give the sensation of *complete* tonal detachment and isolation, a complete *circle of tone* apparently lacking a point of impingement or pressure-contact, and *suspended* in the Vuoto space. We can offer no adequate explanation of this phenomenon of tonal detachment of these three tones which have no focus and therefore do not "lean" against any particular point. Other things being equal, they possess beauty of buoyancy and are of fine carrying power, apart from affording the singer himself very considerable tonal satisfaction.*

The fourth note of the Vuoto series, C♯, while still of the Vuoto quality when the singer so desires, is not felt by him to be so completely detached and suspended as the first three, for the tone commences to "tack on", albeit in small measure. Now this "tacked on" feeling is actually only that which results from the point of impingement or pressure-contact of the top of the sound-beam against a definite spot, which in this case is against practically the middle of the palatal arc. We can say, therefore, that the Vuoto curve is considerably decreased in the case of the C♯. It is even more so in the case of the next note, D♮, the fifth and last of the Vuoto series. Also the D is "tacked on", and more so than the C♯. While not possessing so much Vuoto quality as C, it can be given just sufficient Vuoto to make it reflect the characteristic quality of

* It is possible that the synchronization of the formant (which is only in exceptional situations in multiple relation to the main wave) with the sound-beam is responsible for this tonal effect. This interesting and curious tonal phenomenon occurs in the Stradivarius violin (and apparently in no other) when certain notes are bowed—the natural resonance frequency of the "belly" synchronizing with the harmonic content of the bowed string. In the Vuoto tone, it would appear that the resonator assumes major control. (N. Bonavia-Hunt.)

this zone of resonation. But beware of overdoing the colour by curving the tone more forward along the arc of the palate than it should be, for that will produce unwieldy, booming tone. No, the Vuoto D must be sung upright, with a slight, very slight O-curve forward along the arc. Note that this forward curve is minute in this case.

Although not of true Vuoto quality, A♮ and A♭ (third space) can be produced with a sort of Vuoto feeling when the Vuoto-procuring process is applied.

Regarding the D♮ again, it is for the singer to decide whether or not he wishes to mix it with a small percentage of O. If produced with an unmixed AH³, as in the normal scale, it will obviously not be classed as Vuoto tone. AH and AW must have some O-tint in order to participate in the Vuoto resonation. Even if this D be sung on the OH vowel itself, the tone will not be of the Vuoto timbre when the tonal direction is upright with, if anything, a very slight inclination just back of the vertical (as D should normally be produced, whatever the vowel employed). But if the tonal direction, with the OH, points just in front of the vertical, then it will be of Vuoto quality. It is all very subtle.

When this D is produced with AH² (as occasionally it can and should be, care being taken not to allow the tone to become blatantly open) the sound-beam will be felt by the singer to be very slightly more inclined just back of the vertical than that with AH³. But for all practical purposes the sound-beams of all vowels, including the short ones, soar more or less vertically upwards on D; and if assisted to do so, or allowed to do so, each vowel-cum-beam will tune in to its exact point of impingement. (See p. 161.)

This same D can be effectively produce *mezzavoce* on AH³, AW and OH by adding a small percentage of *oo* on top of these vowel tones. The sensation is that the particular vowel has been *capped* with a tiny *oo*-hood: a mixed tone, therefore. In the singer's sensation, it is precisely this small *oo*-cap on top of the vowelled tone which seems to "puncture" the palate and tune in to the cavity above like a "feeler", just sufficiently to impart to the whole tone a sort of head-voice quality. The old Italian school used to call this "chest tone with head-voice quality" (suono di petto con colore di testa). It can be used only for *p* effects because no real strength, or *crescendo*, is feasible or advisable with the note coupled-in this way.

THE BASSO CANTANTE AND THE BASS VOICES

The foregoing remarks for the baritone are applicable equally to both these bass categories, with slight variations.

The *basso cantante*, or singing bass, is a definite category of voice. It has nothing in common with that nondescript called "bass-baritone", which is just a baritone with some extra low notes that are generally pressed into service in order to produce the supposititious bass part and quality of the voice.

We can consider the *basso cantante* in the light of a somewhat amplified baritone with a definite bass quality tinging the whole voice. It has not the fullness and depth of tone possessed by the true bass which, on the other hand, never displays the brilliance of the *basso cantante*'s high notes. The last-mentioned can sing certain baritone rôles that the true bass would be unable to sustain, however good his production; they merely lighten somewhat the whole mechanism.

The Vuoto Resonating Zone of both these bass categories embraces the same series of five notes as that of the baritone, i.e. from B♭, third line, to D♮, fourth line, inclusive; but they *naturally* round off, or darken, their tones slightly more than does the baritone, and also a little earlier in the scale: the *basso cantante* at A♭ or G, and the bass at F♯ or F♮. Both categories can and do produce A, and A♭ with a Vuoto quality by introducing an OH-tint (as explained above for the baritone); if not of true Vuoto quality, these two notes are a colourful approach to it.

Technically, both categories produce their voices like the baritone, employing the same vowel modifications, the same vowel-mixing processes as described above for the baritone, and the same zones of resonation. Being naturally of heavier calibre than the baritone, the general vowel-colouring and mixing are slightly more accentuated—the bass more so than the *basso cantante*. For instance, the *basso cantante* will employ slightly more OH-tint for the Vuoto from B♭ to D♮; and the bass more still. He will employ slightly more OO-tint or "cap" in the head cavity from E♭ (fourth space) to high A♭ than does the baritone, while the real bass will employ still more up to his highest note, about G. Which is quite in keeping with the nature of these vocal categories.

Recapitulation.—The resonating zones of the Baritone, *Basso*

Cantante and Bass voices, and the series of notes to be tuned therein, are:

ZONE 1: the mouth-pharynx cavity; from lowest note to D♮, fourth line, inclusive;

the so-called Vuoto: same cavity as Zone 1 but employing mainly the front half (mouth) for tuning in the five notes B♭ (third line) to D♮.

ZONE 2: (a) the Intermediate or Super-Vuoto; mainly above and basically on a level with the palate; from E♭, fourth space, to F♮, fifth line.

(b) head cavity above the palate, and a continuation of the Intermediate; from F♯, fifth line, to A♭, or higher.

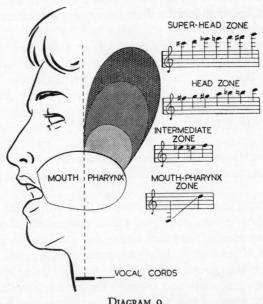

DIAGRAM 9

N.B.—*The shaping and the partitioning off of the three resonating zones is mainly theoretical. Nevertheless, the zones themselves are factual; for the singer they exist as three separate compartments, albeit forming one expanding V-shaped cavity. As each zone is, so to speak, coloured with its individual quality, it tinges with a distinctive and characteristic timbre every note tuned in to it. The "partitioning" between one zone and the next is real in the singer's sensation, even though as tenuous as coloured vapour.*

Concluding Remarks

(1) The following remarks apply to all voices, male and female. The singer producing his voice correctly will experience a three-fold sensation given by the sound-beam:

(*a*) the sound-beam increases in height in obedience to the vocal-acoustical law: the smaller the vibrator in length and depth, the taller the beam; and conversely. Which increase is particularly noticeable as from E♭, fourth space, upwards;

(*b*) the sound-beam decreases in diameter as the effective vibrator length is decreased. Which decrease is marked as the pitch rises from E♮, fourth space. Therefore, the smaller the effective length of vocal cord engaged to satisfy the conditions of a given pitch, the narrower the beam; and conversely;

(*c*) the beam commences from E♮, fourth space, upwards, to incline backwards from the vertical in order to follow its *natural* angle and points of impingement, as the pitch rises, for purposes of correct tonal coupling and subsequent reflection; the very fact of this inclination of the beam back of the vertical provides adequate space for resonation. The singer must not attempt to provide space physically, for he will be sure to overdo things; he can secure space on the principle of the yawn, just the idea of it, nothing more, for actually the yawn is back of the vertical. If the singer just *thinks* "back of the vertical" he automatically loosens and opens his throat, whereupon the sound-beam is free to follow its natural trend.

(2) The very fact of modifying the vowel shape, even in the smallest degree, from its basic or pure tone-colour—AH, AW, OH, OO, EH and EE—and all the short vowels as in *pat, pot, put, pet, pit,* as well as the IR sound, as in *bird,* gives rise to a correspondingly small curving in the pharynx, particularly the upper part, whereupon the *top* of the sound-beam nestles into the tiny curve, the feeling of which on the high notes is very marked, particularly on account of the tonal intensity. On the low notes the modification or rounding of the vowel produces a relatively bigger curve which is of course noticeable to the singer but not so impressive or intense as the compact little curve of the high pitches. The broad sound-beams of the low notes provide ample

"room" for curving and tonal manœuvring, whereas the narrow beams of high notes provide but little. Every curve reflects the degree of modification; and the whole thing is internal. This is why we stress the importance of avoiding all *deliberate* use of the lips in vowel formation and modification; by such use, an unnatural and superfluous curve is added to a natural one, lengthening it unduly in a horizontal direction, whereupon the tone suffers distortion in degree. Only on the low notes, when employing AW, OH and OO vowels, do the lips *of themselves* come into active operation and participation. But even so, only as a finishing medium, because the prime, the basic shaping is internal. However, *as the pitch rises, so the lips participate less and less in the general shaping until, finally, on the high notes their action is reduced practically to nil.** The lips must participate *indirectly* in tone production, that is to say, *only as a result of the internal shaping.* If *allowed* to by the singer, they will surely look after themselves and perform their duty. There is absolutely no need to deliberately push them about. If they are, men's voices will boom and women's hoot. Booming and hooting tone reflect distortion.

Will the student please remember that correct vowel modification has nothing in common with distortion of any kind. For instance, an AH² or AH³, even if mixed with tints of OH and/or OO, is still basically AH; likewise an OO mixed with OH, and vice versa, and EH mixed with EE, or IR, and EE with French *u* (German Ü) retain their basic vowel quality provided that the "tinting" with the other vowel or vowels is not overdone. Moreover, the collective ear of an audience hears just the basic vowel while subconsciously appreciating the tonal results of the masterly mixing.

(3) We assumed in this chapter an ascending scale on the AH vowel. But no matter what vowel is employed, long or short, the fixed series of notes belonging acoustically to a given resonating zone must be allowed, or assisted, to tune in to that resonator, *and to no other.* IT IS THE PITCH OF THE NOTE THAT DETERMINES THE LOCATION OF A RESONATING CAVITY, irrespective of the vowel employed to produce that pitch, and IT IS THE VOWEL employed on a given pitch THAT DETERMINES THE ANGLE OF INCLINATION AND POINT OF

* From E♭ (fourth space) upwards, *the pharynx takes over* the shaping gradually more and more as the pitch rises.

IMPINGEMENT OF THE RESULTANT SOUND-BEAM IN RELATION TO THE GIVEN RESONATOR.

(4) No chest note can be tuned in to a head-voice cavity or resonator; in other words, no pitch from the lowest to D♮, fourth line, that naturally have to be tuned in to the mouth-pharynx resonator, can be tuned in to the head cavity above the palate. It is a physical impossibility; no sound-beam of any one of these pitches is "tall" enough for the purpose. BUT, unfortunately, a so-called head tone, or rather a pitch acoustically belonging to the head resonating zone, can be forced into the mouth-pharynx cavity; the thus distorted product is wholly bad for physiological and acoustical reasons.

(5) The AH, and EH (a monophthong, as in *there, Mary*) more than the other vowels, afford the singer a poignant sensation of the gradual "compressing" (or gathering up) of the tone as the pitch rises, a compressing due to the gradual narrowing of the sound-beam that results from, and reflects, the process of gradual elimination of the vocal cord mass in length and depth. The sensation of tonal compression is also aroused by the increasing frequency as the pitch rises. A high note means a *small* focus in a *big* space.

(6) When we speak of "colour" in relation to vocal tone accruing from the different vowels and modifications thereof, we are not juggling with an abstract, for what actual colour is to the eye, vocal colour is to the ear. Basically, both are sensations aroused by vibratory motion of varying rates: that of visual colours reaching astronomical figures (see Chapter XIV). It is a term of the old School, and is still used in Italy.

(7) Today, in every country, singers want to bawl, to make as much noise as possible. The usual reason adduced for this predilection over artistic singing is that they "want to be heard". It is a psychological sign of the times, and of all time, since "the desire to be important" is, according to Professor John Dewey, the American philosopher, the deepest urge in human nature. By some strange mental twist the majority of modern singers consider noise and importance as synonymous. Quality and beauty do not seem to mean much, if anything, at all to them. Is it because modern training has not inculcated in sufficient measure appreciation of beauty in vocal tone? We are inclined to think it is. But it is also partly due to the dwarfing influence of the

vulgarity, the cult of ugliness, that has permeated and degraded all art today. Line is losing its true function. All art seems to be reverting to the prehistoric, to the primeval attempts of cavemen.

RESONATORS
SCIENTIFIC ADDENDUM
by NOEL BONAVIA-HUNT, M.A.

There are two main kinds of resonators: (1) the resonating body and (2) the resonating cavity. Both types are employed in the production of the human voice, and it must be stressed that both are employed together and simultaneously, since the human body is a correlated structural organism in which all its parts are intimately woven together.

Every resonating body has one or more natural vibrating frequencies: that is, it vibrates more readily and easily if adjusted to a certain frequency. This is known as the "natural period" of the resonating body. The resonator may be set into vibration by (a) another body vibrating in sympathy with it, in which case both vibrators are in tune or "at resonance" with one another, or by (b) another vibrator forcing it into vibration even though the frequency of the energizer is out of tune with that of the resonator. We may give a ready illustration of the two kinds of resonance, sympathetic and forced, by referring to the *natural* production of the human voice whereby the vocal cords are so adjusted in length, depth and tension as to initiate a sound at the required frequency and set in sympathetic vibration other parts and cavities of the head. In this case, the "other parts and cavities" are not forced into vibration but vibrate readily of themselves without compulsion from any generator—a very important point for singers. If, however, the vocal cords are so adjusted in length, depth and tension that they are not in tune with any of the "other parts and cavities" of the head, then it is only possible to get these other parts to vibrate and become resonators by increasing the pressure of breath from the lungs until the vocal cords are forced into tune with these other parts. This is not the whole story of vocal generation plus vocal resonance, but as an illustration of the basic difference between natural and forced production it is sufficient for the purpose at the moment.

There are three important points in connection with vocal resonance that must be stressed:

(1) When the resonator starts to resonate and vibrate at the appropriate frequency it becomes *the master sound-producer*. The original generator (in the human anatomy, the vocal cords) sets in motion forces which overmaster it completely, and if the vocal cord mechanism is *slightly* out of tune with the natural frequency of the resonator, the latter will draw the vocal cord vibration to its own frequency. If the vocal cord vibration is badly out of tune, the resonator can only (if at all) be forced into co-operation by an excessive muscular effort. Now in the manipulation of orchestral instruments forced vibrations are unavoidable, the resonating material and resonating cavities are both compelled to vibrate in combination with the initiating sound and so amplify it as required by the performer. But the singer is able to adjust the generator as well as the resonator (within practical limits) so that the marriage between generator (the female) and the resonator (the male) may be an ideal relationship. In many vocal-producing methods the generator is treated as if it were incapable of adjustment, with the result that the resonators are *forced* into vibration at the required frequency or frequencies (alas, very often producing tone that is abominably flat and occasionally sharp). Generally speaking, one of two things must happen: either the tone is forced into the desired loudness by excessive lung blast, or by reason of ill-matched periodicity between cords and resonators the tone is attenuated and insipid. It is therefore of the highest importance that the generator should do as little work as possible consistent with the vocal result aimed at, while the resonator should be given the major share of the work. The actual ratio of work done in this relationship of generator and resonator depends on the pitch of the note produced: the cleavage widens as the pitch ascends, that is, the higher the note the greater the proportion of mastery which the resonator obtains over the generator.

(2) The vocal cord generator has a highly efficient assistant which acts as a kind of intermediary or ambassador between itself and the head resonators. These latter resonators consist of both vibrating bodies and vibrating cavities. The bodies are the bony and the cartilaginous structures of the head: the septum of cartilaginous plate that divides the nose into two parts. The skull and its structural parts are the most important of the vibrant bodies in

the head, while the nasal and frontal cavities are the most important of the air resonators.

I have said that the resonators should, as far as possible, be encouraged by the singer to vibrate naturally and without forcing from the vocal cord generator; but fortunately the singer possesses a truly wonderful piece of mechanism which Nature has most obligingly provided with the object of stimulating the head resonators into action. This assistant is none other than the *soft palate*—an assistant, however, which must not be directly or consciously pressed into service by a deliberate attempt to raise or lower it (or groove it, or otherwise manipulate it) as unfortunately is advocated by certain misguided methods.

The soft palate is neither generator nor resonator: it is something in between. It is a *vibrational relay*. It carries the original sound vibrations generated by the vocal cords (and their vortices) to the head resonators. How? By itself mimicking the vibrations of the generator below in the throat. It is set in motion by the *sound waves* reaching it from the larynx. The soft palate thus vibrates in sympathy with the vocal cords. The palate must be given its rightful place in the vocal chain and network as intermediary between generator and resonators. Its vibrations, at the appropriate frequency for each note produced by the singer, set in motion the head resonators. But further, the palate controls the amount of opening between the mouth-pharynx chamber and the cavities above in the head. It is a vibrant door, and it greatly increases the efficiency of the resonators. Thus the singer possesses three main sound producers (using the word "producer" in its technical sense to connote that which develops into ultimate being)—vocal cords, soft palate, resonators.

Another extremely important function of the soft palate is that of neutralizing unwanted resonance in the mouth-pharynx chamber. Any cavity or chamber which possesses such a vibrant diaphragm can only resonate at its natural frequency—or at worst, will resonate at its natural frequency at the expense of all other frequencies. This enables the different vowels to be formed purely and without the accompaniment of parasitic frequencies set up by an uncontrolled air column. It can be seen that the palate must so adjust itself as to effect the neutralization of unwanted frequencies above-mentioned. (Be it noted that any such adjustment must not be consciously performed by the singer, it must never be a deliberate physical act, because it is part and parcel of the general vibrator-resonator adjustment for every pitch.)

This adjustment results in the palate vibrating at a frequency which is in phase with that of the vocal cord generator.

Note the structure of the soft palate: (*a*) it is "hinged"; (*b*) it consists of just the right kind of material for its purpose, namely of material that is soft, flexible, and massive. The third characteristic is vitally important, since no material is of any use in connection with sound-production unless it possesses sufficient *density*. If it is also soft and flexible, it is ideal for its purpose. Again, it is *loaded at its head end*. Nature has placed the uvula at the correct point of the palate to enable the palate to operate without executing tortional vibrations. And this loading also reduces the frequency of the vibrations with the express object of preventing the palate from getting out of control. The real reason why the uvula load is there is because the palate is somewhat on the short side: it has to be if the human head is not to be all out of proportion to the rest of the body or to assume an ugly shape. But the loading completely solves the problem, so that the apparent shortness of the palate is no handicap but actually a help, since a longer palate would have made the production of the higher notes an extremely awkward proposition.

(3) Lastly, the mention of high-note production leads me to say a few words by way of conclusion on the head resonators. These consist of both body and cavity vibrators, as already stated. It is important to observe that the body type are mainly responsible for *amplifying* the note sung, while the cavity type introduces certain fixed * formant frequencies which *colour* the note, that is, lend a certain personality or individuality to the tone. When producing the higher notes the singer must see to it that the resonators carry the mastery, that the vocal cord generator is subservient.†
And the *right* resonator must be given the mastery. When the *highest* notes are sung, the hard, bony structure at the top of the head must be engaged: that part must be engaged which vibrates *naturally* at the nearest frequency to the note sung. Now, if the top of the head is tapped by the fingers from the crown in a direct line down to the bridge of the nose and even down to the upper lip, a

* i.e. independent of the harmonic frequencies of the note sung.

† This it will always be, provided appropriate elimination of the vocal-cord mass is effected for every pitch. (Author's note.)

lower-pitched sound or note will be heard at each successive tap, until at the upper lip the lowest pitch is reached. This shows that the natural resonance frequency is diminished from the crown at the top to the nose at the front, the reason being that as the finger taps down and round the head surface certain inner cavities are engaged which possess lower-frequency resonances. It should be obvious to any singer that these resonators should be engaged at the appropriate pitches produced by the vocal cord generator, which means that the voice (or sound-beam) should be directed *backwards* (in varying degree) for the higher notes, with all vowels, and only forward (in varying degree) for the lower notes on certain vowels. Since the various vowels are formed by various shapings of the mouth-pharynx, including appropriate action of the tongue,* it is also obvious that notes sung on these vowels must be directed backwards or forwards (relatively to the vertical) according to the pitch or frequency of the main harmonic characteristic of the vowel produced. Thus the vowel AH (as in *father*) having a high-frequency characteristic is naturally produced, on high notes, with the voice directed backward from the vertical line, while the vowel OO is produced, on low notes, with a forward direction, since it possesses a low-frequency characteristic. (The OO possesses on the high notes more or less the same high-frequency characteristic as AH; in fact, the frequency characteristic of all vowels *on the same high note* is, for all practical purposes, very much the same.)

* The extremely slight action of the soft palate for shaping and modifying the vowel (all vowels) on high pitches induces, and therefore controls, the equally slight movements of the tongue from pitch to pitch and change of vowel. (Author's note.)

CHAPTER XII

THE VERTICAL

THE STUDENT is asked to pay serious attention to a certain technical operation the full understanding and proper application of which is of vital importance to good singing. We refer to what we term "The Vertical".

For our purpose the Vertical is an imaginary line passing upwards from the throat so as to bisect, firstly, the mouth-pharynx cavity at the point where hard and soft palate meet in the middle of the palatal arc, and, secondly, the front and back parts of the head above this arc. We say "imaginary", though actually part of this line is real in the sense that the sound-beam of the AH vowel from the normally lowest note to D♮, fourth line, inclusive, soars vertically upwards, even as do those of the EH and EE vowels. And this in all voices, male and female. Consequently, we can say that up to this D the imaginary line is identifiable with the real vertically-soaring sound-beam. But from the next note, E♭, fourth space, upwards, the *imaginary* line is continued vertically, dividing the head into two parts, while the sound-beam proper commences to come *behind* the vertical in varying degree as the pitch rises, and according to the vowel employed. It is precisely the imaginary portion of the vertical dividing line continuing from the palatal arc upwards which is our particular concern in this chapter, for it is highly important in relation:

(1) to the direction taken *naturally* by the sound-beams as the pitch rises above E♭, fourth space, and (2) to the vowel reflected by the sound-wave system.

The singer should think of the vertical as a line which forms part of his technique and its control: he should think of it as a frontier which it is dangerous to cross tonally from said E♭ upwards.

Singers would avoid many pitfalls of production if they had a clear conception of this partitioning, dividing line, this vertical. To illustrate: As explained on p. 150, all vowels and their associated sound-beams have a common direction and meeting place at D, fourth line; in fact on this D all sound-beams point straight upwards more or less centrally within the mouth-pharynx cavity. Whereas all notes (all vowels and their beams) up to said D tune in to the mouth-pharynx cavity, at different points according to the pitch and vowel (but never higher than the arc of the palate, because the sound-beam, whatever the vowel, does not extend upward noticeably until *after* the D), the very next note, E♭, tunes in *just above* the palatal arc, and *just back of the vertical*, whatever the vowel may be.

From E♭, fourth space, upwards, ALL notes, whatever the vowel employed, must tune in BEHIND the vertical, and in varying degree according to the pitch and vowel.

Let the student mark well that our imaginary dividing line, or vertical, comes into play from E♭, fourth space, upwards, and greatly influences production right up to the highest note.

As the E♭, sung on AH, is therefore only just back of the vertical, the next note (E♮) will be slightly further back, apart from being tuned in a little higher (due to the now lengthening sound-beam); the next note, F♮, is again slightly further back of the vertical than is the E♮, and also a little higher up. And so on, note by note, to the normally highest pitch.

As explained in pp. 252–3, the sound-beams of EH and EE (and their short derivatives as in *pen*, *pin*) do not deviate from the vertical, from E♭ upwards, as much as do those of the AH-AW-OH-OO group and their short English derivatives, as in *pat*, *pot*, *put*, but soar straight upwards as the pitch rises and tunes in just back of the vertical all the time. The student should also note this phenomenon. (See Diagram 1, p. 57.)

Let us now consider the first three notes—E♭, E♮, F♮—the very first notes to fall victims to the practitioners of the constant forward production method so much in use today. What happens if any one of these notes (on any vowel) is MENTALLY directed behind the vertical? The answer is simplicity itself: The physical reaction to the conception of the vertical and to the slight *mental* pull-back from it results in an equally slight adjustment of the pharynx, *loosening and freeing the throat* and permitting the sound-beam to soar and tune *naturally* in to the cavity above the palate. How important it is to *think* of the correct direction the particular beam should take, and *allow* it to do so by loosening the throat.

To think and sing "back of the vertical" is *a simple throat-opening process* which allows the sound-beam to follow its *natural* trend. Another point to be noted is that when we have to sing back of the vertical the particular vowel *must* be rounded in degree. The two processes are simultaneous and inseparable. The student should bear this well in mind.

And what happens if any one of these three notes (with any vowel) is deliberately "placed" or thrust forward against or in front of what we call the vertical? The answer is equally simple: The issuing tone is hard because the forward thrust closes the throat at its narrowest and most sensitive point (the zone just above the larynx) and distorts the internal shaping (mouth-pharynx cavity) and with it the vowel itself, of course; it is often flat, since this method prevents the beam from soaring to its appropriate height, the vibrator adjustment having been deranged in the sense that the cords unduly thicken and their frequency in consequence is slightly lowered. If for any cause the vocal cord mechanism is unduly thickened in depth for a given pitch, the relative beam cannot possibly attain to the exact height required by the particular pitch.

Any note from E♭ upwards that is thrust against, or in front of, the vertical and points, say, towards the lips, the tip or bridge of the nose, the eyes, or the forehead, must suffer tonal distortion accordingly and will therefore be hard, heavy, laboured and inclined to "stick"; and added to this it will require boosting and bolstering up by an excessive breath pressure. This is how that iniquitous couple: forward production and diaphragmatic drive —came to be solidly wed. Such notes never really "sing", never vibrate with buoyant freedom. How can they, when they issue from a distorted medium, a badly-shaped resonating cavity.

Bad advice, misnamed teaching, advises this forward thrust of the tone right against, and more often right through, the vertical on to the so-called "mask", tragically labelled the "key" to the head voice and grandiose resonance. By so many it is known as "covering". Such ignorance borders on the fantastic! The poor misguided student feels the discomfort of the first attempts to "cover" the tone in this way, and often notes the ambiguity of the term and the process. But the human mind readily adapts itself to anything bad, and the vocal organs with it; eventually it may warmly defend the false principle.

Let us examine the following:

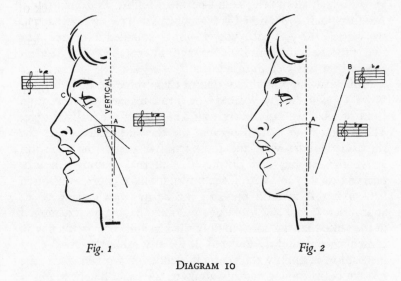

Fig. 1   Fig. 2

DIAGRAM 10

Note how in Fig. 1 at A the sound-beam of the AH vowel for the pitch of E♭, fourth space, is well directed but the *top* of it still in the mouth-pharynx cavity, and how at B it is pushed forward of the vertical with the top of it still in the mouth on a level with the arc of the palate; note also how at C the beam is thrust forward in front of the vertical, pointing "over the eyes", or "bridge of nose", for high B♭. All three "placings", A, B, C, are wrong. While A is only a little out, the beam not being tall enough, B and C are hopelessly so.

Be it remembered that the available space from the back of the tongue to the wall of the throat is very small in every individual, and is easily constricted. And the tone will always reflect the slightest constriction.

Now look at Fig. 2 carefully, comparing it with Fig. 1, and note how at A the beam line (on E♭, fourth space) is not only slightly back of the vertical, as it should be, but the *top* of it is tuned in just above the level of the arc of the palate, and therefore above and outside the mouth-pharynx cavity. Now note direction of the beam at B for the high B♭. And what does this mean? It means that the linear directions of Fig. 2 are *natural* and acoustically correct. They leave the throat "loosely" open and properly shaped for the particular vowel. (By "loosely" we mean unobstructed, with the parts flexibly free to adjust themselves correctly in accordance with the mental orders.) Be it noted: If the singer *thinks* "back of the vertical", at a certain angle, the throat obeys the thought, releasing the parts concerned and assuming the right shape; whereupon the sound-beam will *of itself* soar upwards into the head cavities at the correct angle with respect to the vertical. It is really all very simple. And the very *thought* of this angle, this "back of the vertical", is sufficient of itself to secure adequate throat opening. Moreover, this freedom of action of the parts enables the throat to adjust itself automatically so that the conditions of vowel and pitch are accurately complied with.*

The singer has not anything mechanical or physical to do. He must NOT try deliberately to drive the sound-beam in this direction or that to comply with certain methods in vogue, nor mechanically open his throat (for he is sure to overdo things). It is specifically a *mental operation* (not a physical action such as moving a limb or opening the mouth) to which the physical will faithfully respond if *allowed* to by the singer. The student will soon learn to sense the exact position of the vertical, and make all back-of-the-vertical adjustments and vowelled tuning with delicate assurance.

Some singers tilt the head slightly back, so the angle the imaginary dividing or bisecting line takes is still the "vertical" for the singer himself, still *his* vertical. Which is all that matters. Whereas a true vertical is an unvarying plumb-line perpendicular, the singer's vertical dividing line *moves with his head* thereby maintaining constantly our imaginary partition.

There is a scientific explanation of this back-of-the-vertical principle: As the pitch rises the sound-beam draws back gradually further away from the outside atmospheric pressure *in order to be conserved* instead of being dissipated. The higher the note the more necessary it becomes to screen the beam from outside interference. By soaring back of the vertical into the head cavities it screens

---

* The vertical line, when given considerable thought and "exercise", becomes a live mental structure. Because it is then an effective dividing line it is of very considerable assistance to the singer as regards guiding and checking the accuracy of the angle of travel of the varying sound-beams in relation to vowel and pitch.

itself completely. Up to and including D♮, fourth line, the beam has no need to be screened, whatever vowel is employed.

The diagram hereunder is drawn from an actual photograph of Gigli singing. Note the angle at which the head is tilted backwards, and the angle of the "vertical" dividing line. Note also the perfect poise of the head and general relaxation.

(From a drawing by Victor Caesari)

DIAGRAM 11

CHAPTER XIII

HOW THE MOUTH-PHARYNX AFFECTS
THE CORD MECHANISM

IT IS SO LITTLE KNOWN and appreciated how the mouth-pharynx cavity plays a really vital part in the adjustment of the vocal cord mechanism; for weal or woe, its influence on it is enormous. In fact, the actual shaping of this cavity affects the vibrator to the extent that it can make or mar the adjustment proper and the tone issuing from it. Hence the importance of knowing the exact shaping of the vowelled tones to be produced on every pitch.

Now, the vowel is the key to the exact adjustment of the vibrator mechanism at all pitches; but its actual shaping must be properly related to the pitch in the sense that every vowel *must* be modified, or rounded off, as the pitch rises from the normally lowest note to the highest. Which gradual modification is the direct result, of course, of the gradual rounding of the mouth-pharynx cavity, as in an ascending scale. As a guide to students in this sense we are giving on pp. 277–8 a Table of Vowel Modification for all vowel sounds. (See also p. 276, last paragraph, and footnote.)

The basic training of the old School was simply this: If the singer will just THINK vowel, that is, the SOUND AND SHAPE OF IT, in pure or modified form according to pitch (and expression), and NOT attempt any direct physical shaping inside or outside the mouth, the parts concerned—soft palate, pharynx, tongue—will automatically adjust themselves accordingly, the tonal product, or vowelled tone, being the exact reproduction of the previously *mentally conceived* vowel *shape* and *sound*. In other words, in order to stress this very important point, if the MENTAL SHAPING and MENTAL CONCEPTION OF THE SOUND of a particular vowel, or some modification thereof, is correct, then the actual physical shaping of the mouth-pharynx cavity will follow suit and the tone thought out will be *exactly* reproduced. If there is no direct physical interference, these mobile parts will always adjust themselves in obedience exactly to the shaping thought.

And what is a vowel? It is a vocal shape quivering within the confines of the mouth-pharynx cavity, properly adjusted, and projected into the listener's world. Therefore, a *vowel is shaped vibration*.

Normally, in most voices, the physical reaction closely follows the mental shaping, that is, if *allowed* to do so by the singer; and to allow means that he must *not* do any deliberate physical shaping of the cavity and that he must leave his lips well alone because the external mouth (lip aperture) looks after itself in that it reflects automatically the internal shaping, and completes it. Lip protrusion, or funnelling, upsets the internal shaping in no small degree, and often induces tonal distortion: "cavernous" tone in men and hooting in women are two signs of such distortion.

In ordinary speech, vowels as a rule are not deliberately or consciously shaped, even though some are stressed. Their physical formation primarily is the result of subconscious thought; therefore it is automatic, mentally and physically, having been acquired by the human race as a well-established habit after many æons of evolution. But in singing, vowels require a different treatment because we have higher pitches than speech, and an adjustable vibrating mechanism coupled with resonating cavities which demand accurate setting, particularly on all those pitches not touched by the spoken voice. Singing is an art that embraces a unique set of manipulative processes. The technique of speech is comparatively simple and is limited to a few pitches; that of song is quite intricate and extends to three octaves. Moreover, in singing, especially on account of the big compass, we come up against adamant acoustical law which must be understood and obeyed if good tonal results are to accrue. Consequently, vowel shaping must be deliberately thought out.

The pure (unmodified) vowel as used in normal speech is confined to the lower fundamental pitches of the voice and there sits comfortably, so to speak, on the relatively long cords having little tension. But as the pitch rises beyond the maximum reached in speech we have to handle a vibrating cord mechanism ever-varying from pitch to pitch in length, thickness, and tension, as well as highly sensitive and pliable resonating cavities. Both systems need very careful adjusting; and the higher the pitch the more delicate and precise becomes the dual adjustment. As the pitch continues to rise, as in a scale, the shape and sound of the vowel must, from its pure (spoken) state, be modified (rounded) very gradually, imperceptibly almost from note to note, as already stated above. The rounding process imparts a gradually darker hue to the tone, still retaining, however, a bright "head" or top on it.

Initially, this vowel shaping and modifying must be done MENTALLY, and accompanied by the right "feeling-tone"; but *never physically*, because the deliberate physical formation is a waste of effort and is sure to be overdone in some way. In fact, nobody knows or ever can know the *exact* physical adjustment of the parts concerned, how much or how little. Only in the singer's mind can this shaping-cum-tone modification take place with absolute accuracy, provided of course his mental conception of shape and sound is correct for all vowels on all pitches. And if this conception is faulty, as is the case with so many singers? Well, then, we get words that more often than not are unintelligible; we get songs without words. If it were not tragic for the art, it would be ludicrous. We never could understand why an individual wants to get up before an audience and sing a song or aria merely to produce sounds audibly divorced from every known language. Nothing is less convincing or seductive. A wordless declaration of love would be funny indeed. How many singers have perfect diction?

When vowel formation is indifferent or bad, the distortion is due (1) to bad training, (2) slovenly habits of speech, (3) wrong mental conception of vowel formation and sounds.

How does the shaping of the mouth-pharynx cavity affect and assist the adjustment of the vocal cord mechanism? Well, the very fact of (1) *mentally* rounding the vowel in appropriate degree as the pitch rises causes (2) the mouth-pharynx cavity *automatically* to shape itself exactly in accordance with the mental shaping, and while doing so it (3) reacts in turn on the vibrator below in the larynx to the extent of actively inducing and assisting the cord-shortening and thinning processes to a degree that secures the correct adjustment for the particular pitch. And this assistance is by no means negligible. If to this is added the tonal "lift-up" (see Chapter XVI) as we pass to a higher pitch, even if only a semi-tone, the thinning process will be wholly assured. By this means we get balanced tonal results on all pitches, with all vowels.

If, on the other hand, the vowel is kept pure (unmodified), as in speech, or is badly shaped, as the pitch rises to the high notes, the cord-shortening and thinning processes cannot accurately take place, and may even be impeded, partially or completely, at certain points; consequently, with a vibrator too big for a given high note, the tonal product invariably reveals the strain due to a bad adjustment.

True technique in singing is the art of following and assisting Nature, a co-ordinating network of ideas which, accurately expressed by means of an acquired technique, effectively produce the desired adjustments within the vibrator and resonator systems.

The student must be on his guard against the pseudo-technique of many present-day methods of voice production because largely conjectural in origin, blind in theory, and often brutal in practice, obstructing the natural processes most of the time.

Given a correct mental vowel-shaping (that naturally includes the correlative sound conception) the physical adjustment should be *allowed* to follow suit automatically without the singer attempting any direct assistance of the kind, and the issuing tone will then have for singer and listener that *suspended* (or "ballooned") feeling as of a shaped vowel resting on the moving surface of the tonal stream: a feeling of disembodied tone. The student must therefore guard against either involuntary or deliberate physical shaping of the vowel after the mental shaping. The mental and physical shaping will never coincide exactly unless the physical is *allowed* to obtain *automatically* on its own. Any *direct*, deliberate physical shaping superimposed on the mental can only lead to a general weighting of the adjusted parts, and so unbalance the whole.

Let us picture the vocal edifice as follows:

First Floor   .   .   Singer's Mind
Ground Floor   .   Mouth-pharynx Cavity
Basement   .   .   Larynx-vibrator Mechanism

and bear in mind that while the adjustment of the mouth-pharynx cavity is directly affected (for good or ill) by the conscious or subconscious thought in the singer's mind, the vibrator mechanism in the larynx is, in turn, directly affected by the mouth-pharynx shaping, also for good or ill. Consequently, the vibrator adjustments within the larynx proper are controlled by the singer's mind *indirectly* through the mouth-pharynx shaping. Therefore, the sequence of events is:

Mind directly affects the mouth-pharynx shaping, and the
Mouth-pharynx, in turn, directly affects the vibrator adjustment.

We warmly advise the student to retain a clear picture of this very important aspect of vocal technique.

Let us now enlarge our picture of the vocal edifice and imagine an "operator" residing within the laryngeal basement: (1) By forming mentally the vowel, the Mind-Boss on the First Floor causes the mouth-pharynx cavity on the Ground Floor to adjust itself accurately to this shaping, and in doing so automatically relays the particular thought-order to the Laryngeal Basement, whereupon our imaginary operator adjusts with split-second motion the vibrator in length, thickness, and tension to suit perfectly the conditions of the particular pitch. It is just as if he had under him a finely tooled unit, precision-marked for every pitch, with a sliding "zip" arrangement for the *simultaneous* adjustment of cord length, thickness, and tension (see footnote, p. 78). As our operator adjusts the mechanism in this way, a sound-beam of exact width, height, and pitch is shot upwards, and the direction it takes will depend (1) on the pitch, (2) on the vowel employed on that pitch, (3) on the shape given the mouth-pharynx cavity and throat in general, (4) on the singer's trend of thought. Given a good vibrator adjustment, a good internal shaping, and a continuance of correct thinking, the sound-beam will automatically take its *natural* direction, if *allowed* to by the singer. *Given favourable conditions as above*, the singer has no need to do any tonal "placing" himself: *the beam will find the right point of impingement all on its own, instinctively as it were.* The art lies in remembering the varying directions taken by the sound-beams pertinent to the different vowels, and foreseeing mentally the direction a particular sound-beam will, and should, take. If the behaviour of the sound-beams is always carefully noted, the singer finally will succeed in *memorizing and visualizing* the location of the point of impingement of every beam within the appropriate resonating zone, according to the pitch and vowel; this applies particularly to the upper medium and high notes.

To secure accurate vibrator adjustment for every pitch (and absolute accuracy *is* possible) the deliberate mental formation of the vowel followed by the automatic physical shaping of the mouth-pharynx cavity must be correct in relation to pitch. (See Table of Vowel Modification, p. 277.) If it is not, then our imaginary operator within the laryngeal chamber can only make approximate, and perhaps muddled, adjustments all along the line, with a greater tendency to wrong than right. Without the illumination brought to the chamber by correct thought, the operator has to work in the dark; in which case most of his adjustments will be part automatic and part guesswork, with more or less disastrous results for the tonal product. If (1) the vowel-forming thought on the first floor of the vocal edifice (Mind) is wrong, then (2) the physical shaping on the ground floor (Mouth-pharynx cavity) will perforce also be wrong; consequently, (3) the operator in the basement (Larynx) is rendered *physically incapable* of adjusting the vibrator mechanism properly, notwithstanding the percentage, high or low, of automatic adjustment inherent in every voice. That he adjusts the cord mechanism in most cases through darkened spectacles and with considerable guesswork (often against his will, i.e. against inherent natural processes) is very obvious, very audible today in which a general low standard of singing is so much to the fore.

Will the student please remember on every occasion that the *very thought* of a rounded (modified) vowel tone finds immediate reaction, through the mouth-pharynx cavity, in the vibrator mechanism, causing it to shorten in appropriate degree; such adjustment, of course, is practically instantaneous.

Unfortunately, in so many cases the student's mental conception of vowel formation, of vowel sounds, is faulty. And where the high notes are concerned it is apparently non-existent. Modern methods of so-called training are chiefly to blame.

If to the *correct* mental formation of the AH, or AW, or OH vowels on the high pitches we add the *mere thought* of a miniature *oo* sound (as in *pool*), or that of the short *u* sound (as in *put*), there is a split-second reaction within the mouth-pharynx cavity; in fact, a *minute* curving is thereby *automatically* induced and super-imposed on the basic shaping that, in turn, reacts physically on the vibrator mechanism to the extent of causing just that little extra shortening of the cord which will secure a sound-beam of *exact* width and height for the pitch in question. In some voices this can be achieved without adding the small percentage of *oo*. However, apart from the mechanical assistance it affords, this small tinge of *oo* (or *u*, as the choice may be) adds balance, colour and beauty to the tone itself.

As part of the vocal technique imparted by the old School the student's mind was very carefully trained to MENTALLY choose, visualize, hear and form the vowel so as to make it coincide with, and satisfy the conditions of, every pitch. He was taught which vowel sounds or colours (colori), which vowel shapings or modifications were required for a given note or phrase. And he was taught to paint the whole song with this adjusting brush.

The relation of the singer's mind to the mouth-pharynx cavity is that of a hand in a glove. To illustrate: Even as the slightest movement or curving of one finger, or of all fingers together, reacts in equal degree on the glove, so the slightest mental formation causes the mouth-pharynx to assume physically the same shaping in equal degree. The hand is the mind, and the glove the cavity. The relationship of mental formation and physical shaping is as intimate and as highly sensitive as hand and glove.

Let us now examine what happens, and what are the singer's sensations, when the vibrator mechanism is accurately adjusted for a high pitch. We know that when the right feeling-hearing of pitch plus a correct vowel shaping in relation to the given pitch has induced a correct vibrator adjustment, a tall, narrow sound-beam is shot upwards from the larynx to soar right through the mouth-pharynx cavity and tune in to the head resonating zone at its *natural* point of impingement, well above the arc of the palate. After piercing this cavity on its way up, it seemingly, as a sensation, carries with it, so to speak, a tinge or shadowy outline of the particular vowel, and on tuning in we get what could be called a vowelled focus (platform). Actually, of course, the focus itself (which is merely the *top* of the sound-beam) does not, indeed cannot possibly carry the vowel proper. How can it, seeing that the top of the beam is tuned in at a point in the head cavity well *above* the arc of the palate, while the actual vowel is under this arc and inside the mouth-pharynx cavity. And there it must always reside, for there it is created and there it must live, move, and have its being for the entire duration of the note.

We will now bring into relief a highly important aspect of vocal technique, a sensation of tone which the singer must accept and build permanently into his mind because scientifically, acoustically correct: Once the sound-beam of the high note is tuned in to the head resonating zone at its exact point of impingement, the singer knows that, in a sense, his work is finished, and all he has to do is to keep the top of the beam (focus) on the same spot, feed and sustain it for the duration of the note. In what sense is his work "finished"? Well, as the top of the sound-beam is focused, so it *recoils from its focal point* and flows downwards into the mouth-pharynx and out through the lip aperture into the world of listeners, *taking with it the shaped vowel-tone* obtaining for the moment within that mouth-pharynx cavity (where we know the actual vowel is born). The listener hears the vowelled tone only; he doesn't hear the small focus, except perhaps vaguely as a central point of compression within the vowelled tone. On the other hand, the singer himself feels *only* the small focal point (platform) vibrating, purring, and glittering high up in the head. Having created it, he *knows* what vowel it reflects, and what the listener hears.

Now, the curious part of this tonal sensation is: That the singer does *not* feel the whole of the upsoaring sound-beam but ONLY the top of it, known as a focal point or platform, nor does he feel its recoil from this focal point and its downward travel into, and out of, the mouth.

Furthermore, let the student note this: As the beam recoils from the focus, passing on and downwards as explained above, so the upsurging part of the beam continually replenishes the focal point itself. And this process goes on, of course, for the duration of the note. The following diagram illustrates the uprush of the sound-beam of AH on, say, high B♭, the approximate location of its focus, and direction of recoil therefrom:

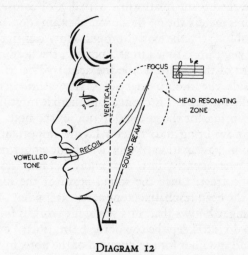

DIAGRAM 12

in which the sound-beam of, say, AH, on high B♭, soars upwards from the vocal cords right through the mouth-pharynx cavity, pierces the palate, and tunes in at *f* (focus) within the head resonating zone, and *rebounds downwards* into, and then out of, the mouth as vowel. (Note line of recoil in diagram.) The singer has *only* the sensation of focus (platform) or tonal point of impingement (*top* of sound-beam) tinged minutely, so to speak, with the colour of the particular vowel; the listener has *only* the impression of vowel sound. (See Chapter XVII.)

The vowel is always in the mouth-pharynx, and remains there whatever the pitch, high or low; but the sound-beam, from E♭, fourth space, upwards, pierces the palate in order to tune in to the head cavity at different heights according to the pitch, and at different angles *behind* the vertical according to the vowel used. This applies to all voices, male and female.

The above-described acoustical phenomena and tonal sensations are present in all notes tuned in to the head cavities *above* the arc of the palate, whatever vowel is used.

On p. 277 we give a Table of Vowel Modifications applicable, say, to an ascending scale of two octaves. This should be studied very carefully in connection with the above explanations. To become a good singer, other things being equal, the student must have in mind a well planned scale of *gradual modification* of the vowel (all vowels) as the pitch rises from the normally lowest to the normally highest note in his voice. He must know primarily what modification or rounding of the original, or pure, vowel sound he has to aim for, and what *tonal change* any given modification introduces into the vowel, whether on an ascending scale or when attacking any note—high, medium or low—with any vowel.

It should finally be noted that the fact of modifying or rounding the vowel imparts a darker colour to the tone, equal in degree to the modification itself. After all, the gradual darkening of the tone as we go, for example, from AH to AW and then on to OH and OO on the same note, is merely the result of the gradual rounding of the mouth-pharynx cavity. The pharynx, of course, is the pliable rounding medium; it is the singer's real mouth, and mainly it is his tonal "drum".

CHAPTER XIV

VOCAL ATTACK

AN EXQUISITE SENSE OF TOUCH is what we would define as true vocal attack. In a highly specialized touch-sense we have the sensitive key to correct attack of the tone.

We know that colour is vibration, as are light and sound. Colour waves reach staggering figures. Take, for instance, the colour violet: Science informs us that the retina of the eye vibrates 727 million million times per second when we look at it; the retina of the eye, therefore, vibrates in one second as many times as it would take a watch to tick in about 23 million years!*

Because of its relevancy, we will press into service a true account, cited by Cesare Lombroso (1836–1909), professor of forensic medicine and psychiatry, of an experiment made on a fourteen-year-old Italian girl whom an accident had totally deprived of sight. After much patient endeavour the blind girl was able unerringly to pick out any coloured ribbon from a quantity of ribbons of different colours merely by *feeling them with her fingertips*. The touch-sense was afterwards developed at the tip of the girl's nose, the lobe of the left ear, and finally the right toe, to the same degree of colour-selecting sensitivity.

Early in 1919, shortly after the First World War, the author was visiting an exhibition of modern paintings in Rome, when his attention was drawn to a blind Italian soldier led by another soldier. Standing in front of a fine oil painting the blind soldier,

* The vibrations affecting the retina in order to produce the sensation of colour come within the following range: They must not be of slower rate than 458 million million for red, nor of faster rate than 727 million million for violet. (Colours are really selective light waves.) If faster or slower than these two extreme limits, the sensation of vision will not be aroused. All the other colours of the spectrum are produced by vibrations, the respective rates of which lie between the said limits. The retina is composed of nine layers, which together are no thicker than thin paper. The innermost layer is made up of something like thirty million rods and three million cones.

with the fingertips of his right hand was, with slow deliberation, feeling the form and colour of everything depicted thereon. The touch of his fingertips on the canvas was extremely light. For a heavy touch would dull the sensitiveness of the neurones: nature's pressure-registering agents.

The experiments with the blind girl leapt to memory. The author motioned the soldier guide to one side, knowing already what the latter's answer would be to the query, "What is he doing?" The guide's reply corroborated the experiments: "He was an artist; this is now his way of 'seeing' and enjoying a picture." As an alternative to sight, the blinded soldier had developed a fine touch-sense in his fingertips.

If vibration of astronomical velocities such as arouse in us the sensation of colour can be "felt" not only by the eye but also by the tips of finger, nose, ear lobe, and big toe, how much more can the comparatively slow and cumbrous vibrations we identify as sound, or voice, be *felt*, particularly when the vibrations are generated within us as part of ourselves primarily by vocal cord action. And how very much easier is it to develop an exquisitely fine touch in the vocal cords themselves with their network of sensitive neurones. Where the generation of vocal tone is concerned, the singer's touch-sense is capable of the highest development. (See *N.B.*, p. 92.)

Inappropriate as it is, the word Attack is used to define the movement of close approximation of the vocal cords for tone production or origination. When we take a deep breath the vocal cords (two horizontal bands lying back to front within the larynx) open out sideways to form an oval. The deeper the breath, the bigger and more complete the oval shape. Then follows the *will* to produce tone. Whereupon, automatically and with inconceivable rapidity the cords return from this oval shape to form a horizontal line; actually a thin slit, or glottis, separates the two cords that must *never touch*, not even in the act of initiating a note. It is precisely this oval-to-linear movement of the cords that constitutes, and is called, the "attack". (A very misleading term, by the way, as it is generally misunderstood and misapplied.) Almost simultaneously, the air, which becomes somewhat compressed immediately under the larynx, endeavours to pass through its natural and only exit. We say *almost* simultaneously because, theoretically, the vocal cords should approximate a split-second

M

before the air from the lungs sets them into vibratory motion. Vibration is the result of resisted pressure; the resistance of the cords being, of course, slightly less than the air pressure.

The oval-to-linear movement of the cords (attack) must be directed by a quick, light thought of a *gliding* nature. If the singer's conception of the attack contains an element of roughness, no matter how slight, the vocal cords will not approximate properly. Roughness or heaviness of thought causes an equivalent roughness or heaviness of action, i.e. abruptness. A rough attacking movement causes the vocal cords to strike one another thereby producing a "knocked" attack. (This is the harmful *coup de glotte*.) If the rough attack is accompanied by an excess of breath pressure, the cords will not merely strike against each other but possibly overlap, as they will grip spasmodically in an instinctive, automatic attempt to resist the excessive breath pressure.

As the essence of good singing is *legato*, and the essence of *legato* primarily a perfectly smooth, gliding attack (oval-to-linear movement of the cords) plus a smooth continuity of the tone, we advise the student to *visualize* the attacking movement, or tone-generating movement, as we would prefer to call it. The oval-to-linear movement of the cords constituting the attack must be made smoothly, the cords themselves joining rectilinearly, at the moment of approach, with perfect tightness so that the only air allowed to pass through the extremely thin, razor-edge slit or glottis is *vibrant* air or sound-producing eddies. If the attack is smooth there will be no knocking or colliding, no overlapping of the cords. Never jab in the vowelled tone, but *glide it in.*

Once the tone is launched it is up to the singer to *allow* and maintain an absolutely smooth continuity. If the singer *wills* and *thinks* this regularity of motion, if he visualizes this fluidity of vibration, this fast-moving stream, the neurones of the vocal cords will obey the command.

"Let the cords sing", was an adage of the old School. But the singer must *allow* them to do so by *thinking* and *willing* a smooth continuity. The vocal cords must first be made to purr, and then *allowed* to continue to purr like a well-balanced engine of Rolls Royce quality. A good singer does not attack with a knock, even as a good driver does not let in his clutch with a bang. (The perpetration of a peccadillo of this kind even by a great singer, as sometimes occurs, is to be deprecated). Rough attacks are definitely harmful to cords and larynx. All man-made machinery is designed and built to run smoothly; so is vocal machinery, but few singers let it do so.

For this reason the term "Launching of the tone" is far preferable to "attack", for the cords must, from the aforesaid oval shape, *glide* into the linear.

To illustrate this gliding movement we would ask the student to imagine the simultaneous launching, down an inclined plane, of two ships which, before being released, are at the two open ends of an inverted V. On being released, at first slowly and then with ever-increasing speed they glide down the incline towards each other. Just before meeting at the point of the Λ they turn slightly outwards to continue their forward motion parallel to each other. The ships do not meet, nor collide, but continue to glide forward very close together. Make a *gliding* tonal attack; never jab the tone in.*

There is a poetry of motion in correct attack, in this "launching" of the tone, and it lies in the fact that there is no striking, no colliding, no touching even, of the cords as they approximate from their oval shape to the rectilinear. Any striking and knocking of the cords is extremely harmful; if habitual, the continual irritation produces corns on the cords themselves which, with constant abuse, are also apt to become "knock-kneed". The tone invariably suffers, as it is impossible to secure the exact laryngo-pharyngeal adjustment on any pitch where violence and excess in any form are present (see p. 267). Banish, therefore, every "coup".

The basic requirement of all machinery is smoothness of action, out of which come regular movement and continuity. The cords open out to the oval shape to permit the inflow of outside air; they return to the rectilinear in order to offer resistance to the air outflowing from the lungs. Singing, therefore, is the harnessing of resisted pressure, the pressure being slightly more than the resistance. The act of singing consists, in its basic mechanical element,

---

* As soon as you produce a vowelled tone, "balloon" it by mentally lifting it up on to an imaginary fast-moving stream. Because of its reaction on the breathing machinery, inducing as it invariably does a perfectly smooth action of the parts concerned, this thought of a *straight*, smooth, *moving* tonal line irons out the tonal wrinkles that may have wormed their way into the adjustment. Imagine the vowel, as a shape, to be riding *on* this stream and moving smoothly away from you in a dead-straight line.

of a *vibrating line* of flexible resistance. To create this vibrating line of resistance is the object of the movement called attack. And because this *flexible* line of resistance vibrates, and is both plastic and elastic, it gives rise to a definite sensation that we call "feel". This FEEL is the base of the issuing tone, *the base of all vocal tone*. Where there is feel there is touch. It is this touch, this feel of the live, vibrating principle *on* which vocal tone is based, that must be created by a smooth, gliding movement. When this movement is smooth we say that the attack is clean and good. It is *on* and *with* this vibrating line of resistance that the singer should develop an exquisite sense of touch. (The principle of attack is very closely related to the bow-laying movement by a fine violinist.) By vibrating-line we mean the linear adjustment of the vocal cords during phonation.

The fine network of neurones in the vocal cords themselves constitute a superlative touch-centre that, by the exercise of a constantly accurate attack, can be sensitized to a very high degree. Once developed and perpetuated, this centre of exquisite touch or feel becomes the source, the base of all vocal tone. For the singer it is and with exercise becomes the pivot of voice, which he adjusts, readjusts, and manipulates at will.

The act of attack (tone-launching or tone initiation) consists firstly of a *mentally* well-shaped vowel which is "placed" with an imaginary downward and then forward gliding movement. (The line described is very similar to that of an aeroplane diving and flattening out, or of a man diving off a high platform and then straightening out in the water, without so much as a splash; in these two cases the downward and forward movement is of course physical, whereas the downward-forward launching of the tone is purely mental, imaginary.) The word "placed" is put in inverted commas above as obviously the singer cannot physically place or lay a vowel downwards on the surface of the adducted vocal cords.* What is called a vowel is the result, or effect, of a mass of vibrations pouring into and through a *shape* given by an appropriately adjusted mouth-pharynx.

Note.—Even as a liquid has no definite shape unless placed in a solid containing vessel whose shape it temporarily takes, so a mass of vibrating air has no definite *shape* unless passed into and through

---

* See *The Science and Sensations of Vocal Tone*, p. 29.

a cavity whose shaping it takes temporarily. Now the temporary shaping of the mouth-pharynx, filled and bathed with vibrations, constitutes what is called a vowel. Therefore, *a vowel is shaped vibration*. When molten metal is poured into a mould it first takes temporarily the shape of the mould, and then, when cool, permanently adopts that shape. Like liquids, vibrations delight in ferreting out every little curve and cranny when injected into a shaped cavity. To produce all the different vowels it means that the mouth-pharynx cavity has to be given different shapings; the difference in shape between one vowel and another is slight in some cases, and marked in others (on the low notes, but not on the high notes). From the standpoint of intelligible vocal tone, vibrations become meaningless unless properly *shaped* within a well-adjusted cavity. Hence the importance of correct vowel formation on all pitches.

If by an imaginary movement we can secure a correct physical result, it is legitimate to employ it. In this case the above-described mental movement physically helps the singer to obtain a correct initial adduction of the vocal cords, or, in other words, a good attack. Imagination is an important factor in our life and work; its uses by the singer are many and varied.

On the other hand, given a good cord adduction, natural or acquired, it matters little whether the attack is downward or upward. Good cord approximation creates a perfectly flat, horizontal vibrating base for the best tone possible in relation to the particular individual voice. However, by *mentally* describing such a downward curve we help nature to do her work properly. To assist nature is, after all, an intrinsic part of the singer's art.*

When the principle of attack has been mastered, the imaginary downward and forward vowel-laying movement should be combined simultaneously with an upward thought accompanying, and riding up on, the actual physical sound-beams themselves as they soar upwards from the laryngeal source to seek out their respective points of impingement in relation to the pitch and

* Attack a high note on an imaginary ready-made tonal stream, and at the same time imagine you have available a sufficient quantity of breath in the head. These two mental devices have proved their worth. Also, when attacking a high note on AH, AW, OH or OO, have in mind the *sound and shape* of a miniature *u* (as in *put*) with which to "hook in" the vowelled focus. Simple but effective. (See p. 307.)

vowel. All this has been treated in detail in *The Science and Sensations of Vocal Tone.*

Whatever the attributes of a voice, quality of tone depends basically on a correct attack. A jerked or knocked, or high-pressure attack induces a faulty adduction-adjustment of the vocal cords themselves, and in turn passes the evil on to the resonators so that they, too, fail to respond correctly; it is apt, moreover, to produce tone that is heavy, or sagging, or draggy, or squeaky, or rasping, or throaty, or nasal, or in fact any defective timbre singly or in combined form.

Every attack must be dead on the pitch; there must be no scooping or dragging up to any note. (We don't slide our finger up the wall or door to press the doorbell: we put our finger straight on to the push-button.) A nicely executed *portamento* is not scooping.

Knocked or jerked attack (*coup de glotte*) is now a widespread feature among singers in every country; this is but one sign of the general decline of singing. So many singers unwittingly employ it, and many deliberately cultivate it. Some teachers even encourage it because it is supposed to produce "manly" tone; manly tone on all fours, for actually it is *barked* tone. Men are the greatest sinners in this respect because, perhaps, of an innate desire to show their manliness! If they only knew what harm it does and what bad results accrue.

A SCIENTIFIC ADDENDUM
by Noel Bonavia-Hunt, M.A.

Nature has endowed various parts of our body with what are called "neurones": these are found in the skin and in the muscles. The neurones are placed there to register pressure. Reference has been made to the artistic "touch-sense" of the blind man, and this sense is entirely due to the existence of special neurones with which the nerve endings situated in the fingers are equipped and which can be stimulated by simple pressure. It is not my intention to enter into this question of an intuitive complex percept that forms the basis of all artistic performance; I am more concerned to show that the touch-sense is equally at the disposal of the singer for precisely the same reason as it is, for instance, at the disposal of the violinist or pianist, and that it is due to the existence of the neurones supplied by nature exactly in the positions required.*

What exactly is "vocal attack"? The adductor muscles, which are provided with neurones, close the cords in order that the pressure air from the lungs may set them in stable vibration. The cords must never touch each other. Can they be made to touch? Yes, percussion is possible by means of a spasmodic adduction of the cords, though the collision occurs only for a fraction of a second and is due to momentum or impetus of the motion in question. The cords will also touch each other when a nodule or corn is situated on one of their edges. Now it is the manner in which the adductor muscles bring the cords together that constitutes the "attack" in producing the note required, and this technique is also accompanied by the tempering of the pressure of breath from the lungs. First the adjustment of the cords to the optimum approximation and resistance, then the push of air from below: that is the order of events, and the "timing" of the two operations is as precise as the batsman's "cut".

The vibrator of an organ reed pipe is set in motion by the wind striking it, but the correct position of the vibrator in relation to the orifice that has to be closed at each vibration is artistically arranged by the voicer, and the resistance is that of a constant tension of the material itself: in other words, the vibrator is a spring and acts as such. It is also of vital importance that the vibrator should execute its closing and opening movements in such a manner that the orifice or slit shall have its area reduced from maximum to minimum (or vice versa) without introducing any abrupt discontinuities or irregularities into the process—in other words, there must be a uniform rate of closure and opening, a perfectly smooth and regulated gradualness of motion from start to finish; otherwise inharmonic overtones are introduced and the tone is harsh and strident. This same rule applies with equal force to the vocal cord mechanism, and for this reason a correct "launching" of the note is essential.

The tensioning of the vocal cords is controlled by the adductor muscles and their neurones, so that the voicing operation has to be

---

* We teachers and singers know, however, that our touch-sense is much more intimate and sensitive than that of the instrumentalist, as the live vibrator (vocal cords) is part of ourselves, constituting as it does a terminus of the sympathetic nervous system. (See *N.B.*, p. 92.) (Author's note.)

carried out with each note produced and forms an integral part of the technique of production. The operation is four-dimensional, since it involves an intuitive appreciation of space, mass, time and force; or, to express it mathematically, energy multiplied by time.

Another point connected with the vibration of the cords is that the displacement should be proportional to the pressure, since this ensures an acoustic output that is a linear function of the input. Breach of this rule is responsible for the introduction of alien harmonics in the tone produced, the positive and negative half-cycles of the wave not being symmetrical. *It is the duty of the neurones of the adductor muscles to transmit to the brain the sense of proportional pressure and resistance* occurring at the moment of attack, and it is easily possible for the singer to cultivate this fine sense of proportion under the guidance of a sympathetic teacher.

Lastly, Nature has beautifully ensured the correct ratio of cordal energy to applied pressure by providing the ventricles and false cords which act, in *right* production, as "traffic controllers". (See also p. 104.)

CHAPTER XV

THE TRUE BREATH-GOVERNING PRINCIPLE

A MISAPPREHENSION that has wrought very considerable havoc in the sphere of vocal technique is responsible for certain distorted conceptions of the mainspring of singing: the breath and its control. The perversion is universal, in varying degree. All voices, with few exceptions, have suffered from the pernicious influence, because in their search for the truth, the teacher, the student, and the singer are in most cases much too ready, unchallengingly, to accept writings and sayings of known and unknown pens and tongues. Fame is not necessarily synonymous with accuracy: it assuredly is not in the world of vocal technique and singing.

Many are the mistaken views on the control of the breath for and during the act of singing. That there should be antagonistic opinions on such a natural function, visible and tangible, as is breathing, passes all comprehension.

The oft-quoted adage: "He who knows how to breathe well, knows how to sing well", is less than a half-truth. It borders on stupidity. Are we to deduce that a bulging chest and powerful breathing machinery make the singer or, indeed, induce good singing? Good singing includes very much more than mere breathing capacity or efficiency. It means primarily a fine technique, a voice well produced with all vowels on all pitches within the individual compass; it means painting a vocal picture with appropriate vowel-colours, conveying a message, delineating life at its best and worst, the moods and emotions, the playful fancy, and the passions that move men; it means telling a story well. It means all that and more, for, in the words of Horatio Bonar:

> *Thy soul must overflow, if thou*
> *Another's soul wouldst reach;*
> *It needs the overflow of heart*
> *To give the lips full speech.*

185

Such niceties, however, are not secured by false methods of "breath control" which in the main connote forced-breath blast with more than a measure of indiscretion.

Let us reverse the adage and postulate: "He who sings well, breathes well". For good singing, technically speaking, must necessarily assume and include good breathing, and by "good" is meant, physiologically correct.

A fine vocal technique is a question of delicate adjustment all along the line; consequently, where the breathing factor is concerned, we demand measured quality in the right place, and not unmeasured quantity in the wrong place.

To breathe correctly is to lay the foundation for good singing, technically and artistically. It is not the size, but the flexible strength of the breathing machinery that counts. The office of breath is not only to give life and continuity to voice, but also to *sustain* it. Breath energizes, feeds, and supports voice; but the energizing, feeding, and supporting must be nicely balanced and correctly correlated.

How often do we hear and read of "breath control"; how often does it roll glibly on the tongue alike of teacher, student, and singer? Few, however, are able to offer a really satisfactory explanation of the exact meaning of this term. For so many it means, unfortunately, a "masterful" propulsion of the air stream by means of the diaphragm developed to a noble degree of hardness. The propulsion can never be "masterful" because based on brute force in this case, and the much-vaunted "control" is no real control, as the diaphragmatic drive is blind and brainless.

One can exercise a certain degree of deliberate control over the diaphragm itself as a muscle, but there "control" ends because it is impossible, by means of this muscle, to calculate the *exact* quantity of air forced upwards to the vibrator. *The diaphragm has no tactile terminal or telephonic nerve-line capable of transmitting to the brain advance information of this kind.*

The "breath control" fetishist is quite convinced that the control of the breath directly by means of the diaphragm is his by right of muscular development and drive. Self-deception was ever the deadly nightshade of the human mind. And our muscular-minded votary practises auto-deception in that his idea of breath control is centred solely on the fibro-muscular diaphragm. Interrogation reveals, however, that not one of these enthusiasts gives a thought to the mathematical *effect* of the drive, to the actual quantity of breath thus forced upward to the vocal cords. But *it is the gauging of this quantity* with (almost) mathematical exactness *that constitutes the fulcrum of good singing* from the technical standpoint.

It is impossible to supply to the vocal organs the EXACT quantity of breath for the generation, maintenance, development and support of any note, high or low, by a deliberate, conscious supply of air through direct, willed control of the expiratory muscles. By this we mean to convey that whereas the singer is free to contract, drive, and punch with his diaphragm as much as he pleases, never under any circumstances is he able to release, *with calculated precision*, by this direct muscular action, a quantity of air that for a given note represents a true requirement.

Because he knows how to secure vibrator-resonator adjustments for maximum efficiency, the good singer employs an exact quantity of breath to satisfy the requirements of tonal intensity from *p* to *f*. Never will he employ a pointless maximum but a finely balanced, indispensable "minimum" in every case.

Before explaining how the singer gauges and effectively releases and controls this exact quantity of air, we must point out that this exact quantity of air (which we also call an indispensable minimum) is in itself insufficient. It, together with the laryngeal adjustment (which we call platform) must be vitalized and made very intense by concentrated mental-nervous energy. This energy, nerving as it does every muscle concerned, affords extraordinary support (*not* thrust) to the tone.

At this juncture we would warn the student against the following erroneous methods: (1) raising the shoulders; (2) deliberate drawing in of the abdomen; (3) excessive protrusion of the abdomen resulting from the forced descent of the diaphragm; (4) lateral expansion of the lower ribs. Taken singly, or in any combined form, all four methods are taboo: (4) or costal breathing is harmless but incomplete, and therefore inadequate; (3) or abdominal breathing, employed singly and particularly with forced descent of the diaphragm, is as harmful as it is incomplete. When carried to extremes, as it often is, it is the sin of sins; it has done untold harm to so many voices, and, in the case of female singers it can cause some trouble internally.

The combined forms of diaphragmatic and rib breathing constitute the right way; with a normal and natural descent of the diaphragm (and not a forced descent, as in (3) above). All great singers employ this combination, whatever their nationality. A significant fact.

Correct breathing consists of:

PHASE 1.—*Inspiration* or taking breath: of which the two movements are (*a*) vertical descent of the diaphragm, a large and powerful muscle dividing the chest from the abdomen and which, in a state of rest, has the shape of a basin put upside down; (*b*) sideways extension of the *lower* (or "floating") ribs. The two movements are therefore vertical and horizontal: (*b*) following (*a*) in one oil-smooth action. They increase the capacity of the chest in height, depth and width. After the diaphragm has been lowered (flattened), the lateral expansion of the lower ribs has the effect of slightly raising the *lower* part of the chest (which must *never* be raised deliberately, as advocated by some). As a result of the descent of the diaphragm, the abdomen (abdominal wall) will protrude somewhat and in varying degree according to the individual; but owing to the lateral expansion of the ribs, it will not only return to normal but will be *slightly* drawn inwards. This is a perfectly natural process and should not be interfered with under any circumstances. All men take breath as above described.

Women, however (with few abnormal exceptions) do NOT first lower the diaphragm and then expand sideways the lower or floating ribs in two separate, albeit consecutive, movements. No, with then *the two inbreathing movements are simultaneous* and resolve therefore into *one down-and-out movement*. Modern ignorance actually teaches women to breathe like men, as above described, and the *forced* descent of the diaphragm, often to the total exclusion of rib employment; this inversion of nature's ruling can lead and has led to internal injury in some cases. Women should never attempt, or be made, to alter their natural breathing mechanism.

PHASE 2.—*Expiration* or breathing out: this embraces the gradual *synchronized* return of ribs and diaphragm to the initial state of rest. As the breath is expired, the return of the diaphragm and ribs to their normal position must occur with a perfectly smooth and *regular* action. For the return excursion (expiration), the flattened diaphragm gradually arches again, effecting a gradual upward pressure on the base of the lungs, while the laterally expanded lower ribs, as they return to their normal position horizontally in an inward direction, also exert pressure sideways

on the lungs. Expiration, therefore, has two synchronized movements. All men, and women, outbreathe in this way.*

For the purposes of singing, the too *rapid* return of both diaphragm and ribs to the initial state of rest must be *governed*, not
with a rigid, but with a smooth, regular, elastic action. Why has
the *rapid* return of these parts to be governed? Because the breath
itself must be governed during expiration in order to permit
correct initial and subsequent laryngo-pharyngeal adjustments,
and also to prevent any *excess* of breath pressure against the vocal
cords, overloading them and thereby obstructing correct, balanced
adjustment. How is this governing effected? NOT by the deliberate
and rigid downward jamming of the diaphragm; NOT by the
deliberate and rigid sideways retention of the ribs: not either of
these, singly or combined. How then?

For the purposes of good, mechanically correct singing (and we
are concerned in this chapter solely with the technical aspect of
singing), the breath must reach the larynx in a smooth, *regular*
stream exercising normal pressure, and *never* forced pressure. The
larynx, of its own and instinctively, as it were, will take up the
exact quantity of breath for the correct production of a note when,
and if, the singer is able correctly to adjust his vocal cords and
resonators in relation to, and satisfying the conditions of, pitch and
vowel. This exact quantity of breath, representing what we called
above the indispensable minimum, is determined to a nicety by
instinctive calculation—an instinct developing from the experience
of true sensations of vocal tone accruing from oft-repeated correct
vibrator-resonator adjustments for the production of all notes
with all vowels.

We would here stress the importance of the student and singer
making a practice of visualizing the tonal sensations accruing from
such correct adjustments. Which sensations consist mainly of the
focal points, or *platforms* as we also call them, that are actually the
TOP of the sound-beams, impinging against definite spots within

* An excellent illustration of these synchronized movements is obtained by
laying a single sheet of notepaper lengthwise flat on a table and then, after
placing the middle finger of each hand firmly on both ends, pressing slowly
inward until the paper is nicely arched. The inward movement of the ends
represents the return excursion of the ribs, and the arching of the sheet the
return of the diaphragm. If in this arched position we reverse the movement,
we get an illustration of the above-mentioned down-and-out inspiratory
movement occurring *naturally* in the majority of WOMEN.

the resonating cavities. After considerable concentration and oft-repeated attempts at the retention of the sensations, definite *mental images* of the sensations of focused tone gradually form, hazily, perhaps, at first, finally to emerge clearly. These images, being mainly linear, as actually they are the *top* of the sound-beams, vary in size, intensity and location according to the pitch and vowel. The individual "feel" of these varying images must be committed to memory. Visualization is applicable particularly to the upper medium and high notes, and the higher the pitch the clearer and more "illuminated" becomes the image of the focal point or platform. Inversely, the focal points of all notes from the lowest up to D, fourth line, never become marked in themselves, because the sound-beams go no higher than the arc of the palate and the mouth-pharynx cavity is felt to be full of vowel (which is not the case of the notes from E♭, fourth space, upwards, as explained elsewhere).

For instance: a high A♭ sung on AH has its own individual and characteristic sensation intimately related to size, intensity and location of its focal point or platform; it differs from the sensations accruing from the A♮ or G♮ immediately above and below it if sung with the same vowel. The difference, mind you, is marked. But is much more marked if high B♭ is sung, or the F♮ a fourth below. If we repeat the experiment on, say, the EH vowel, the focal sensations again differ materially; the new combination of vowel and focal position providing a different and characteristic sensation.

Because the tension increases with the rise in pitch and the tonal focus changes position according to the pitch and vowel, with every change of pitch with the same or with another vowel, there is a positive change in the tonal (focal) sensation; there is a difference in the tonal "feel" qualitatively and as regards location, size, intensity. And again, the fact of changing the vowel without altering the pitch introduces new characteristics as regard "feel", location, and general quality; however, the higher the note, any change from one vowel to another on the same pitch is accompanied by no marked change of sensation.

Clear-cut mental images of such tactile feeling provided by the impinging sound-beam are possible of retention only after the varying tonal sensations have been developed as a result of oft-repeated production on a correct basis and permanently built into the voice. They must be made part and parcel of production itself, for they are the most cherished possessions of all great singers. As Joseph Hislop exclaimed, when discussing deliberate tonal creation and visualization: "Yes, *every* note has to be *painted in*."

In tonal creation the singer must *seek* the tension and therefore the "feel" of the platform (which is nothing but the setting or adjustment of the vocal cords) on the principle of the downward attack. Hence our advice to pupils in the studio: "Seek your tension, your platform, mentally downwards through the vowel shape." In other words, first *mentally shape your vowel* and then attack *mentally* downwards through the shaping (vowel) to seek and feel, or shall we say create, the right platform that purrs and "sings". And by platform is meant vibrator adjustment. (See p. 223.)

It must be remembered that vibrator (and resonator) adjustment and the breathing process are inseparable concomitants, acting and reacting on each other, beneficially or otherwise. For instance: a forced adjustment engenders reflexly an equally forced expiration; and, vice versa, a smooth, balanced adjustment induces an equally smooth and balanced expiration. We earnestly ask the student to study carefully this important aspect of vocal mechanics. The issue is vital. It is the basic principle of speech in song. If the *speaking principle* is applied to singing there can be, and will be, no excess breath pressure (unless deliberately or wilfully employed), for it is this very principle that helps to create correct vibrator and resonator adjustments. (It is a characteristic of all truly great singers.) Moreover it engenders a *braking action* on the breathing muscles during expiration. Which action is extremely slight and does not imply or induce rigidity or jerkiness of movement. It is in fact an "ironing-out" action which with smooth continuity retards, as required, the return of ribs and diaphragm to normal. Retarding does NOT mean halting or holding back with an effort of the will, for that produces rigidity in some degree—the worst enemy of the vocal machine.

In the case of a *crescendo*, or of producing a note, a bar, or a phrase *forte*, a greater amount of breath is of course released instinctively to satisfy all conditions; even so, the slight braking or governing action still persists and will absolutely prevent any excess of breath pressure against the vibrator, by preventing the too rapid return of the ribs–diaphragm combination; it prevents, therefore, all *excess* of muscular action.

To grasp this principle of speech in singing, to grasp the true breath-governing principle, the student by way of experiment should *speak* a few words, preferable on the same pitch. He will observe that no thought is given to the breath: in fact, all he feels is voice—vowels and consonants. He feels that vowel formation and enunciation obtain on top of the breath, sitting on it, so to speak, and that during phonation the vocal organs, and particularly the vocal cords, take up a sufficient quantity of breath for the purpose, a quantity that is exact, with no excess and no shortage. Consequently, no undue or excess pressure is felt by him in the region of the larynx, no discomfort anywhere. With very little breath, therefore, corresponding to an indispensable minimum, he enunciates and sustains speech. He neither seeks nor desires to employ consciously, or to control directly, the action of ribs and diaphragm. His main thought is his speech; and provided the formation and the release of the vowels and consonants are good, speech is clear, flowing, unimpeded, effortless.

Again, let the student first say a word, *song*, for instance, stressing the vowel sound (in this instance, a modified AH) and then, without stopping or altering the tone, *sing* it a few pitches higher, stressing still more the vowel sound. He will note that there was no deliberate or conscious attempt on his part to create and control any muscular action of the ribs and diaphragm, the extra work required of both being accomplished as a result of a reflex action due to the initial demands of the larynx (and specifically the vocal cords) prompted by an instinctively calculated need.

The few brilliant individual exceptions in the world of song prove eloquently that it pays to obey natural laws and follow nature's dictates, man-discovered, if you will, and not the many preposterous man-concocted methods that are mainly guesswork.

Mediocrity invariably employs a blind, uncontrolled and uncompromising maximum breath pressure; quality singers use a perfectly controlled indispensable minimum.

That most pernicious of breathing methods, dubbed diaphragmatic or abdominal, is responsible for the wrecking of many thousands of voices. The normal functioning of the diaphragmatic muscle is one thing; its glorification as a single form of breathing, as the alpha and omega of vocal technique, is criminal. As a breathing system it employs the diaphragm in the rôle of a high-pressure piston. But do the diaphragm obsessionists realize, among other things, that the *slightest* stiffness in this muscle produces a corresponding rigidity in the vocal organs, larynx and pharynx? (See p. 27.)

When the diaphragmatic obsession is carried to the point of not merely driving it downward with force but keeping it down (flattened out) with still more force during expiration, rigidity is increased tenfold, whereupon the singer's larynx, throat, neck and jaw are affected in varying degree. Have these people ever experienced seasickness and noted how the line of muscular rigidity goes from stomach to throat? How can the vocal machine do its work under such adverse conditions? *Flexible* firmness is the soul of vocal vibration and is therefore the antithesis of rigidity. In singing, the vocal organs must have flexible firmness: every part, even as the whole, must have a certain elastic "give" in it. Flexibility in any engine spells efficiency, and rigidity functional failure in equal degree, for all work must be fluid.

Even as the good violinist regulates to a nicety the "weight" of the downward movement of the bow to the string as he attacks, and also the degree of frictional contact, so the good player of a wind instrument regulates his output of breath for the production of every tone; the exact quantity for every note, *forte* or *piano*, is for him a matter of instinctive calculation, or rather pre-calculation born of the feel at the central point of expenditure and resistance: feel of shape, feel of quality, feel of quantity, feel of intensity, all in one.

In the singer's case this "feel" of *the central point of expenditure and resistance* is much more intimate, real, and alive, for his vibrator is within him, part of him. Now this "feel", varying in intensity according to the pitch and vowel and what he has to express, accrues basically from vibrator adjustment, from the setting of the vocal cords as they vibrate. This setting or adjustment we call *platform* because it gives the singer the feeling of flexible firmness and resistance. On the upper medium and high notes the setting or platform is reflected, as a sensation, by the TOP of the sound-beam impinging at different angles and "heights" within the resonating system: a *tactile feeling*, therefore. For the good singer this *feel*, platform or focus, this live, vibrating resistance-point (or line) is an intelligible, intelligent entity with a soul all its own. It is born from, and *exactly* reflects, the particular vibrator adjustment, or setting, obtaining at the time: in other words, length, thickness and tension of the vocal cords appropriate to pitch, and giving

N

rise to a sound-beam of definite height and diameter to satisfy conditions of pitch.

The *feel*, we said, has shape, size, quality and intensity, varying according to pitch and purpose; it is both plastic and elastic, possessing flexible firmness. For, it must be remembered, singing is basically resisted pressure, the actual resistance having a certain elastic "give" in it.*

Provided his breathing muscles function correctly and have had appropriate exercise, the singer can profitably forget all about his diaphragm, his ribs, his chest: no attention need be focused on their action. Responding to appropriate messages dictated by the singer's mind to satisfy the requirements *at the point of expenditure* (focal feel or platform) as described above, expiration will be, muscularly, as automatic as inspiration should be. Sluggishness of muscular action, however, is sometimes as inevitable as it is inexplicable; only in such cases recourse may be had to deliberate muscular action, as necessity dictates, but only as far as the *intake* of breath is concerned.

It is precisely by the tonal *feel* that the singer is able to determine the *exact* amount of breath to be employed at any pitch, *forte* or *piano*, and intervening grades of intensity, and the *exact* degree of vibrator resistance to oppose thereto. By observation, analysis, and exercise of this feel, the aforesaid determining becomes simply a matter of *instinctive calculation*, as we said before. It is also an instrument of pre-calculation to the same ends.

A really good singer knows the feel accruing from every single adjustment in the sense that if the feel goes awry, as is possible at times, he knows where to look for the trouble. This is particularly the case of the upper medium and high notes, which he definitely visualizes. Now this *vision of the feel* of the vibrator adjustment, reflected as it is by the TOP of the sound-beam (which top we call focus or platform), is no chimera, no figment of the author's imagination, but a live, a real thing acquirable by one and all.

* Whether the *feel* lives and has its being as a tonal focus, or platform (seemingly containing within itself the sum total of the vibrator adjustment of the moment, as is particularly the case of the head notes) or is a direct original sensation of the vibrator, apparently shorn of resonance as in the case of the owest notes particularly of the heavier categories of voice, whether it is one or the other, the facts of adjustment remain unchanged, for the *feel* in the first instance is merely a reflected image, vibrationally alive, of the actual cord setting operating within the larynx.

The more accurate the vibrator adjustment the closer the approach to exactness of quantity of breath required for the creation and continuity of a particular note.

The indiscriminate blasting of the breath upwards against the adducted cords (vibrator adjustment) by conscious, deliberate driving action of the breathing machinery and the deified diaphragm in particular can but result in vocal distortion in degree. Any attempt at *direct* control of diaphragm and/or ribs must result in what we call failure, as the exact quantity of breath required for a given pitch and intensity is, mathematically, an unknown quantity.

It must be remembered that the laryngeal mechanism feeds and functions primarily on the "head" of compressed air located immediately below. The vocal vibrator knows no more about the lungs-cum-diaphragm than does a petrol engine about the tank.

Now the true breath-governing principle amounts to this: The *instinctive calculation* of the exact quantity of breath required *is born of the vibratory feel;* and because this feel reflects the vibrator adjustment and its working, the singer is able through its adroit manipulation and perfect *balancing* to regulate the flow of the breath. Acting like a sensitive valve, the feel governs by reflex action the breathing machinery.

The feel, which is synonymous with focus, platform, point of impingement, has *vibratory equilibrium* (a wonderful feeling) duly appraised by the mind-brain unit which, keen to maintain the *status quo*, transmits an appropriate order to the breathing muscles to *subordinate* their action to that of the vibrator adjustment and its normal requirements. On receiving the above order, the only desire of the expiratory muscles is to promote the well-being of the vibrator setting, or different settings, with the same breath so long as it is in being. When a new breath is taken and a new (good) adjustment made, the mind-brain again appraises the feeling of vibratory equilibrium, and again transmits the same order to the expiratory muscles. Once the message is received, the muscles start their governing action and continue to do so automatically as long as the adjustment lasts. If a *crescendo* is required, the extra quantity of breath is released as a result of a fresh message from the mind-brain duly impressed by the feel, the sensation of the adjustment and *its* call for more "juice". You, reader, will perhaps say that we are thus endowing the "feel" with consciousness. Well, this is so, because as platform or focus it includes, as we know, especially on the high notes, an important part of the singer's being. Yet it is a strange reflection that the singer himself is unaware of the actual messages sent by his mind-brain unit to his breathing machinery, although immediately conscious of the effects thereof. *The vocal cords*, undoubtedly, *are an ancillary organ of mind.* Will the student please bear this in mind.

The sequence is: Sensation or feel of vibrator adjustment, reflected by the top of the sound-beam, transmitted to brain-mind that appraises the vibratory equilibrium and transmits appropriate order to expiratory muscles to feed the laryngeal mechanism with the required amount of breath which, in turn, continually recreates and sustains the feel. And so this cycle of events goes on for as long as the particular breath lasts: "Feel" to brain-mind, brain-mind to breathing machinery, measured breath to "feel" (focus or platform), and then off again on the same round. Truly a happy family circle, a circle of whirling thought. This is what is meant by *indirect* control of the breath. It is indirect because it is mainly subconscious.

If different adjustments on varying pitches are made with one breath, the whirling thought-circle proceeds apace and intelligently provides for the varying pressures and intensities. As a new breath is taken, the merry circle is momentarily broken, immediately to lock and function again as before as soon as the new adjustment is launched on its vibratory career.

Be it noted, this governing action is perfectly smooth, devoid of jerks, jabs and knocks, devoid of rigidity. *It is as if the breathing machinery were bedded in oil.* The whirling thought-circle is essentially elastic; it contains no element of stiffness.

Mark well, a *crescendo* must be felt to develop directly, locally, at the *feel* or platform (focus); and this is particularly the case of the upper medium and high notes on which *only* the top of the sound-beam *impresses the mind*, when production is correct. And the higher the pitch the higher in the head resonators will the platform or focal resistance-point be felt; it seems to the singer that nature thus brings the control of a complex instrument to a focal point from which the whole may be governed to a nicety; it seems to him, as a sensation, that his very being is concentrated solely in and around the point or platform, almost to the exclusion of all else. A truly wonderful feeling of superb detachment. Body seemingly does not exist, but just the mind and the focused tone. It is therefore *the voice of the mind*.

We repeat that this point, this focused top of the sound-beam, is what we call "feel". The student must bear in mind that sound-beams are live, vibrating things that should be treated with the greatest respect; he should also remember that, particularly on the high notes, the *real strength* of vocal tone is, as a sensation, to be found at the *top* of the sound-beam itself.*

The aforementioned principle of *crescendo* applies to the entire vocal compass. The *crescendo*, we repeat, must be made and be felt to take place *with* and right *in* the focused top of the beam itself, and nowhere else. Part of the singer's mind nestles within the focus, and part hovers over it, thereby exercising a dual control.

As we know, the focused top of the sound-beam is merely the *resonant reflection* of the actual mechanical adjustment within the larynx below, a live, reflected image, a working model of the actual vibrator in action. The reflection is so true a likeness, so real, so vital, so substantial (particularly on the high notes) that the singer feels and could take oath that the vibrator (his vocal cords) itself was located and was functioning right in the head cavities.

The reflected image or "feel" of the vibrating mechanism, understood and manipulated with the right kind of thought, is *the pivot of good singing* from the technical standpoint.

If the old School, instead of saying "Voce sul fiato" (voice on the breath), had said voice, or vowel, on *top* of the sound-beam, the student would have felt the warmth of enlightenment that is generally lacking in such ambiguous adages that leave posterity guessing and wondering. Which "voice" is synonymous with focus, "feel", platform.

The same breath-governing principle applies to *decrescendo*, reversed of course in a sense as regards operation, for the braking action on the expiratory muscles is in this case obviously more

---

* On the very lowest notes, for the production of which the vibrator mass is more or less at its maximum and therefore arousing the major sensation for the singer, the "feel" of the adjustment-resistance of the vibrator is unmistakably located in the laryngeal area; quite a normal phenomenon; inversely, the impinging of the resultant sound-beams is faint and hazy. On the high notes, there is no sensation in the laryngeal area. (See footnote, p. 225.)

marked (but never stiff or "sticky"). And the smoother the operation of this focal *decrescendo* the smoother will be the action of the expiratory machinery. *Such smoothness of action must be first in the mind.* The interdependence and interaction of vocal cords and breathing apparatus is so extremely intimate and sensitive that to caress, iron out, or "oil" the first is to secure an oil-smooth action in the second. If the breath-flow is jerky, irregular, spasmodic, excessive and rigidly "controlled", the niceties of vibrator adjustment are disturbed and the tone will reveal certain impurities and distortions. In a jerked or knocked attack, the breathing machinery is not properly poised. A smooth attack and *fluid* tonal continuation is invariably accompanied by a correspondingly smooth action of the expiratory muscles. To sing *legato* is to breathe out *legato;* it is to *think legato.*

TOUCH is the primitive, the original sense in living organisms, from the microscopic amœba to the elephant; it is the only sense distributed over the whole body. From certain logical aspects, touch might be considered as the lowest conceivable degree of consciousness. Our other senses are derivates or specialized extensions of touch. The eye *feels* the vibrations we call light; the ear *feels* the vibrations we call sound; the nose *feels* the volatile molecules of odour; the taste-buds of the mouth *feel* the molecules peculiar to foodstuffs and beverages. With these senses it is plainly a question of *contact,* of touch.

In the singer's case, the sense of touch or "feel" of focus must be allowed a maximum of sensitive development. There is *touch* when he creates and launches a tone, and there is *touch* in the top of the impinging sound-beam for the duration of the tone. The vocal cords, endowed as they are with neurones, *feel* the breath pressure against them as they adduct to oppose resistance. (We all know by experience how hypersensitive the cords are when a tiny drop of liquid, or worse still a crumb, has gone "the wrong way".) In every case this touch, this "feel" is a sensation accruing from extreme sensitiveness to external stimuli, and as such transmits appropriate messages to the brain-mind. The "feel" of the vibrating cords is exactly reflected in the "feel" of the focus, or platform. Actually the feel is one—like the sun and its rays.

With the above explanations, in which there is purposely much repetition, the student should be able to understand why and how by means of this "feel", this *touch*, highly sensitive and intimate, the true breath-governing action is reflexly or automatically induced.

The foregoing analysis of artistic breathing is worthy of the deepest consideration. From its study and application high results accrue.

The author has known and knows intimately many world-famous singers, male and female, of different nationalities. Discussions on technique revealed that not one of them exercised or attempted to exercise direct, deliberately-willed control of the expiratory machinery. They all exercised indirect control over the breath by reflex action which, as explained above, is the only true breath-governing principle. (See Gigli's remarks in Chapter I.)

To conclude, we will say with Dean Inge: "Illumination is not granted to the mere thinker, but to him who acts while he thinks, and thinks while he acts."

N.B.—On p. 177 of *The Science and Sensations of Vocal Tone* is given an excellent breathing exercise.

CHAPTER XVI

THE LIFT-UP PRINCIPLE

O NE OF THE MOST IMPORTANT manipulative props in the singer's technical field is the principle of the "lift-up". Of what exactly does it consist? As previously explained, and stressed on every occasion, the mass of the vocal cords has to undergo gradual elimination in both length and depth as the pitch rises from the lowest to the highest note. Rarely in this respect do the sixty-odd muscles actuating the laryngeal mechanism function correctly on their own; too often their action, individual and collective, is incomplete, undeveloped. One erroneous concept is sufficient to cause a certain group of these, and other muscles, to function imperfectly. Even one wrong thought, in an otherwise accurate grouping of right thoughts culminating in a terse message to the vocal machinery, assuredly is going to prevent that equipoise of vibrator and resonance which is the basic desideratum of all vocal study. With the exception of the few completely natural voices, practically every untutored voice is defective, or incomplete, in some respect, in some detail of mechanical procedure and adjustment. It may be in some instances merely a lack of muscular development; it often is, as nature seems well content at times to establish the basic structure, the design, and leave the question of muscular development to the ingenuity of man.

It is really surprising how the simple process of "lifting up" the tone is a direct and effectual aid to correct laryngeal adjustment not only as we ascend the scale diatonically or chromatically, but also when there is an interval to sing, be it a second, a third, or an octave or more. It definitely assists the particular group of muscles to actuate the thinning process of the cords. And if combined with the simultaneous rounding of the vowel in due relation to the pitch, the effective cord length is thereby secured. Appropriate tension should come in automatically as a result of thinking pitch. Furthermore, the "lift-up" offers the vocal organs a greater freedom of action.

Note that we place the term "lift-up" between inverted commas, for obviously one cannot lift up the tone. But the very *thought* of doing so and the attempted shadowy action accompanying it, react on the laryngeal muscles concerned, suggesting and inducing *lightness* of mechanism through the thinning process *in* degree.

Now, as already explained, the fact of securing a laryngeal adjustment that offers an appropriately short and thin vibrator for employment on a higher pitch, that is, a shorter and thinner vibrator than the one employed for the lower pitch (be the interval a second or an octave, or any interval) is of physiological and acoustical significance. In fact, from this shorter, thinner, and altogether lighter vibrator that satisfies physiological conditions accrues a taller and narrower sound-beam that satisfies acoustical requirements. This means, therefore, equipoise of vibrator and resonance in relation to pitch.

As the tonal lift-up is not physical but essentially mental, it includes a *mental* pull-back movement which induces appropriate space backwards, horizontally and vertically, and helps to keep up the tension. So the mental line is a pull-back lift-up. In all this the singer has nothing physical to do; and that is the beauty and simplicity of it.

Particularly in the completely natural voice the lift-up obtains automatically on an ascending scale and with any interval; it is noticeably present also on a descending scale or interval. Seemingly it is inherent in and part of the mental-physical make-up of such voices, although often the singer himself is unaware of the action as such; but they instinctively sense the need of, and aim for, this buoyancy of production accruing from the lift-up.

If a voice does not naturally execute the lift-up from note to note as the pitch rises, whether in a scale or an interval, then art must require the singer to make it consciously, and make a practice of it until the principle is embedded in the subconscious and becomes a habit. After all, it was precisely by observing, testing, and putting into practice the idiosyncrasies and technicalities of the completely natural voice that the old Italian School was founded and developed.*

* A few known examples of the completely natural voice are: Giuseppe Krismer, Aristodemo Giorgini, Beniamino Gigli, Giacomo Lauri Volpi, John McCormack (all tenors); Viglione Borghese, the most extraordinary baritone

On rapidly ascending runs a continuous lift-up thought is of very considerable aid to note-to-note adjustment. Also on descending runs this thought should prevail, for it ensures accurate tuning, preventing also any over-release of tension as can easily occur when coming down to a lower note.

If the singer is *mentally* behind his tones, as he should always be, apart from being mentally on top of them in the upper medium and high pitches, the lift-up can be likened to taking a peg out of one hole in a perpendicular shaft, lifting it up (not vertically, but with a pull-back and slight curving-over movement) and putting it into the desired hole situate at an exact height in the shaft. The lift-up thought is invariably one of soaring lightness and smoothness. (See p. 276, para.)

Whatever the direction a sound-beam should take, and whatever the interval, even if only a semitone, the singer should never pump, push, or drag up the tone for such procedure will prevent vibrator elimination. Even the small interval of a semitone exacts a degree of vibrator elimination, and the lift-up is of considerable assistance in this respect.

Only a mere gossamer thread of tone should unite note to note, and never a thick tonal line. Which connecting thread expresses lightness and continuity, and ensures a perfect *legato*. What is this gossamer thread of tone connecting two *forte* notes on two different pitches? It is merely a *pianissimo* tone.

To enable the student to grasp our meaning we give hereunder a sort of slow-motion picture of what actually takes place in a "lift-up": When we pass from one *f* note to a higher one, whatever the interval, we first make a rapid *decrescendo* to *p* (and this means rapidly reducing the breath pressure in due proportion) and then bridge the interval or gap with the aforesaid thread-like tone; then, as we alight on the new pitch, we make a rapid *crescendo* to *f*, "talking in" or, if you like, "thinking in" the vowelled tone out of the void, so to speak, appropriately modified in relation to pitch. Naturally, the greater the interval the longer the connecting tonal thread; and conversely. This *decrescendo* to *p* and

voice for quality, power, and flawless production the author has ever heard, and moreover a great singer and actor; Gaetano Rebonato (a pupil of the author's teacher), a light baritone of crystalline beauty, a model of vocal perfection. They all studied for many years, however, to build up voice and art. (See footnotes, pp. 32, 348.) Caruso and Bonci were products of schooling.

subsequent *crescendo* to *f* is performed so quickly as to pass un-noticed by the listener; this is important.

The lift-up is actually a *portamento*, lightning-fast and impercep-tible to the listener who, however, is quick to appreciate the tonal results accruing from the procedure. Hence the above picture of the lift-up mechanism, rapid and inaudible, exactly reflects the mechanism of the *portamento*, which is comparatively slow and audible. The term *portamento* literally means a tonal "carrying" up or down, a gliding with continuous tone, from one pitch to another. In the *portamento* the connecting tonal thread is deliber-ately made audible. If instead of a gossamer thread the *portamento* is made with a thick tonal line it becomes "moanamento"; assuredly not a vocal ornament. The downward *portamento* must also be executed on a thin tonal line which is maintained by the simple process of keeping the tone up high and light as the descent is being made.

In lifting up the tone from one pitch to a higher one the sensation is one of "carrying" the tonal focus of the first note up to the higher position within the same, or to a different resonating zone higher up, according to the requirements of the new pitch. And on the way up we feel the gradual increase in tension-resistance and of course the gradual decrease of the focus; however, the smaller focus finds ample compensation in increased flexible firmness producing greater tonal intensity.

The feeling is somewhat similar to holding one end of a small, thin elastic band between thumb and index of the left hand in a fixed position, and grasping the other end with the right thumb and index-finger, then stretching it upwards a little with the right hand so as to get a certain tension and height to represent the jumping-off pitch. Next stretch the elastic band, not straight up vertically but with a slight pull-back-and-up movement, thereby carrying the *top* part to a higher position (the left hand not moving, of course). The top part represents the tonal focus.

Now we advise the student to experiment with the elastic band (1) by keeping hold of the band as before and, without moving the left hand, stretching the elastic gradually more and more by carrying the top part, between right thumb and forefinger, verti-cally upwards to a normal maximum of tension. He will note that the *feel* of the ever-increasing tension obtains chiefly at the *top* of the elastic; this reflects by analogy the ever-increasing tension-resistance of the rising tonal focus (or *top* of the beam) distinctly felt by the singer as the pitch rises; (2) let him now lower his right hand slowly and note the feel of the gradually decreasing tension of the elastic band; this reflects by analogy the sensation of decreasing tonal tension-resistance as the pitch falls.

We repeat that the lift-up from note to note must be lightning-fast: there must be no slow deliberation such as to make it obvious. Nothing detracts from beauty and appreciation so much as the denuding of technical procedure; a technicality in the raw is most uninspiring, even as the loveliest lady would be unlovely if she walked abroad partly or wholly skeletonized. Technique must be nicely fleshed and clothed.

The connecting gossamer tonal thread of the lift-up can and should be made so light and airy that it feels almost at breaking-point; but thin as it is, the connection must not be a slack, lifeless thing, but flexibly taut—like the thread of a spider's web.

When the singer has to come off a high pitch to a lower one, whether a semitone or an octave, or more, *the tone must be kept up*, as high as the pitch permits, and supported in order to prevent any possible excess release of the tension. As the pitch lowers, so there is, naturally, a drop in tension; but as we are dealing with an art, it is after all unnatural in a sense to have such extraordinary tension within the larynx—consequently, the natural "instinct" of the cords is to get rid of as much tension as they can when opportunity arises. Even the descent of only a semitone is an "opportunity" for them to over-release the tension. This is one of the reasons why so many singers go flat as they descend to a lower pitch. We have, however, a remedy for checking this waywardness: We tell the student to "keep or lift the tone up as you come down". Simple but effectual. A rising thought regulates descending tone.

CHAPTER XVII

THE SINGER'S SENSATIONS AND THE LISTENER'S IMPRESSIONS

As PART OF HIS TRAINING, it is vitally important for the singer to be able to differentiate between the tonal sensations he himself experiences and the impressions received by the listener. If on the lower pitches there is a certain similarity of perception, on the higher pitches they are, in a sense, diametrically opposed.

The first essential in the matter of differentiation is that *the singer should never attempt to listen outside himself*, never attempt to listen to the tone as a listener external to himself. Because the aural perspective is different, never at any time will he, the creator of the tones, be able to appraise their ultimate form and pattern such as is perceived in aural impressions by the listener. The singer is essentially the active creator; the listener the passive receiver.

We have devoted in this work a whole chapter to the sound-beams because, from the singer's standpoint, they are the alpha and omega of vocal tone. By sound-beam, to which reference is often made, is meant specifically the *main stream* of the vibration which, as a sensation, impresses the singer's mind the most. It is the main stream of the tone with which his mind is chiefly exercised and on which his attention is focused; it is the main stream or sound-beam which he manipulates, directs and focuses; it is the main stream that in the last analysis constitutes the singer's all-in-all, the quintessence of his tones, which embody and reflect tonal form (vowel), colour, pattern and texture.

By way of adding to the student's knowledge of things vocal it is well for him to be informed of the fact that, be the pitch high or low, the motion of air is not only longitudinal (up and down) as depicted in our diagrams both in this and in the parent work, but also vibrates laterally. So apart from its main up-soaring stream, the effective sound energy must and does form a vibrant component in the mouth and pharynx. However, where the higher and high pitches are concerned (from E♭, fourth space, upwards) the relative sound-beams soar upwards through the mouth-pharynx cavity and pierce the soft palate to enter the head cavities where they are coupled and focused at appropriate points. After the singer has created, directed, and focused the sound-beam, it rebounds downwards into the mouth whence, after bathing the internal shaping of the mouth-pharynx cavity appropriately adjusted for a particular vowel, it passes into outer space carrying with it, so to speak, the vowel shape encountered at the moment within this cavity; thus is the vowelled tone propagated for perception by the listener. (See diagram, p. 174.)

The student, therefore, can form pictorially in his mind how the vibration, after swirling within the mouth-pharynx cavity appropriately shaped for the particular vowel, passes through the lip aperture into outer space, winging its way in vowel form with its tonal pattern, characteristic colour, and emotional tints, if any, introduced in varying intensity as the singer wills; and naturally this is what happens on every pitch, high or low.

The tonal shape we identify as vowel should always contain certain willed *mental vibration* that often constitutes the most potent factor of attractiveness in vocal tone. (See p. 249.)

When the singer creates tone on the low and medium pitches the sound-beam is, in his sensation, relatively broad of base and short of stature. On these pitches, up to and including D, fourth line, the chief coupling and reflecting surface consists of the arc of the palate whose relatively low ceiling is of adequate height to accommodate the beams of said pitches; but it cannot be employed, with physiological balance and acoustical accuracy, for the coupling and focusing of the high pitches with their tall, narrow beams which, on the highest notes, are practically double the height of the ceiling provided by the palatal arc.

An analysis of the singer's sensations reveals, in all voices, that up to D, fourth line, from the lowest note, the mouth-pharynx cavity feels to be full of vowel. This is because the sound-beams go no higher than the arc of the palate (indeed, they cannot go higher), and because, as stated above, the motion is not merely longitudinal but also lateral. However, with the sideways vibration the singer should not preoccupy himself, for it is the up-soaring sound-beam that is his chief vocal tool. Even though the mouth-pharynx cavity is full of vowelled tone on the aforesaid pitches, the alert singer cultivates an intimate acquaintance with the behaviour of the beams in order the better to focus them, according to vowel and pitch.

As explained fully in previous chapters, the sound-beam undergoes rapid and marked changes once D, fourth line, is passed. (We are assuming an ascending scale on the AH vowel). In fact, as a sensation of tone, all singers, male and female, feel (when their production is correct) that from E♭, fourth space, upwards, vowel no longer completely fills the mouth-pharynx cavity, part of the tone having pierced the palate to tune in to the head cavity immediately above. As the pitch rises above said E♭ so the vowel tone is felt, as a sensation, gradually to depart from the mouth-pharynx cavity and to be gathered up by degrees and compressed into the simple sensation of a very short and thin tonal line (which we call platform or focus). As explained elsewhere, this line is merely the TOP of the now rising sound-beam; and the higher the pitch the "taller" and narrower becomes the beam; consequently the highest pitch produces the sensation of a really minute platform. And where in the head cavities there is just this sensation of platform there can be no sensation of vowel for the singer himself, because vowel tone resides *solely* within the mouth-pharynx cavity.

The vowel-vanishing or gathering-up process is rapid from the aforesaid E♭ upwards, and as "platform" appears on the scene to take the place of the vowel-in-mouth sensation, the singer, producing his voice correctly, will feel that *underneath* it everything is non-existent. The feeling is that of a void and that everything tonal, and physical, has converged to just a focal point, to a glittering platform which even seems to attract to itself and encompass the whole (almost) of the mental and physical self. And the higher the pitch in the head resonating cavities the more marked is this feeling of emptiness *under* the platform which, thus poised, seems to the singer to be isolated in space. A wonderful feeling. Actually, all head notes should give this feeling of splendid detachment, of balloon-like suspension.

And so we come to a curious phenomenon: Whereas in the singer's case these high notes are felt as *linear* platforms, varying in length according to the pitch, and nothing else, in the listener's case they come floating over the auditorium in vowel form— "disembodied" globular tone. What a difference between the singer's sensation and the listener's impression! Practically, they are diametrically opposed where the high notes are concerned. Of course the singer himself knows exactly the shape and colour of vowel he is producing through the tiny platform.

To attack and tune in a head tone the singer merely thinks vowel (shape and sound) duly modified in relation to pitch and possibly "mixed" with another vowel tint. *The mere thought of the pre-selected vowel shape is sufficient to create the appropriate platform* as the mental moulding reacts both on the shaping of the mouth-pharynx cavity and on the laryngeal mechanism to the favourable extent of assisting adjustment. If the mental shaping is correct, the mechanical adjustment will be equally correct. And the well-trained singer *knows* by experience that on a high or head note such preconceived vowel shape and sound (that to him resolves itself purely into tonal platform, and nothing else) actually induces (automatically) the correct adjustment of the mouth-pharynx cavity down below, even though he is not conscious of any tonal sensation therein, as explained above. He knows, moreover, that the tonal platform is merely the *top* of the tall, narrow sound-beam produced as a result of the aforesaid mental pre-shaping. He knows that although he feels no vowel, hears no vowel, and no tone below the platform itself of a high note, there is of course a vowel singing all the time within the mouth-pharynx cavity. He knows that the sound-beam of a high note, of which the top monopolizes his attention to the exclusion of all else tonal, re-bounds back into the mouth where, after swirling within its preconceived and adjusted vowel shape, it is despatched as vowel into outer space for the delight, we trust, of an appreciative audience. (See diagram, p. 174.)

On a high (head) note the singer, therefore, should never feel a full-bodied AH or EH or any other vowel either in pure or modified form ringing in the mouth-pharynx cavity; if he does, he is producing his voice badly. (See footnote, p. 54.) Indeed, where *high notes* are concerned, *no tone should be felt in the mouth at all.* He certainly cannot feel or hear a real vowel ringing in the head cavity (above the palate), for that is a physical impossibility. On a head note a large-size vowel and a small focus cannot possibly co-exist: acoustic law puts its foot down on this point in no uncertain terms. But because the thought is of considerable assistance to some students we can compromise in the matter by suggesting that the *top* of the sound-beam carries a *miniature* vowel. As a matter of observed fact the *thought* of creating a miniature vowel high up in the head cavity when attacking a high note is of considerable assistance to the laryngeal mechanism as regards adjustment.

When it is a question of the medium and low notes (from D, fourth line, downwards) it is also a fact that all the tones, all vowels, are felt by the singer to be flooding his mouth and to be no higher than the arc of the palate. The singer is here more or less on a speaking basis. When these notes are produced the impression of vowel tone received by the listener overrides, in amplitude, the sensation of vowel experienced by the singer himself, although there is a certain affinity of perception. On these pitches the listener hears vowel, while the singer both feels and hears vowel; and as the singer can only go by his *internal* sensations and cannot really listen outside himself to advantage (as so many singers try to do in vain), it stands to reason that the tonal perceptions of the listener must be of fuller form. The truth of the matter is that the singer is too close to, too intimately associated with, his own mechanical processes and resonant effects to render possible a complete aural reception and appreciation of the vowelled products (as is possible to the listener), for these, as they pass from him to outer space in finished vowel form replete with harmonic high-lights, colour, and vibrational pattern, can only be fully appreciated at a certain distance from the originator. After all, when any object is too close to the eye no useful visual perception is possible, even as when sound is too close to the ear no distinct or character-istic aural perception is possible. In both cases there is a blurring of sight and hearing because no focusing is possible to eye and ear at such close quarters.

Furthermore, in any attempt the singer may make at external listening and tonal appreciation of his own voice, the external sounds are masked by the more intimate sound motion at work within, which competes against the outer sensation and carries its message more effectively to the brain-cum-mind.

The singer's most profitable work is that of focusing his atten-tion inwards on the mechanical processes and resonant effects that, in the last analysis, bear the same relation to one another as the sun and its rays. And the closer he gets mentally and physically to these tonal sensations and the more intimate his association with

o

them, the more they reveal themselves, the more they "speak" to him in unmistakably clear terms. Consequently, he is better able not only to create but to control and direct them. The most intimate contactual association in this sense can never blur internal perception and appreciation.

The audience as a whole hears vowelled tone from the lowest to the highest pitch and generally takes no cognizance of the vowel modifications necessary to satisfy the mechanical and acoustical requirements of pitch. It takes no cognizance of the decreasing vibrator mass as the pitch rises; and why should it, when such decrease of the primary element is masked to its ears, and more than amply compensated for, by an ever-increasing resonance (which after all is the main thing with which the listener concerns himself, other things being equal), a resonance carrying vowel forms, tonal colours and emotional tints. To illustrate, we could say that the vowelled resonance heard by the listener is the size of a football, and the tonal focus felt by the singer the size of a pin-head when producing his highest note.

CHAPTER XVIII

THAT MECHANICAL MARVEL

SINGERS GENERALLY are not conscious of possessing one of the most wonderful mechanisms of which it is possible to conceive—apart from the beauty of tone it is instrumental in producing.

The vocal cords, actuated by the sixty-odd muscles within the larynx, perform miracles of adjustment with split-second accuracy and vibrate at speeds that the mind's eye is unable to distinguish. And by speeds is meant the number of times they open and close in alternate succession per second, for and during phonation; which number varies according to the pitch.

We know how the cords vary their length, thickness and tension as the singer goes from pitch to pitch. With good production, their note-to-note adjustment is exact. By way of example let us consider the work performed by the soprano mechanism—that we assume to be complete in compass and correct in action. Pictorially we can say that the vibrational structure is built up on three main pillars: The middle C, for which the cords vibrate or, in other words, open and close in alternate succession at the rate of 261 times per second (New Philharmonic pitch); C, third space, for which they vibrate at double the speed, i.e. 522 times per second; and high C, for which the rate is again doubled—1,044 times per second.

Pause just a moment to reflect, while our soprano is producing a high C: in one second of time the cords open and close no less than 1,044 times! This means 62,640 times in one minute if she could hold the note all that time. If we compare with this the 8,000 revolutions per minute, or 133 per second, of a racing-car engine, we shall see that this is a poor performance by the side of the much higher "revs" of the vocal vibrator.

If our soprano sings first, say, middle C and then with the same breath produces high C, the cords adjust themselves with extraordinary rapidity to produce the higher pitch and make a vibrational leap from 261 to 1,044 cycles per second; if she then takes the F in alt, the rate rises to about 1,400 cycles per second.

Consider again for a moment what happens within the larynx as our soprano soars rapidly up the scale with, say, a two-octave spin from the normally lowest to the highest note, and back again. Think of the speed with which a first-class coloratura can ascend and descend the two-octave scale: she may do it in about three seconds. In that short time her cords, to produce the 29 notes, not only adjust themselves by varying in length, thickness and tension, from pitch to pitch 29 times in all, but on ascending, they gradually increase the number of cycles per second from pitch to pitch while getting shorter and thinner and more tensioned gradually all the way up. Inversely, on descending, the cords gradually increase in length and thickness from pitch to pitch while their tension gradually diminishes and the vibrations per second get less and less.

If we divide the three seconds of time expended in the complete run by 29 (the number of notes sung) we find that each adjustment is made in about 1/10th of a second. And to think, furthermore, that each adjustment varies dimensionally and in tension as well as in frequency, according to the pitch; in fact, it has barely time to make one adjustment, vibrate, and produce the tone when the message is flashed for the next tone to appear, which means a slightly different adjustment in length, thickness, tension and frequency; and so on until the play is over. What subordination and obedience to thought, what tractability, what powers of adjustment have been conferred on this relatively minute mechanism! And is it not a further source of wonder and admiration that the speedy adjustments and frequencies obtain in obedience to messages that are mainly subconscious? Mainly, but not entirely, for there must always be a certain degree of conscious ordering, guidance and control.

Think also of the work entailed for the cord mechanism in the case of a song, or more eloquent still, an operatic aria. Think what happens in terms of adjustment and frequency when our singer flits authoritatively, albeit with light touch, from pitch to pitch. We have calculated that when singing the "Caro nome" aria from *Rigoletto*, the soprano's cords open and close approximately 84,000 times, producing therefore an equal number of vibrations as a result of 408 separate adjustments.

The duration of the actual singing in this aria is about four and a half minutes. And if we take the above number as an average and assume a soprano rôle to have an actual singing total of 30 minutes, the opening-closing movements of the cords then reach a grand total of 560,000! Quite a spot of work for them even though, as we assume, it is all done correctly from the mechanical standpoint.*

What hard labour for them when production is not correct and when it is based on sheer physical strength, whatever the length of the rôle.

It is all very wonderful; and so let us conclude by saying with Browning that

> *To know*
> *Rather consists in opening out a way*
> *Whence the imprisoned splendour may escape.*

---

* Dwell for a moment on the marvel of mechanism when we produce a high note, sustain it, then pronounce another syllable or word on it. The consonant finishing the syllable or word and that beginning the new one, interrupts the tone momentarily; the beam stops, but returns to the same spot (if the singer retains the picture of focal height, size and location) as soon as the new vowel sound is produced. In a split second the vocal cords abandon the adjustment for the said high pitch, stop vibrating, readjust themselves in length, thickness and tension *exactly* as before the consonantal "cut", and shoot up the sound-beam again for the same tuning-in.

CHAPTER XIX

PRECEPT AND PRACTICE

IN THE FOREGOING CHAPTERS the extreme importance of the mental factor has repeatedly been stressed. And because physique is far from being all, every possible mental aid must be enlisted by the singer in the practical application of the principles governing vocal mechanism. It is surprising how many pitfalls beset his path in the purely mechanical field; and yet, the technique of singing is merely the concatenation of a few simple processes. And because of the simplicity and delicacy of co-ordinated adjustment of the whole, demanding an exquisite touch, the motive and controlling power is, and should be, mental. In fact, in the sensations of tone experienced by the singer whose production is correct there is apparently little or no physique; and this is particularly true where the upper medium and high notes are concerned.

Matter is ponderous only to the senses of sight and touch. We cannot see the physical basis of vocal tone, but we can *feel* the resultant vibrations, culminating in the sound-beam. Actually it is a feeling-hearing. Over fifty years ago, Lord Kelvin defined matter as being "made up of thought forces". So, in reality, all is mind.

The analysis of vocal technique must have small beginnings, and thought must be educated with slow deliberation. "Slowness is beauty", affirmed Rodin, the famous sculptor. When was a thing of beauty the product of hurry?

If the mind is slow at first to follow and control the varying sensations aroused by the sound-beams, it soon acquires extraordinary dexterity as a result of repeated attempts on the same line. The thought-wave, Science postulates, is the fastest in the universe: faster than light, faster than the radio wave, both of which travel at the rate of 186,000 miles per second. There is nothing the mind cannot accomplish in the sense of creating and controlling vocal tone; and as for following the sensations aroused by the sound-beams and their varying points of impingement of different sizes and intensity of touch, in short, all their regalia, it is mere child's play once the procedure has become habitual. If a student could assume the rôle of passive observer within the mind of a great singer when in action, he would be astounded at the incredible speed and accuracy of his thought—finely subdivided and distributed, creating, adjusting, readjusting, controlling here, there, and everywhere within his tonal domain, expressing so much with such apparent ease and such economy of mental and physical means.

Assuming in the student a certain measure of comprehension of the principles of vocal technique as expounded in the foregoing chapters, and in the parent work, *The Science and Sensations of Vocal Tone*, we offer hereunder some practical suggestions:

THE ASCENDING SCALE

The slow, ascending scale is the finest medium for building up the voice; and this building is very materially assisted if the singer listens inside (never outside) himself.* Commencing from the normally lowest note of the individual voice, the scale should be sung from the tonic to the octave and back again to tonic; then the next scale half a tone higher: tonic to octave and back again; then the next scale; and so on until the normally highest note is reached. Exercise first on the AH vowel, then on AW, OH, OO, EH, EE. Once these classic, or basic, vowels have been thoroughly worked in, the so-called English short vowels, as in *pat*, *pot*, *put*, *pet*, *pit*, readily fall into line and take up their exact positions as they are merely derivatives of the former. Also these short vowels must be gradually modified (rounded) as the pitch rises.

It is the slow climb that provides the finest muscular education for the vocal cords proper and the entire muscular system within the larynx; it builds up stamina and resistance to fatigue. A succession of ascending scales sung slowly is apt to be tiring at first, for they demand an ever-increasing tension as the pitch rises. (It is tantamount to climbing a rope: not the first yard but the last is difficult, on account of fatigue.) The laryngeal muscles have extraordinary powers of rapid recovery, so short bouts of rest work wonders during the daily study. Furthermore, the slow scale affords the student the opportunity and time to feel, listen, analyse, visualize and control the sound-beam as it increases in height, decreases in breadth, and tunes in as the top of it impinges

* The voice-strengthening ascending scale symbolizes life's upward climb tempering mind and soul.

against different points within the resonating cavities as the pitch rises. The ascending scale is all-revealing in every sense; it is a most effectual betrayer of defects, for it makes the product of faulty adjustment stand out in strong relief. The ascending scale is an education *per se* of both mind and voice.

The feeling—which, when marked, becomes visualization—of the gradually increasing height of the beam as the scale is ascended from the normally lowest to the highest note, reminds one of the rise of the mercury in a thermometer when artificial heat is applied to it: it has that fascinatingly smooth rise in the tube which is characteristic of the *feel* of the gradually rising beam within the tonal chamber, taken as a whole.

An added advantage of the slow ascending scale is that it allows for the building in of *the note-to-note lift-up* principle in a much shorter time than otherwise would be the case. And the quicker the student forms the lift-up habit the better. After all, the end of all exercise is habit forming, of both mind and muscle.

Hereunder is an excellent slow scale used by every exponent of the old Italian School in the past (today it is rarely used and is practically forgotten):

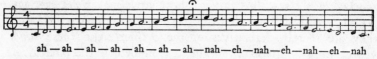

ah — ah — ah — ah — ah — ah — ah — nah — eh — nah — eh — nah — eh — nah

Then transpose up a semitone at a time so that progressively the scales of D♭, D♮, E♭, E♮, F, F♯, G, and so on, will be sung up and down until the normally highest note is reached.

In the foregoing chapters we have already explained in detail how and why the vowels must be modified gradually as the pitch rises. The student must be careful not to overdo the vowel modification or colouring, as distortion is just round the corner.

When the tenor, soprano, mezzo or contralto enter the so-called head resonator on F♯, fifth line (whatever the vowel used), it is a good plan, as explained on p. 139, to approximate the tonal shaping and quality as well as the focal height, size and location, to the G. Note that we say "approximate" only. Therefore the singer should:

Produce F♯ more like G than F♮
    „   G   „   „ A♭   „ F♯
    „   A♭ „   „ A♮ „ G
    „   A♮ „   „ B♭ „ A♭
    „   B♭ „   „ B♮ „ A♮

For tenors, sopranos, mezzos and contraltos.

and so on.

Not that the lower will sound like the higher note because, particularly on the head pitches, each note is quite an individual with its own characteristic form and quality. But the very fact of approximating the lower to the higher note in this way is of considerable assistance to general adjustment. It also assists exact "tuning".

As regards the head resonator of baritones and basses, the singer should effect the above-mentioned approximation, and

Produce E♭ more like E♮ than D
    „   E♮   „   „ F♮ „ E♭
    „   F   „   „ F♯ „ E♮
    „   F♯   „   „ G   „ F♮
    „   G   „   „ A♭ „ F♯
    „   A♭   „   „ A♮ „ G

All this, of course, on general lines only, because there must not be any hard and fast rule where vocal colours are concerned, except to confine them within certain physiological and acoustical limits. For instance, it is not always desirable for tenors and sopranos (and mezzos and contraltos) to produce F♯, fifth line, with a G approximation; the mood or emotion to be expressed might well require a slightly more open tone, albeit perfectly "tuned". Equally, it is not always desirable for the baritone and bass to produce E♭, fourth space, with a typical head voice quality, Or E♮, such as to approximate the F♮, fifth line, which latter *must* be of head voice quality, and never openish. More often than not these two categories will produce E♭ and E♮ with a nicely rounded open*ish* tone which seems merely a rounded continuation of the D♮, fourth line, which should always be openish in quality, except occasionally when it can be given a head voice quality for *mezzavoce* purposes, as explained elsewhere. Note that we say "open*ish*", i.e. with the "corner" rounded off, which does not mean wide-open or blatant tone. Most tenors, sopranos and mezzos can and should produce the F and F♯ (the head voice entry note) with nicely open tone, the vowel being just sufficiently rounded off, which must never be blatant. In every individual voice there is a point beyond which tone-opening must never go.

The whole idea of such approximation is chiefly to assist the mechanical adjustment of the cords and the shaping of the mouth-pharynx in relation to pitch and vowel; consequently, it is particularly useful in scale work, and *vocalizzi* in general.

WHEN DESCENDING

As each scale is descended in turn the student should be alert to the tonal sensations, of which the changes of direction of the sound-beam, of location, and of focal size are particularly marked when the descent occurs from the highest to the medium notes.

It is an excellent plan, when the singer comes down even only a semitone, to retain, as far as possible, the same tonal feeling of size and quality. For example, if we are singing high Ab and then have to descend to G, we should bear in mind and voice the Ab quality and general feeling of height, size, and location, and produce the G accordingly; whereupon it will maintain adequate tension and the intrinsic qualities of lightness and firmness as well as of rotundity. We call this tonal *grooving*. This mental process prevents any possible excessive "drop" or spreading of the tone. By the same token if a soprano has to sing a rapidly descending run of five notes or more, from a high pitch, it is well for her to keep in mind the general quality, shaping, and size of this high note and then "groove" in, so to speak, all the descending notes. Which simple process effectually prevents tonal splaying, or opening to excess, as the lower notes are being produced.

With a descending phrase, a drop of a second, or third, a whole octave or more, there is a tendency in all voices to over-release the vibrator tension and splay out the tone. To obviate this we tell the student (apart from the "grooving" mentioned above) to "come down on a thin tonal line" and "keep the tone up as you come down". These ideas work wonders.

THE TONAL TRIANGLE

Great prominence was given in the parent work, *The Science and Sensations of Vocal Tone*, to this phenomenon of resonance, in view of its paramount importance in the domain of vocal sensations. We called it "The Triangle of Laryngeal Platforms" because the tonal sensations as experienced by the singer whose production is correct are, particularly on the upper medium and high notes, linear in form, exactly reflecting the varying vibrator adjustments or, in other words, the amount of vocal cord in length and vertical thickness employed in relation to pitch. Which linear form is given by the *top* of the sound-beam which, as we know, is short and broad on the lowest note, tall and narrow on the highest note, with all the well-graduated sizes intervening between these two extremes. Consequently, the tonal sensation of the lowest note is compounded as a relatively long and thickish *horizontal* vibrating line, or platform, lying crosswise within the mouth-pharynx cavity, and that of the highest note, say top C, or higher, an extremely short and thin line of vocal vibration (actually more a focused point than a line). The base of the tonal triangle is formed by the biggest platform, and the apex by the smallest platform (a mere tonal point on the extreme high notes). From the lowest pitch up to and including D, fourth line (in all voices), the singer can feel both a full-bodied vowel and "platform" within the mouth-pharynx cavity, whereas from E♭ (fourth space) upwards, he no longer feels a full-orbed vowel but just *platform* (the *top* of the sound-beam) as it gets gradually smaller and smaller while soaring into the head cavities with the rising pitch. And not only do the platforms get smaller as the pitch rises, but brighter and more intense, more highly "polished", arousing in the singer the sensation of something akin to a miniature limelight.

We know that as the pitch rises from the lowest to the highest note, the effective cord length (in good production) gets gradually shorter and thinner, and, in consequence, the sound-beam gradually narrows as it increases in height. Hence the sensation, for the singer himself, of small platforms or foci on high notes. It is a wonderful phenomenon, yet so simple that its apprehension is easily possible to all.*

If we take a complete vocal scale of, say, two octaves and consider only the *top* of the ascending sound-beam resulting there-

---

* If the student will persevere in concentrating on his tonal sensations inside the resonating spaces (and *never* listen to the tone outside himself) he will ultimately succeed in clearly visualizing these ever-decreasing platforms, forming a Tonal Triangle as the pitch rises. It is precisely the constant exercise of this hearing-feeling (the sound, internal sound, and *touch* of the top of the beam) which sharpens the mind's eye in no small degree. (See diagram on title-page.)

from, it is easy to grasp the principle of the Triangle of tonal sensations. (We speak here of beam in the singular, as we are assuming the complete scale to be sung on one breath and one vowel, either AH or EH, which are the best for revealing the triangle). Particularly on the upper medium and high notes, it is not the beam itself in its entirety, from vibrator to point of impingement, that impresses the mind of the singer, but just the *top* thereof as it impinges, or "leans" (appoggio) against certain well-defined points within the resonating cavities. And this phenomenon applies to the beams of all the vowels.

Now the extraordinary part of it all is that whereas the vocal cords lie horizontally, but pointing forwards within the larynx (a protective cartilaginous box), the tonal "lines" (platforms) are crosswise (at right angles) to them, or rather to the line they form when fully adducted.

This linear form assumed by the tonal sensations (felt and ultimately visualized by the singer as lying crosswise within the resonating space), exactly reflects or mirrors the diameter of the beam; which diameter exactly reflects in turn the effective length and vertical thickness of the vocal cords employed, and varying, naturally, according to the pitch. Therefore as the pitch rises (and this means a rising frequency) and the beam with it, the linear sensation of the tone gets gradually shorter and thinner. Hence the sensation of a tonal triangle.* The mirrored images of vocal tone

---

* These reflected or mirrored images of the vibrator adjustments constitute the linchpin of vocal technique and production; and the constant noting by the student of their tonal *feel* will help him ultimately to *see* them and memorize their varying sizes in relation to pitch. Through such touch-visualization the singer is able immediately to gauge to a fine degree of accuracy the amount of vibrator he is employing at the moment. If excessive, he is made aware of the excess, however slight, by means of this *measuring feel* coupled to *mental vision*, and so is able correctly to readjust the particular laryngeal setting.

The student will be interested to know that two famous singers, whose technique was outstanding—Dinh Gilly, the French baritone, and Giovanni Inghilleri, the Italian baritone—used exactly the same words, albeit in their respective languages, when referring to the Tonal Triangle after perusal of the manuscript of *The Science and Sensations of Vocal Tone*. The words are verbatim; and be it noted, that at the time (1929) the two artists had never met: "The triangle is *so true;* but I should never have thought of putting it in diagrammatic form like that." Tetrazzini, Gigli, Schipa, Hislop, and the other famous singers who commended in writing the parent work, remarked on the "truth" of the tonal triangle.

are particularly sharp on the highest notes, almost approaching the quality and sensation of light, concentrated light.

The top of the vertically-soaring beam of the AH vowel sung on the lowest note impinges against the arc of the palate, practically in the middle; however, this impinging, *appoggio*, is not at all marked; consequently the singer's mind is not very impressed. It is only just *after* the first octave that it really begins to take notice of the touch and live presence of the top of the beam. Another phenomenon is that the beam itself does not seem to increase in height or narrow perceptibly during this first octave (though it does both these things almost imperceptibly). The observant student will note a very gradual and almost imperceptible rise of the beam and decrease in tonal size even on the first octave. His best plan, however, is to "lean" the tone even of the lowest pitch against the arc of the palate. It will only be perhaps a "vapour" touch, but will be sufficient to tune in the beam. After the first octave the touch of the top of the beam will no longer be "vapoury"; the feather-touch gives way to a touch, a "leaning", which becomes more marked the higher the pitch rises. On the highest notes, the frequency of the extremely narrow beam is such that it gives the feeling of a miniature drill, a tiny tonal drill which is very vital, and *glowing* high up in a V-shaped cavity.

When the heavier categories produce their lowest note, the basic tone is so preponderant (their thickness of cord is such that its forcible vibration overmasters the resonating partner) that *their* first tonal line of the triangle is felt by them to be on a level with the larynx itself or, say, in the laryngeal region. Their basic rumble is quite marked, whereas that of the lighter calibres (tenors and sopranos) is sometimes barely noticeable to the singers themselves; by way of compensation, however, they feel more resonance than rumble. So the only difference between the light and the heavy calibres lies in the fact that the first few tonal lines of the triangle are more marked in the latter than in the former.

The AH and the EH (we mean here a single sound as in *where, said*) are the best for visualizing a well-defined tonal triangle. Let the student make the following test by singing on one and the same low note slowly (stressing the vowel):

Bella Where Led Lid Been

with an EH-tone pointing vertically upwards. As he does so he will note the four degrees of narrowing of the EH sound (the sensation being that of parallel lines gradually narrowing, like sliding doors closing a gap); after which comes the EE sound which narrows the gap still more. We have included the EE vowel as we consider it a very closed, compacted *eh* (even as *oo* is a closely compacted AH, when viewed in the proper light). This sensation of five successively narrowing vertical spaces is due to the tongue rising, and the soft palate lowering in equal degree, in order to form these variations of actually one vowel sound. After all, they are merely modifications of the open EH sound in *bella*, which the Romans pronounce quite open without being blatant. In other words, the five sensations are due to the gradual narrowing of the mouth-pharynx chamber. The EH in *bella* requires a mouth more vertically open than for the EH in *where*, and a progressively closer lip-to-lip aperture for *led*, *lid*, *been*. The extremely narrow space felt in the mouth when singing EE on a low note is due to the fact that in order to form and produce this sound the tongue is raised almost to the point of touching the arc of the palate, while the soft palate descends in equal degree, thus leaving a very narrow space for the tone to squeeze into and come out of the mouth.

The next experiment consists of singing slowly up the scale from the lowest to the normally highest note on the EH vowel (not a diphthong, but one sound, as stated above) which, to begin with, and for our present purposes, should be open as that in *bella*. As the pitch rises the EH should undergo gradual modification, passing through the narrowing colours as in *where*, then that of *led*, and finally, on the highest notes, of the still narrower *eh* as in *lid*. (Actually, as found also in such words as *kin*, *fin*, *mint*, this sound is composed of *two* "short" vowels, intoned simultaneously, i.e. the *eh* in *fed*, *met*, etc., and a much "shortened" *ee*. It is a fifty-fifty combination, with the *ee* half resting on top of the *eh* half. It is wonderful how the pharynx adjusts itself in this way. The student can prove the existence of this double vowel by intoning it on not too low a note, and gradually releasing the *eh* sound, which is the under half, and leaving only the *ee* singing, or vice versa, gradually releasing the *ee* sound, which is the upper half, and leaving only the *eh* singing.)

Now this test on the ascending scale reveals a tonal narrowing due *solely* to the gradual narrowing of the sound-beam as the pitch rises, whereas the first test revealed a narrowing of the tone due to the gradual narrowing of the actual chamber in the mouth-pharynx. Two totally different sensations, two totally different causes.

By way of experiment, the student should now reverse the first test and sing, on the same low note, *been, lid, led, where, bella,* and note the gradual opening of the vertical tonal shaft; this is due to the tongue and soft palate working in reverse action to the first test, gradually withdrawing from the palatal arc and thereby increasing the cavital space.

Will the student please remember that all vowel modifications must be made mentally, whereupon the parts concerned will automatically adjust themselves in obedience to the thought. There must be no deliberate physical modification of the shape of the mouth-pharynx cavity, because this inevitably leads to over-emphasis and consequent tonal distortion.

THE MEANING OF "PLATFORM"

The term "platform" was first used in the parent work, and is also mentioned so often in the present volume that it calls for more detailed explanation.*

We chose this word as it adequately expresses not merely a physical fact but also a tonal sensation. It reflects the sensation aroused by the close approximation of the vocal cords when tone is being produced. The curious part of it is that whereas, for the purposes of phonation, the cords open and close in rapid alternate succession, the singer has only the sensation of the actual approximation, and never of their opening. In fact, as a sensation, they feel to be closed all the time a note is being produced. Furthermore, the singer feels that he is mentally and tonally "leaning", or say "standing", on a small vibrating surface or platform offering a certain degree of resistance; the feeling is one of flexible firmness, and resolves into the sensation of a tonal line. It is

* Although the meaning of "platform" was adequately explained in the parent work, a certain type of individual thinks fit to discredit, with enamelled sneers, verbally or in writing, not merely the term itself but also its significance. Its importance to the singer escapes them. One of the most contemptible traits of the human mind is to pooh-pooh that which is new, or strange, or not understood for lack of knowledge. Which lack, of course, must be filled in somehow as a save-face.

precisely *on* this tonal line or platform that the singer builds his vowelled tone, and lives, moves, and has his vocal being. Due to the ever-increasing tension as the pitch rises, the high notes, resolving themselves into tonal lines greatly decreased in length and thickness, more than ever give the sensation of resilient little platforms that, even though coupled in and resonating high up within the head cavities, are so vital, so exactly *reflecting* the life and substance of the laryngeal source, as to cause the singer almost to believe that his vocal cords were actually located and vibrating in the head cavities themselves. Indeed an extraordinary phenomenon of resonance.

In order to make this point clear, we give hereunder an exercise which will help the student to understand what we mean by "platform":

Moderato

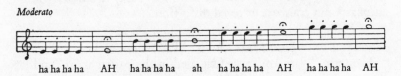

ha ha ha ha   AH   ha ha ha ha   ah   ha ha ha ha   AH   ha ha ha ha   AH

As the first four notes of each group are being sung *staccato* (with a short aspirate preceding the *a* sound, as in *father*) the student will note, or rather feel-hear, four small tonal "taps", so to speak. These are produced by the approximated cords, and although of short duration he will feel (if the *a* is produced clearly) a short line or point of resistance which, however, has a certain resilient firmness about it. As he passes to the AH on the semibreve, with the same breath, the sensation is that he is mentally and tonally *on* a tiny, resilient platform which, while vibrating, is *flexibly* solid. Platform is vibrational contact. The idea of platform and its function is all-important for the singer, for it is, and reflects, the very source of vocal tone, the source of the sound-beam. As we know, this source or base gets smaller and smaller as the pitch rises to the highest note. While the platform on the lowest notes is felt (in all voices, but in varying degree) as a vibrational contact in the region of the larynx, it does not remain there; it assumes gradually a higher position as the pitch rises and the sound-beam with it, firstly in the mouth-pharynx cavity up to D, fourth line (all voices), and then from E♭, fourth space, upwards, in the head cavities. The platform rises rapidly with the pitch from this E♭ upwards, and noticeably so for the singer himself. And what is this rising platform? It is merely the *top* of the sound-beam which the singer feels as a gradually decreasing tonal line, decreasing in length and thickness as the pitch rises to the highest note. Furthermore, as the pitch rises so the platform becomes clearer and brighter as a line, as well as getting "tougher"; this is due to the increasing tension and frequency as the pitch rises. On the other hand, from the lowest note up to D, fourth line, the platforms are not so clean-cut or bright, or firm; and this is due to the relatively lower tension and frequency.

We said elsewhere that on the lowest note the sound-beam was not at all distinct as a sensation and that its touch against the arc of the palate was rather "vapoury"; on the other hand, the basic rumble of the cords vibrating in their entire length and thickness on the lowest notes is much more impressive as far as the singer's mind is concerned. So that is why we say the first platforms are felt in the laryngeal region.* It is only about after the first octave (from the lowest note) has been sung that the *top* of the sound-beam begins to make itself felt by the singer as it impinges against the arc of the palate at given points according to the vowel and the pitch. What has happened? Quite an appreciable amount of vocal cord in length and depth will have been "eliminated" (when production is correct) during that first octave, and the rumble, therefore, is less impressive, with the sound-beam coming into its own gradually more and more. In other words, the basic rumble (platform) of the lowest note has risen to reveal itself, after the first octave, as the *top* of the beam. Added to this sensation, the singer will also feel, up to D, fourth line, full-bodied

* This is quite a normal and natural sensation because (1) the vocal cords, on the lowest notes, are engaged practically in their entire length and depth, and (2) part of the resonance is sublaryngeal, or below the larynx, where it can be felt and heard by gently tapping the chest with the fingertips just where the neck ends, while the low note is being produced. While sound is always produced *above* the cords, it does excite the sympathetic vibration of the lower bone structure and thoracic cavity; and this sublaryngeal vibration is what the old School also called chest voice (*voce di petto*). Inversely, if the chest is tapped in the same place while a well-produced high note is being held, no sound is felt or heard in this region. This phenomenon is due to the fact that a well-produced high note engages little cord; consequently the basic rumble is not sufficient to excite any sympathetic vibration of the lower bone structure. (See footnote, p. 197.)

P

vowels filling his mouth-pharynx cavity. As soon as platform is felt as the *top* of the beam impinging against a given point within the resonating system, the sensation of laryngeal rumble will be practically non-existent.

From E♭, fourth space, upwards, the sensation of vowel filling the mouth-pharynx cavity begins to leave the singer, and gradually as the pitch rises all he feels is platform ever-decreasing in size (length and thickness) until the highest note is reached. This is due to the gradual narrowing of the sound-beam as it soars gradually higher and higher in the head cavities. This completes the tonal triangle of "platforms" (or tonal lines), the base of which, felt in the laryngeal region, is the lowest note being produced by the vocal cords in their entire length and vertical thickness (depth); while the apex, felt high up in the head cavities, is the highest note being produced by the merest front tip of the vocal cords. As a matter of fact, the sensation aroused when a coloratura or light soprano is correctly producing E♭, E♮ or F in alt is not a tonal line but just a tonal point, flexibly tough, feels like a tiny drill and that it is emitting light, so to speak. The following spot gives the student an idea of the size of this tonal point:*

.

Naturally, the sensation aroused by the highest note, or notes, of all the different calibres of voices, male and female, will vary as regards size of tonal focus; the bigger the individual calibre, the relatively bigger will be the tonal focus of the highest note, but still very small. The size of the focus reflects exactly the amount of cord used. All coloraturas and light sopranos should feel their very highest notes as no bigger than the above focal point (when produced correctly). Even the high C has only a tiny focus, whatever the calibre of the voice. (A tiny focus in a big V-shaped space.)

If the mental picture of the whole process is clear in one's mind, it is really quite simple. But simple things are often overlooked and made quite complicated.

It is the *top* of the sound-beam which arouses in the singer the

---

* This point was put on paper by the author's daughter, Alma, a coloratura, to illustrate *the size of the tonal sensation* (or focus) aroused when producing a perfect E♮ in alt. And by this we mean a perfectly adjusted and produced note of glittering quality, warmth, and power (having nothing in common with that species of whistle which so many light sopranos produce on the extreme pitches).

sensation of platform, as it becomes clearly delineated from about
C or C♯, third space, in tenor and all female voices, and increasingly so as from E♭, fourth space. (In baritones and basses this
occurs a little lower.) As the pitch rises from these points, so the
platform gets clearer, and easier to visualize through feeling-
hearing. Now the top of the beam exactly reflects the effective
cord length (and depth) being engaged at the time, and of course
the frequency. And the top of the beam, which we call platform,
is so alive, so vivid, that the singer could swear that his vocal cords
were actually vibrating in the head cavities; this is the case *in all
well-produced upper medium and high notes* inasmuch as *the singer
himself has no tonal sensation whatever in his throat.* The platform is
merely the projected image, so to speak, of the effective length of
the cords working down below in the larynx. If, for example, the
effective cord length for a given high note were no bigger than a
pinhead (as illustrated above for E in alt), the "projected image"
carried by the top of the beam would naturally be no bigger than
a pinhead—the beam itself being just a pencil line of equal
diameter. (Any light soprano producing a *good* high C or more
will tell you that she feels only "a pinpoint" of tone, and nothing
else. It is quite obvious that only a pinpoint of cord could produce
such a tiny tonal focus by means of an equally narrow beam:
See footnote, p. 226.)

It is similar to the picture thrown on the screen by means of a
beam of light. At the cinema the picture we see is only the *top* of
the projected beam of light carrying the reflected image of the
actual picture located within the operator's cabin. But this projected, or reflected, picture on the screen is as real to us as the
actual one in the cabin which we are not permitted to see. Likewise the real vibrational "picture", or amount of cord, is located
in the larynx, and the image thereof is carried up to the resonating
cavities by the sound-beam and there "projected" against certain
points, according to the vowel and pitch. The higher the pitch, the
smaller the "picture" in the larynx, and therefore the smaller the
reflected image carried by the top of the sound-beam. Whereas in
the cinema the picture on the screen is a very big enlargement of
the tiny 35 mm. film in the operator's cabin, the tonal "picture",
or platform, projected in the head cavities is exactly the same size
as the original one in the larynx (see footnote, p. 220).

A clean attack means creating a good platform, the foundation of all vowelled tone. This vibrational contact must be maintained all the time a note is being produced. By good platform we mean a clear-cut vibration, and not a foggy, mushy thing of little life and tone. A woolly platform is no platform; it has no firmness and seemingly with a hole in the centre through which the tone, as a sensation, falls through. Such a badly adjusted platform can never produce good, clean, bright tone. What happens is that the cords do not approximate sufficiently, and apart from having insufficient tension, they thus permit an escape of breath through the too-open cords. Muscular re-education is the only remedy, and special exercises must be used. The above exercise is extremely useful in such cases for it will help the student to acquire a neatly adjusted platform, which means well approximated cords. A clean, resilient, brightly vibrant platform is the base, the mother of vocal tone—the father being the breath and the pressure it exerts against the approximated cords. So this exercise should be practised daily on every note for a time, as it also develops the *feel* of platform.

To acquire the idea and the substance of platform the student has the following operational "keys": (1) good vowel shaping in relation to pitch; (2) smooth tonal attack; (3) tonal flow; (4) exact knowledge of the *natural* direction taken by the sound-beams of the different vowels, from the lowest to the highest note; (5) well-governed application of the breath pressure.

Hereunder is an exercise which will help to tone up the laryngeal

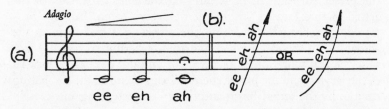

Then transpose up a semitone at a time. The *eh* sound must be very narrow indeed, almost like that in *pin*, and therefore very close to the *ee* sound. The transition from *ee* to *eh*, and *eh* to *ah* must be made with oil-smoothness *without loss of tension*. To achieve this, the student must, so to speak, pull the *eh* ou. of the *ee* in an upward-backward direction, and the same with the *ah* out of the *eh*. The upward-backward pull is mainly mental. The angle of the upward-backward pull is as at (*b*). The *eh* must be a single sound as in *egg*, and should be sung as narrow as the *i* in *fig*.

muscles and so induce a closer approximation of the cords as soon as they are called upon to sing. It is a strenuous exercise, so a short period of rest half-way up the scale may be advisable. Also the tone-closing exercises on p. 231 are a wonderful "tonic", and should be practised daily.

ON TONE-CLOSING

The tone-closing principle and process is enshrouded in the main today in, frankly, something approaching complete ignorance. Students everywhere are told "to cover" the tone, to put it "in the mask", "over the eyes", and, above all, "well forward" all the time. These wonderful "formulas" are supposed to produce the head voice. They certainly succeed in closing and humping the singer's throat and bottling up the tone into unintelligible vowels and words. One and all they spell tonal distortion in varying degree, for the simple reason that the vibrator and resonator systems are thrown right out of gear by such blind procedure. These same methods are not peculiar to any one country; indeed, they are in vogue everywhere, for to teach them requires no particular study, no thought, no hard work, no art. And is it not symptomatic that the number of first-rate singers all over the world is fast decreasing? Their number can actually be counted on the fingers, whereas mediocrity is countless. And yet there are thousands of really fine voices, as good as Dame Nature ever created; but there are thousands of bad teachers waiting for them, to pump in the above false methods and so ruin many potential singers. But for this, so many would have made the grade.

In our own small way we can say that these lurid facts are borne out too eloquently. In the last thirty years literally hundreds of students, including teachers and professional singers, have sought our advice. Nearly every one of them had been taught "to cover" and put the voice ' well forward". Interrogation as to the meaning of "cover" and *how* the tone had to be "covered", and what with, elicited no intelligent answer from any one of them, but merely a confused state of thought on the subject. Not one mentioned *vowel*. When we hinted that possibly something had to be done with the vowel in order to produce what is called head tones, we were rewarded in most cases with a blank stare. It is a pitiful state of affairs which a referendum, even in this country alone, would forcibly reveal. With the blind thus leading the blind, where do we go?

This is no tirade against teachers' integrity. We are trying to expose systems that are as false and harmful as they are stupid. To anyone truly in love with the divine art (and there are countless thousands who are) it is all the more galling to contemplate the present vocal ruin when we consider how simple is the tone-closing principle and process, how beautifully natural, as we now propose to explain in a practical way. But the student must make up his mind that to get results certain physiological and acoustical laws *must* be obeyed; these laws, as far as they govern vocal mechanism and tone, have been adequately explained in foregoing chapters. However, it will be necessary to refer to them again.

We know that as the pitch rises from the lowest to the highest note the vowel (shape and tone) must be gradually modified or rounded in order to "close" the tone, particularly on the upper medium and high pitches. *What is this tone-closing?* Acoustically speaking, *it is nothing but the gradual narrowing of the sound-beam as the pitch rises,* which is the indirect outcome of the vowel-rounding process (as explained in Chapter XIII).

By way of preliminary experiment let the student sing, slowly and deliberately, AH-AW-OH-OO on the same low pitch. In doing so he will note that for the transition from AH to AW the mouth closes slightly, from AW to OH considerably more so, and from OH to OO still more; let him then swing backwards from OO to AH and forward again to OO, and back again to AH, and so on several times in succession. The narrowing of the tone felt on passing from AH to OO is merely due to the gradual closing of the mouth; and vice versa, the widening of the tone felt when passing from OO to AH is merely the result of the gradual opening of the mouth. There is no question here of any *actual* closing of the tone itself, because the sound-beam really remains unaltered in size, as indeed it must in order to express the particular pitch on which the test was made. As already explained in previous chapters, to every pitch corresponds a sound-beam of definite size, height and width. In good production this requirement of acoustic law is seldom if ever really violated; but cockeyed methods, such as are listed above, are directly instrumental in violating this particularly vital law, with the dire results we are invited to applaud.

The next experiment clearly reveals the true tone-closing process. No personal method or fad is involved, no guesswork, no humbug, but just plain acoustical facts as revealed in tonal sensations.

The following exercises will not only drill and mould both the vibrator and resonator systems but also help the student to visualize, through tonal feeling-hearing, the gradual narrowing (closing) of the tone, and by tone we mean here sound-beam:

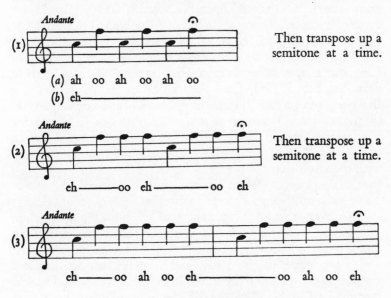

(1) (a) ah oo ah oo ah oo
(b) eh————————

Then transpose up a semitone at a time.

(2) eh————oo eh————oo eh

Then transpose up a semitone at a time.

(3) eh————oo ah oo eh————————oo ah oo eh

Then transpose up a semitone at a time.

The above are for sopranos, tenors, mezzos and contraltos. Baritones and basses should start a little lower.

EXERCISE 1: First of all we assume that the student has now some knowledge of the behaviour of the sound-beam, the direction it takes in relation to a given pitch and vowel, and the height to which it rises.

As the singer goes from C to F he must *allow* (by thinking) the tone (sound-beam) to swing slightly back from the vertical and then up. Let him get *mentally behind* the AH tone on C and ride up on it to the F, on OO, and he will feel-hear how the tone narrows on the way up and curls over slightly as OO is produced. Transpose up and repeat the process from C♯ to F♯, and then from D to G, E♭ to A♭, and so on. And the higher he goes in this way the more noticeable the narrowing or "closing" of the tone. Actually it is the sound-beam which is getting narrower. When we said that the singer must "ride up on the tone" when moving to the higher pitch, we really mean on and with the platform, because, as a tonal sensation, it is the platform which gets gradually smaller, being the top of the beam. The student will remember that as the pitch rises the OO should open out towards OH, a mixed tone therefore; let him *think in* the *u* in *put*, from high G upwards.

The next on our programme is (*b*) of Exercise 1. Before making the test, the student should refresh his memory by referring to Diagrams 1, 2, 8. Whereas in exercise (*a*) the OO-beam tends to draw away backwards from the vertical as the pitch rises, the EH-beam of exercise (*b*) tunes in just back of the vertical also on the highest pitch. But in going to the higher note on EH the singer must not go straight up vertically (just because the beam is close to the vertical) as that may stiffen the parts and cramp his throat, with the result that the tone will "stick". He must *mentally* pull-back, lift-up, and more or less straighten up afterwards, and in doing so he must narrow the EH vowel by *thinking* of (not doing) the narrower *eh* sound in *egg*, or even of *bid* on the highest pitches. The mental pull-back frees and opens the throat, permitting the sound-beam to soar without obstruction. By mentally shaping the vowel according to the pitch, and mentally anticipating and visualizing the direction the sound-beam of a given vowel should take (and will take, if *allowed* to), the beam will soar up at that same angle and automatically tune in to the right spot within the appropriate resonating zone. The singer, therefore, has no actual "tone placing" to do, physically speaking. The more physique he clears out of the way, within reason, the better. With few exceptions, the average singer today is earthbound; what little thought he employs for and during production is mostly embedded in his diaphragm and his face (forward production), with brute force striving to make both ends meet! This modern conception is called "technique", but it is a travesty.

EXERCISE 2: As written, it is suitable for sopranos, tenors, mezzos and contraltos. Baritones and basses should start a little lower.

First, the student rides up from C to F on the EH-beam with a mental pull-back, lift-up, and straightening of the tone to just back of the vertical on F (*thinking* the while of a slightly narrower *eh* sound, as stated above); he then pulls back to the OO, which on F is not far back from the vertical and therefore fairly close to the EH position. A very important point to remember when pulling back on the F from EH to OO is to keep the tone exactly the same "size" during the transition; we tell the pupil to "groove" the tone. In other words, it means keeping the same size of platform without widening it in the slightest. (It means, again in other words, maintaining the same width of beam. Which is in keeping with the acoustical fact that *pitch determines the width of the beam*, and two or ten different vowels sung on the same pitch must not change the width of the beam natural to that pitch. Should the singer open the focus when passing from one vowel to another *on the same pitch*, he will derange the laryngeal setting and engage a length of cord which is in excess of the true effective length required for that pitch. The tonal product will therefore not be good.) As he passes from OO back to EH, on F, the same tonal grooving must be made, by *thinking* and *willing* it, whereupon the parts will react to the thought accordingly. Then down the vertical EH shaft again to the C, and repeat the exercise once more, as above. *If the tone produced is consistently good*, verily *it is the voice of the mind*. The next thing is to transpose up a semitone, and repeat the process. And so on, semitone by semitone, up to, say, the interval F to B, or G to C. As the interval gets higher and higher, so the *eh* vowel must be modified or narrowed towards that in *bed* and finally to that in *bid*. Remember also that the swing back to *oo* from the *eh* position, and the forward travel back to the *eh* again, must be grooved, as stated above; and the higher the pitch the narrower becomes the grooving, or, in other words, the smaller the platform. On these head notes (from high G upwards) do *not* use the lips to produce the *oo*, for that is fatal to good production. As stated above, the *oo* must be "loose", which means mixed with a percentage of *oh;* to this end you can think of the *u* in *put*, which will be felt to be formed and produced well back of the vertical on high notes. The starting note of the exercise, which is a C, should be sung with openish EH vowel, as in *Mary*. As the starting note gets higher and higher, this EH sound should be slightly narrowed towards that of *nest* (without actually touching the latter's narrowness which is best reserved for the higher notes), while the mouth, internally and externally, takes on the shape of an inverted U. The student should make every effort to get a complete mental picture of these tonal things; when he does, he will be well on his way to technical success.

The next is EXERCISE 3, which is an amplification of Exercise 2 with the added vowel of AH. The remarks for (2) apply to (3) in every way. We would point out, however, that when passing from OO to AH on the F there is a certain backward movement noticeable to the student. But as the exercise is transposed up gradually higher and higher, so this OO to AH pull-back movement becomes gradually less until on A or B♭ the movement is practically nil; this is due to the fact that on such high pitches the OO vowel opens out somewhat to OH (or rather must be allowed to by the singer) in order to produce a mixed vowel tone very similar to the *u* in *put*, and, on the other hand, the AH on those

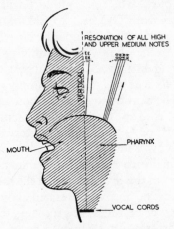

DIAGRAM 13

N.B.—*On all high or head notes none of the shaded part in the above diagram is, in the singer's sensation, engaged for tuning or focusing purposes; in other words, all sound-beams of the high notes, whatever the vowel employed, long or short, tune into the head resonating zone above the palatal arc and behind the vertical. Consequently, the singer has no sensation whatever of focused tone in the mouth-pharynx cavity. Furthermore, the shaded part is non-existent as sensation—that is when the singer is producing his head notes correctly; he must not attempt, therefore, to employ this part for creating or even assisting tonal tuning or focusing. (The reverberation some singers feel, or imagine they feel, in the frontal bone structure has nothing in common with the actual focusing of the sound-beam; reverberation must not be confused with focusing. It is because of the cartilaginous reverberation in the nose that the "on the mask" and "over the eyes" methods were evolved; but that is mistaking the shadow for the substance.*

pitches must be rounded off towards AW with an added tinge of *oh* or *oo;* consequently, also the AH becomes a mixed vowel tone. As a result, the AH focus is, so to speak, half merged into the *oo* focus. Notwithstanding this close proximity of focus (platform) the singer must *think* and *will in* this minute and almost imperceptible pull-back from *oo* to *ah* on the same high pitch. He must be careful to "groove" the tone or platform during this backward movement, and also on the return journey *ah-oo-eh* on the same note. If the student transposes the exercise up to F-B♭, or higher, he will note how the tone (sound-beam) gets narrower and narrower the higher the note, as revealed in the decreasing size of the platform.

The above exercises are sufficient to give the student a good idea of the tone-closing process producing what is called head voice. He will realize how simple the whole process is, how there is absolutely nothing to "cover", and how *all* high notes, whatever the vowel used, *are far removed from his face*, being well back of the vertical (see Diagram 13, p. 234). He will note the difference between the seeming tone-closing of the above-mentioned experimental test on the low note, due to the closing of the mouth, and the actual tone-closing or gradual narrowing of the sound-beam itself as the pitch rises. These exercises are also extremely useful for *drilling and toning-up the entire muscular system* governing the mechanism of the vocal cords and the action of the parts responsible for shaping the mouth-pharynx cavity, the importance of which shaping is revealed in preceding chapters.

N.B.—These exercises may be found rather fatiguing; an occasional rest of about a minute is salutary.

The above forms a substantial part of what is called technique. *This tone-closing process,* whereby correct head tones are produced, *is what thousands upon thousands of students and singers in every country are searching for,* and in vain in most cases. Instead they are told to "cover", and what not. To cover is hump and to smother. To think that such a simple process should be so overlooked and warped into a parody, as indeed it is today more than ever. It requires no professional intelligence to understand and apply it; but it does demand honest, unremitting study and application, which not all are willing to give. The wrong way, however idiotic, is more easily "mastered", and because of it the thousands fall an easy victim.

The student is well advised never to attempt listening outside himself to the tone he is producing; on the contrary, he must listen inside himself (mouth-pharynx and head cavities), and all the time be *behind* every tone he produces. And particularly on the upper medium and high notes he must be both *behind and on top of every tone.* He must *mentally ride up* with and on the tonal platform as it soars to another and higher pitch, *and watch and feel it getting gradually smaller* as it does so (as a result of the mental vowel-rounding).

We wish to impress upon students the importance of always securing a well-balanced and *perfectly level* adduction of the vocal cords for every note. To this end, a correct "attack" is necessary; which term embraces not only a correct vowel shape in relation to pitch and the employment of only an indispensable minimum of breath, but also *thought* and *will* to produce vocal tone. As a result of this thought and will, and the desire to sing, the laryngeal muscles cause the cords to approximate in order to meet and oppose a certain resistance to the breath pressure (which also comes into being in obedience to the thought-will-attack combination); and if they approximate correctly, only a thin razor-edge slit divides them every time they come together after separating. (The number of times they open and close per second varies according to the pitch.) While they *should* come so very close together at each approximation, *the cords must never meet*, never touch one another. And when they come close together like that on a perfectly level basis, we get what we call a clean-cut, freely vibrating *platform*. Whether the tone be *f* or *p*, the platform must be brightly vibrant, with the feeling of burnished silver wire adequately tensioned in relation to pitch. Will the student please bear in mind that *it is precisely the clean-cut, vibrant platform which imparts carrying-power to the tone* (and never the thick cord rumble indulged in by so many singers under the impression that it is "rich and big", which, while possibly impressive in a room, fails to carry in the theatre, except in a dull, dead way, wholly unconvincing).

If the student assiduously practises internal observation of tonal sensations as above described, if he by this means develops a fine hearing-feeling of these sensations, which are mainly produced by the sound-beam, the mind's eye develops to an extraordinary degree, and real visualization results. Platforms are *seen* as tonal lines ever-decreasing in length and thickness as the pitch rises higher and higher; whereupon the vision of the tonal triangle is crystal clear. In time, every tonal sensation is brought right into the focus of the mind's eye. Which, of course, spells mastery.

The Tonal "Wheel"

We now come to an extremely helpful prop for securing tonal lightness coupled to oil-smooth action of the vocal cords and consequent *tonal flow*. It is a mental concept of a ready-made revolving tonal "wheel" located within the singer's resonating system, i.e. mouth-pharynx and head cavity, considered in the light of one cavity for simplicity's sake. It eliminates (1) general stiffening of the parts and (2) halting of the breath flow: two bad vocal defects widely prevalent.

If, for example, with *vocalizzi* like the following:

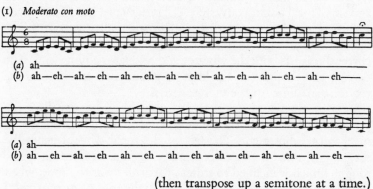

(1) *Moderato con moto*

(a) ah————
(b) ah — eh — ah — eh — ah — eh — ah — eh — ah — eh — ah — eh — ah — eh——

(a) ah————
(b) ah — eh — ah — eh — ah — eh — ah — eh — ah — eh — ah — eh — ah — eh——

(then transpose up a semitone at a time.)

the singer imagines the tonal wheel to revolve at the same rate as the exercise (with a back-to-front movement), production is greatly facilitated. Each bar of six notes equals one complete turn of the wheel. The mental wheel should be made to "turn" before attacking the first note. The student can either play the first bar two or three times on the piano, or rehearse it mentally. This induces the idea of *motion*. Whereupon the first note, C, is attacked and the AH vowel placed, so to speak, on the "rim" of the revolving wheel; and as it is carried up and over on the already revolving wheel, so the six notes of the first bar are produced. One complete turn of the wheel accounts for the first bar, and the next turn for the second bar, and so on. Thus the scale of C is sung up and down again to starting point. Whereupon the next scale, D♭, is sung, then D♮, and so on until the normally highest note is reached. We know that as the pitch rises so the sound-beam grows in height and decreases in width, so on the first octave or little more the rim of the wheel will be fairly broad but gradually is felt to be narrower as the pitch rises towards and on the high notes. (This reflects the process of gradual elimination of the vibrator mass and the consequent gradual narrowing of the sound-beam.)

These and all true sensations of vocal tone are so definite and incisive that they assert themselves through any mental artifice or "crutch" we may employ, for the simple reason that all such imagining must be based on and ultimately conform to physico-acoustic law.

If the singer *thinks* "narrow rim" on a high note, or series of high notes, he gets a modified vowel and therefore a narrow beam and small focal point; conversely, the *thought* of a modified vowel, a narrow tonal stream and a small focus, will give rise to the sensation of a narrow rim. Either thought, separately or concurrently, assists both the vibrator and resonator adjustments. The narrow rim thought on the high notes connotes and induces the requisite smallness of the vibrator mass.

In print, the wheel idea may well seem absurd;* actually it is a powerful adjunct to thought, and of material assistance to mechanical adjustment. The feel of the tonal wheel teaches the meaning of tonal flow and continuity; it imparts freedom to the tongue which is inclined to stiffen, particularly at the root, when the EH and EE vowels are sung—verily the root of many a vocal evil.

As the pitch rises, so the wheel increases vertically in size; on the high notes, therefore, the top of it will be high up in the head cavity. When producing her highest notes the soprano has the feeling that the rim of the wheel is no broader than a pencil line.

Elsewhere we said that the singer should always be mentally behind his tones; consequently, as he is behind it, his view of the wheel is not broadside but just of the rim itself soaring upwards and away from him, turning downwards and back to starting point.

As gradually from the highest scale normally sung with the

* As a matter of fact, the wheel idea is far nearer to the actual aerodynamic phenomenon than is realized. (Noel Bonavia-Hunt.)

above exercise we work our way down again, scale by scale, to the starting scale of middle C, so the rim of the wheel gets gradually broader and the wheel itself smaller. Which broadening of the rim and decrease in the size of the wheel reflect the broadening and shortening of the sound-beam. So we see how a mental prop, as above, is intimately related to and reflects the physical facts of voice.

Here is another exercise that can be sung on the wheel principle:

(2) *Andante*

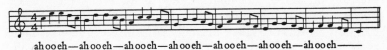

ah oo eh — ah oo eh — ah oo eh — ah oo eh — ah oo eh — ah oo eh — ah oo eh ——

As the tempo is *andante*, the wheel will turn more slowly than for the first exercise. The student can start in the above key and then transpose it up a semitone at a time, so that with six such transpositions he will reach the G♭ to B♭ group. Baritones and basses can start a minor or major third, or a fourth lower than the above.

If, as suggested above, the wheel is made to "turn" mentally before one starts to sing, the attack of the tone looks after itself, so to speak, for it obtains on a *moving* principle. The mental act of placing or laying the vowel (tonal shape) on the rim of the already revolving wheel is sufficient to induce the proper adduction of the cords. While it is a good plan to exercise the adduction of the cords (attack) with the downward mental sweep, it is immaterial, once the cords habitually adduct with precision, whether the so-called attack is downward or upward. However, the downward attack has the added advantage in that it assists in consolidating the resultant adjustment.

Hereunder is another exercise applicable to the wheel principle:

(3) *Andante, molto legato*   *

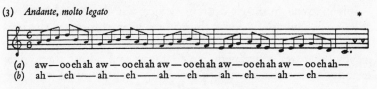

(a) aw — oo eh ah aw — oo eh ah aw — oo eh ah aw — oo eh ah aw — oo eh ah —
(b) ah — eh —— ah — eh —— ah — eh —— ah — eh —— ah — eh ——

* From the author's *Fifty Vowelization Exercises* (Ricordi & Co.). By kind permission.

Take care when passing from OO to EH to sing two distinct, clean-cut vowels, and not OO-Way; this applies equally to Exercise 2 above.

The tonal wheel will help the student to realize the importance of keeping the breath flowing freely when he is singing.

A THROAT-OPENING DEVICE

Because it is absolutely necessary, when on the point of attacking a note, to give the throat and mouth-pharynx complete freedom of action, the singer should enlist every aid to such preparedness. In this sense we have found the following most useful: It consists of a curve mentally visualized and described just as the tone comes into being. This mental curve is one that pulls back from the vertical and moves upwards, as shown in the following diagram:

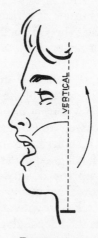

DIAGRAM 14

It is an excellent throat-opening device, wholly mental, without the singer having anything physical to do in this sense; the preparatory mental curve is all-sufficing because the reaction thereto leaves the parts concerned free to move and adjust themselves exactly in accordance with the mentally-shaped vowel.

The very fact of the mental pull-back from the vertical loosens the whole throat, and also the tongue and soft palate together with the muscles operating them, whereupon the unobstructed passage of the upsoaring sound-beam is assured. The upward trend of the mental curve is merely a lift-up which induces tonal lightness and flexibility.

ON EXECUTION

(1) The general trend of modern singers is to *plough* their way through a song, aria or rôle, a process which overburdens the voice without getting really good results. By a curious kink, so many look upon singing as hard labour and attack the job with a navvy's verve. This finds encouragement from certain audiences that seemingly admire the red-necked high note produced with a display of muscularity, mostly misplaced, strained face and heaving shoulders; in short, a bashing competition.

Inversely, the good singer gives the impression of gliding or "skating" *on* the tonal line with light but firm motion, and reminds one of the light, positive touch of the ballerina as she moves across the stage on her toes; for her, there is no flatfooted "ploughing".

(2) Particularly when the *eh* and *ee* vowels are sung it is easy to "clutch" the adjustment and constrict the throat, whereupon the tone (sound-beam) is not free to move to its appointed place; in which case it will "stick", and the singer feels impeded motion, just as the motorist would if driving with his brakes half on. This is due to the excessive elevation of the tongue in relation to the pitch, and consequent lowering of the soft palate in equal degree. Basically the fault lies with the mouth opening that in such cases will be slot-like as in the spoken word with *eh* and/or *ee* in it. And a slot-like opening for a high pitch spells disaster, for the tongue is able to ride up and the soft palate down, almost blocking up the internal mouth (as when *ee* is sung on a low pitch). The remedy lies in *doming* the mouth shape, inside and out, with an inverted U-shape when producing these vowels on a high pitch, because then the tongue *cannot* rise, nor the soft palate fall, too much. Apart from these considerations, many singers are inclined to stiffen the tongue and soft palate as soon as they produce tone. If we stiffen one part of the machinery, all the other parts will be adversely affected in degree. This will also occur in any man-made machine. The obvious remedy to this lies in singing *loosely;* by which is meant relaxing everything round and above the larynx

while maintaining the vibrational contact firm and resilient, and keeping the tone *purring* contentedly all the time in unrestricted surroundings. In other words, the vocal cords must be made, and allowed, to *sing*, and the resultant sound-beam allowed to follow its natural trend.

(3) Through the sense of touch—tonal-aural touch—the author, when teaching, is able to *see* with the mind's eye clearly and unerringly the exact size of the platform, its exact location within the resonating cavities (height and angle with respect to the vertical) and therefore also the effective length (and depth) of cord employed, when a pupil produces vowelled tone on a given pitch. By this means he is able to correct errors of adjustment and production, whereupon the relative sound-beam, of corrected width and height and direction, will tune in *naturally* to the exact point according to the particular pitch and vowel. It is easy for him to detect the slightest error in the direction given to the sound-beam, as, for instance, when it, and its platform, is too close to the vertical for a given pitch and vowel, or when it tunes in to a point in front, instead of at the back, of the vertical, or when, on the same pitch, a vowelled tone is placed in front instead of behind another vowelled tone. (For instance, after E♭, fourth space, the vowels AH, AW, OH, OO must all be *behind*, and never in front of, EH and EE.) Such vision-through-aural touch of the tones was acquired by long practice. It can be acquired by one and all, but one must know what to listen for.

(4) *Paint in* (talk in) the vowels (shape and tone-colours) with the same smooth, sleek, delicate thought actuating a skilled painter as he lays on his colours with firm but delicate touch or sweep of the brush and gradually builds up his picture. The good singer has much in common with the good painter; both have the same inward urge, the same creative force waiting at the standpoint of expectancy for outward expression, expansion, and exaltation. Both deal with line, shape, and colour.

(5) To punch at the vocal cords with excess breath-blast is the worst kind of muscular education; the whole muscular system inside and above the larynx is thereby constrained to effect exaggerated and oft-times unnatural adjustments, resulting in marked tonal distortion. Under the stress of excess breath pressure there cannot possibly be any nicety of adjustment.

If you just *think* of a rounded vowel shape and dark*ish* tone you get a small platform; inversely, if you think and aim to produce a small platform (with, of course, a given vowel correctly shaped in mind) you get a rounded, darkish tone. Correct thinking finds immediate reaction, and correct physical adjustment occurs automatically.

(6) Fundamentally, there are two ways to sing: the wrong and right. The wrong way (generally adopted today) is that which causes the vocal cords to adjust themselves as best they can under the impact of excess breath pressure. Where there is the will to sing, the cords are bound to approximate; but it is the way they do so that matters.

The right way is when the singer, with an indispensable minimum of breath pressure, seeks and assists correct muscular adjustment within and outside the larynx by deliberately *thinking* a vowel shape-cum-tone, appropriate to pitch, and *willing in* normal muscular energy. The higher the pitch the more the energy employed. To get a high note means additional effort, additional muscular energy braced up by increased mental energy, by increased *will*. Once the tone is launched with the aforesaid minimum of breath and a *crescendo* becomes necessary, the breath pressure will be increased in controlled degree. Seeing that only the front tip of the cords is employed for producing the high notes, it stands to reason that because the mass of this mere tip is so small and light, little breath is required to move it and initiate the tone; on the other hand, considerable muscular tension and energy suitably braced up by nerves and will is required. The singer must *will* in this muscular energy in relation to the pitch; the higher the pitch the greater the will and the muscular energy coupled to nervous *support*. This *willing* braces the nerves, and the nerves the muscles. We tell the student "Gather up your forces to a point, and then attack the high note. Be all excited. Be like a wild rabbit, not a tame one." The singer, when in action, must be "nervy" and in a state of almost suppressed excitement, even when singing *mezzavoce*.

Although modern methods would have us believe it is so, singing, as we understand it, is not a blind, slogging match between forced pressure from the lungs and riotous resistance thereto of the vocal cords.

Above all this, the first requisite is for the singer to have an exact conception (feeling-hearing) of the particular vowel to be sung,

either in pure form, or modified (rounded off), according to the
pitch—for we know that the different pitches demand slightly
different vowel shapings.

(7) A very common fault is noticeable in the downward *portamento*. The average singer will not only come down to a lower
note (be the interval a second, third, fourth, or more) on a thick,
slurring tonal line instead of with a thin, uplifted one, but will
intone the landing note with the vowel he comes down with and
then repeat the same note with its rightful vowel or syllable, thus
making two notes instead of one. To illustrate:

love—ly love—ly   love—ly night   I   am yours

In all three examples the small notes show the fault complained
of. In (*a*) two F's and two E's are sung, instead of one; in (*b*) two
F's and two E's instead of one; and in (*c*) three F's instead of two.
This procedure is inartistic and ugly; it becomes "moanamento"
instead of *portamento*. The correct way is to come down on a thin
tonal thread to the lower note on which the next syllable (or
word) is pronounced without the latter note being intoned beforehand—as indicated by the small notes at (*a*) (*b*) (*c*). When coming
down in this way the singer must lift up and lighten the tone in
order to keep the tonal thread *as thin as possible* (almost at breaking
point) and then "land" nicely on the lower note, enunciating the
new syllable (or vowel). This makes for a clean-cut and refined
portamento and tonal continuity. (See (23), p. 271.)

TONAL PLAY

(8) Sometimes, when a student is singing exercises, we tell him
to "play with the tone", that is, make a quick occasional *decrescendo* to *p* and then back again to *f*; in other words, execute a
rapid *messa di voce*. The object of this tonal play is to encourage the
laryngeal muscles to operate with varying degrees of firmness, and
so constitute a simple system of graded gymnastics, imparting to
the cords muscular suppleness and responsiveness.

The way is thus prepared for delicate *p* attacks, rapid *crescendos*,
and fine *decrescendos*. When assiduously practised, tonal play

imparts ultimately to the cords a fine sensitiveness of touch, of responsiveness to the slightest pressure of the breath. In all this the breathing muscles *have* to come into line and are indirectly drilled to share in the tonal play with fine judgment.

In this connection, to secure a well-graded breath pressure for purposes of tonal development we employ a term that appeals to the majority of students, conveying as it does the thought of an air-flow devoid of brutality, namely: "Blow upwards from the platform." This induces appropriate muscular action, with the result that the singer feels he has under control a *steady* increase of breath pressure. Inversely, for *p* singing we advise the student merely to "breathe" on the platform, so to speak; which idea conveys in practice lightness of tonal touch. If we *gradually* reduce the "blowing" to mere "breathing" on the platform, we secure a perfect *decrescendo*, and, conversely, if we gradually increase the "breathing" to "blowing" we get a perfect *crescendo*.

THE TRILLO OR SHAKE

(9) There is perhaps no more exquisite embellishment than the *trillo*. Cultivated in the past by all singers, male and female, its study has been much neglected in these so-called modern times. Some voices possess a natural and well developed *trillo*, others only in embryonic form awaiting development. Rarely is it brought to a fine art today.

A good, natural *trillo* connotes in the main a good production, at least as far as the pitch or pitches on which it is executed are concerned. By "good" we mean a very fast, short-wave, closely-knit throb. It is produced by a peculiar mechanism in that it consists of a sustained basic note, produced in the usual way, and of a second note superimposed—generally a tone higher. This superimposed note is not actually or, say, deliberately made by the singer but is the result of a piston-like action of the entire larynx, lightly and almost imperceptibly bobbing up and down in the throat automatically with extraordinary rapidity.

A well-developed *trillo* is readily started without any preparation. However, the preliminary movement is sometimes effective. To prepare it, the singer must first produce the basic note (which of course is actually made by the laryngeal vibrations in the usual way), and then a second note, usually a whole tone higher, which is also a *sung* note. Slowly at first, then gradually faster and faster, both notes are sung alternately until, suddenly, the *trillo* itself bursts into life and takes charge of the proceedings. The basic note remains, but the second note which, during the preparatory movement, had been deliberately sung, is now transformed in the sense that no longer is it made by an actual adjustment of the vocal cords, but is a "throbbed" tone produced as a result of the air in the throat, mouth-pharynx, and head cavities being jogged at *regular* intervals with great rapidity through the aforementioned piston-like action of the larynx proper.

This rapid alternation or oscillation must be perfectly even with an oil-smooth action, very fast and short-waved. As a sensation, the *trillo*, once launched, is apparently outside the immediate control of the singer herself during the vibrational momentum. Yet she can stop it at will. In the singer's sensation the higher (superimposed) note is so "elusive" that it almost passes into the realm of the intangible; but the basic note is felt to be under immediate control. The preparation reminds one of pressing the self-starter switch on a car, and the *trillo* of the bursting into life of the engine.

Whatever the pitch on which the *trillo* is produced, the adjustment must conform to the mainspring of vocal mechanism; in other words, to the principle of gradual elimination of the vibrator mass as the pitch rises. Should the basic note of a *trillo* be produced with a length and thickness of vocal cord excessive in relation to the particular pitch, the product will be cumbersome and of the slow, long-wave type that possibly will degenerate, as it is being sustained, into a low-pitched (under pitch) tone which of course is the reverse of beautiful and never spectacular. It can remind one of gargling!

The lower the pitch, the relatively "fatter" the two-note preparation and therefore also the *trillo* itself (due of course to the relatively big vibrator in length and thickness); inversely, the higher the pitch the closer and smaller must be the two-note preparation, while the *trillo* itself will be equally small and closely-knit (due to the now much reduced vibrator in length and thickness). In other words, *the basic note of the "trillo", whether with or without preparation, must have the same size of platform as when a given note is sung in the ordinary way;* and this size, as we know, is governed by pitch. *A "trillo" on a high note must be very small, closely-knit, and fast moving.*

The two-note preparation can also be made *staccato*, and is quite effective. As a matter of fact such *staccato* preparation assists some voices to launch the *trillo*. After all, *staccato* notes are merely crisp little platforms.

ON ATTACK

(10) Pitch relies primarily upon tension—not upon breath-blast. Tension that is independent of excess breath pressure is secured by *willing* it in with little breath, whereupon we get appropriate muscular action within the larynx and also the breathing apparatus. After mentally shaping the vowel in relation to the particular pitch:

Mental line

Seek
Your
Tension
Downwards
Through
The
Vowel
To
Find
And
Create
A
Resilient
Platform

The student should experiment first by singing, on the same *low* note, the syllable KA four times, and then, still on the same note, BA, BA, BA, BA, or SE, SE, SE, SE, or any other syllable, and he will feel first the consonant on top, then the vowel, and finally the resilient, vibrating platform of resistance. So we have the consonant roof, the vowel building, and the vibrator foundation. The next test, on the same lines, should be made on a medium note, then on an upper medium, and finally on a high note. Although on the upper medium and high notes the tonal sensation will have risen well above the mouth level, the above order of progression should be kept mentally intact, for the sensation of height of beam cannot and does not invalidate the physical fact that the consonant and the mouth-pharynx shaping for vowel are, as a unit, always and ever on top of the vibrator.

If, when you are going to produce a *high* note, you form and put out a full-size open-toned AH vowel (or any other broad vowel) in its pure form without modification, as in speech, you cannot possibly create a tall and narrow sound-beam—such as acoustically belongs to the said high pitch, for the simple reason that such a broad vowel induces the employment of a considerable length (and possibly thickness) of cord. With a big section of cord it is an acoustical impossibility to produce a tall, narrow beam. When a mistake of this kind is made the frequency is liable to fall perceptibly, and the only remedy for the untutored singer is to forcibly increase his breath pressure in an effort to boost up the vibrations to the exact pitch. He rarely succeeds in doing so (see footnote, p. 54).

If, on the other hand, you visualize, form (mentally) and produce a high note *based on the thought* of a small, rounded-off or modified vowel (a miniature vowel, if you like) you create a tall, narrow beam, because such thinking reacts on the cord mechanism and induces and assists in reducing the amount of cord to be engaged in effective length and thickness. Only a small piece of cord can produce a tall, narrow beam, and only a tall, narrow beam can reflect a well-rounded tone on a high note. If the vowel to be sung is AH, AW, or OH, your *first* thought must be that of a *tiny oo* vowel (or *u* in *put*).*

If, after correctly attacking a high note with a small vibrator (small tonal platform, brought into being by the *thought* of a rounded vowel) the vowel sound is "opened" beyond a certain limit, the cords will inevitably lengthen somewhat; whereupon the sound-beam becomes shorter and broader in degree. The original adjustment within the larynx is thereby thrown out of gear; pitch and quality suffer in consequence. If the vowel sound is

* We tell the student to "nip" or "pinch" the small focus of high notes. To "pinch" a tonal focus is of course a physical impossibility. But as the focus is a projected image of the exact amount of cord being engaged at the moment, the very thought of a small "nervy pinch" reacts on the muscles actuating the cord mechanism, inducing appropriate tensioning, without stiffening, of the adjustment. Actually, the feeling of "pinch" is the *tiny* slit between the much shortened cords, and vibrating (that is, opening and closing in rapid alternate sequence) at high frequency. To get this idea of "pinch" tie a knot, fairly tightly, in an ordinary elastic band and feel its flexible firmness; tighten it gradually more and more, and note how the knot gets gradually smaller and firmer—just like the feel of a tonal focus as the pitch rises higher and higher. The small focus of a high note must have the same firm "give" in it that you feel in the tight elastic knot.

thus "opened" it means that actually the mouth-pharynx shaping has been somewhat flattened. Never must one open the sound on the extreme high notes, but it is admissible to do so (up to a point, of course) on all notes right up to the upper medium; even so, much will depend on the individual voice as to the actual permissible degree of tonal "opening" without it degenerating into blatancy.

Apart from deliberately thinking and willing in pitch-cum-tension, the mental-physical preparation to produce a tall and narrow beam requires *anticipation of the height and of the direction* the forthcoming beam will and should take *naturally*, according to the pitch and vowel. Coupled to appropriate vowel-shaping, the very *thought* of the direction a given beam will take frees and opens the throat naturally; and in this sense the singer has nothing to do physically. In singing, so much takes place automatically as a reaction to thought.

TONE AND PERSONALITY

(11) The following diagram and explanations are intended to stress *the importance of producing vocal tone that is always vivified by thought, and emotion.* So much depends on what tone must express. Vocal tone denuded of intensified thought is merely a plain, empty mechanical sound, as unconvincing as it is brainless. We call tone brainless when it means just nothing.

Hereunder is a diagram illustrating a sound-beam charged with what we call a "central core" of vivifying thought-waves:*

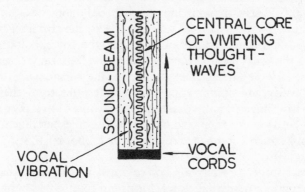

DIAGRAM 15

* It reminds one of the central bore containing mercury in a thermometer.

A sound-beam is the main stream of vocal tone; even if of good "quality" it may be just a mechanical sound, cold and unconvincing. But add to it the vivifying central core of thought and we produce tone charged with expression and feeling; and the *meaning* it thus conveys captivates the listener. The singer's whole being must always be *in* his voice, as the whole being of the violinist must be *in* his violin—which is invariably the case where great artists are concerned.

The sound-beam itself is composed of physical vibrations, whereas the central core is composed of mental vibrations: *intensified thought waves, emotional waves, nerve-energy, imagination* and *will*. The central core gives life and soul to the issuing tone which, thus loaded, stirs the heartstrings of an audience. Such *completed* tone expresses the combined personalities of poet, composer and singer. When every tone, every word, is thus made to *live*, we have what is called "interpretation" at its highest. (See p. 300.)

In the words of Robert Hamilton: "True personality proceeds not from the assertion of self, but from the loss of self in something greater which reflects it back in a fuller and deeper integration." In fact, the great singer loses his self in his art, in his song which, together, reflect back his personality in an enhanced and completed form.

The intangible substance we call thought *is* vibration; when intensified and injected into the vocal stream we get a "fuller and deeper integration". Life is a function of thought; and so if vocal tone is to have real life it must be vested with thought. What kind of thought? Firstly, thought appertaining to the song or aria to be sung, the story it tells, the picture it conveys, the character to be portrayed; secondly, thought of technique, the vowel-colours for painting the tonal picture; thirdly, expression, emotion, accent as delineated by the melodic line and underlying harmonies. All this is the quality and combination of thought (vibration) that we wish to have injected into vocal tone by way of a central core (like a spinal cord) which then, and only then, becomes intelligent and intelligible. Such a completed tonal picture cannot fail to stimulate the imagination of an audience.

A great singer is really a tonal colourist in the sense that he deliberately chooses certain vowel forms and colours with which to express thoughts and things, incidents of life and the whole gamut of human emotions. Tonal colouring is a potent factor of success, and it reveals the singer's personality. In this way is established the subtle psychic link-line connecting singer and audience.

To what do we owe the beautiful tone of a Stradivarius or Guarneri violin? To the exquisite artistic *love* and idealistic *thought* of the originators actually *embedded therein;* we owe it also to their technical skill and painstaking labour. And so it is with pianos such as Bechstein, Blüthner and Steinway. Strange to relate, the Strad violin and the Bechstein piano are both of brilliant and powerful tone, whereas the Guarneri violin and the Blüthner piano are both of softer tone. Today, however, so many makes of violins and pianos have a pronounced £ s. d. tone.

THE EH, EE, AND OO VOWELS

(12) To judge by the way they are produced, these three vowels are the bugbear of most students and singers. Shorn, however, of their seeming difficulties, they are as readily produced as all other vowels. In most cases, difficulties are of the singer's making. What is required is the intelligent understanding of the correct shaping of the vowels themselves, as well as of the direction taken by the respective sound-beams, in relation to pitch. When carefully explained, the student should have no trouble with them once they have been worked in.

First of all, why are EH and EE different sounds to, say, AH? The main physical reason is that in order to produce EH (one sound as in *Mary, there*) the tongue arches somewhat more than it does for the formation of AH, and the soft palate descends in equal degree; as a result, the internal shaping of the mouth-pharynx undergoes a change, while the actual space within it is made narrower than for AH. For the formation of the EE vowel, the tongue arches more than it does for EH, while the soft palate descends in equal degree; consequently, the internal space is still more restricted. We can test this by singing on the same *low* note first AH, then EH and EE. Note how the tone itself narrows during the transition. Particularly the EE vowel sung on a low note feels very confined, and the tone very narrow; this is quite in keeping with the condition of arched tongue and lowered soft palate, appertaining to the low pitches, referred to above. (Which condition obtains *naturally* as a result of *thinking in* the vowel sound; never must it be the result of a deliberate act, as some methods advocate.)

So many students are taught to "smile", or show half a dozen teeth or so when singing; and this letterbox slot is to be maintained regardless of pitch and vowel! This method, or fad, is as murderous as it is stupid, having absolutely no foundation in tonal fact.

We know that the sound-beam rises with the pitch and eventually soars into the head cavities; and because it should do so naturally, it is up to the singer to assist matters by *allowing* it to follow its natural trend. But it cannot possibly follow its natural direction and tune in accurately to the head resonating zone if, on the upper medium, and more particularly on the high notes, the singer keeps a flat, slot-like mouth opening internally and externally. And the very fact of a slotted mouth (toothy-smile method) when producing EH and EE means that the tongue is free to arch considerably and the soft palate to descend. While this condition is normal for the lower medium and low pitches, it is the height of folly to impose this same condition when high notes have to be produced. In Chapter XIII we explained how the shaping of the mouth-pharynx affects the cord mechanism, favourably, or adversely. The noxious effect that the slotted-mouth opening has on the cord mechanism where high pitches are concerned, is marked. The tone is invariably hard, shrill and "catty", never of good quality on account of the general distortion. The slotted mouth on high notes induces the employment of an excessive amount of cord in length and depth; consequently the resultant sound-beam is much too short and broad, to satisfy the acoustical conditions of high pitches. Finally, the restricted space on high pitches makes the tone "stick", and this in turn induces the singer to exert an excessive breath pressure in order to free it, and merely succeeds in making things worse.

If, on the other hand, the singer *rounds* his mouth, internally and externally, with an inverted U-shape for producing EH and EE on high pitches (by *thinking* rounded vowel-cum-tone), the tongue cannot possibly arch too much for the pitch, nor can the soft palate descend except in measured degree, because the reduced arching movement of the tongue curtails the descent of the soft palate. Notwithstanding this reduced movement of tongue and palate, the EH and EE vowels are perfectly shaped and intelligible to the listener.

The sound-beams of EH and EE are upright on the low notes;

but as the pitch rises above E♭, fourth space, they incline slightly back of the vertical. (Both beams travel practically in the same direction.) (See diagram hereunder.)

Few singers realize that not only EH but also the EE vowel *must*, on high pitches, be produced with a well-opened (dome-shape) mouth, internally and externally, because for the same pitch the sound-beam of the EE is just as tall as that of AH, EH, or any other vowel, and consequently requires a nicely-domed space. And it is precisely the internal dome or vault shape that

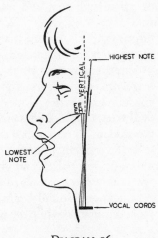

DIAGRAM 16

prevents the tongue from arching excessively; adequate space is thereby provided for the upsoaring beam.

It must be remembered that the movement of the tongue to produce EH and EE on *high* notes should be so slight as to pass unnoticed by the singer himself; and it is only by "doming" the internal mouth that the tongue movement can be limited, as it must be.

However, the singer need not worry about the actual degree of arching of the tongue for a given pitch on either EH or EE (or of any vowel, for that matter), for neither he, nor anyone else, can ever possibly know the exact degree of arching. It is fatal to even attempt to control the tongue movement directly. If the tone is good, freely produced, the tongue evidently has contributed to the shaping automatically as a result of the vowel shape-cum-tone being *thought in* (not deliberately made). And if the tongue does its work in this sense automatically as a result of such thinking, who should worry about how much it arches, or doesn't arch, on a given pitch? Our advice to singers is to stop meddling with the tongue and soft palate.

The singer must learn to relax, to sing "loosely" (that is, everything flexibly loose except the vibrator mechanism), and, provided the EH and EE vowels are mentally well shaped, with the right sound also in mind in relation to pitch, the tongue will look after itself, as the soft palate will too, and assist in the general shaping and production.

We are trying to impress on the student that on high notes in particular, and on the upper medium pitches, he *must* resist the tendency (which most students have) to think of EH and EE in terms of the spoken vowel on a more or less low pitch, as that will induce inevitably (automatically) the slotted-mouth opening which, we repeat, is fatal where high pitches are concerned.*

It is necessary for the student to remember that the higher the pitch the smaller must be the movement of the parts concerned in vowel-shaping (i.e. of tongue, soft palate, and pharynx generally). As the pitch rises, so everything mechanical grows beautifully less: vibrator (in length and thickness), sound-beam (in width), tonal focus, and articulation of consonants, while the resonance increases more and more.

Finally, the student should experiment and note the difference of feeling of "space" when the upright narrow, or closed, *eh* (as in *met* or even *bid*) and the upright broader and more open EH (as in *Mary, there*) are sung on the same low, or lower-medium, note. The first is felt to be a very narrow tonal shaft, whereas the second is felt to be a comfortably broad shaft. The difference in space is due, of course, to the different degree of arching of the tongue and lowering of the soft palate, as explained above.

* Produce all EH vowels upright between two imaginary parallel lines, so to speak. On the low notes the open EH of *where* to be sung straight upwards between two lines the breadth of a school ruler; on medium notes the *eh* of *egg*, *breast* between upright parallel lines the breadth of a pencil; and on high notes the *eh* sound in *fig, big*, between upright parallel lines the breadth of a knitting-needle. The above three breadths, and intervening one, are intended to illustrate the sensation of gradual narrowing of the sound-beam from the lowest to the highest note.

Also the OO is considered by so many singers a difficult vowel to produce properly. Every vowel is "difficult" when its exact shaping in relation to pitch and the direction its sound-beam takes as the scale is ascended from the lowest to the highest pitch are unknown to the singer. But once these things are explained, understood, and put into practice, the OO loses all its seeming terrors. Knowledge dissolves most difficulties. (See diagram, p. 144.)

Like all the other vowels, the correct shape and sound of the OO must first be mentally conceived, whereupon the actual production obtains automatically without any deliberate act on the singer's part.

OO is produced with appropriate internal shaping (round) and naturally puckered lips on the lowest note, while its sound-beam points well forward to tune in just over the front upper teeth. One must not try on the lower notes to get the same tonal brightness and "power" that we associate with more open vowels such as AH or EH, because OO is in itself a sombre, velvety tone; and due to the restricted frontal area in which the beam finds itself on the low pitches there cannot be much amplitude. There is compensation, however, in the richly "gathered-up" tonal qualities which make the OO colourful and expressive.

As the scale is ascended from the lowest note it should be kept true to shape and sound without any modification up to about C♮, third space; after which, very, very gradually, note by note, it must be allowed to follow a natural tendency to modify by opening out slightly with a backward movement so as to introduce a tint of OH in the tone. The beam, from its initial much-curved position on the lowest note, gradually shifts its point of impingement backwards along the arc of the hard palate as the pitch rises, so that on reaching the said C it will be pointing upright, more or less. The next two notes (C♯ and D) will not really require any more *oh*-tint than C; but at E♭, fourth space, it demands a trifle more *oh*-tint as the beam *must* point just back of the vertical. If at E♭ the beam is not tuned in just behind the vertical, and instead points bolt upright, or even in front of the vertical, the tone will "stick", and suffer distortion in degree. To introduce this slight *oh*-tint, the singer has only to "loosen" the OO ever so slightly backwards. The *oh*-tints thus introduced will not be heard as such by the average listener, who will only hear the basic OO sound—provided only a tint, and not a preponderance of OH is introduced. As the pitch rises above the said E♭, so the percentage of *oh*-tint must be allowed to increase, but only in very small degrees, until on the highest note there will be a nicely mixed tone of 40 or 45 per cent. of *oh* and 60 or 55 per cent. of OO. The OH percentage must never outgrow the basic OO, for then the former and not the latter vowel would be heard. Which would be bad for diction. From the said E♭, upwards, the OO beam increases gradually in height and pulls away backwards from the vertical more and more gradually as the pitch rises to the highest note, opening out as it does so gradually with stronger OH-tints.

If the OO is sung pure (unmixed with *oh*) with *f* tone all the way up the scale to the highest pitch (as so many singers try to do), the singer will feel that from about E♭, fourth space, upwards, his throat is getting constricted more and more as the pitch rises, until a tonal deadlock is reached. By thus holding the OO pure (which inevitably induces pursed-up lips) the vibrator mechanism cannot shorten or get thinner as it should; consequently the beam cannot soar as it should, because too broad and too short; nor can it swing back of, and tune in behind, the vertical as from E♭, fourth space, upwards, because obliged to point forward against, or in front of, the vertical. The very fact of thrusting the beam forward against, or in front of, the vertical when it should tune in behind it (even if only in minor degree as it does on the said E♭) cramps the already limited space between back of tongue and the pharyngeal wall, and severely restricts the resonating zones appropriate to the upper medium and high pitches. All these things added cause marked tonal distortion. (See diagrams, pp. 164, 174.)

If we contemplate singing an OO *p* from the lowest note right up the scale, an essential factor is the *support* to be given to the whole adjustment by the simple process of puckering the lips; the degree of puckered tautness and approximation creates a small "drum-like" terminal to the general resonating area, and offers a coupling surface within a confined space which has the result of "pointing" the tone. As we ascend the scale slowly with the same *p* tone, the OO must be kept pure in shape and sound, and it must be small and "pointed". (By "pure" we mean exactly as spoken.)

As already explained above, the OO beam travels backwards from the front of the mouth (on lowest note) along the arc of the hard palate as the pitch rises, until at D♮, fourth line, it is practically upright. As the pitch rises from the lowest note the lips must be kept well puckered all the time—the lip tautness seems by reflex action to "lock" the vocal apparatus.* As the tone, from E♭, fourth space, climbs backwards and upwards step by step, the lip-to-lip aperture gradually increases, the lips themselves retaining, however, their tautness; for without it the tone may well collapse. And the bigger the vocal category, the more this support is necessary. Even though the OO-tone is felt to be very small and pointed already on the low notes, it actually gets smaller and smaller as a focus as the pitch rises to the highest note. Be the tone *p* or *f,* the beam direction and movement is exactly the same.†

When passing from *p* to *f,* particularly on pitches above the said E♭, the tautness of the lips must be gradually released as the *crescendo* develops; as it does so, the mouth (lip aperture) opens more and more, but always relative to the pitch. On the highest pitches it is as open as for AH or AW, for we must remember that when singing OO *f* it must *not* be kept pure but "loosened" some-what backwards in order to introduce a percentage of *oh* into the tone. Moreover, we know that the lips are *not* used for any vowel on the high notes.

We might add that one can sing OO *p* on a high note with a small lip aperture, provided there be adequate *internal* space and the tonal focus tuned well in behind the vertical and high up in the head resonating zone. But the inexperienced singer is liable unconsciously to over-thicken the vibrator by coupling in the

---

* The taut position of the lips serves as a " frein harmonique", and helps to preserve the fundamental harmonic without detriment to the overtone develop-ment. Thus the tone is still buoyant, in spite of the close position of the lips and the reduced power. (Noel Bonavia-Hunt.)

† If the OO feels small on the low notes (especially when compared to the more open vowels) whether it is sung *f* or *p,* it is not because the actual sound-beam is narrow but because the resonating space at its point of impingement is considerably restricted by reason of the small lip-to-lip aperture. As the pitch rises, from the lowest note, this small OO feeling undergoes a change in the sense that while the resonating space is gradually increased by the singer instinctively in order to accommodate exactly the gradually rising beam, so the actual tonal focus gets smaller and smaller; the higher the pitch the bigger the lip-to-lip aperture (although the actual degree of mouth opening varies from individual to individual). So on the low notes we have a small OO feeling within a restricted area, and on the high notes a smaller tonal focus within a (relatively) big space.

R

tone at an insufficient height. The danger lies, in this case, in the mental and physical forward pull of the small puckered-lip aperture that introduces a rival resonator at the mouth, whereas all high notes, *piano* or *forte*, demand a *vertical lengthening* of the resonator.

STACCATO

(13) This Italian word means "detached". *Staccato* tone results from the cords being set in motion, and then the vibratory action being suddenly stopped. In a series of *staccato* notes, this go-and-stop occurs in alternate sequence. The *staccato* is not merely an ornament in song: it is also a healthy gymnastic for the cords themselves and the muscles actuating them. It is employed to advantage as a corrective of tonal flabbiness due to inadequate adduction.

In many voices, the first octave (where the cord tension is moderate) is inclined to be "woolly"—the tone being attenuated through air passing the cordal barrier. This means that the cords do not approximate sufficiently, and a certain amount of pressure air escapes to mingle with the tonal vibrations (i.e. the vortices), impoverishing the product in varying degree. Sometimes the weakish adduction is confined to the first two or three notes only. In such cases we press the *staccato* exercise into service because it causes the laryngeal adductor muscles to contract and relax in alternate sequence; it is somewhat analogous to flexing and relaxing the arm in order to develop the biceps. *Staccato* work must not be overdone, as it is rather tiring on this account and should be alternated with an ordinary *legato* exercise. By the way, *staccato* gives a very clear idea of "platform"; in fact, a series of *staccato* tones is just so many little platforms. (See p. 224.)

VOWEL-BEAMS

(14) As every vowel, long and short, is the result of appropriate internal shaping (of the mouth-pharynx cavity), it stands to reason that each and every basic change in this shaping necessary to produce a given clear-cut vowel must, *by the very nature of that shape*, cause the relative sound-beam to take a direction that is individually its own, and therefore different from that taken by the beam of any other vowel. Mind you, the difference may be only very slight in certain cases. The beams of certain short English vowels follow closely the direction taken by those of

certain long, classic vowels from which individually they are derivates. For instance, the short *i* and *e* in *pit*, *pet*, follow the classic EH and EE beams (which themselves have an identical direction); then the short *a* in *pat*, rather a distant derivate of classic EH, follows the latter's beam direction; then the short *o* in *pot*, which is not really "short" but actually a rounded classic AH (AH² modification we call it) as it is identical to the vowel sound in *sorry*, *song*, etc.; therefore it follows the beam direction of AH; then the short *u* of *put*, etc. is a derivate of classic OO, and actually a mixed tone of *oo* and *oh;* consequently its beam follows the same direction as that of the classic OO (as in *pool*, etc.); then we have the *ir* vowel, as in *bird* (of the same family as the French *eu*, as in *yeux*, but more open than the latter which is a very narrow and flat tone); the *ir* beam is just between classic AH and EH, with a marked tendency to follow the direction of the EH beam as the pitch rises to the upper medium and high notes. As a matter of fact, the *a*, as in *pat*, already mentioned above, has the same beam direction as the *ir* from the lowest to the highest note.

As we know, every vowel intoned by the singer has its own sound-beam which, according to the individual vowel, points in a given initial direction on the lowest note and moves on at definite angles gradually as the pitch rises. The vowel-beam is the main stream of vocal tone, the main tonal sensation with which the singer has to deal; it is the chief manipulative prop of the singer's art. It is therefore highly important for the singer himself to be familiar with the behaviour of the sound-beams relative to all the vowels, long and short, because it is only through such knowledge that he can expect to produce his voice correctly with every vowel on all pitches. Only thus can he exercise a really intelligent control over every tone he produces: a prize worth working for. A correct angle of the beam means a correct mouth-pharynx shaping (vowel shape) and, vice versa, a correct vowel shape, in relation to pitch, induces automatically the correct angle or direction for the beam to take, as it will under such ideal conditions, if allowed to by the singer, according to the pitch. If the internal shaping for a given vowel is not correct in relation to a given pitch, and the singer does not *mentally* foresee and fore-provide for the angle and road up which the beam has to travel, it is obvious that the beam itself will be forced into another path or direction not its own, with the inevitable result that the tone

suffers distortion in degree. The singer cannot afford to thrust a
beam in a wrong direction; and "thrust" he does when he
deliberately places a tone "well forward", or "covers" it, when
its natural direction is, say, back of the vertical and pointing upwards (as it would if the vowel sung were EH or EE or IR, or
any vowel on an upper medium or high pitch).

Again, if, for instance, we sing OO and then EH on the same
low note, the OO beam points forward just above the upper
front teeth, whereas the EH beam soars straight upwards; consequently, on low notes the OO is in front of EH. But if we now
sing these same two vowels on a high pitch, the OO is well
behind the EH, which latter is still soaring upwards, albeit slant-
ing just back of the vertical—see Diagram 1, p. 57, and note the
difference. The same phenomenon is noticeable if we sing OH or
AW instead of OO, and EE instead of EH. The student should
test it out for himself.

When on the same high note we go from EH (or EE) to OO
(or to OH, AW or AH) the amount of pull-back from vowel to
vowel is more marked in some individuals than it is in others,
according to the size and shape of the cavities. Even though the
variations are often slight, every individual must be a law unto
himself in the matter.

Again, if we sing AH and then EH (or EE) on the same low
note, the EH will be felt to be just in front of AH—both beams
being more or less vertical.* Now, this relation never changes
whatever the pitch, high or low. (*No vowel-beam comes back of
AH*, whatever the pitch.) The difference in the vowel-to-vowel
movement is noticeable when the pitch rises (as in an ascending
scale); the higher the pitch, the greater the space between them.
This is explained by the fact that whereas the EH (or EE) beam
continues to soar straight upwards, and is just back of the vertical
on the high pitches, the AH beam gradually pulls backwards
away from the vertical as it soars with the rising pitch.

---

* On the low notes, the open EH vowel (as in *Mary*) is an upright beam,
whereas the more closed *eh* sound (as in *egg*), the short *i*, as in *bid*, and the long
ee, as in *seen*, can, on the low notes, be produced either upright or horizontal,
more or less, pointing forwards. (On the high pitches, the beams of all four are
quasi-vertical.) In most cases, however, all four vowels should be sung upright
on the low notes—and not horizontally forward, for the latter is inclined to
cramp some voices.

When producing OO on high pitches, the mouth must be as wide open as for AH, seeing that the relative sound-beam impinges high up in the head cavity close to that of AH. The lips being thus widely separated, have no part in the OO formation on high pitches, not even as a finishing medium, as is the case on the lower notes. Be the note high or low, it is primarily the pharynx which shapes the OO (and all vowels), the lips merely *finish* the general shaping. On the high, or head, notes the pharynx alone performs the dual task of formation and finish of the OO.

We give hereunder just a few examples of vowel-to-vowel movement in order to emphasize the importance for the singer of knowing the directions the different vowel-beams should take naturally, particularly when two different vowels are sung on the same pitch. Even a slight mistake in beam direction when passing from one vowel to another is sufficient to cramp the throat and distort the tone in degree. Considerations of space do not permit of a full range of examples; but the discerning student will be able to analyse many more on his own account in songs and arias of all kinds, and thus get thoroughly familiar with all combinations of vowel-beam directions, not merely on the same pitch, but different pitches with small or big intervals and different vowels. He should make a practice of such analysis. It is a real throat-moulding work and the vocal organs soon get the habit of doing the right thing every time. But the informing thought must always be present, for automatism can never really be trusted.

As an important aid to good production the singer must sing "loosely", that is, without stiffening in the slightest the facial and neck muscles, or the jaw. Only the vocal machinery—the muscles actuating the breathing apparatus, the laryngeal mechanism, and the pharyngeal parts—must be adequately tensioned, and braced by the *will* and nerve energy, and in varying degree according to the pitch. Normal muscular tension of this kind has nothing in common with rigidity.* Abnormal tension, due to excess breath pressure, produces stiffening in degree. So we constantly tell the

---

* Don't misunderstand this idea of "using the muscles". We are not suggesting direct, but *indirect* action of the laryngeal muscles through operation of the *will* to produce tone. The muscles actuating the vocal cords and their mechanism are moved by the *will* through the nerve from the brain. The higher the pitch the more will is required, and vice versa, the lower the pitch the less will required.

student to "sing loosely" and "relax" everything *but* the parts of the vocal machine, everything but *the central core of tone*, everything round this core. The laryngeal motor must be alive and alert, and well braced whether the tone be loud or soft.

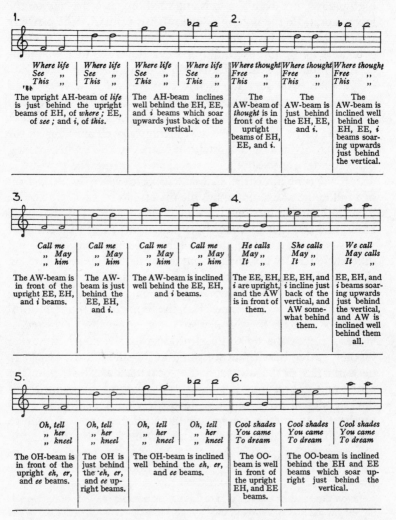

1.

Where life	Where life	Where life	Where life
See ,,	See ,,	See ,,	See ,,
This ,,	This ,,	This ,,	This ,,

| The upright AH-beam of *life* is just behind the upright beams of EH, of *where*; EE, of *see*; and *i*, of *this*. | | The AH-beam inclines well behind the EH, EE, and *i* beams which soar upwards just back of the vertical. |

2.

Where thought	Where thought	Where thought
Free ,,	Free ,,	Free ,,
This ,,	This ,,	This ,,

| The AW-beam of *thought* is in front of the upright beams of EH, EE, and *i*. | The AW-beam is just behind the EH, EE, and *i*. | The AW-beam is inclined well behind the EH, EE, *i* beams soaring upwards just behind the vertical. |

3.

Call me	Call me	Call me	Call me
,, May	,, May	,, May	,, May
,, him	,, him	,, him	,, him

| The AW-beam is in front of the upright EE, EH, and *i* beams. | The AW-beam is just behind the EE, EH, and *i*. | The AW-beam is inclined well behind the EE, EH, and *i* beams. |

4.

He calls	She calls	We call
May ,,	May ,,	May calls
It ,,	It ,,	It ,,

| The EE, EH, *i* are upright, and the AW is in front of them. | EE, EH, and *i* incline just back of the vertical, and AW somewhat behind them. | EE, EH, and *i* beams soaring upwards just behind the vertical, and AW is inclined well behind them all. |

5.

Oh, tell	Oh, tell	Oh, tell	Oh, tell
,, her	,, her	,, her	,, her
,, kneel	,, kneel	,, kneel	,, kneel

| The OH-beam is in front of the upright *eh, er,* and *ee* beams. | The OH is just behind the *eh, er,* and *ee* upright beams. | The OH-beam is inclined well behind the *eh, er,* and *ee* beams. |

6.

Cool shades	Cool shades	Cool shades
You came	You came	You came
To dream	To dream	To dream

| The OO-beam is in front of the upright EH, and EE beams. | | The OO-beam is inclined behind the EH and EE beams which soar upright just behind the vertical. |

N.B.—If you place a vowel-beam in front of another when it should go behind it, you will cramp your throat and get tonal distortion in degree. A correct direction of a vowel-beam in relation to pitch means a correct internal adjustment. (Study Diagram 1, p. 57.)

A Technical Instrument

(15) Hereunder we give a technical instrument of considerable importance:

(1) *Think* of, mentally *see*, and physically *hear* the VOWEL, while mentally shaping and physically producing it.

(2) Let the breath FLOW.

(3) Let the vowel flow along with the tonal stream.

(4) *Inside:* Be mentally very alert, alive, constructive all the time, with mind and mechanism braced, but with everything else relaxed (tongue, soft palate, and throat generally).

(5) *Outside:* Be apparently most unconcerned (relaxed) in order not to "show the works".

Except for purposes of expression, the face should remain calm and unaffected even when producing the highest notes and singing the most difficult phrases and passages; never at any time should there be a tugging of the facial and neck muscles, or stiffening of chin and jaw.

As you are about to produce vowelled tone, think of, mentally shape and "see", and physically hear (*inside*, and never outside yourself) first the particular vowel and then the whole word—which you should "see" mentally projected in front of you, as it were. You must be conscious of every vowel sound contained within the projected word. For example, take the phrase "Your soul is locked in mine". Firstly, what *sounds* make up the first word? *Your* is made up of two vowel sounds, i.e. a short *i* (as in *bit*) and *or*, as in *floor* (it is also pronounced y*oor*). The *ōr* is the chief vowel sound of this word, so you must flit over the short *i* and get right on to the *ōr*. *See* the complete word as you are producing the *ōr* tone; the next word, *soul*, includes two vowels, i.e. long *oh* (as in *police*) and short *u* (as in *put*), with the stress on the first; so sing the *oh*, see the whole word before you, and finish off with a short *ul* sound. And so on with the other words. At the same time, the innermost *meaning* of each word as it comes along must be given life and substance. Finally, you must have before you the picture or story a series of words convey. (See p. 301.)

With the vowel (the *singing* medium) and the complete word before you in this way, you can put into it what feeling, expression and accent you are able to muster for the duration of the note on which a particular vowel, syllable, or word happens to be.

Every vowel, particularly the one carrying the accent, every syllable, every word, particularly the important ones, should mean something, or everything, to you, even as the notes on which they are sung and the whole melodic line should; the very harmony under the note should be felt, and the *meaning* of its colour appreciated.

This is what great singers have always done. With them this mental shaping-seeing-cum-physical (internal) hearing was and is an ingrained habit. It conforms to the teaching of the old School, and one could say their motto was: "Think more to do less." (Today it seems to be: "Think less, or not at all, to do more.")

The habit is easily acquired with practice, and well worth the mental labour entailed.

The Soul of the Word

(16) The student is advised to work on vowel analysis until he is thoroughly conversant with the *sound* of every vowel, long and short, he meets with in the words of a song, aria, or operatic rôle. The vowel is the soul of the word; the word is the song. In English, many hundreds of words are written with letters of which the sounds do not correspond to those we are wont to associate with these particular letters in the alphabet. For instance, in words such as *song, sorry, solid*, the *o* is not an *oh* sound, as it is in the alphabet, but a modified *ah* sound; the same sound occurs in *of*. In words like *rough, us, up, convulse*, the *u* is not the *you* sound of the alphabetical letter, but is a derivative of *ah;* in the word *rough*, moreover, the *o* is unvoiced and quite superfluous therefore.

It is only by knowing the exact *sound* of every vowel (whatever letter is used to represent it) that the singer can hope to transmit the appropriate message to the vocal organs, which will always respond automatically to the *thought* of the exact sound and shape of a vowel, or vowels, he wants to produce; added to the vowel, of course, is the well prepared and released consonant completing the word.

So many singers think just of "tone", the vowel being for them a sort of vague background. Vowel necessarily includes tone; but tone may well be a nondescript affair, as it often is. How many singers are intelligible all the time? The majority regale us with "songs without words", which the good violinist will "put over" so much more effectively.

Good diction needs groundwork. The student should set about analysing his vowel sounds as follows: It is not sufficient to just look at a word—the important thing is to extract the sound, or sounds, as conveyed by the letters composing it. Let us take the word *song*, and extract the sound of this *o*. As stated above, it is a modified *ah*. So first *think* of the sound, and shape, then whisper it *staccato* several times, then voice it several times *staccato*, and finally sing it on a sustained low note, listening carefully all the time to the *sound*, and feeling the internal shaping that goes with it. No deliberate attempt to form the vowel must be made; it is sufficient to *think it in*, sound and shape. Next take a word like *sing:* What have we? We extract a sound which has nothing whatever to do with the sound we associate with the letter *i* of the alphabet, viz. a so-called short *i*. Now put it through the same processes as above, and in so doing listen to the *sound* of the *i* and feel the internal shaping that goes with it, and commit both to memory. (Note that "commit" has the two vowel sounds we have just examined.) Be careful to produce the *exact* sound to be "processed" in this way, and shape will look after itself; a correct vowel sound in-evitably connotes a correct shaping. Let us now examine the vowel sound in *egg* and *said;* in both words we have a so-called short *eh*, which is not so open as the EH in *Mary* or *where*. If we whisper and then voice the *eh* of *egg* and then that of *said*, we feel and hear a slightly more closed or flatter *eh* in the latter; the difference is extremely slight. When both are spoken, and sung on low and medium pitches, we detect this subtle difference, but not when sung on the upper medium and high notes, as the vowel itself undergoes modification, viz. a narrowing towards the *i* in *fig*.

Now take the word *sat*. What *sound* have we? Not the *ehi* of the *a* of the alphabet. It is a hybrid sound lying between *ah* and *eh*, partaking a little of each without actually being either. If the student will now "process" this sound, as above, he will note first its peculiarities of timbre, and secondly how its beam lies between the AH, as in I, and the EH. Test this by singing, on a lowish pitch, first AH, then the *a*, then EH, and back again. Thus: AH-*a*-EH-*a*-AH-*a*-EH, and so on, to and fro slowly several times in succession to get the feeling of the movements. Try to memorize the exact sound, and shape, of this *a*. If you now sing AH-*a*-EH slowly on every note up the full vocal scale you will feel how the *a* tends, on the high notes, more towards the *eh* in *egg* (and also a tendency towards *ir* (*bird*)), with an upright direction just back of the vertical. This hybrid *a* sound is found in many words, such as *and, have, had, sand, sad, pander,* etc.

If we now analyse the word *life* we find, firstly, that the *i* is spoken as in the alphabet, and secondly that it is a diphthong, consisting of two vowel sounds (as in I) viz.: an open AH (not quite so open as that in *far*) upon which the stress is laid in both speech and song, and a short *i* (as in *fig*), which is "flicked off" right at the end of the time value. *N.B.*—In this connection the student should be careful when singing diphthongs, that abound in English, such as AH*i* (in *life, bind, find,* etc.), OH*u* (in *rose, dome, roam, Rome, go,* etc), EH*i* (in *may, say, play,* etc.) to always give the *first* vowel about *9/10ths of the note value,* and retain, say, 1/10th to "flick off" the second and less important vowel sound. Too often we hear *lah*I——*f* instead of *l*AH——*if,* or *shah*I——*ne* instead of *sh*AH——*ine.* All English diphthongs must be sung like the Italian *mio,* which has the stress on the EE; it means *mine,* which also has the stress on the first vowel of this diphthong, viz. the AH.

In *go* and *do,* for example, the same letter is used to represent different vowels: the first is the alphabetical diphthong OH*u,* but the second is OO (one sound only). In words like *put* and *foot,* however, we have the same short *u* sound represented by different letters (English is not more inconsistent in this respect than most languages); when sung on the same low note the short *u* of *put* is just behind the long *oo* as in *pool,* being actually a mixed sound of *oo* and *oh.* As a matter of fact, the *u* and *oo* become, on the high notes, one and the same vowel sound and tune in at the same spot because the long OO should open out slightly as the pitch rises, to take on percentages of OH and so become a mixed vowel like the short *u.* The student should "process" this *u* in order to memorize its exact sound, *mixed* sound.

The above few examples are intended to point the way to vowel-sound analysis which the student is well advised to practise daily until all the vowels, long and short, and their internal shaping, are *memorized.* The task is not arduous or long, and it is superfluous to enumerate the advantages accruing therefrom.

We dealt with the analysis of the consonant in Chapter X, Part II, pp. 110–20. In this connection, we tell the student to "bunch the fingertips to represent the consonant" and then "spring them apart quickly but smoothly to represent the vowel". One must always get rid of the working parts of the consonant (tongue, soft palate, lips) and make for the vowel quickly, smoothly, without jerking or stiffness; the vowel shape must be free of every impediment.

TONAL UNSTEADINESS

(17) The wobble apart, there is a kind of tonal unsteadiness which may be confined to an occasional note, to a series of notes— as in a phrase, or present in all notes of a voice. This unsteadiness or irregular "pulsing" is caused very often by an irregular breath pressure; by a momentary intermittent halting of the breath flow, of which the singer is generally not conscious; by a constant excessive breath pressure.

The average length of vocal cord in women is half an inch, that in men three-quarters of an inch. When we compare this tiny and beautifully fashioned instrument, in which is embedded a phenomenal mechanism, to the big and powerful breathing apparatus, we shudder to think of the fearful abuse to which it is subjected by the forced-breath-pressure method so much in vogue.

Under normal conditions the vocal cords vibrate, i.e. open and close horizontally with a to-and-fro sideways motion. When subjected to excess breath pressure they are liable to give way and arch upwards slightly; as a result their vibratory motion is dual: (1) the normal sideways opening-closing during which the cords are absolutely horizontal; (2) the abnormal up-and-down movement as the cords endeavour to return to their normal horizontal position only to be arched upwards again by the continued blast. Which dual movement makes the tone "sticky" and heavy, imparting to it an irregular throb. Apart from this, it is exhausting work for the cords themselves and the muscles actuating them. If the excess pressure is habitual, the laryngeal muscles first harden, then get "knotty" (muscle-bound), and finally become exhausted and flabby. The fearful wobble makes its appearance. In certain cases, one cord will be found to be folded over the other (like crossing one's legs); in others, the cords have become "knock-kneed". This is what an habitual excess breath pressure and its fool brother—the *coup de glotte*—will do to the vocal cords of misguided singers. The *cough* de glotte! (See pp. 178-9.)

ON DETAILED INSTRUCTION

(18) Whereas some students will revel in the details of this exposition, others may find them irksome and the whole work too "complicated". A certain type of mind is unable to probe into the depths of things. To such as these, our advice is that each should do his own condensing of the work by extracting therefrom just what appeals to him and what he thinks he will require and can absorb. (See para. 6, p. 287.)

Our purpose in this detailed exposition is to bring thought, that has long been educated away from the fundamental principles and from even the simplest precepts, back to a burning focus, not of passing interest but of detailed inquiry and searching analysis. It is only by making adequate enlargements separately of the "pictures" reflecting the various vocal-mechanical functions, the resonant effects resulting therefrom and the sensations they produce in the singer himself, and it is only by enlarging every part of the vocal whole of sensations that they can be brought nearer to the student for examination. Enlargement is analysis. To merely make a statement, by word of mouth or in writing, is not sufficient, even if it is a fact; to be really constructive, a detailed explanation must follow. To our thinking, details simplify matters.*

THE REST FACTOR

(19) Few singers realize the importance of rest where actual vocal work is concerned. Too many use their voices for one or even two hours without a pause, and some put in three or four hours a day, and boast about it. But eventually they pay for it in coins of premature ageing of the voice, and disappointment. You cannot afford to "slog" any machine, however good. Every muscle, or group of muscles, must be given periods of rest; work without rest in the laryngo-pharyngeal region produces, firstly, congestion of the parts; secondly, abnormal fatigue; and finally local inflammation. The plethora of blood thus established at the part affected by excessive exercise is increasingly demanded by that part for subsequent functioning and cannot be supplied without abnormal effort. It becomes a vicious circle.

* The author will be pleased to answer any question that may perplex the reader of this work, or of the parent work—*The Science and Sensations of Vocal Tone* (Dent).

For instance, during a whole hour's singing the voice should be rested several times at intervals for one or two minutes at a time. This is highly beneficial, and not "a waste of time". The voice responds gaily to this treatment. Muscles can get "fed up" just as much as minds do. Every singer must use his own discretion as to the amount of rest his own voice needs. Thus real strength and stamina are built up.

Even with reasonable periods of rest there is such a thing as normal "athletic" fatigue, which is constructive and invigorating; as the vocal organs gain strength, so this fatigue gradually decreases almost to vanishing point.

ON MEZZAVOCE

(20) *Piano* or *pianissimo* effects can also be made with the mouth barely open, no attempt being made to pucker or otherwise shape the lips, whatever the vowel may be. Miniature vowel tones can thus be produced.* An indispensable condition, however, is a good vowel shaping *within* the mouth-pharynx cavity. (In this connection the following test is instructive: With lips barely separated—just sufficient to let the sound out—let the student sing *mp*, on middle C, the five vowels AH, EH, EE, OH, OO, in this or any order, three or four times in succession, *smoothly*, with one breath and in moderately fast tempo, making absolutely no attempt to "place" any tone and *without any lip movement* whatever. He will hear, and feel, five distinct well-shaped "miniature" vowels. Let him now make this test, still *mp*, *p* or *pp* on different, higher pitches. (An added advantage is that it proves to the student that *the pharynx is the real mouth of the singer*.)

Singers with flexible voices can carry the test to the high pitches; in which case a little more mouth aperture may be necessary. Care, however, must be taken when singing the vowels AW, OH and OO *piano* with a small lip aperture on pitches above E♭, fourth space, *not* to associate them with the direction they take in speech, viz. forward in varying degree on the arc of the hard palate. On the contrary, as explained elsewhere, they must be

---

* The usual *p* tone produced in the studio or drawing-room may suffice for the concert hall, even a vast one, but only if with pianoforte accompaniment. Singing with the orchestra in concert hall or opera house requires that the *p* be less *piano* and the *f* more *forte*. It is all relative. This more *f* means more tonal *appoggio* (not bawling).

behind the vertical and pointing upwards, from said E♭ up to the highest pitches. The inexperienced singer, when producing these three vowels on a high pitch with small lip aperture, is apt (because thinking of the low pitch of speech) to place the tone forward against the vertical or in front of it, with the result that the note will be coupled in at insufficient height. If to assist this forward thrust of the tone he adds the forward pull of the puckered lips, he unwittingly introduces a rival resonator at the mouth—whereas all high notes, whatever the vowel used, *p* or *f*, demand a *vertical lengthening* of the resonator, and never a horizontal lengthening; the latter spells tonal distortion in no small degree.

ON EXPRESSION

(21) Love, hate, joy, sadness, fear, courage, resentment, sarcasm, bitterness, anger, suffering, anguish, mental and physical pain, and so forth, each have their characteristic timbre that is readily detected in the spoken word, and every human being, as circumstances arise, unconsciously injects into his speech the timbre peculiar to each of these moods and emotions. It comes natural to one and all. But why is it that so many singers seem unable to include in their singing tone, even in moderate degree, these varicoloured inflections? Is it lack of imagination, or are they reluctant, too self-conscious or "shy", to show any feeling? Are they incapable of being moved by poignant situations in which imaginary characters laugh and cry, and live and die? Are they not capable of being moved by words and music, and what they express, to a point of make-believe bordering on the real, even as the dramatist and composer were while creating their work? The good actor feels his rôle and is able to identify himself with the character he is portraying, and rouses an audience to enthusiastic approval mainly through the varied tones of the spoken word. Likewise, *the singer must paint the picture and tell the story* of song, aria or operatic rôle with varicoloured vocal tones; he must learn to act with his voice. He who is not moved, cannot expect to move others.

RESONATING SPACE

(22) When attacking a high note directly, or producing it at the end of a rising phrase, it is necessary always *to anticipate the space* for the soaring sound-beam. We tell the student to create an "air-ball"; which simple *thought* of an air-ball is instrumental in

creating adequate space without stiffening. In fact, the idea of an
air-ball is the exact opposite of rigidity, and it induces automatically the expansion of the pharyngeal cavity; hence we get an
enlargement of the resonating space. (See Gigli's practice, p. 22.)

Two Bad Habits

(23) To scoop up from one pitch to a higher one, or moan
down from a high to a lower pitch, even if only a semitone, on a
thick tonal line is the essence of inartistic ugliness; it is also bad craftsmanship. Many mistake the upward scoop and downward moan
for *portamento-legato*, which double term means a "carrying up
and joining" one note to the next with smooth tonal continuity.
Whereas the *portamento* is purposely made audible, the *legato* is a
practically inaudible tonal line joining note to note. The true upward *portamento* should be made on a tenuous gossamer-like tonal
thread; if on a thick tonal line it becomes a "scoop". Also, the downward *portamento* should be executed on a very thin tonal line; if on
a thick line, it moans—a "moanamento", therefore. (See p. 244.)

There must be no scooping or gliding up to a note when attacking it; tonal attack must be direct on the pitch—like pressing the
button of an electric bell. To this end we tell the student to "talk
the vowel in", right on the pitch.

Exercises for Diction

(24) Hereunder are a few exercises that are excellent not only
for moulding the vocal organs, and therefore acquiring good
technique, but also as an aid to good diction. And what is good
diction but a well-shaped vowel and an appropriately formed and
released consonant. Basses, baritones and contraltos should transpose accordingly to suit their voices:

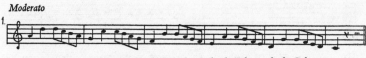

ah eh Bah... ah eh Cah... ah eh Dah...ah eh Fah...ah eh Gah......

First, sing this as written, then transpose up a semitone at a time,
viz., into the keys successively of Db, D, Eb, E, F, and so on, in
order to reach the normally highest note, say Bb, for tenors,
sopranos and mezzos. Basses, baritones and contraltos should start

in the key of G and transpose up, as above mentioned, and so reach their normally highest note, say G or A♭. (Some contraltos, of course, go as high as the mezzo.)

To derive full benefit from this exercise the student will remember that the AH must *always* come behind the EH, whatever the pitch. All consonants must be exercised in turn; when single consonants have been worked in, syllables with two and three consonants should be used, as, for instance, *Flah, grah, strah, sprah,* and so forth. After a time the AW, OH and OO vowels should successively be used instead of AH, and worked in as above. Mainly, the above remarks apply also to the following exercises:

Moderato

(AH)	1. ah ...	balm .	ah ... calm .	ah ... darn ..	ah ... farm .	ah .... guard ....
(AW)	2. ah ...	born .	ah ... corn .	ah ... dawn .	ah ... fawn .	ah .... gaunt ....
(OH)	3. ah ...	bone .	ah ... cone .	ah ... dome .	ah ... foam .	ah .... goad ....
(OO)	4. ah ...	boom	ah ... cool .	ah ... doom.	ah ... fool ..	ah .... goose ....
(EH)	5. ah ...	where	ah ... bear .	ah ... dare ..	ah ... flare .	ah .... glare ...
(EE)	6. ah ...	been .	ah ... seen ..	ah ... dream.	ah ... stream	ah .... gleam....

The student, as he transposes up from key to key, as mentioned above, should choose different words and so make the exercise more useful and interesting. He is reminded that all vowels, long and short, are in front of the AH, whatever the pitch. Apart from the above six long vowels, also the short vowels should be exercised, as in *pat, pot, put, pet, pit,* as well as the *ir* vowel as in *bird, heard, turf.* It is well to prepare a list of words including these twelve vowels.

Moderato, con moto

(1)	ah.....awehee oo........ah.......awehee oo........ah......awehee
(2)	ah.....aweheecharm.....ah.......aweheecharm.....ah......awehee

oo........ah.....awehee oo.......ah......awehee oo..............
charm.....ah.....aweheecharm.....ah......aweheecharm..........

N.B.—In (2) above, the word "charm" is merely given as an example. From phrase to phrase a different word should be used. There must be no jerking as the vowel springs out of the consonant (see p. 267). Remember that the AH of *charm* is always back of the *ee*.

This exercise is extraordinarily helpful to all voices, as it induces a smooth output of breath and consequently flowing tone. To assist matters we press into service a mental device that (1) indirectly obviates all stiffening of the breathing muscles, inducing their smooth action which, in turn, provides a smooth and regular breath stream, and (2) prevents forced breath pressure—the bane of modern singers; (3) loosens the whole throat.

As he starts to sing this exercise, let the student picture a tonal wheel revolving *horizontally* (clockwise) *inside* the mouth-pharynx cavity; he should be *mentally underneath* the spinning wheel, and each vowel as it comes along should be seated on the rim. The speed of the wheel is determined by the tempo at which the exercise is taken. The physical reaction to the very thought of a turning wheel is highly beneficial, as stated above. It also ensures the smooth merging of one vowel into another without jerking or halting of the breath-cum-tone.*

Sopranos, mezzos and tenors should start the exercise in the above key, and the other categories two or three keys lower; then transpose up a semitone at a time until the normally highest note in the particular compass is reached. As the pitch rises, so the wheel gets gradually smaller. If it were, say, the size of a half-crown when singing the exercise on the lowest key, it will be reduced to the size of a threepenny bit, or less, on the highest key. The feeling of gradual decrease in the size of the wheel as the pitch rises is due to the gradual decrease in the internal movement as one vowel after another is brought into play. Be it remembered that when singing different vowels on the same high pitch, or on different high pitches close together, the internal movement of adjustment from vowel to vowel is reduced to a minimum. (The modern methods of "placing" the tone forward, or on "the mask", and "covering", induce brusque, erroneous and exaggerated movements of the throat which absolutely distort the vowel shaping.)

* Instead of a spinning wheel one can imagine a *revolving globe:* the size of a golf ball on the lower notes, and of a pea on the highest pitches.

S

The turning wheel does not, of course, take into account the directions taken by the varying vowel-beams, nor does it interfere with their natural trend. And because the wheel imparts to the throat the required freedom of action, the beams will seek and find their natural points of impingement. We are assuming in all this, vowels well shaped in relation to pitch.

May we again impress upon the student that the actual internal rounding for vowel modification is *so slight* that the mere *thought* of the more rounded and darker vowel tone is sufficient to induce the right adjustment. The physical reaction to the rounding-thought is immediate and exact. To *do* the rounding physically, deliberately, is to overdo it every time, because nobody (neither teacher nor the singer himself, neither scientist nor physiologist) knows or indeed ever can know the *exact* amount of internal adjustment, i.e. movement of tongue, soft palate and throat generally, for a given vowel and its modification; it is physically immeasurable. Only the mind, guided on the right lines by think-ing the exact vowel tone and exact modification required, can induce the exact physical adjustment. It all demands a certain delicacy of procedure, the same delicacy of thought that guides and controls the touch of the painter's pencil and brush.

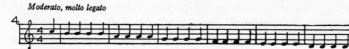

Bah kay ee aw dah fay ee aw cah gay ee aw sah jay ee aw pah lay ee aw tah may ee aw BAH

Then transpose up, as stated above, changing the consonant at every bar. Sing the exercise very *legato*, very smoothly. There must be no jerking or stiffening as the consonant is released.

ah eh ah *love*. . . ah eh ee *me* . . . ah eh aw *for* . . . . ah eh ee *ev-*   *er* ah eh oh *do* . . . .

Tenors, sopranos and mezzos should start in the key of G, as above, and transpose down a semitone at a time until the normally lowest note is reached. Basses, baritones and contraltos, however, will start, say, a third lower (all depending on the individual voice), and then transpose down from key to key. The words to be sung should be changed as the new key is entered; fresh combinations are good for diction.

The idea of starting in a high key is to exercise the pronunciation of words on high notes. Remember that the consonant must always be *mentally* formed and released right on top of the focal point (platform); this makes for lightness and crispness of consonantal action that never disturbs the vocal cord adjustment for the ensuing vowelled tone. (See Diagram 3, p. 110.)

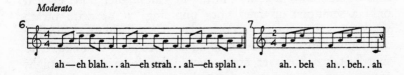

All voices can start in this key, or lower. Then transpose up a semitone at a time. Different syllables should be used every time, with one, two, or three consonants before the vowel.

Then transpose up a semitone (D♭ major), and so on, key by key, until the highest note is reached. All the vowels should be sung-in in this way; also the short vowels should be tuned in with scale work.

The importance of singing scales cannot be overestimated. The gradual climb as the scale is sung up and down again in the different keys, getting higher and higher, develops, strengthens and "tones up" the muscular systems actuating the cord mechanism, the pharyngeal parts, and the breathing apparatus. Only such scale work can really fashion the vocal instrument and finally build into it a high degree of automatism whereby the varying adjustments of all the parts concerned obtain with fine accuracy and a minimum of thought directing and controlling.

The arrows in the above sample scale represent the note-to-note lift-up both up and down the scale (the importance of which is explained in Chapter XVI), which should be assiduously culti-vated until it becomes a habit of mind and a habit of voice. If he gives the principle sufficient thought and practice, the student will find himself automatically "lifting-in" the higher note, even if only a semitone up (and not "pumping" it up with breath pressure, as so many singers do today, particularly on the higher and high pitches), and also keeping all descending tones up. Care must be taken, however, not to overdo the lift-up idea, as it might fog the tone. A characteristic of the completely natural voice is precisely this tonal lift-up when going to a higher note and also when descending to lower pitches. The lift-up assists the cord-thinning process within the larynx. We learn from nature's *completed* examples, completed designs; and that is how *the* glorious School of natural vocal technique was built up in the past.

In a two-octave scale, when the pitch rises from the normally lowest to the normally highest notes of the individual voice, there *must* be, either naturally or assisted by deliberate thought, a gradual rounding (modification) of the vowel tone-cum-shape. This applies in degree to all vowels, long and short. *One cannot separate shape and tone*, for the slightest change in the shaping of the mouth-pharynx cavity alters the tonal quality in equal degree; and *if you change the tone you are actually changing the shape of this cavity in some degree.**

* If we draw a series of quarter-circle curves varying in size gradually until only that of a pinhead is left, it is because the *mind* has estimated every curving. This is obvious to us all. What is not obvious, however, to the average student, is that the mind can and *must* be allowed to estimate the different curvings within the pharyngeal region that physically reflect the varying and often subtle tonal modifications. As explained in Chapter XIII, the *shaping thought* reacts automatically upon the shaping of the mouth-pharynx cavity. The singer must *not* do any deliberate vowel shaping, or curving.

The principle modifications of all the vowels applicable, say, to an ascending scale of two octaves, are as follow:

Long Vowels

AH (as in *far, father*), modifying gradually to the *ah* sound in *god, sorry,* then towards *aw* with final tints of *oh* and *oo*.

AW (as in *awe, ought*), modifying gradually towards *oh* with final tints of *oo*.

OH (as in *polite, rose*), modifying gradually towards *oo* (or *u* in *put*) on the high notes.

OO (as in *pool, cool*), modifying gradually by opening out to introduce percentages of *oh,* to finally produce the *u* (as in *put, good*).

EH (as in *may, Mary*), modifying gradually by narrowing first to *eh* in *egg, breast,* and finally to the *i* sound in *fig, pit*.

EE (as in *sea, feel*), modifying gradually by curving towards the French *u* sound.

Short Vowels

a (as in *pat, have*), modifying gradually by darkening the sound towards *eh* (in *egg*), to finally take on a slight *ir* tinge.

o (as in *pot, song*), actually a modified AH sound, undergoing further rounding off as given above for this vowel.

u (as in *put, could*), maintains its mixed tone of *oh–oo,* as above for OO.

e (as in *pet, egg*), actually a modified or narrowed EH, gradually narrowing towards *i* (in *fig, pit*), itself a mixed tone of *eh* and *ee*.

i (as in *pit, rim*), a mixed tone of *eh* and *ee,* gradually takes on a tinge of French *u,* as for *ee* above.

ir (as in *bird, absurd*), gradually darkening and narrowing as the pitch rises.

While on the subject of vowel modification, it is well to point to the four basic modifications of AH in the English language, i.e.:

AH[1] (as in *far, father*), corresponding exactly to the Italian A, as in *padre*.

AH[1¼] (as in *I, eye*), which is merely a slightly rounded AH[1].

AH[1½] (as in *one, won*), which is slightly more rounded than AH[1¼].

AH² (as in *sorry*, *song*), which is more modified or rounded than AH¹ᶻ.

There is no word reflecting the next modification—AH³, a dark edition of AH², before reaching the rounded AW vowel sound (which could almost be called AH⁴).

THE MENTAL "SOUNDBOARD"

(25) So many singers are inclined to close and tighten their throats, due possibly to the forward production methods, to "covering", or to a general tendency to constriction. Apart from the obvious disadvantages accruing therefrom, they fail to secure adequate space for tonal reinforcement and prevent the sound-beams from following their natural direction. To counteract all this we press into service a very effective mental device, i.e. an imaginary soundboard inclined backwards with respect to the vertical. The physical reaction to this idea is extraordinary: (1) the whole throat is left free and easy, and nicely open; (2) adequate space is provided automatically, whereupon (3) the sound-beam is free to soar to its natural sensation-point for accurate tuning-in; (4) it acts as an anti-forward production device, and (5) as an anti-"covering" device, and therefore (6) as an anti-humping of the throat with its resultant tonal distortion.

It is particularly useful for tenors. But all voices can apply it. Due to its angle of inclination, the "soundboard" becomes operative from about C, third space, upwards. The AH vowel should be worked in first, then AW, and afterwards OH and OO. On the AH vowel, however, one can start the scale work from middle C. You just picture this soundboard inclined back of the vertical, as in the diagram below, and tapering towards the top end, and place your vowel on the surface, keeping it there all the time as you go up and down the different scales, or exercises. Don't let the vowel tone come away from the "surface" of the soundboard, for that will mean that you are "humping" your throat. Once you get the idea you will soon feel any cramping of the throat. You need not worry about "placing" the tones; the beams, having now a free right of way, will seek out their own natural points of impingement. You can "walk" up the scale on the surface of the soundboard with the vowels *ee, eh, ah, aw, ee, eh, ah, aw,* or any combination thereof, and down again. The EH and EE vowels can also be worked in separately on the soundboard; for these two vowels you can, if you like, somewhat straighten up the soundboard so that it will not be so far from the vertical. As you sing up the surface, don't forget a *slight* lift-up from note to note, and to round off the vowel in the usual way as the pitch rises. Feel that you are, so to speak, laying the vowel backwards against the surface of the board.

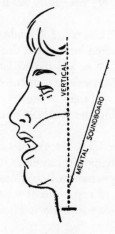

DIAGRAM 17

The angle at which we mentally create the soundboard is actually that of the AH vowel when sung from E♭, fourth space upwards; so actually you sing AW, OH and OO *up this AH-road*. The idea of the soundboard was born out of the fact that the AH is the farthest back of all vowels, whatever the pitch, high or low, and that no vowel can ever come behind it.

Before starting to sing, the soundboard should be mentally created and "set" at the correct angle in readiness for the oncoming tones.

When this mental artifice has served its purpose, it should be abandoned, and the voice built up by normal procedure.

N.B.—The author's *Fifty Vowelization Exercises*, published by Ricordi & Co. (E.R.945), will be found extremely useful and beneficial.

CHAPTER XX

ON INTERPRETATION

Iₙ Giuseppe Verdi's "Letters", *I Copialettere di Giuseppe Verdi*, two of the letters, quoted hereunder, dealing with the mooted question of interpretation, are particularly enlightening. The truth underlying the Master's statement is obvious. Years of practice and experience will shape a mechanism for extracting the fine essence hidden behind the symbols of thought we call notes, melody, and harmony.

Verdi wrote, in Letter CCXXI, April 11, 1871, that:

"When singers take it upon themselves to *create* (as the French still say) their parts, nonsense and confusion result. No! I want only one creator, and will rest content when performance is *just simply and exactly as the music is written*. The mischief is that music is never rendered as written. For my part, I have never found the 'effects not imagined by the composer' that we often read about in the papers. I do not admit the right of singers, or conductors, to *create*, because that is a principle which leads to the bottomless pit." Again, in Letter CCXXXIV, he states: "It is indispensable to know the composer's intentions. No success is possible, whatever the music, without intelligent, aye, *devoted* rendition."

The following extract from an article in *The Musical Times*, July 1, 1930, by the Editor, Dr. Harvey Grace (reprinted with permission), offers strong British views on the same subject:

TECHNIQUE AND INTERPRETATION
by Dr. Harvey Grace

Technique was probably never less esteemed than it is today. On all sides we see the half-taught dabbler with a temperament (or with plenty of assurance) acclaimed above the man who knows his job so well that he does it without fuss. Musical journalism is now being invaded by writers whose literary ability cannot atone for their ignorance of the fundamentals of music, and one of their favourite and most damnable heresies is that technical knowledge and pedantry are almost synonymous terms. Apparently they hold the view that the more you know about music, the less you enjoy it—that, in fact, ignorance being bliss, it is sheer waste of time to be wise. The blessed (I almost used another adjective)—the blessed word "interpretation" is always at the end of their pen.

Toscanini showed that, performed with superlative technique and with faithfulness to the score, *great music is almost always its own interpreter.* Why should so many conductors distort rhythm, retard already slow second subjects, add an extra *f* to *fortissimo*, another *p* to *pianissimo*, and so forth, when (as Toscanini has shown) all the variety that is necessary has been provided by the composer?

Toscanini and his players reminded us thus of the primary importance of technique. Was it Bulow who said that the first thing in pianoforte playing was technique, the second, technique, and the third, technique? Before hastily deciding that he was wrong, let us try to make a list of great performers and composers who have failed through having too much technique. We shall soon give it up, and turn to the far easier task of naming those who have failed through having too little. So, after this triumphant vindication of technique by the New York Philharmonic Orchestra, let us have heaps more of it, and a good deal less of that confounded "interpretation". Often it is sheer impertinence prompted by vanity; and sometimes (to adopt a witticism of Beerbohm Tree's) it may even be described as the "loincloth of the incompetent".

On all sides it is agreed that the outstanding feature of the playing under Toscanini was its straightforwardness and its freedom from point-making and underlining—almost all the features, in fact, that mark the performances under conductors of the so-called "interpretative" type. Yet have we ever heard more moving or impressive playing than that of such familiar things as the "Eroica"? The general feeling that all sorts of fresh beauties and details were revealed, was due, as Mr. Ernest Newman pointed out, simply to the fact that for once in a way *we heard the music as the composer wrote it,* with all its niceties of balance and nuance duly respected. The players had the necessary technique, and the conductor's reverence and modesty prevented him from coming between us and the composer.

*   *   *

We should now like to advance our own views, for what they are worth, on this thorny matter: What, then, should be the attitude of the singer towards a composition? The first essential is to get self out of the way. By this we mean that the singer, before he moves in to render a vocal work, must view things in their correct perspective. He must consider the composition (1) to be an emanation compounded of two sources springing from two individual minds: the poet's and the composer's; (2) the poet writes his words, mere symbols to express his ideas, imaginings, feelings, moods and emotions that he injects into imaginary persons, things, situations, happenings. And to convey sometimes a flood of such thoughts he has as a vehicle mere words that speak to the mind through the eye, and to the ear through the voice. Words are often inadequate to express the full chain of ideas; but they are eloquent signposts pointing to the hamlets, villages, towns, cities, and capitals of mind in which the poet lives, moves and has his being; (3) the composer reads the words, and the choice of words, the verses and stanzas reveal to him the poet's intentions and so form a picture of events. Much depends on the quality of this picture, on its clarity and details; if pronounced, the poet's original picture will be reinforced by the composer's. Actually, it will be one and the same thing, with the possible and probable addition of delicate beauties from the fine mind of the musician. Thus the two minds vibrate in unison: two more or less identical pictures, one superimposed on the other.

The next step is when the composer puts down in musical notation this dual or joint picture representing a story into which he injects his own feelings, moods and emotions, developing a vocal line with a majestic harmonic support. This tonal picture dovetails perfectly into the poet's symphony, forming, as it does so, a complete work. In one sense the composer's tone-colouring work is more limited than the poet's effort, in that the written or spoken word conveys much more meaning to the average person and to the masses than do the symbols we call musical notation and the melodies and harmonies accruing therefrom. Observe that the composer has to compress within the narrow limits of mere notes strung on a melodic line that rides on more notes compounded into a harmonic structure, *all* the paraphernalia of human thought, the full gamut of moods and emotions, with a few added markings of expression. It is asking much. To help him he has the thrilling voice of melody and the wonderful colouring of harmonic combinations that accompany, support, and embellish the throbbing tones as they rise and fall in stately undulation; a change of key and of time reflecting a change of mood or emotion, an added sharp, or flat, or natural, meaning worlds, or just a fleeting emphasis.

And as he writes, the good composer has in mind his ideas, and ideals of production and execution: perfect attack, well-shaped, colourful vowels, smooth tonal continuity, expansion and shrinkage of *crescendo* and *diminuendo*, the forward surge of *accelerando*, the delaying of *rit.* and *rall;* he also builds in terms of varying tempi, rhythm, accent and expression, with an occasional *rubato*— a very important auxiliary much neglected by executants in general. As he composes he *hears* in his mind the particular voice for which he has to raise a melodic-harmonic edifice. He sees and hears *his* creatures—who, originally, are the poet's creations—and he lives with them, laughs, cries, suffers for and with them. To him the characters of an opera, or even of a song, are real, live beings; and he loves them all whether they are good or bad.*

The actual notes, of long or short duration, are after all mere pointers to, and hieroglyphs of, the inner substance of the joint poetic-musical concept—like portholes in a ship affording light and vision to the various cabins and trappings within. Notes are small peepholes in the curtain separating composer and performer through which can be seen the tonal realm that the latter has to "interpret", or explain, and make clear to the audience. In other words, he has to describe the joint picture.

As the melody-cum-harmony is merely the skeleton of the real picture behind, so to speak, it is up to the singer to convey to the audience everything that he sees and *feels*.

Whatever the nationality of the composer, he speaks the universal language of music. Of course there is both a melodic and harmonic idiom characteristic of national music, the product of a race-mind, just as there is a national idiom in all spoken languages. Even as moods and emotions have their degrees of intensity according to racial idiosyncrasy, so certain individuals of one race will externalize with greater emphasis than others of another, and different individuals of the same race will vary in the degree of intensity of expression. So with a piece of music before him the

* Puccini, at 4 a.m., was found in tears at the piano by his wife: "Mimi is dead," he muttered. Verdi shed tears when Aida died.

singer should remember above all that the composer (alive or dead) has a tale to tell, which is also the poet's, that he will speak to you in frank terms, that he will bare and reveal his most intimate thoughts provided you let him by getting *self out of the way*— at least while you are analysing and extracting the essence out of the aria, or song; the composer will conduct you round his musical workshop, show you his creations, and guide you bar by bar, phrase by phrase. Let *him* do all the talking, and you all the listening: *then wait for your reaction*. But wait in a receptive mood and be ready to grasp and make yours, as it were, the composition as a whole. Thus does self take a back seat—for the moment.

If a good one, the composer has already done all the "interpreting" that *you* will ever need to score a success, other things being equal; but you must not merely follow and carry out his markings of expression; the thing to do is to get right into the melodic line and ride on it as it rises and falls. Let each note-cum-word, or syllable, literally speak to you and express its entire being, for in a good composition every single note has meaning. Until you get the real feeling of the song, try not to allow your own thoughts on how *you* think "it ought to go", to intrude on the newborn atmosphere; if they do, they will spoil reception exactly as atmospherics or another incoming station will spoil reception on a radio set. There must be no interference; so just tune in to the composer's station and let *him* do all the broadcasting. With practice and in time, you, the singer, will be able to relay it clearly, faithfully, interpretatively.

What passes in the poet's mind and what in the composer's as they write? What do they see, hear, and feel? *That* is what you, as a singer, must get at, contact, and tune in to. Their respective forms of composition reflect and manifest the respective images of thought; they will therefore speak to you as a beautiful rose does, as the sun and moon and stars do, if you know how to feel, listen, and read aright.

Some composers, like some writers, do not always express themselves with sufficient clarity, and the inner meaning appears elusive, impossible to grasp. Much of the so-called ultra-modern music is just "clever" manipulation of notes, and conveys "pictures" that are as intelligible and visible as a Raffaello in total darkness; the mental image behind the cacophony may well be cubistic, but tonal cubes are not inspiring.

Compositions vary in quality as do speech, letter and essay writing. A language when spoken can be mutilated, painful to hear; and letter writing varies from puerile to perfection. By the same token a musical composition can be anything from soggy to sublime. Given a really good composition, the singer must not attempt to "paint the lily", or the peach. Cabbage combinations, however, do require a lot of make-up. The ordinary ballad is not generally the product of a master mind, but can be materially improved by a good and imaginative singer.

He would be a bold man that attempted to improve on or even touch up the work of a Michelangelo, Da Vinci, Raffaello or Reynolds. Has anybody attempted to improve Shakespeare? Or Verdi, Puccini, Wagner, Beethoven? The idea is preposterous. Why then in the name of reason do singers, and conductors, vainly imagine that they are "interpreting", aye, improving, the work of a master-composer by adding personal frills of "expression", exaggerated displays of emotion, fake feeling, stabbed and hammered accents, mostly in the wrong places; *andante* slowed down to funereal, *moderato* whipped up to a gallop, turning *p* into *f*, and so forth. Verdi once said, "I write five *p*'s to get one".

Interpretation, reduced to its simplest terms, is nothing but the possibility of being roused emotionally in the same degree as that of the composer when he was actually writing the particular aria or song (or whatever music is being performed). If we can contact his thoughts, and feel what he felt, as they lie imprisoned within note, bar and phrase, and an occasional marking, if we can do this without injecting any personal twists of fancy, we shall have what is called interpretation at its best and highest, as the composer himself would wish it. It is for the discerning singer to release the imprisoned wealth through appropriate tonal colours, expression, and accent.

The good singer stamps that undefinable substance called personality on everything he sings, his atmosphere of mind commingling with that of the composer, and with that of the poet. Actually, a song or aria well rendered is a product of three minds. (See pp. 250, 299–302.)

CHAPTER XXI

OCCASIONAL JOTTINGS AND ADDENDA

(A)

ART IS LONG TO LEARN: its pupils pass through stages when they seem bewilderingly to go backwards. But this is merely a reaction to impatience.

The singer can durably improve and master nature only by obeying her laws, not by violating them.

The student must keep alive that zest, that spirit of enthusiasm that alone can nerve him for the struggle towards achievement.

A new work, a novel presentation, a new idea can quicken the faculties: Education, to be successful, must not only inform but inspire. The first essential of learning is an open mind.

The student must learn gradually to teach himself to think for himself.

It is the intangible that is inclined to be overlooked or ignored; consequently, a disproportionate amount of attention is devoted to purely physical effort, forgetting that singing is mainly mental.

Behaviour results from beliefs: if the belief is wrong, the behaviour that follows it is always wrong; and conversely.

Not one of the various factors of vocal technique can be interpreted as an isolated phenomenon, for each of them fits into a perfect scheme that may look complicated when viewed from the circumference but is certainly simple at the centre. As it is in the physical universe, so it is in the realm of vocal technique: dependence is everywhere; independence nowhere. Hence the detailed elaboration in the present work.

From the technical standpoint there is no discernible difference between a *completely* natural voice and a perfectly trained one.

The singer, if he wishes to reveal his powers of artistry to the full, must be ever on the alert to guard against and hold in check that streak of brutality, that something lurking in the human mind ready to engulf or destroy the finer traits—even as the frosts of earth destroy flower and fruit.

In singing, physique is in inverse proportion to pitch. Meaning that the lower the note, the relatively greater the vibrator mass used; and, vice versa, the higher the note, the greater the tendency towards a dwindling percentage of vibrator mass.

Whether he is taking a lesson, or studying by himself, the student should retire within a mental circle of song that severely excludes the usual annoyances of life and that petty feverishness which we are wont to associate with civilization.

Too often the attitude of an individual when contemplating a work of art, reading a book, or listening to a voice, is dictated not by knowledge but by the emotional response in himself.

Abbreviation can easily degenerate into dullness, but detail arouses the faculties and makes for interesting and constructive reading. "Details," wrote Oscar Wilde, "are the only things that interest." (See (18), p. 268.)

Why this low standard of art and craftsmanship in singing as compared to the much higher one of all other instrumental performances? It is due mainly to the total or partial lack of real technical knowledge in both the teaching and the performing realms.

When his production is mediocre or bad, the singer's mind is unconsciously imprisoned within the narrow precincts of the false tonal products of his own creating.

The first inkling of the falsity of a concept marks the parting of the ways towards its ultimate disappearance.

A figure of speech, or an analogy, is always admissible if it helps an idea to reach the student's understanding.

A teacher who allows a vocal defect to persist can be taken to task as much as if he had actually taught it.

Some students think of progress in terms of prolonged effort rather than of accomplishment; and others in terms of increased power of tone, with quality at vanishing point. Ambition often far outruns performance.

The constant aim of the student should be tonal *quality:* true art has nothing in common with noise. When purchasing an object do we not demand first of all quality of material, design and workmanship, from cars to cows, and furs to fish? Quality of tone resides primarily in the mind.

Sometimes embedded in the lower strata of subconsciousness and lying in a completely dormant state there are rare flowers of wisdom. It may be that, vested with truth, probing contact will ultimately cut their anchorage, whereupon they rise to the conscious surface. If we are wise we shall welcome them as titled guests, intelligent and compelling.

This and the parent work, *The Science and Sensations of Vocal Tone* (Dent, 1936), constitute for all students, teachers and singers a buttress of solid learning that has found favour in the minds of such vocal seers as Luisa Tetrazzini, Beniamino Gigli, Tito Schipa, Dinh Gilly, Giovanni Inghilleri, Joseph Hislop, and other world-famous singers as well as in the British press. Their commendations in writing are a source of considerable encouragement to all students of the art.

A singer must be a delineator of life at its best and worst. For this a command of vocal colours, that can only accrue from a correct technique, is essential.

Vocal tone, though offensively loud, is often scarcely intelligible.

A singer should have a range of interests apart from his art, to which he can turn for change and refreshment and so touch life at many points to stimulate his imagination.

A student who feels the moral impulsion of progress cannot stay in a rut; he cannot be content with the same level of achievement year after year. Ability never can be cheated of scope and expression.

For a good attack, *stroke or caress the tone out* with the delicate touch of the artist's brush, pencil or pen. To stroke is to caress, denoting gentle action. First "point in" the vowelled tone and then "talk" it in, *glide* it in. The soul of touch is lightness; lightness of touch, of attack, is the first principle of vocal economy. Let us have *caresse de glotte*, and NOT *coup de glotte*—because *coup* means "blow", something violent.*

Attack with absolute smoothness and carry the smoothness right through the *crescendo* to *f*. And attack dead on the pitch by deliberately thinking the particular pitch; there must be no scooping or sliding up to the note. (Nobody slides finger or thumb up the wall to press the electric bell.) (See footnote, p. 181.)

It is really astonishing how audiences more than ever today will accept the idea of a singer producing any kind of sound or noise which they would never tolerate in an instrumentalist producing an equivalent series of bad tones; would-be serious singers produce noises which the serious instrumentalist would never lower himself to produce.

(B)

Employ always an indispensable minimum of breath for the attack and then develop the tone with a light, flowing, measured increase of breath pressure. This lightning-fast *crescendo* appears to the listener to be a forthright *f* attack.

Let the breath *flow* after the initial adjustment-attack has been made. Be the tone *f* or *p*, *the breath must have motion;* it must flow freely and evenly.

* The vowelled tone must *flow* as smoothly as the fingertip moves on oiled glass.

T

A perfectly even outflow-cum-pressure of the breath is induced by *thinking, willing* and *visualizing* a smooth tonal flow. And the breath stream or jet for and during production should be considered *linear*, never of wedge form which connotes excess and brutality.

It is a good plan *mentally* to "carry up the breath" beforehand to the height at which the tone is to be produced. This is impossible, of course, and sounds silly, but the result is not silly, as excess breath pressure is avoided and the fear of attacking high notes abated. (See footnote, p. 181.)

To convince the student that little breath (indispensable minimum) is needed to launch vocal tone into the outer world we require him to "Take no breath, attack a high note, sing a series of high notes, or a phrase, or up and down the scale".

For tonal attack a relatively light initial breath pressure gives the laryngo-pharyngeal muscles a much better chance of adjusting themselves correctly than when they are jabbed or even punched into position (modern "technique") with a blind, brutal, unmeasured breath thrust.

The breathing muscles must be strong yet highly responsive, in order to permit the singer to intake an amount of breath adequate for the moment, even if only a half or quarter breath. Particularly the lower or floating ribs and the diaphragm must play their part with alacrity. For a quick intake of breath just *think* of inspiring *only* at the bottom of the lungs; whereupon the diaphragm descends somewhat and the lower ribs move sideways. The dual action must be rapid and smooth. Elasticity of rib movement is the keystone. (See diagram, p. 306.)

Let the breath flow while singing: *keep it moving* evenly also when singing *p* or *pp* (when so many singers are inclined to hold back the breath and thereby stiffen the machinery in degree). If the breath flows, say, at the rate of two inches per second for normal *f*, it should still move at this rate during *p* singing; in the latter case less breath moves and therefore less all-round pressure is exerted. If the breath-flow is not maintained at the above speed (assumed for purposes of illustration) in both *f* and *p* singing, the vibrating mechanism of the vocal cords will stick, falter or stall, and produce faltering tone. (Analogously, an aeroplane slowed down to stalling speed will falter and drop.)

It is highly important to take the breath pressure off as you come down the scale, or an interval, or even from one note to the next below. This is particularly necessary when coming down from a high note. The pressure must be carefully *decreased* and kept *light* and *up;* by so doing, the cord tension will be released to a nicety. The general tendency of most singers, when coming down to a lower pitch, is to exert even more pressure, or retain the same pressure they had on the high note they are leaving. Which procedure retains too much cord tension on every pitch passed over during the downward sweep, and moreover unduly thickens the vibrator adjustment. The net result of which is tonal heaviness, and often flatness. Furthermore, tonal scratch accompanies the ungraceful swoop. Hence our constant advice to students: "Lift up as you come down," or "keep the tone up as high as possible as you come down on a *thin* tonal line."

Most students ask: "Why is it that I lack breath more when coming down the scale than going up?" Our answer is that in ascending the scale the cord tension increases gradually and, other things being equal, there is no escape of air through the cords themselves; the tension factor is therefore all-important. Inversely, when descending, the cords that should relax their tension with perfect graduation from pitch to pitch rarely do so on their own, and instead are very much inclined to over-relax, thereby permitting a certain escape of air through the cords from note to note. (Be it noted that such extraordinary tension as exists not only in the cords proper but in the whole of the muscular system within the larynx, is rather unnatural as we don't go about the world with tensed cords in our throat; but it is part of the *art*. Consequently the cords, as if endowed with a measure of intelligence, are only too glad and ready at the slightest opportunity to "get rid of the load". And opportunity is offered as soon as the singer starts to descend to a lower pitch, and particularly from a high pitch where tension is considerable.) The remedy lies in *keeping the tone up as high as possible during the tonal descent—as* explained in the preceding paragraph. The immediate reaction to this *thought* is that over-release of tension is prevented.

When a phrase is almost finished and you have to take breath, don't carry the tone right through to the full value of the last note and then suck in a little breath with a spasmodic jerk and expect to sustain the new phrase with well-balanced tone; also don't wait until the orchestra, or piano, has practically finished the introduction to a song or aria, or a short intermezzo between one verse and the next, and then suddenly and hastily snatch or gasp in some breath at the very last moment. That won't do. Where possible, take in the breath slowly, one, two, or three bars before starting to sing. To steal a little of the time value of the last note before taking a new breath spoils neither the phrase nor the phrasing (the composer foresees the necessity), but permits the next note and phrase to be taken with unhurried poise and assurance. It gives the singer just that modicum of time to gather up his forces: a very important factor.

Take sufficient breath and so regulate its expenditure as to finish every phrase with a margin left with which to carry on, if necessary, another two or three notes.

(C)

A rising sound-beam means (1) a rising pitch; (2) increasing resonance.

The sensations of tone aroused by the sound-beam must always be associated with the particular vowel giving rise to it. And, inversely, the vowel must always be considered as part and parcel of its relative beam; they are in fact inseparable concomitants.

The sound-beam is, so to speak, a "stick" of tone, and the top of it must touch, tune in, and press or "lean" against a hard surface at a definite spot, otherwise it will hang loose, as it were. In other words, the tone must always be *braced up*, be it *f* or *p*.

Sound-beams on low notes (up to about the first octave, in all voices) have, so to speak, only a "vapour" touch; the focal point (*punto d'appoggio* or "leaning" point) is hazy and rather indefinite.

It is only when the pitch rises above the first octave that the "leaning" touch or sensation-point becomes firm and definite as a sensation. We often suggest, however, to the student to attack the tone with a "vapour vowel" in order to secure a free and smooth tone initiation, whatever the pitch.

The *proof* of the cord-shortening process obtaining as the scale is ascended from the lowest to the highest pitch, lies in the established fact of the small focus on high notes. The *small* focus is merely the *top* of an equally small (narrow) sound-beam which is shot up from an equally small effective length of vibrating cord—an exact length in relation to pitch. Now, the small length left for producing a high note means actually a tiny slit or "loop" between the two extreme front ends of the cords, which slit, because of its minuteness, is able to open and close rapidly as demanded by the particular high pitch, just as nature intended. Consequently, only a thin (a pencil line) but highly condensed stream of air should be applied against this really minute length of cord. And it stands to reason that only a narrow sound-beam, the exact diameter of the tiny loop, can be created and shot upwards—and never a big, broad beam (see footnote, p. 226). Unmeasured breath pressure can, however, widen the loop to the detriment of the tone; the tone deteriorates because widening the loop means employing too much cord in relation to the pitch. The singer must always bear in mind that a small vibrator and a thin, highly concentrated breath stream constitute a single concept.

The vibrating mechanism of the vocal cords has no predilection for any particular vowel, word, or language; its main concern is (as a result of correct vowel shaping in relation to pitch) just to secure pitch by shooting upwards into the mouth-pharynx and head cavities a sound-beam of varying height and direction. *The vibrator is interested in pitch alone*, and not at all in the vowel as such.

The shaping of the mouth-pharynx cavity (mainly responsible for the vowels and their modifications and directly affecting, for weal or woe, the varying adjustments within the larynx) should be such as not to interfere with or disturb the vibrator mechanism which must be allowed unimpeded freedom of action. Any change of internal shaping when passing from one vowel to another must obtain with an oil-smooth action in order to avoid the slightest jerking or roughness; consequently it must be performed *mentally* (see pp. 21-2). And, provided the subjective conception of such shaping is correct, all will be well. If the singer deliberately attempts physical shaping of the vowels he is sure to overdo things, because no one knows, not even the singer himself, in physical terms the varying degrees of internal adjustment whether within the larynx or the resonating cavities. But if his *mind*, naturally or through training, is able to correctly order the shaping of the vowels, every mental message will find an exact physical response of the parts concerned. The mind is both the managing director and mechanic of the singing machine.

The student may ask what is the use of knowing the different directions taken by the sound-beams of the different vowels, and their relationship or distances one from the other on the varying pitches. The answer is that the entire network is a highly important aid to correct internal shaping and the maintenance of that shaping; it moulds the voice and helps to keep it perfectly "tuned".

A *crescendo* must be very carefully executed. The more you "bore" (within limits, of course) into a tonal focus with a thin, concentrated breath stream, without however increasing the size of the focus itself except in minor degree, the greater will be the tonal strength in relation to the maximum capacity of the particular voice. To initiate the *crescendo* and carry it through to its controlled maximum, the pressure of a mentally conceived and *willed* thin stream of breath must be increased gradually with an oil-smooth action. It is similar to exerting pressure with an electric drill. Furthermore, during a *crescendo* the singer should *keep always in mind* the vowel-colour or shaping, and size and height of the tonal focus, as well as its exact location with respect to the vertical. By this means a note can be "drilled" without altering in the slightest the network of adjustment. By holding in mind and voice the vowel shaping which produced the tonal focus, for the duration of the note and without a moment's distraction, the setting will remain unaltered. This is an important point as so many singers, when holding a note, unconsciously distort the vowel and thereby upset the whole adjustment.

When sound-beams are *allowed* by the singer to take their natural directions, adequate resonating space is made available by this very fact. On the other hand, when requisite space has been pre-arranged through correct thinking, the sound-beams will take their natural directions all on their own. Merely to think "back of the vertical" (as from E♭, fourth space) frees and opens the throat, thereby automatically providing space at the correct angle.

> *Arouse thy courage ere it fails and faints;*
> *God props no gospel up with sinking saints.*
> (Langbridge)

(D)
A defect or a difficulty is often half solved as soon as its precise nature is disclosed.

Serious study and careful preparation lasting years ensure a successful début lasting minutes (other things being equal); meticulous preparation is the great thing, and it applies to every human enterprise.

(E)
Expression is impossible without *form*, without exact vowel shaping in relation to pitch.

There should be no scheming for effect, and therefore no spurious or fake emotion, for this hybrid mental mechanism masquerading as emotion is readily detected by most members of the audience; the accompanying physical movements will leave them cold. To move an audience, the singer himself must be genuinely moved. His mental message must be telepathic. To what was due the phenomenal success of Tetrazzini, Caruso, Gigli, and scores of others in vocal history but the fact of positively genuine mental and emotional vibrations artistically interrelated with the vocal vibrations perfectly shaped and produced in the form we call vowels—apart from the question of superlative tonal quality and an exquisite sense of vocal art as a whole?

The key to correct vocal mechanism is the gradual elimination of the vibrator mass as the pitch rises. To fill the requirements of acoustic law, nature has made it possible for the singer so to adjust his vocal cords as to employ only a very small effective length for producing the high notes. This minute length (forming a tiny slit or "loop") of the extreme front tip of the two cords executes the opening and closing cycles many hundreds of times per second (frequency). To obey the same law, the violinist slides his finger up the string to shorten it in order to produce high notes; the players of oboe, clarinet and saxophone reduce the effective vibrating length of their reeds (with their tongue and lips) to produce the high pitches; the harp is so made that for every pitch, from the lowest to the highest, the string is slightly shorter and thinner (and given gradually more tension); on the piano every string is shorter as the pitch rises, although the thickness is not so beautifully graded as in the harp. As we whistle up the scale, the aperture of the pursed-up lips becomes gradually smaller: the higher the pitch the smaller the aperture and the tighter the pursed lips. The ballerina cannot perform flatfooted, and so for her evolutions and rapid pirouettes she discards the mass of the whole foot and gets on her toes. Certain speedboats are flat-bottomed in order to offer the least resistance to forward motion; and as speed increases so the front part of the boat rises gradually off the water until at maximum speed only the back part touches or skims the water, in obedience to natural law. No record was ever made by a runner in overcoat and hobnailed boots. These are all illustrations of "elimination" of mass, everyone and everything obeying natural law. But the majority of singers today, through no fault of their own in most cases, but thanks to the colossal ignorance of modern teaching that shuts its very eyes to basic principles, blandly reverse the order of things. Is it any wonder that we rejoice in a general vocal decline, and in a world-wobble?

We are all inclined to over enthuse about things for which we have paid in good coin of the realm. But too often the interest on capital expenditure is disillusionment and disappointment—ruined voice and broken hopes. (The author has tasted of the bitterest cup.)

One of the main objects of vocal exercises, prolonged over a number of years, apart from the actual strengthening, developing and general "toning" of the muscles concerned, is to form a *habit* in both the vibrator and the resonator systems so that whatever the vowel employed on any pitch, high or low, the degree of automatism that habit confers will take over efficient control, but not full control because, as oft-repeated, the singer must never wholly rely on automatic manipulation of the mechanical processes, and therefore must retain a certain necessary degree of *formative* and *directional* control.

By muscular development through rational exercise of the laryngo-pharyngeal parts and of the breathing machinery is meant a loose-muscled, lithe fitness in which rigidity has no part. Those singers who habitually subject their vocal organs to high breath pressure are unable ultimately to sing a true *mezzavoce* or execute the refinements of *diminuendo* and *messa di voce*, because under the constant forcing the vocal cords and all the muscles within the larynx, some sixty-odd, become "knotty". For a singer can become muscle-bound as can the athlete through over-emphasis; he can still shout, but cannot *sing* any more.

(F)
"Feeling is a grasper of the truth without seeing it" (Leigh Hunt).

The student should endeavour to turn feeling into definite formulation and so give the intellect the possibility of grasping what emotion glimpsed, thereby fusing reason and feeling.

Forcing weakens the effect by narrowing the natural quality of the voice.

Fear or stage fright finds an antidote in the courage acquired from the knowledge of possessing a sound technique.

The small tonal foci or platforms of high pitches demand a maximum space for resonant development; but don't open the vowelled tone while attempting to open the throat. And don't narrow or otherwise tighten the throat in a mistaken endeavour to secure a small focus.

Particularly on high notes, *breath, tone and thought must be brought to one point,*

Tonal flatness means an insufficient number of vibrations per second for a given pitch. When a note is flat the cause invariably lies in the employment of too thick a vibrator in relation to pitch, and possibly it is also too long. It can also be due, on a descending scale, or interval, to excessive loss of cord tension which is brought about by allowing the mind to come down too much with the pitch. Hence our dictum to students: "Keep the tone up as you come down." And tone up means mind up. Be on the alert *not* to let the tone overdrop as the mind comes down with the decreasing pitch or pitches.

The term "frequency" is applied to the number of vibrations, or "cycles", per second set up by any particular note. The lower the note the fewer are the vibrations per second, and, vice versa, the higher the note the greater the number of vibrations per second. Therefore as the scale is ascended the sound-waves become smaller and more frequent. A sound-wave is a disturbance in the atmosphere; the cause of it in the singer's case is initiated in the larynx. The singer should learn, therefore, through correct technique, how not to distort the wave-form from its inception (larynx) to its point of issue (mouth).

(G)

The vocal instrument must be treated with a gentleness that embodies strength, intelligence and authority; it must be handled with that delicate firmness which reveals its intrinsic qualities with unimpeded, unlaboured motion. Gentleness is not weakness. An ancient Chinese philosopher spoke of "The strength of gentleness", and St. Francis de Sales wrote: "Nothing is so strong as gentleness; nothing so gentle as real strength." The greatest of all, Shakespeare, expressed the same thought:

> *What would you have?*
> *Your gentleness shall force*
> *More than your force move us to gentleness.*

(H)

When singing, hesitating thought makes hesitating breath produce hesitating tone.

A well-produced high note is felt by the singer to be merely a small tonal focus which is naturally associated with the particular vowel; but he feels and hears no actual vowel as such, although he well knows that one is being produced. This is due to the acoustical fact that no vowel, as such, can possibly tune in to the head resonator above the palate. If, however, while producing the tone he cups one ear with the curved palm of the hand facing forward, he will hear clearly the exact vowel colour or modification, and added vowel-tint, if any; this proves to him that also on high notes the actual vowel is always in the mouth-pharynx cavity, while the focus of the sound-beam relative to the vowel is tuned in the head cavity. On taking his hand away while still singing the same note he will no longer hear the vowel, but only the tonal focus high up in the head. This is wholly a natural phenomenon. The singer, if he wishes, can associate the tonal focus with a *miniature* vowel.

Seeing that *only* the sound-beam can tune in to the head cavity, don't try to get, place, produce, or feel *a full-size vowel in the head*, for it *is an acoustical impossibility;* in other words, don't try to get the same sensation of full-size vowel on high notes (above D, fourth line) as you can, and should get, in the mouth-pharynx on all notes from said D downwards. (See Chapter XII and Diagram 1, p. 57.)

(I)

Imagination is the keynote to what is called "interpretation" (see Chapter XX); it is a real force, urging, forming, directing. Students, singers and teachers are well advised to exercise it much more than they do if they wish to touch more than the hem of truth.

The singer should endeavour to become a brilliant suggestionist, through the medium of his voice, of the great variety of tonal colours at his disposal. To this end it is well to cultivate the power of conveying to others what he himself feels. And while rendering himself almost unconscious of his audience and without dwelling upon the effect he is making, he should plunge boldly into the very depth of words and music, and live and enact the life and drama of the people he is portraying. Only then will he be able to identify himself completely with the part and with what he is singing; only then will he be able to suggest and paint the picture, and compellingly tell the story. A vivid imagination unlocks the door. And the more genuine feeling he can inject into the words and tones (vowels) the greater will be their influence on the listener: for only what comes from the heart can reach the heart.

Within the usually accepted meaning of the word "interpretation" we could well state that one hundred, or one hundred thousand, singers would sing a song or aria by a great composer in more or less an equal number of different ways, each adding something of his own idea as to "how" the song should go. For instance, where the composer has marked, say, *più mosso*, the singer will slow it down because *he* "feels it ought to go slower here". Or maybe the composer's markings are not noticed, or respected, or given no particular importance. The beauty of the melodic line is not followed through; and so forth. The composer is seemingly just an incident. Be it remembered, however, first and foremost, that the singer who is able to reflect closely and faithfully the composer's thoughts and intentions—the mood or moods he was in and the varying emotions or shades of emotion he felt when composing the particular song or aria, will indeed be a first-class "interpreter". (See p. 250.)

Great composers know, intuitively it seems, the various vocal colours with which the words of their composition should be painted, and as through his mind and on to paper note follows note on a moving melodic line, so the vocal (vowel) colours go with and into them. (And what is also the orchestral accompaniment thereof but a mass of well co-ordinated tone-colours?) We all know the human voice changes its colours or timbres to reflect the varying thoughts, moods and emotions of the moment. Without seeing him we can tell at once what mood a man is in by the peculiar timbre of his voice as he is speaking, quietly or noisily, or when shouting. Joy, sadness, laughter, sorrow, fear, pain, politeness, kindness, sympathy, and so forth, are each expressed with a peculiar and characteristic timbre which is unmistakable. There is the easily recognizable timbre of open sarcasm; veiled sarcasm carries an extra tint. There is the polite word spoken with smiling lips and unsmiling eyes, the open and the veiled threat, the openly angry word and the cold, cutting undertone of suppressed anger.

One and all are reflected with a peculiarly characteristic timbre which everyone readily recognizes. Most individuals inject these varying timbres into their speech as they go through life, some tinting them more heavily than others. It is, however, a strange but observed fact that so very few singers seem able to inject these varying timbres into their singing tone. Why? Do they lack imagination and are therefore unable to develop the art of make-believe? Are they incapable of being moved by even the finest composition? Are they insensitive to other people's troubles and sorrows and love affairs when brought to life in song and opera? Are they ashamed or afraid to publicly express any feeling? The student can answer one and all for himself.

With imagination, high sensitiveness, and receptive thought, true interpretation is not difficult to achieve, for, as Emerson wrote, "A man cannot bury his meanings so deep in his book but time and like-minded men will not find them". And the key to it all is to be, or endeavour to be, "like-minded". Given a fine composition, the words, the notes, the melodic line (often in wave-form reflecting, perhaps momentarily, a passing thought, mood or emotion) together with markings of time, expression, accent, build a picture. It is up to the singer to reconstruct this very picture with his imagination and paint in the colours, and light and shade, with his *words*,* his *vowels* in both pure and modified form, with or without added tints. If the singer will devote sufficient time and thought to such analysis of his songs, and give rein to his imagination (which needs exercising constantly even as a muscle does) he will be pleasantly surprised at the results; if he perseveres he will in time develop a sensitive mechanism whereby he will be able instantly to get in more or less the *same state of mind* in which the composer was at the time of composing the particular piece. Again Emerson encourages us to persevere, when he writes: "The

* On her deathbed a great Italian soprano, racked with disease, albeit barely in her forties, asked to be propped up. After singing the first four words of Margherita's death song in Boito's *Mefistofele*—"Spunta l'aurora pallida"—with unsurpassable clarity of diction, accent, and expression, she stopped and said with dramatic emphasis: "Ah, the *word*, the WORD; without it there is *no song*, NO SINGER." Her beautiful face was suffused with a strange light as she sang the entire song with such emotional intensity that the very air seemed charged with the drama of an ebbing life that was more poignant than death itself. Three hours later she passed on.

years teach much which the days never know. It is long ere we discover how rich we are. We are wiser than we know."

The *tempo* of a composition comes within the field of "interpretation". A composer writes a song or aria with a definite tempo in mind, and marks it accordingly. Even if unmarked, the music itself speaks clearly in this respect. Now, if the tempo is slowed down, or hurried, even in slight degree, it will probably lose many of its characteristics, and the music itself much of its idiosyncrasy, charm, attraction, atmosphere, personality, form, colouring, expression, and so forth, to the extent almost of no longer being an emanation of the composer's mind. Furthermore, the more subtle effects are completely submerged. Why will singers, conductors, coaches and accompanists not be guided *solely* by the music itself, particularly when it is the music of a first-class composer, instead of stamping, and therefore spoiling, it in degree with their own personality which, from the point of view of composition, *is* inferior. (See Chapter XX.)

When passing from one pitch to a higher one, particularly when the interval is fairly big, we tell the student to "bounce" the tone up. The effect of this thought of "bouncing up the tone" is to *lighten* the vibrating mechanism of the vocal cords as the pitch rises, the upward soaring being effected with and on a gossamer thread of tone (*legato*). To "bounce" the tone up is to "lift" it: two expressions to get the same reaction within the laryngeal mechanism, i.e. an appropriate thinning of the cords (elimination in depth).

(K)

Here is the master-key of vocal mechanism: (1) Round (darken) the vowel gradually as the pitch rises from note to note up the scale, or ascending interval, in order to assist the *cord-shortening process* within the larynx; (2) simultaneously lift up the tone from note to note (up the scale or ascending interval) in order to lighten the mechanism and assist the *cord-thinning process;* (3) *mentally* pull back as you lift up from one note to the next highest in order to release all the parts concerned, free the throat and induce a *natural* opening thereof. The note-to-note increasing tension is automatically induced through the very thought of increased pitch, which itself is materially helped to be exact by reason of (1) (2) (3) above. Tension can also be *willed in* appropriately in conjunction with the thought of pitch. Some mechanisms more than others require the assistance provided above.

(L)

Deliberate lip protrusion on the upper medium and the high notes particularly (with added the forward thrust of the tone) makes either for mushy, woolly tone, or, as is more often the case, too heavy or "lumpy" tone, due to engaging too much cord in depth. Such lip protrusion causes tonal distortion in degree, due to constriction of the throat. On *high* notes the resonating cavities must be "extended" in a vertical direction, *never* horizontally as happens with inappropriate lip protrusion. And it is precisely the forward thrust of the tone on high pitches which causes too much cord to be engaged in depth.

The Italian term *legato* means tied, joined; actually it is meant to convey the idea of continuous, smooth, tonal flow. Due to certain consonants there are inevitable "cuts" or interruptions in the tonal flow, albeit of short duration. Now the whole art of *legato* singing consists, therefore, firstly of a perfect, imperceptible merging of one vowel into the next and, secondly, of making these interruptions or cuts in the tonal line as small and as unnoticeable as possible, compatible with good diction, and so convey to the audience the impression of an uninterrupted vocal stream. With consonants such as B, P, M, the mouth must close completely, and half close with G, K, S, N, etc. But in every case, in order to produce the ensuing vowel the lips must spring apart and the chin drop with a quick, gliding movement devoid of jerking and stiffness.

On the lower medium and low notes the lips participate in the formation of the OO, OH and AW vowels merely as an external finishing medium; the greater part of the shaping of these vowels obtains *in* the pharynx. Indeed, all vowels are due to internal shaping. As the pitch rises so the lips, as from D, fourth line, upwards, should be employed gradually less until from about G, or A♭, or A (according to the individual) the lips barely participate, if at all, whatever the vowel employed. This applies to all vocal categories except baritones and basses; in their case it is about E♮, fourth space, F, or F♯, according to the individual.

Too many singers, in blind obedience to that miserable forward production method, funnel their lips also on the highest notes; they look silly and produce stupid, distorted tone in consequence. And whatever the vowel, the funnelling of the lips on high notes is the antithesis of good production.

Until they learn their technique most pupils find it difficult to understand why lip participation is not called for in the formation of the OO vowel on high notes. They must remember that the formation of all vowels obtains primarily in the mouth-pharynx cavity, and that the back part of this cavity, the pharynx, starts to take over most of this formative work as from E♭, fourth space, and as the pitch rises therefrom it gradually takes over the entire formation. Consequently, to use the lips as an "aid" (unwanted and unnecessary), is fatal to good production.

The singer must always be careful *how* he finishes, particularly a sustained note on a high pitch, which has considerable cord tension. We advise students to "lift" the tone upwards as he is about to leave it; by this means the cords open out smoothly and the tone trails away imperceptibly. Inversely, if the high note (especially) is terminated with a downward thrust and un-diminished breath pressure (as most singers do) the cords will open with a rough jerk, whereupon the tone cuts off with a grunt. This is all the more pronounced where there is an excess of diaphragmatic drive.

(N)

All great singers will tell you, if you are sufficiently intimate with them to ask, that they feel small, compact tonal foci on high notes, and that the higher the pitch the smaller the tonal focus.

The small, compact tonal foci (platforms) of high notes give the feeling of being "tuned" or plugged into a tiny socket. The actual locating or tuning requires something of the delicate tuning-in of short-wave stations on a wireless receiving set.

Analogies are useful. When a student produces a high note

with too big a mechanism, due mainly to insufficient cord tension, we say: "If you tighten the knot of a shoelace it gets smaller and more compact." And better still, "If you tie a knot in an elastic band, and then tighten it gradually more and more, the knot itself gets smaller and more compact but is still resilient and 'springy' as we press it between finger and thumb." This feeling of a small elastic knot gives a very good idea of the sensation given by the compact tonal focus of a perfectly produced high note.

The student is apt at first to query the smallness and apparent insignificance of the tiny tonal foci of high notes: "Will it carry?" "Is it big (or loud) enough?" "Isn't that tinny?" (This is something the singer with the *completely natural* voice never queries, for he senses that all is well.) The tonal focus is merely the top of the sound-beam, and is so highly compressed that the singer's mind fastens itself mainly to the brilliant point, and takes no notice whatever of the actual vowel churning down below in the mouth-pharynx cavity. This is an extraordinary phenomenon. However, after tuning in at the correct height relative to pitch and correct angle relative to the vowel employed, the tone (sound-beam) rebounds downwards from the head cavity into the mouth and out into the world of listeners, carrying with it the vowel of the moment. Too many singers today want to make, and feel, big, fat, meaty, full-size vowels or tones also on the highest pitches, and in the same breath talk about "head voice". *Only* the sound-beam can soar into the head cavities (above, and via, the palate); the vowel never. (See footnote, p. 54, and diagram, p. 234.)

As regards sustained tone, don't produce a note, particularly a high one, and then leave it there on its own, so to speak, expecting it to "stay put" as regards height, size, angle, location and intensity. It might wander (like a car, bicycle or a donkey would) without that indispensable minimum of control. So keep the mind focused on these five factors, and of course also on the particular vowel shaping, appertaining to the sustained note for its entire duration. Controlling thought must never be relaxed.

When going from one high note to a higher one, or from a medium, or low note to a high pitch, we tell the student to

U

"bounce up" his tone from point to point, *gathering it up* on the upward journey. To "gather up" the tone means making a gradually decreasing focus (platform) as the pitch rises, and the key to this gathering-up process is of course the gradual rounding of the vowel plus the mental lift-up-pull-back of the tone. This tonal gathering-up comes from the old Italian saying: *Raccogliere il suono*, an expression which certainly reflects the process of decreasing tonal focus as the pitch rises. To "bounce up" the tone is to "lift it" up, quickly and lightly.*

Even as a horse instinctively slows down, if the rider lets him, before making a high jump, in order to gather up his forces, so the good singer will prepare himself for a climbing phrase, or for attacking a high note, not with a hurried intake of breath nor with a lung-cramming one, but with a fast, finely measured, *poised* intake simultaneously gathering up his forces, mainly mental and nervous, to a point of effective output. This betokens a cool mastery based on sound technique and experience. A quick intake demands a *flash* message to the breathing machinery in order to promote the fast but smooth action of diaphragm-cum-lower ribs. The following diagram illustrates the directions of the mental message inducing a down-and-out movement right at the base of the lungs: (1) the diaphragm moves downwards; (2) the lower ribs move sideways, left and right.

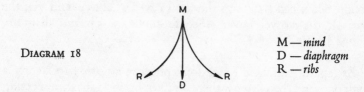

DIAGRAM 18

M — *mind*
D — *diaphragm*
R — *ribs*

When making a *crescendo* on a sustained high note in particular, the size of the focal point should increase but little; there are definite limits to such increase, and the higher the pitch the smaller the amount of permissible increase. To increase a focus beyond its

* Always give a mental pull-back-and-up when going to a higher note (even if only a semitone) whatever the vowel; the reaction to this thought is immediate, and it automatically loosens all the parts and opens the throat with fine delicacy of action.

true limits actually means increasing unduly the amount of cord employed for the particular pitch, thus throwing the mechanism out of gear. With training and observation the singer will be able accurately to *feel* and sense when he has reached the permissible limit of tonal development of a focus in size. There is an un-mistakable feeling of balance and buoyancy from which *excess* breath pressure is absent.

For the attack of a high note, or final phrase of high *tessitura*, we advise the student to take a normal breath, and then for the attack proper mentally take just a short "stick of breath" (say, three inches of needle thickness) and imagine it already poised in the head cavity ready to be used. The reaction to this apparently absurd thought of a "mental length of breath" is such that it positively inhibits the employment of excess breath pressure; fuss and fear also vanish. (See footnote, p. 181.)

How often have we heard the remark, after producing a good high note perhaps for the first time: "There is so little to hold on to; I feel I must *do* someting about it as I fear it will crack." Whereupon we explain to the student that one cannot physically "hold on" to a tonal focus which is more or less an insubstantial thing, being merely the top of the sound-beam, and that if the small focus is well tuned in to the head cavity it is because the general adjustment in both the vibrator and resonator systems was good; consequently all he has to do is maintain the setting which initiated the tone, holding the same thought in mind and voice, and leave all else well alone. No extraneous physique is to be introduced, such as forcing with the breathing muscles, tightening the neck muscles, stiffening the chin and jaw.

If we have to produce a high note on AH, AW or OH, it is a good plan to *think* (back of the vertical) towards the *oo* sound as in *moon*, or the short *u* sound as in *put* (which is actually a mixture of *oo* and *oh*). Supposing the word is *far*: Before attacking the note the *preparatory thought* lies first in rounding off the AH, thinking of it as an AH^3, which in fact closely approximates the AW sound (as in *saw*), and then *thinking* towards, or of, a tiny, miniature *oo* or *u* shape and sound. (The physical reaction to this thinking is an appropriate shortening of the cord mechanism.) The listener will only hear a nicely rounded AH, and not the added tint of *oo* or *u*, because the singer has in mind and voice *basically* the word *far*, and because the percentage of the AH is greater. Of course, if too much OO were introduced, the AH sound would be over-modified and we should get a distorted, unintelligible word.

For the singer, a well-produced high note gives the sensation of a small, compact, *glowing* focus into which he seems to have gathered up his whole being, the waves of thought commingling with and beautifying the vocal waves. (Electroencephalography has proved the existence of "brain waves".) It is the mental-nervous excitement of feeling and emotion which the singer pours into a tonal focus that makes it glow. Sheer physical tone of itself is really neither attractive nor convincing; to give it personality the vocal waves must be injected with thought, or brain-waves of a high-keyed imagination. It is the very presence of dominating thought-waves ingressing within the accurately vowelled tone which imparts to it that quality of magnetic attractiveness which never fails to enthuse an audience. The emotional output must however be controlled in order not to swamp the vocal adjust-ment, altering, distorting, or coarsening it to the detriment of quality. Faithfulness to the ideal tone is far more important than mere loudness. (See (11), p. 249.)

If only the singer, on certain phrases, could pour into the vocal stream the same waves of thought that cause the wondrous quality of glowing love-light to appear in a woman's eyes, tremulous in its soft loveliness, to what heights of expression and personality could a vowelled tone not be brought! Where *intense feeling* is present in all its majesty to produce such glowing thought (or vibration, for that is really what it amounts to), it can and should be directed through the vocal organs right into the tonal stream, tinting and beautifying it.

Low notes sing by themselves, so to speak, requiring little effort, mental and physical, and little breath to produce and sustain them. Once launched, the low note seems to be able to support itself with a minimum of attention. Therefore beware of "digging down" to produce them, for it strains the cords and distorts the natural quality. So do little, and let them sing comfortably.

(P)

Physical energy in singing is only part of the story. The greater part must consist of mental-nervous energy. There must be intellect, too. We increase the energy of our whole organism by increasing the intensity of thought; and conversely. Mental energy and physical energy vitalize thought; vitalized thought replenishes physical energy.

Progress is always microscopical where the mechanical development of the voice is concerned. It is like building a brick wall, brick upon brick, plus cement, in total darkness just by touch. Then comes a flash of light (of knowledge and understanding) suddenly to reveal the work so far accomplished. The student finds he is able to do things considered impossible before. Then darkness again, and the work of construction by touch goes on. Another flash reveals the progress made. And so on in alternating sequence: light and darkness, the former gradually growing until all is light. Again, study is a dark room, and every step forward is punctuated by a pinprick in the blind. Little light enters the tiny hole, and little can be seen through it. But gradually as hole upon hole punctuates progress, so the light increases, the light of knowledge, understanding and experience, until there is no blind left, and therefore no darkness. Students on the whole are apt to be impatient and want immediate tangible results. It can't be done. Nature doesn't work that way.

Progress that is considered in terms of increased power is a noisy regression. Instead of the healthy, slow, normal growth resulting from rational exercise on a long-term basis, there can be the unhealthy, rapid increase of vocal strength as a result of habitual forcing; unfortunately these quick "results", called progress, are highly flattering to so many students. Quality of vocal tone does not seem to count much in so many cases. Cheap power and plenty of it is the modern trend. Indeed, noise is the symbol of what is called "modern" art: witness also the loudness of those footling figures in "surrealist" and "impressionist" daubs (two expressions possibly to camouflage the lack of real drawing and painting ability), and the monstrosities hacked out of marble (seemingly with eyes closed). Is not also the drunkard an "impressionist" when he sees "pink" elephants, and everybody with two noses? The impressionistic daubs we decry are closely reminiscent of the caveman's puerile efforts.

When practising, give your voice frequent spells of rest. Never sing for a whole hour uninterruptedly. Muscles need periods of rest in order to recuperate. Even inanimate objects such as steel suffer from fatigue when subjected to continuous work. It is also known that by continual use musical instruments are apt to become tired, and that the finest Stradivarius or Guarneri violin can virtually be killed by excessive use without periods of rest. A watch performing erratically will often pick up again if rested for a fortnight or so.

Portamento means carrying the tone from one note to another, upward or downward. In every case, whatever the interval, the tonal joining must be as thin as gossamer, like that of a spider's web. If the *portamento* is executed upwards with a thick tonal line we get a nasty scooping effect, and if downwards we get "moana-mento"; there is nothing dainty or artistic about either. To prevent the latter, the tone must be lifted up and lightened almost to breaking point, no matter what the descending interval may be. Similarly, the upward *portamento* must be made by lifting and lightening the tone almost to breaking point, as it were, all the way up.

If the note, prior to a downward or upward *portamento*, is being sung *f*, a rapid *decrescendo*, which includes a tonal lift-up, must be made in order to create the desired gossamer thread of tone. The singer should *mentally ride up* on the vowelled tonal stream to the higher note, or down to the lower pitch, as the case may be.

Rising pitch connotes increasing cord tension. To get the idea of gradually increasing tension, as on an ascending scale from the lowest to the highest note, hold one end of an ordinary elastic band between thumb and index of left hand and the other end between thumb and index of the right hand—the latter being held vertically above the former. Now, without moving the left hand, pull the band slowly upwards with the right hand, occasionally bouncing it slightly up and down as the stretching or tensioning proceeds. Particularly after the stretching has proceeded apace we note on bouncing the band slightly up and down how the point of maximum tension is felt to be at the *top* of the band we are holding with the right hand, and not at the bottom held by the left hand. Even when the band is stretched to its maximum it is always at the top end that the point of maximum tension is felt; we do not seem to feel either the bottom end or the middle piece. And so it is with voice: It is the TOP of the sound-beam that gives the sensation of increasing tension as the pitch rises and impresses the mind the most. This is particularly marked after the first octave of the voice has been ascended.

The good singer gives himself up to the expression of his song in the presence of others, but never *at* them, for he is mainly oblivious of his audience. To get inside the skin of the rôle, aria or song is the secret of detachment.

Good production depends, primarily, on the singer's power of representing ROUNDNESS; for does not nature abound in rotundities, spheroids, loops, and an infinite variety of curves? Roundness has a definite function. In the case of vocal tone the gradual rounding of the vowel that must obtain as the pitch rises is necessary for, and the outcome of, a gradually decreasing vibrator.

The difference between *p* and *f* singing is primarily a question of degree of muscular action. For example, if we represent *p* by holding a piece of paper between thumb and index with only just sufficient pressure to keep it from falling—even though it can easily be removed with the other hand, we can represent *f* by a much firmer grip of the paper so that it cannot easily be removed. We can reduce the tone to a *p* which gives the feeling almost of breaking point, so thin and tender is the vocal line (analogously to the paper almost falling from finger and thumb but kept up by *tender* pressure nicely calculated to hold it indefinitely). It is easy in both cases to grip the paper excessively. And it is easy to exercise an excess of pressure in *f* singing, and insufficient pressure in *p* singing. In the latter case the tone falls.

When a tone is slightly sharp or flat it is sometimes due to the singer not thinking pitch *deliberately*, as he should particularly on important and telling notes.

Youthful facility sometimes spurns the drudgery of technical exercises; but how often has the career of a gifted and promising singer been cut short on this account.

(R)

We tell the student to "sing loosely", which means giving absolute freedom (relaxation) to neck, jaw, and facial muscles generally, as well as to the internal parts of the mouth-pharynx, tongue, soft palate, gullet. It means to loosen everything except the vibrating mechanism: this must be alive and alert, and the tone isolated and properly braced up at all times. Such is the real meaning of relaxation.

Keep before you a mental picture of the resonator as one cavity gradually extending like a big V from the mouth upwards as the pitch rises. (See pp. 221, 226.)

The relation of vibrator and resonance can be analogized by the roller-blind and the light: the longer and thicker the vocal cord employed, the smaller the resonance, even as the more the blind is lowered the less light available from outside; and vice versa, the shorter and thinner the effective piece of cord (in relation to pitch) the greater the resonance, as the less blind is lowered the greater the light.

(S)

The attitude of the mathematician towards the principle of mathematics is conditioned by the knowledge that no personal opinion, whim, or fad or guesswork can change or divert in the slightest degree the operation of the laws of that principle. The solution of every problem is *there* already, and exact obedience to the rules puts the solution within his reach. This should also be the attitude of the teacher, student, and singer towards the principle of vocal mechanics. It rarely is. (See para. 4, p. 29.)

Psychologically speaking, suggestion means a method of instilling an idea or series of ideas in a way that will make it acceptable and thus by-pass the critical faculty, or Reason, and so embed itself in the subconscious of the person concerned. Power is conferred to suggestion by reason of (1) the superior knowledge of the person making the suggestion orally or in writing; (2) repetition—because we all tend to believe what we see written and hear stated, if we see or hear it often enough; (3) the emotional state of the moment, for when disillusionment and frustration are strong and a new thought or idea holds the promise of rehabilitation, the reasoning or critical faculty is inhibited. And when Reason is off guard suggestion slips in, for good or evil. This accounts for the unthinking adoption of false vocal methods by thousands of students in every country.

It is a sheer waste of vocal capital to learn songs and rôles with your voice. It is far better to (1) get thoroughly familiar with the words; (2) learn the melody; (3) sing the melody first on AH to get the idea of line, phrasing and continuity; (4) seated at the piano, play the melody and *speak* the words as it unfolds: that is, speak them rhythmically on one low pitch. Thus eye and ear absorb. Then stand up and sing.

Learn all songs off by heart; only then can the singer make them, so to speak, an extemporization of his own creating. Eyes glued to the music detracts considerably from performance.

Particularly on the high notes, if you do not allow for the sound-beam sufficient "ceiling" or height, or space, for its upsurging and focused impingement, it will revert downwards and derange the particular adjustment of the cords. If you THINK "lift up and back" as you are about to soar or are soaring to the high notes, sufficient space will be provided. (See Gigli's remarks, p. 22.) Space is also secured by thinking of an "air-ball" high up in the head cavity above the anticipated height the soaring beam will reach. On no account must you do any actual physical stretching to get space because you will surely overdo it. No one, teacher or singer, can possibly know or gauge exactly how much the soft palate must be raised; consequently, all such stretching is just a blind action and asking for faulty adjustment.

When an individual sets out to do or make something the question of *shape* presents itself, be it painting, sculpturing, modelling, woodcarving, making a last, a die, etc. The operator must have in mind definite ideas as to shape, colour, effectiveness, utility, adaptability, and so on. Also in the singer's mind the question of shape (vowel-shaping and vowel modification) must arise primarily, for the varying moods and emotions can only be expressed through an appropriate medium. Few singers today shape their vowels *mentally* with deliberation. That was the basis of the singer's art as the old Italian School taught it. It was the first thing told to the author in 1907 in Rome by Antonio Cotogni, admittedly the greatest baritone of all time, product of the old School and exponent *in excelsis* of the true Bel Canto. We cannot conceive of a painter not pre-selecting shape and colour before committing them to paper or canvas. Most singers seem nonchalantly to ignore tonal shape and colour, and genuinely expect to express poetical and musical thought through a mis-shapen and often colourless medium; and this is one of the main reasons why the average singer fails to "put over" his song.

To sing well one must be in a (controlled) state of excitement both in *f* and *p*, all the time. When singing be alert, be "nervy", be all of a *mental glow*, for only thus will the tone glow and be braced up.

In the main, we encounter everywhere "blind" singers and their blundering guesswork tone. Blind in the sense that true vocal technique is more or less an unknown factor to the majority (although they call a lot of funny ideas "technique"); and therefore they rely on a certain automatism of mechanism inherent in every voice. This may be anything from 30 to 70 per cent., with or without training. In which case the missing 70 to 30 per cent. are mechanical incompletenesses in varying degree, or say mechanical "blanks" filled by the singer with a feeling of incompetence that engenders fear.

Beware of a corroding self-satisfaction. But do cultivate self-encouragement, and in this sense: When a particular tone is produced, or a phrase sung, say, just fairly well, the worst thing for the student himself is to condemn it out of hand with a "that's awful", which effectively blinds his appreciation of the good in his effort. On the contrary, let him encourage himself with the reflection that the note, or phrase, was "not so bad after all" or was "pretty good", and then make another and another attempt. He should encourage the slightest improvement; if he doesn't, he may find subsequent attempts much worse than the first. It is psychological.

True vocal strength is secured not by brutal lung blast but by tonal intensification through a vivifying mental-nervous energy, bordering a state of excitement, pouring into and through the vocal mechanism culminating in the glowing focal point. We call this "local" strength, in that true power is embedded in the larynx proper. (See footnote, p. 261.)

When making a *crescendo* hold fast to the particular vowel shape for the entire duration of the note—unless of course a slight change in shape and colour is deliberately planned. If the shape and colour are not *mentally* retained, the tone will be in danger of sliding into irritating vagaries of quality and timbre.

Staccato singing is more difficult of execution on the lower medium and low notes than on the high pitches on account of the relatively low cord tension. On high pitches in particular, well adjusted and rounded *staccato* acts as a "pointer" or "feeler" for the sustained note. Properly executed, *staccato* singing, in moderation, is an excellent "tonic" for the entire muscular system within the larynx. The high pitches must, however, be produced with in mind the rounding influence of *oo* as in *pool* or *u* as in *put*.

No singer's top notes are ever really "lost"; rather is it the art of producing them properly which is lost—if ever it was won. The habitual forced production of the high notes, particularly when the tone is too open and when too much cord is engaged in both length and depth in relation to the pitch, imposes an enormous strain on the entire muscular system within the larynx; a muscle-bound knottiness eventually sets in, and together with the cords themselves the whole system loses its pristine freshness of resilient adjustability and responsiveness. Finally nature calls a halt; a deadlock appears in the vibrating mechanism, and adjustment for high frequencies is no longer possible so long as the untoward conditions persist.

Light sopranos particularly are inclined to sing sharp at times on high notes; the remedy lies in lowering the tonal height by darkening the vowel somewhat (rounding it off).

"Can I sing songs?" is the usual question asked by new students. Our invariable reply is that it is not advisable to do so until the vowel-shaping on all pitches has made substantial headway, as consonants are liable to upset the shaping before it has consolidated. All vowels on all pitches have to be worked in by dint of repetition (sometimes hundreds of times) over a period of many months' study. Every repeated attempt to produce correctly a certain vowel on a particular pitch, when based on true technique, of course, is constructive, even if only the target itself is hit; slowly and surely every well-thought-out attempt brings us closer to the centre, the tonal bull's-eye.

The singer must be a creator-observer: As he creates his tones (sound-beams) he must observe *inwardly* what they do, where they go, what they feel like, what is their size, intensity, vitality, height and direction within the resonating system, whether properly poised and flowing, and so forth. And as progress is made on the technical side he can mentally sit back more and more, and so *allow* the voice to perform its own work without being bullied by pedantic, domineering thought. The voice must be given due credit for some of the work and results. The technical progress achieved, step by step, reflects increasing degrees of built-in automatism. Besides, the voice thrives on encouragement.

Never must the singer attempt to listen outside himself. The singer and the song are one and *internal*.

Too many singers make such a terrible "do" of singing as if it entailed really hard labour, physical stuff. Whereas the truth is that *good singing is mainly a mental creation mentally operated*.

The well-trained singer allows his whole being to be brought to a focal point of control that in turn regulates the entire vocal machinery—even as a lever or switch controls a machine. The true singer keeps body and bodily bits out of mind, for he is just mind-cum-tone.

The singer must cultivate listening and feeling inside the mouth-pharynx cavity from the lowest note to D, fourth line, inclusive, and in the head cavity above the palate from E♮, fourth space, upwards, to the highest note. He must be *mentally behind every tone:* creating, observing, directing, controlling.

Sing with the same beautiful *legato* line as that produced by a great violinist. *Caress* the melodic line with the vowels, as the bow caresses the string of the violin, and carry the vowel-tone along on the breath stream. The singer's mind should ride *with* and *on* the vowels. Let the vowel move like a good bow; let the moving bow be both vowel and breath. Let there be *motion* of breath and tone (vowel).

The impatient attitude of most students towards study and the results they anticipate without reckoning the time factor is as unreasonable as that of impatiently waiting for the kettle to boil.

In the realm of vocal study the forgotten hour and day that add to our experience, growth in grace, strength and ability, finally—

> *Cast their kingdoms old,*
> *Into another mould.*

(T)

Every category of voice has distinctive tonal characteristics, on certain pitches and vowels, that are peculiar to it. To illustrate: Assuming a well-produced tenor's high G, sung on the AH vowel, we can say that it has certain technical and tonal characteristics that distinguish it from any other note above or below in his voice; that this G has a definite *shape*, a characteristic *tone-pattern* which is unmistakable to the expert ear. One hundred tenors, representing different calibres from light to dramatic, of all nationalities, producing this G on AH with the same *technical* accuracy, would reveal in their tonal products the same tenor-G pattern of the AH-shaping, the same *characteristic* pattern. Because it is a thing apart, we are not thinking here of the actual individual quality of the tone that would unmistakably differentiate each of the hundred tenors from all the others. (No two voices are tonally alike, even as no two faces are alike in feature and expression.) But we are contemplating solely the basic and "external" structure of the G-tone accruing from a more or less identical, correct mechanical adjustment of the laryngo-pharyngeal parts.

Given, therefore, an equally good mechanical adjustment, the G of a really beautiful voice will have the same characteristic "tenory" G-sound (from the standpoint of basic structure) as that of a downright ugly or quality-less voice. Change the vowel on this high G and we get a different characteristic tonal colour; but there will be no change in the actual tenory G-sound because the basic structure undergoes no alteration on account of a change of vowel. In other words, the mechanical adjustment remains unchanged because *the cord mechanism concerns itself mainly with pitch* and is quite indifferent to the vowel that is being employed.

Again, the F♯ below and G♯ above said high G have each a different *basic and structural sound* (even though the difference is slight), typifying, from the mechanical standpoint, the one universal tenor voice, or model. Of course, here again on to this basic sound is grafted the individual quality of every single one of our hundred (or million) tenors. Which *individual quality* is characteristic and expressive of just that one person, and of no other. And so it is with the other notes, particularly from E♭, fourth space, upwards, each of which has its own characteristics.

Similarly, the different categories of male and female voice have each their characteristic and distinguishing tonal *patterns* on every pitch, particularly as from the said E♭ upwards. On these structural patterns lie the individual qualities (like clothes on a body).

We believe that this knowledge is the foundation of the true art of teaching. Without it, what does a master listen for? Without it, what can he really teach from the technical standpoint? (See footnote, p. 70.)

Vocal tones, prior to study, may be like the juices of unripe fruit that have not had sufficient time to mature into sweetness.

A teacher should be grateful for certain mechanically incomplete and really defective voices, as they tax his knowledge and resources to the utmost, and sometimes to the extent of opening up a fresh field of thought and investigation.

The teacher, in order to reinstate a control proper to nature, must primarily redress perplexed states of thought in the student. But of these he must have none himself.

The singer creates and produces the tone, but only the listener is able to appreciate it at its full value. We have an analogy in tapestry making: Before the weaver's eye is the *wrong* side of the tapestry; and on the other side of the loom, where he cannot see it, is the picture he is weaving. Yet he seldom makes a serious mistake for he *knows* from training and long experience how to get the unseen effects at which he aims. Likewise the well-trained singer *knows* first of all what he is doing, knows what to expect, knows what the audience is hearing.

Hidden away in the dark recesses of the laryngeal chamber the minute vibrator basically responsible for producing a glittering high note does not get the credit for it. The popinjay focus (the top of the sound-beam) takes all the credit of creator and created. Likewise the humble caterpillar is invariably forgotten in the presence of the gaudy butterfly. What credit does a teacher get? If the pupil is successful it is due to his own intelligence; but if a failure, it is the master's fault. Human nature, in the main, is made like that. The gift of gratitude is rare.

From the lowest note up to and including D♮, fourth line, the tone produced is felt by the singer as vowel filling the mouth-pharynx cavity. The sensation aroused by the sound-beam (main stream of tone) as it soars into this cavity at different angles according to the vowel employed and to the pitch, is relatively weak on the low notes but gradually makes itself felt as the pitch rises towards said D. Constant observation of the behaviour of the sound-beam brings it into a sharper relief as a tonal sensation.

As the pitch rises above E♭, fourth space, and the sound-beam with it, the vowelled tone becomes more attenuated to converge ultimately, as a sensation, into a simple focus. This is because the sound-beam proper starts, from E♭ upwards (in all voices) to soar into the head cavities above the palate, irrespective of the vowel employed, and the singer's mind fastens mainly or rather exclusively on to the TOP of the beam (focus) rather than on to the vowel-shape underlying in the mouth-pharynx. The phenomenal part of it all is that when high notes are well produced the singer has no sensation of tone whatever underneath the focus.

To modify a vowel, don't close, cramp, clamp or otherwise

stiffen your throat, and don't do any physical shaping deliberately. You must remember that in every case any modification that is made consists of a *very slight* movement of the parts within the mouth-pharynx occurring, automatically, as a reaction to the mere *thought* of the slight shaping of the vowel and of the particular tone one wants to produce.

On high notes the *thought* of a rounded vowel shape and tone is instrumental in securing a small vibrator mechanism, and, conversely, the thought of a small tonal focus produces a rounded vowel tone. Even as the mouth-pharynx cavity reacts with exact conformity to correct thought, so the vibrator mechanism reacts, with correct adjustments, to the shaping of this cavity when it is correct in relation to pitch. Consequently, all adjustments of the cord mechanism are controlled by thought indirectly through the mouth-cavity shaping. Hence the importance of having correct thoughts as regards cavity and tonal shaping, with all vowels and on all pitches.

To produce a certain vowel or modification thereof the singer has merely to shape it mentally (never must it be a deliberate act) and hold in thought the selected vowel shape and colour for the duration of the note on which it is being produced. Many singers give only a passing thought to the word as a whole. And it sounds like it, too.

It is most unwise to cultivate, as many do, over-opulence of vibrator; in other words, too much cord in depth. This elaborate digging produces a grand fundamental rumble which gives the illusion of tonal "richness" and certainly increases the individual's feeling of self-importance. Not only does it tax and tire the voice uselessly; the snag is that the rumble feels and sounds grand in a room, powerful and rich, and all that, *but* because it is practically bereft of harmonics or overtones it cannot and does not "carry" in a large hall or theatre. (See footnote, p. 54.)

The so-called dark vocal tone can and should be independent of vibrator heaviness, for the darkish quality is merely the result of a rounded mouth-pharynx cavity, and of nothing else. The rounding process which should result *only* from the thought of vowel roundness can, but need not necessarily, induce the employment of too much vocal cord in depth in relation to the pitch. Which excess inevitably produces heavy tone. And heavy tone produced in this way is often flat, or under pitch.

A vocal tone will "stick" and fail to sing properly (1) if too much cord is being used for the particular pitch; (2) if there is stiffening of the internal parts and externally of the neck, jaw and facial muscles; (3) if the breath is unduly held back deliberately or unconsciously.

Normally, one cannot engage too small a vibrator length in relation to pitch; but it is so easy to fall into the error of engaging too big a vibrator.

To prevent excessive engaging of the cords in depth when making a *crescendo*, the student is advised to "blow upwards" from the focal level as he sustains the note. (See para. 5, p. 324.)

F singing does not and should not imply, or necessarily induce, tonal heaviness.

Tonal colouring or darkening must never decrease brightness of focus.

Vowel *shaping* and breath *flow* go hand in hand.

Many teachers and singers as well as a few physiologists erroneously believe that the laryngeal mechanism is *wholly* of pre-determined action, incapable of subjective adjustment and entirely automatic in operation. If it were true, why does not everybody with a voice sing with perfect production without training? Now and again we have a medical man asserting dogmatically that "the singer has no control whatever over the cord mechanism". These good men are generally voiceless, and once they invade the realm of song they really don't know what they are talking about. (See *N.B.*, p. 92.)

One of the objects of rational exercises for the voice is to over-come primary fatigue, and subsequently the so-called secondary

X

fatigue (the "second wind" of the runner). Singing must never be so prolonged or strenuous as to reach the condition of "staleness" of overstrain.

The presence and emotional stimulus of an audience brings out the best from a singer.

To prevent the possibility of tonal "spreading" on a descending phrase, or run, we tell the student to "come down in a groove".

Don't overload the chest voice colour. Sopranos and mezzos are prone to this. It can become as vulgar as the display of too much rouge on cheeks and lips.

The student should absorb and appropriate the finer points from great singers, but without mimicry.

Pure emotion, appropriately injected into song, is the golden key that unlocks all hearts.

The main object of learning the varying directions taken by the sound-beams of the different vowels are (1) to allow for the correct shaping of the resonating cavities in relation to vowel and pitch, and (2) the exact tuning-in of the sound-beams themselves.

In a *diminuendo* keep the breath moving, and as the tone is being left, lift it upwards in order to trail or taper it off, after the manner of a pencil line of ever-decreasing fineness, to vanishing point. In fact, every tone terminated at the end of a phrase, or before a new breath is taken, should be thus treated for it prevents the oft-heard blunt tonal ending which reminds one of a grunt. The upward tone-tapering, however, must be executed rapidly, except in the case of deliberate *diminuendo*.

For the true technique of tonal attack, let us have "*caresse* de glotte", and never *coup de glotte* (*cough* de glotte).

We tell pupils to "bounce" the tone up from a lower to a higher pitch on a gossamer thread of connecting tone. The effect of this thought is the thinning and lightening of the vibrator mechanism. If to the "bounce" we add appropriate vowel modification, we are assured of an exact vibrator adjustment. The lower note is considered in the light of a tonal "springboard".

"Came the whisper, came the vision, came the power with the need" (Rudyard Kipling).

Some singers have a slight "lisp" when singing words containing S, although perhaps not when speaking (and vice versa); this is always due to a slight protrusion of the mere tip of the tongue beyond the level of the front teeth. The remedy lies *not* in deliberately withdrawing the tongue as S is pronounced, but in forming and releasing a complete sibilant; but if the S-hiss be contaminated with a tint of TH, the sibilant will not be pure, and we get THong instead of Song, and so forth.

An idea useful to many voices when coming down from a high to a lower pitch is to *think* of the tone coming down *vertically*, whereupon the next note will automatically assume the correct vocal angle and be prevented from falling in front of the vertical: a thing which must never happen to any note, any vowel, from E♭, fourth space, upwards.

One could well say that the high or head notes demand (1) the *thought* of an inverted U cavity (or narrowish horseshoe shape) for AH, AW, OH, OO and their derivative "short" vowels (as in *pad, pot, put*); (2) the *thought* of an EU- (French) shaped cavity for EH and EE, and derivative short vowels (as in *pen, pin*). These two shapings of the mouth-pharynx cavity are an extraordinary help as regards vowel modification.

The singer must have an intelligent understanding of the fundamental facts concerning the origin of vocal tone, its behaviour as expressed in terms of sound-beams and their "manipulation" and control. Without this exact knowledge the singer is more or less blind, not knowing really what he is trying to do and what to expect. Blind singing in this sense (vocal guesswork) is all too prevalent today as the true art of singing is slowly and surely sinking into the abyss. Blind singing and blind teaching are well wedded. To learn singing merely by imitation (even assuming the teacher's vocal examples to be good) just as a dog learns a trick merely by repetition, cannot possibly lead to a real understanding of the whole problem of vocal technique: processes and procedure, precept and practice. The trouble of understanding is a very small price to pay for the ultimate feeling of mastery of any subject worth while.

The singer must cultivate a feeling-hearing inside the mouth-pharynx cavity or head cavity, according to the pitch; never can he hear the tone outside himself as others do, so *all* his listening must be internal.

A remedy for flat tone: (1) lift up, (2) pull back, (3) round off the vowel; because (1) induces a thinning and lightening of the vibrator mechanism, thereby producing a taller sound-beam of correct frequency, (2) creates space, in that the throat opens naturally and freely as a result of the "pull-back" thought, and (3) assists the shortening of the cords. Be it noted that the lift-up and the pull-back is only a thought, a throat-opening thought, and *not* a mechanical movement to be performed by the singer. The throat itself reacts exactly to the thought.

When a student is about to produce or go up to a high note in a rising phrase, we say "Carry some of your breath up with you to the pitch", and then explain that this is of course purely a mental process, but a very helpful one. Every note should be attacked with an indispensable minimum of breath, for it facilitates correct adjustment in the vibrator and resonator systems.

After "talking in", or "lifting in", the vowelled tone with initially a small quantity of breath, keep the breath moving by blowing upwards from the focus, so to speak. This prevents engaging too much cord in depth during the *crescendo* development of the tone. Don't lean on the neck muscles, on your chin and jaw; also get your face out of the running when producing the high notes. Sing loosely, that is relax everything except the vibrator mechanism proper and the breathing machinery; in other words keep out as much physique as you can and give free play to the vital, intense sound-beam-cum-focus. *Good singing is,* and always has been, *mainly mental*. Mediocre singing is mainly physical.

Vocal tone issuing from a perfect mechanism can be said to be disembodied in the sense that, apparently, it is free from corporeal character, just as a perfectly produced violin tone seems to be divorced from the working of bow against finger-pressed string, and from the very body of the violin itself.

Thought is always strengthened by emotion; emotion lends fire to thought. While emotion can be weakened by association with thought, the singer's emotional output must be nicely controlled by a balancing thought that will prevent swamping of the vocal mechanism, with consequent excesses and distortions. Thought can be heated to such a degree of intensity as will cause it to pass into the emotional region. Even as people think, feel, and express themselves on different planes of emotion, so the several qualities of music have their varying planes of emotion. For purposes of good singing, thought without emotion is like coal without fire; and emotion without controlling thought, like live coal scattered on the floorboards.

Tremolo, or wobble, results from an excessive up-and-down oscillation of soft palate, uvula, tongue and larynx. It is a slow-moving, over-amplified *vibrato*. In aggravated form, even parts of the neck rock to and fro. The whole business is the outcome of wrong and/or forced production, as well as excessive use, or abuse, of the voice.

Some students are not clear as to the meaning of "tightness" as applied to voice. When a tone is flabby, woolly or windy it means that the cords do not approximate sufficiently; this is due to general muscular slackness within the larynx proper. So we say to the student "Tighter", meaning that he must seek more tension-resistance within the laryngeal mechanism, *not* by increasing the breath pressure but by bracing up the entire apparatus with the *thought* of nervous tension which, *willed* in, induces a certain degree of internal excitement. In other words, a more compact and sparkling vocal tone. It is tantamount to good compression in an engine.

Blatant tone is the result of "opening" a vowel to excess, whatever the pitch. It is a form of distortion.

The judgment of a student or singer may be so impaired by long companionship with erroneous ideas of technique as not to recognize the true state of affairs when it meets eye and ear.

A bass necessarily has a heavier thought than has a coloratura soprano, even as the thought of a crow is heavier than that of a nightingale. Singers should learn to keep strictly within their particular category, both mentally and physically, and not try to invade the heavier ones by forcing their voices.

Said the old School: "Cantare con l'anima sviluppa la voce" (To sing with feeling develops your voice).

The following are intended to illustrate different tonal qualities:

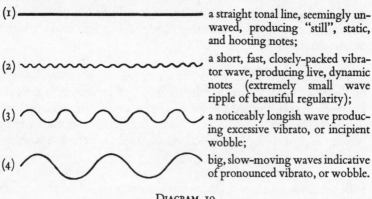

(1) ———————————— a straight tonal line, seemingly unwaved, producing "still", static, and hooting notes;

(2) ∿∿∿∿∿∿∿∿∿∿ a short, fast, closely-packed vibrator wave, producing live, dynamic notes (extremely small wave ripple of beautiful regularity);

(3) ∿∿∿∿∿ a noticeably longish wave producing excessive vibrato, or incipient wobble;

(4) ∿∿∿ big, slow-moving waves indicative of pronounced vibrato, or wobble.

DIAGRAM 19

To sing *p* or *mp* on a mere "thread of tone" (*filo di voce*) may well seem, to those unaccustomed to the sensation, to be almost at breaking point, imparting a feeling that the voice "won't hold". But this lack of confidence is the outcome of singing habitually with a forced breath pressure which, to certain singers, appears to be the only mainstay. A great mistake. It is only a question of muscular training primarily within the larynx proper (in which, remember, over sixty muscles are embedded!). This training is similar to holding a piece of paper (or any object) between index and thumb with only just sufficient pressure to keep it from falling, but no more. This light grip is so nicely calculated that while the object will never slip out of its own, it can readily be pulled away with the left hand. Similarly, *mezzavoce* singing demands only an indispensable minimum of breath expenditure and muscular action, albeit a maximum of mental-nervous support; but the breath must be kept *moving*.

Thought can be made light or heavy at will; the physical reaction thereto will be a correspondingly light or heavy tone— even as the light or heavy touch of an artist's brush, pen or pencil will give a light or heavy tint or line, according to the "weight" of his thought.

It is related that Liszt, on hearing Paganini for the first time, was inspired for, and received from him, "that passion for absolute perfection of technique".

Most modern students, and singers, seemingly prefer to indulge in hard physical labour when singing rather than mental effort that visualizes, forms, guides and controls. "Denken is schwer" (Thinking is hard work) say the Germans, and "the hardest of all work", said Henry Ford, the car magnate. Judging by modern standards it is easier to "let it rip", with barely a thought—and that brutalized.

Tonal overloading makes the product heavy, unwieldy, and lustreless, for it lacks the sparkle of balanced adjustment. The "beefy" fundamental rumble resulting from excessive cord depth (excessive in relation to pitch) is highly attractive to the modern singer; which damaging procedure cuts out the more telling harmonics in the tone. Students must remember that *harmonics are the "carrying" power in vocal tone*, and that the more they dig into the voice the more fundamental rumble they will produce, and the greater the rumble the more noise they create for themselves (the great snag and illusion) and locally in a small room, but are barely heard in a large hall or theatre. The more the rumble the less harmonics in a tone, and conversely. Preponderance of the lower band of harmonics is always fatal to good quality of tone, and excessive cord length and depth produces just this harmonic distortion. (See footnote, p. 54.)

In certain cases, don't give the full time value to a note at the end of which a new breath is necessary for the next phrase, because if you do you will inevitably gasp in a snatch-breath more or less inadequate properly to produce and sustain the ensuing notes. The singer needs a *poised*, not a flurried, intake of breath; for this he must develop a fast-moving breathing machinery. (See p. 306.)

A tonal focus is the culmination of the entire vocal adjustment and effort for a given pitch and vowel. In other words, the vowelled tone is brought, by means of the relative sound-beam, to an acoustical terminal or point, the beam itself being the core or nucleus of the whole physical effort, and the *top* of the beam the focus. Which beam or core must be left undisturbed by the singer, never forced or made rigid by excessive breath pressure, never strangled or damped by bringing chin and jaw, and neck muscles, into the tonal play. Relax everything around this vital central beam.

Due to the modern method of forced breath pressure many voices reveal a kind of flicker or chattering in their tones. Rarely do we hear a clean *legato* line, like the tone produced by a fine violinist. When habitual, excess breath pressure makes for hard, juddering tone, and eventually kills the voice.

When singing, don't be static and stand like a pole, expecting the voice to do all the work. Be dynamic, be mentally alive and alert, be *excited* and brace up the voice with mind and nerves. Use your imagination.

Don't produce a note, particularly a high one, and mentally abandon it, expecting it to "stay put" on its own. You produced and "placed" it, so *consciously* hold it in position for its time value.

What does "placing" the voice really mean? The good singer does not actually "place" the voice; rather does he *allow* the sound-beam to take its appointed, natural direction and height. And this it will do when the internal (vowel) shaping and general adjustment is correct in relation to the pitch. If he *thinks* the right shaping and direction in relation to pitch and vowel, the sound-beam will follow the trend of thought. It is as simple as that. "Placing" the voice originated from the Italian *impostare la voce.*

As you release the well-prepared consonant, *spring open* the parts with a quick, oil-smooth action and rapidly produce your vowelled tone.

Imagine, as you are about to soar to a higher pitch, a ready-made tonal stream, and mentally ride up with it on the particular vowel.

We must distinguish between sentiment and sentimentality. The first is thought prompted by passion or feeling, and is a refined, tender emotion. But sentimentality, so often confused with sentiment, is artificial, affected, often a morbid, mushy tenderness of no substance. True sentiment is found in all good compositions.

(V)

The vanity of certain singers is second only to their bad production.

It is of vital importance to have breath support when singing, and for this the muscles concerned must be carefully developed. When the lower or floating ribs are nicely expanded as a result of the inspiratory act and allowed, as a phrase is being sung, to return smoothly and very gradually to the state of rest, they give the feeling of a horizontal "girder" sustaining the breathing apparatus and indirectly the voice itself.

Vowel is the soul of the word; without it there is no word. The word is the song and the singer. (See footnote, p. 301.)

As an aid to good phrasing, carry through the particular vowel-sound to the end of its note value, and *glide* one vowel into the next.

Carefully think out the particular vowel shape-cum-tone you wish to produce before actually doing so; remember that the vocal organs react immediately and exactly to every shaping thought. So do not try physically to shape the vowels, for you will be sure to overdo things. The mental shaping is all-important.

Don't try to make vowels in the head cavity (above the palate) such as are felt in the mouth-pharynx up to D, fourth line (all voices), for it is a physical impossibility. Only the sound-beam can soar into the head cavity.

As a tonal sensation, vowel commences to fade gradually out of the picture as from E♭, fourth space. From this point, as the pitch rises, the sound-beam proper impresses the singer's mind more and more as it soars into the head cavity, leaving the vowel behind within the mouth-pharynx. Furthermore, on the head notes *only the top* of the sound-beam, which we call platform, or focus, is felt by the singer, and not the beam itself.

Feed the voice with well shaped vowels, good melody, good music.

If by way of experiment the student, with mouth closed and without moving the lips at all, sings lightly in smooth, uninterrupted succession the vowels AH, EH, EE, OH, OO on the same low note, he will feel how they are all formed inside the mouth-pharynx cavity without the aid of the lips. This shows that the lips do not actually form any vowel, not even OH and OO whose shaping, however, is completed by the customary pursing of the lips both in speech and in song, on the *low* notes. The lips are not a vowel forming but a finishing medium.

The necessary lip participation (as a finishing medium) in the formation of OO on low notes gradually gets less and less as the pitch rises, particularly as from E♭, fourth space, until at about high A♭ it is practically nil, for the pharynx has no longer any need of the lips at all. This applies to all voices, male and female. In baritone and bass voices this reduction to nil occurs at about F, fifth line.

The short *u* vowel, as in *put*, can be thought of as a "loose" OO (as in *pool*) when producing a high note on the latter vowel, as it is a mixed sound of OO and OH.

The slightest modification of a vowel shape creates of itself a correspondingly small tonal curve, which of course modifies the sound of the vowel in equal degree. A modified or "darkened" vowel is merely the result of a rounding, in degree, of the mouth-pharynx cavity. The act of modifying a vowel *seems* to produce a marked change internally; actually, the internal curving movement of the pharynx reflecting the modification is often extremely slight. Beware, however, of the mind's tendency to exaggerate all sensations in the head. (Witness the grossly exaggerated "measuring" as the tongue probes and explores a dental cavity, whether the result of decay or of the dentist's drilling.)

Voice training has to reinstate a control proper to nature, a control that gradually has been weakened by bad habits. In all faulty adjustments of the mechanism, nature takes a back seat and error the front. Voice training primarily includes the readjustment of erroneous states of thought regarding technique.

"Nature denies her instructions to none who desire to become her pupils" (Sir Joshua Reynolds).

A voice badly produced and/or habitually ill-treated will soon show—

> *The little rift within the lute,*
> *That by and by will make the music mute,*
> *And ever widening slowly silence all.*
>   Tennyson

If when taking *high* notes on EH or EE you think of the spoken vowel sound, you will automatically adjust your mouth to a slot-like opening, as in speech, whereupon the tongue will rise and the soft palate descend and thus leave only a narrow corridor between palatal arc and tongue. Consequently the tone will be squashed and strident. It can't be otherwise, because the tall or extended sound-beam of high pitches requires the optimum accommodation in both the mouth-pharynx and the head cavities. Inversely, by opening the mouth internally and externally for EH and EE on *high* notes (almost as much as for AH, AW, OH, OO) with the shape of an inverted U, the tongue is prevented from rising and the soft palate from descending to the extent they do in actual speech; this provides sufficient space for resonation. Note, however, that this necessary reduction of tongue and palate movement does *not* prevent the clear formation of EH and EE—although the unenlightened singer may think otherwise. On the other hand, EE and OO cannot be produced on the lowest notes with the mouth well open.

When from an EE vowel you have to sing an EH on the same pitch, it is best to make a slight mental pull-back-lift-up movement in order to place, so to speak, the EH on top of the EE position—not underneath or through it. This thought releases the throat and assists the shaping.

(W)

Words and notes are not the things themselves: they are symbols, or countersigns, used by poets and composers for setting down their ideas and expressing their feelings. For true "interpretation" the singer must translate them back to their original concept.

The words must always be studied first: what they mean, the story they tell, the picture they convey. When read and phrased aloud their significance takes on an added hue and strength. Repetition makes things stand out more clearly. The next step is to spin the story out on the melodic line with colour, meaning, expression and accent.

In words beginning with *w*, such as *white, where, when, was, wall, with, waft*, etc., the singer must be careful *not* to put the vowel sound following the *w* (which is merely a short *u* as in *put*) either on the same spot or in front of it; it must be sung *behind* the *w*, otherwise the tone will "stick" and suffer distortion in some degree.

"During the summer holidays I gave Therese regular lessons in singing, according to a method which has always remained a mystery to me ever since" (Richard Wagner, *My Life*).

CHAPTER XXII

THE "PHARYNGEAL" VOICE

An Ignored Mechanism

ACTUALLY, there is no such thing as a "pharyngeal" voice. The term—a translation from the Italian *voce faringea*, was in usage by the exponents of the old Italian School to distinguish the tonal product of a peculiar but distinctive vocal mechanism, a mechanism that lies between that producing the real of basic voice and that producing the so-called falsetto. It can be engaged by itself, or in combination with either the basic or the falsetto, or both simultaneously. All three mechanisms, each of which can be engaged isolatedly, form part and parcel of the actual cord mechanism.

At one time every teacher and singer trained in the old School employed this mechanism-voice, amalgamating it with the basic and with the falsetto. There is no available data as regards its discovery, but it certainly harks back about 300 years, right into the core of the acknowledged "golden era" of singing. It is safe to assert, however, that today very few teachers in Italy or anywhere else are conversant with the pharyngeal mechanism, its development and possibilities. It may well be that in certain Church circles in Italy a select few have closely guarded the tradition seeing that for so long, and right up to 1870—date of the fall of Papal sovereignty—it was an essential part of the curriculum provided for students destined to enter the churches as soloists, and in particular tenor vocalists—although these were known as "contraltos". Today it seemingly is a lost, or much neglected, faculty in vocal technique. And yet it is of paramount importance. Few teachers possess full knowledge of its function, few teach it (if at all) with the thoroughness it deserves. It appears to have been relegated to the limbo of lost craftsmanship, like so many other things of beauty in all branches of art, due undoubtedly to the fool errand of the "short cut" to accomplishment.

333

The term *falsetto* generally refers to a quality of voice or mechanism. But the terms *falsetti* or *falsettisti* designated in particular the male soprano—that vocal paradox, an importation from Spain in the thirteenth century and essentially a product of eviration. But they were sometimes applied to the real tenor vocalists because the latter's head voice was an admixture of pharyngeal and falsetto. When exercised to the maximum (over a period of about 4 years, depending on the individual voice, of course), these two mechanisms, properly amalgamated, are capable of producing a head voice of extraordinary power.

In Italy, women were not allowed to sing in the churches; consequently, in order to obtain the requisite vocal qualities, the "soprano" was secured through eviration, and the "contralto" by special development of the head voice based on the pharyngeal mechanism, as explained hereunder.

Such specially trained tenors were called "contraltos" because when a tenor sings with a fully developed pharyngeal-falsetto voice from F♮, fifth line, to high C or D, the tonal characteristics are very similar to the medium notes of a contralto or mezzo, from F♮, first space, to D, fourth line, particularly if she also employs the "pharyngeal". Sometimes the two voices are practically indistinguishable as regards quality, but only as far as the above series of notes are concerned; for we must remember that the tenor (and all male voices) actually sings an octave lower than written, and therefore his head notes are of the same frequency as the above series of medium notes of female voices.

The church tenor vocalist known as "contralto" was *not* a product of emasculation.*

* The author's teacher, Giovan, Riccardo Daviesi, was known as the greatest "contralto" singer of the Sistine Chapel in the nineteenth century; and it will not be amiss to quote three press opinions of this great, and much too self-effacing, artist:

Extract from the American *Orpheus*, New York and Boston, January 1, 1870 —the occasion being the first grand performance of Rossini's Mass on September 14, 1869, in the Cathedral of Lucca. The special performance solemnized Rossini's obsequies—the great composer having passed away in Paris, November 14, 1868:

"The Cathedral was magnificently decorated with hangings of crimson and gold, and the blaze of thousands of wax candles in immense crystal chandeliers mingled with rays of many colours that illuminated the pictured windows and lit up the elaborate arches and massive pillars. The bishops and priests in their gorgeous robes, the flowers, the music, the immense orchestra built for the

We said above that the pharyngeal voice or mechanism lies between the basic or real and the falsetto mechanisms. The student will get a clear picture of what we are about to explain if he envisages the three mechanisms as three horizontal layers super-imposed, three *depths* of the vocal cord mechanism producing three different tonal qualities, each of which is characteristic and quite distinct from the others.

Taken by itself, the pharyngeal voice, without any admixture of basic or of falsetto, has a certain quality of steely intensity which is the reverse of beautiful, particularly when produced *f*. Mixed, however, with either the basic or the falsetto (and, better still, with both simultaneously), it assumes very considerable importance.

Before describing this peculiar, outstanding mechanism, we propose to reveal how extremely necessary and important it is, provided it be judiciously employed. In fact, it can be usefully and effectively employed in conjunction with:

occasion, with more than three hundred of the first musicians of Italy, the dense crowd with eager, excited faces that filled every place—all formed a never-to-be-forgotten scene, and a living testimony to the affection with which the memory of Rossini is cherished in the hearts of his countrymen. The principal part of the Mass is written for the 'contralto', and was sung on this occasion by Giovan Riccardo Daviesi, the distinguished 'contralto' of the Papal Choir. *This young artist is beyond doubt the rising star of Italy.* The extension, strength and purity of his voice, the extreme sweetness and marvellous flexibility, the clearness of utterance, the exquisite finish and depth of feeling and expression, places him at a height that admits of no rival. As the fame of a composer must depend somewhat on the manner in which his composition is rendered, if possible the reputation of Rossini must have gained new lustre from the exquisite perfection with which this talented artist expressed the sublime conception of his immortal genius. Of Signor Daviesi, who added so much to the perfection of the execution, we can only say that, in all probability, during the next year Americans will be enabled to form their own judgment in regard to his talents, as he intends visiting that country, where, we are assured, he will meet with the warm welcome with which her children always receive genius. And we trust his advent will be the occasion of an entire revolution in the church music of our country . . .''

Extract from *Musica*, Rome, February 28, 1918: "Giovan Riccardo Daviesi, born in Rome, April 12, 1839, was undoubtedly the greatest 'contralto' ever heard in the Roman churches. He was a pupil of the 'Schola Cantorum' of San Michele. He was first engaged for the Cappella Pia Lateranense, then for the Cappella Giulia, and finally in March, 1864, when nearly twenty-five years old, for the Cappella Sistina."

Extract from the Rome daily, *La Tribuna*, July 10, 1921: "Yesterday, at

(1) the falsetto, for purposes of *pp, p, mp, mf,* and, generally, *mezzavoce* singing;

(2) the real or basic voice—for *f* and *mezzavoce;*

(3) the falsetto and the basic, simultaneously.*

It is extraordinarily useful for:

(4) the full *messa di voce* in its purest form (on the tenor's high notes), starting from a pinpoint *pianissimo* and developing with perfect graduation through *crescendo* to *f*, and back again with graduated *decrescendo* to *pp;*†

(5) the half *messa di voce,* i.e. (*a*) a graduated *crescendo* from *p* to *f*, or (*b*) a graduated *decrescendo* from *f* to *p;*

(6) greatly facilitating the production of, and strengthening, the tenor's high notes;

(7) creating perfect attacks, particularly of the tenor's high notes;

(8) revitalizing the vocal cords (of all voices possessing the mechanism);

7 p.m., Giovan Riccardo Daviesi, teacher of singing, passed away. With the demise of Daviesi, Rome loses one of her greatest singers and teachers. After studying at the 'Schola Cantorum' he entered the Cappella Lateranense, then the Cappella Giulia, and finally the Cappella Sistina. After the fall of Rome in 1870, he repaired to London in order to continue his medical studies under the famous throat specialist, Sir Morell Mackenzie. Subsequently he opened a school of singing there, but shortly afterwards was recalled to Italy by the Vatican. He finally settled in Milan as a teacher of singing. Daviesi was also an excellent composer. At sixty years of age he was engaged as Director of Vocal Studies in the Conservatorium of Irkutsk, Siberia, where he remained seven years, and then went to Moscow. On returning to Italy he settled in Rome. He associated with the most famous composers and singers of his time. He was an intimate friend of Liszt, and of Rossini with whom he lived for some time in Paris, and also of Frezzolini, the celebrated soprano. Gounod, after hearing Daviesi sing in Paris approached him, saying: "Est ce que vous être peintre, Monsieur?" (Are you a painter, Sir?), and on his replying in the negative and demanding the reason for such a curious question, Gounod replied, "Parceque vous chantez avec tant de couleur" (Because you sing with so much colour) . . ."

* All three terms are incorrect: the falsetto is not really a false voice, as it is produced by the vocal cords; the pharyngeal has no more pharynx about it than the other two, and is also part of the vocal cord mechanism; the basic is just the normal voice, which is also called "chest" voice (*voce di petto*), also a misnomer.

† The author's teacher, mentioned above, when eighty years of age, could still execute a perfectly graduated *messa di voce* on a high A or B♭, employing all three mechanisms. The tone was powerful, and rock steady even on attaining the maximum development.

(9) correcting the tremolo or wobble, in tenors, sopranos, mezzos and contraltos;

(10) rehearsing, as it saves the wear and tear of constant repetition of high notes that is so fatiguing to the tenor's normal or basic voice.

The pharyngeal mechanism is found in all sopranos, mezzos, contraltos, tenors, occasionally in light baritones, but not in basses. Consequently, each of these categories has three distinct mechanisms built vertically into the vocal cords in the form of three fibrous "layers": first the falsetto, then the pharyngeal, and finally the basic—the last-mentioned being the lowest and most substantial layer. The pharyngeal, therefore, is sandwiched between the basic and the falsetto; small wonder, then, that it has been ignored or, shall we say, smothered in the folds of indiscriminate thick cord singing so prevalent today.* For, *unless there is adequate elimination of the vibrating mass of the vocal cords* as the pitch rises, *the pharyngeal mechanism cannot engage* and participate in the operational network.

Here is a theoretical diagram illustrating the three mechanisms or vibratory layers of the vocal cords:

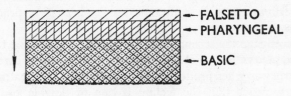

DIAGRAM 20

A number of singers actually employ the pharyngeal in mixed form without, however, knowing what it is all about; they sense its peculiarities but rarely take the trouble to analyse, investigate, and exploit the possibilities. If they only realized what they lose in control and artistry by their want of knowledge or industry! The male alto heard in churches and choirs in England employs mainly the pharyngeal, which for lack of real schooling never attains, however, perfection of development.

* By this we mean that the modern methods of forced breath pressure singing induce the employment mainly of the thick underlying folds of the cords, making it impossible for the pharyngeal to function.

Y

The following explanations will offer a better all-round picture of the three mechanisms. First, the falsetto or uppermost layer: the term *falsetto* (diminutive of the Italian *falso*, false) means "false little voice"; by itself it is worthless for purposes of vocal expression. The old Italian School used to call it *falsettino di testa*, "false little head voice", because, as a sensation, it seems to be generated high up in the head cavities. By no means is it a false voice, as the tone is generated by the thread-like upper edges of the vocal cords which, in order to produce the so-called falsetto, separate much more than is the case for the production of either the pharyngeal or normal tone. And because of the greater space or slit between the cords while producing the falsetto, a much greater quantity of breath is expended, in that not all of it is employed in producing tone (as is, or should be, the case with normal tone) but escapes through the slit, thereby "diluting" the product. It is a "head" voice, but of a pale, insignificant, breathy sort: the tone is anæmic and static. Most voices, male and female, are able to produce falsetto. But some basses, and baritones of the heavier calibres, apparently do not seem able to produce it at all. In its usually undeveloped state, the falsetto is weak, and has little tension-resistance (due to the separation of the cords). We hold the falsetto tone in contempt only when it is produced by itself.

To engage the second layer-mechanism responsible for the so-called pharyngeal voice, the cords approximate considerably more than they do when producing falsetto. As the pharyngeal mechanism comes into action the feeling is one of flexible firmness and resistance (that are lacking in the falsetto). Being the second "layer" it is, as a tonal sensation, slightly lower than the falsetto; and by this we mean that it has slightly more vertical depth, definitely more substance, and is more lifelike.

A little more vertical depth (which is secured by a *slight* downward pressing, mainly mental) will engage the third layer-mechanism, that is the basic mechanism producing what we may call the normal voice. When cord adduction is normal both for the pharyngeal and the basic mechanisms, only a very thin slit (or glottis) separates them—the cords must never meet for and during phonation.

As the singer presses downwards through the pharyngeal layer and engages the basic, the feeling is one of slightly more depth of cord as soon as the latter comes into operation, albeit of flexible firmness and resistance.

Thus we have three mechanisms, three vibrating layers, three vibratory "depths" superimposed, forming one organic vocal cord unit. We could say that they are three consistencies, as the pharyngeal has less cord depth than the basic, and the falsetto less depth than the pharyngeal. Correct sensations inform that the falsetto mechanism consists of the thinnest of thin upper edges of the vocal cords slightly separated with an oval tendency; that the pharyngeal mechanism comes into operation as the cords approximate to linear form, employing the same thin upper edges of the cords with, however, slightly more "depth" of vibrator; that the basic mechanism consists of the remaining layer (the greatest part) of the vibrator mass.

The three mechanisms forming the vocal unit are separable in that it is possible, and usefully so at times, to engage them *singly*; furthermore, either the falsetto and pharyngeal can be employed simultaneously, or the pharyngeal and basic; and when all three are thus engaged, as they can be on certain high notes by the tenor, the tonal product is wonderfully colourful.

If a note is attacked falsetto and then, with unbroken continuity, developed in depth to the maximum of its layer (which is *very* shallow), it will require very little extra downward "pressing" to engage the pharyngeal mechanism—thereby greatly improving the general tonal quality. Upon developing *vertically downwards* the tone to the maximum "depth" of the pharyngeal layer (which is also shallow) only a very slight extra downward pressing is necessary to engage the basic mechanism, thereby improving still more the tonal product. The proportion of basic mechanism can be regulated at will. All of which is not so easy of accomplishment as it appears in print, for reasons that will be explained later. The downward pressing that engages one mechanism after the other must have an oil-smooth action, and be performed with delicate, albeit firm, touch. The singer just *wills* the downward pressing, nothing more; so there must be no deliberate muscular attempt to do so.

The EH vowel, and derivatives thereof, are particularly acceptable to the pharyngeal; by this we mean that it readily engages when these particular vowels are employed, for they act as a "key" or starter. They are: the EH, as in *there*, which is openish;

then the flatter and more closed *eh*, as in *said, fed:* and the short *e*, as in *met, pet;* and finally the *i* sound in *sit, fit* (written *i*, but actually is a mixture of *ee* and of an *e* which is flatter than that of *met*). Another excellent key-starter is the *ir* vowel sound as in *bird, surf*, and the French *eu*, as in *berceuse*, which is flat and compressed. We have therefore five starter-vowels. It is necessary to employ them in the initial period of work in order the better to secure the *isolated* gearing-in of the pharyngeal mechanism, especially when it is undeveloped in an individual. When it has attained sufficient development it will readily engage and "sing" with any and all vowels, although its predilection tends more towards the aforementioned starter or key vowels to which it reacts with elfin delight.

The pharyngeal commences to function effectively in all voices on the same pitch, viz. at F♮, first space. We would remind the student that, although written an octave higher, the tenor's F♮ (fifth line) is *acoustically* on the first space; therefore his first effective pharyngeal note is an upper medium whereas that in women's voices is a relatively low note. Consequently, the pharyngeal mechanism of tenors and of such light baritones that possess it, enters effectively on its career actually on the same *pitch* or frequency as does that of sopranos, mezzos and contraltos. Its effective compass in all voices possessing it is from F♮, first space, to D, fourth line—a matter of ten notes therefore, although in the tenor's case (written an octave higher than he actually sings) modern opera rarely carries notes beyond high C.*

---

* The famous tenor, Domenico Donzelli, wrote to Bellini in 1831 when the latter was composing *Norma*, in which the part of Pollione was being especially written for him: "I do not consider it amiss if I give you some idea of the compass and general nature of my voice, for you will then know better how to write for it and I shall be sure of successfully interpreting in the dual interest of your music and my art. My compass is almost two octaves: from D to high C; I employ chest voice to G only, but up to this pitch I can sustain a vigorous declamation. From this G to high C I employ a falsetto which, when used with art and strength, is extremely ornamental. I have adequate agility."

Obviously, by "falsetto" from G to high C he meant the pharyngeal voice appropriately mixed with what we today know as falsetto—that breathy, useless voice on its own, as explained above. By "chest" voice Donzelli meant the normal voice. In accordance with the training at that time, Donzelli used his normal voice up to F♯ or G, and then the pharyngeal-falsetto combination for the head notes. Several arias in Bellini's and Donizetti's operas include high D♮, obviously intended to be sung with the pharyngeal-falsetto schooling.

The tenor's pharyngeal generally can be extended downwards past the effective starting point (F♮), sometimes as far down as C (an extra five notes, therefore); but the notes below said F are not really serviceable and effective seeing that the mechanism dwindles rapidly from this point and loses its characteristic timbre. The higher the pitch, however, from said F upwards, the more powerful the pharyngeal for it comes into its own more and more as the basic mechanism is gradually eliminated as the pitch rises to the highest notes.

We know that in good singing, from the mechanical standpoint, there must be a gradual elimination of the vibrating mass of the vocal cords as the pitch rises from the lowest to the highest note. On reaching the F in question the pharyngeal starts its career *if the singer so wills it*, and steadily gains in strength and volume as the aforesaid elimination takes place with the gradual rise of pitch. This phenomenon is particularly marked in the tenor voice. If a tenor produces, say, a high B♭ with a well eliminated mechanism, only a small percentage of basic voice is employed; and by way of compensation a goodly percentage of pharyngeal comes into operation automatically.

N.B.—In all correctly produced head notes of the tenor voice there is a goodly proportion of pharyngeal whether or not the singer himself is aware of the fact; and the higher the pitch the greater the percentage. This is a natural phenomenon of which few tenors are conscious. But when trained to do so, the singer can with advantage deliberately increase the proportion of pharyngeal, thereby giving the tone greater brilliance, intensity and carrying power.

When produced *f* in this way, the tenor's high notes should not include any percentage of falsetto, as it might "dilute" the intensity; but as soon as he commences to *decrescendo* or taper the tone from *f* to *p* it is a good plan, although not really necessary, to add finally a small percentage of falsetto to the already mixed basic-pharyngeal mechanisms. It all depends on what has to be expressed, and whether the singer elects to make use of the falsetto, and to what degree. In order to engage this small percentage of falsetto towards the tail end of the *decrescendo* the singer must "lift up" the tone slightly.

If high C is produced *f* with correct mechanism, the pharyngeal undoubtedly predominates, but is given substance by the small percentage of basic still remaining.

From high C upwards, in the tenor voice, the pharyngeal predominates absolutely, with appropriate percentages of falsetto; these notes are worthless today, however, for all practical purposes. A glance at the tenor rôles in the operas of Rossini, Bellini, and Donizetti will reveal convincingly that they were written for voices trained in the old School on the above lines, i.e. for the *tenore di grazia*, light, graceful tenor; the *tessitura*, the runs, with phrases touching high D and even high F, were clearly never meant to be sung with the so-called "chest" voice (the basic mechanism) alone. These composers *knew* what to write for voices, even as Verdi and Puccini did, and a host of others too. It is said that Rossini, Donizetti and Verdi had good tenor voices. As a general rule, the lighter the tenor voice the more the pharyngeal is naturally predominant in the head tones.

Tenors, more than any other category, make much greater use of the pharyngeal and in fact have a greater compass in this operational sphere—provided they have been trained to employ it properly.*

---

* Dramatic accent was not neglected by the "di grazia" tenors; witness also the rôle of Edgardo in *Lucia di Lammermoor*. Donizetti invariably wrote for the "di grazia" tenor; and before and during the Rossini–Bellini period, tenors *never* produced their head notes solely with the so-called "chest" voice (basic mechanism) because their training emphasized the employment of the mixed mechanism: basic-pharyngeal, or pharyngeal-falsetto, or all three simultaneously.

The breakaway from the tradition was initiated by the tenor Marcel Duprez, whose success, however, was all too ephemeral. He is credited with being the first tenor to produce all the head notes, including high C and C#, with the normal voice (unmixed basic mechanism). The French called this "le Do de poitrine", high C in chest voice, which the Italians translated into "il Do di petto". It was the latter who coined the phrase "voce di petto", chest voice, in order to distinguish the real or basic mechanism from the pharyngeal and falsetto. Duprez's vocal collapse and eclipse are instructive under the circumstances. Might is not always right; and in this respect the following extract from *Cantanti Celebri del Secolo XIX* (Celebrated Singers of the XIXth Century), by the impresario Gino Monaldi, is illuminating: "Duprez, through sheer will-power and determination, became one of the most famous tenors in the world. In his case Nature had not been lavish, his voice being both weak and dull; yet by dint of hard unremitting work he succeeded in making it exceptionally robust. After hearing Duprez in *William Tell*, Rossini complimented him with tears in his eyes. When asked the reason for the tears, Rossini replied: 'I weep because those who heard *William Tell* sung tonight by Duprez will not enjoy hearing it sung by other tenors; but, unfortunately, poor Duprez cannot last long.' In fact it was not long before the prediction came true. He sang without producing one single note of falsetto. The effect of his high C was extraordinary. Many

The above recorded phenomenon that provides for an ever-increasing percentage of pharyngeal voice in compensation for a corresponding decrease in basic voice, as from F upwards, is consonant with the acoustical principle of gradual elimination of the mass of the vocal cords in both length and thickness as the pitch rises.

We suggested above that the three mechanisms—Falsetto, Pharyngeal, Basic—built into the vocal cords, can be considered as so many fibrous horizontal layers vertically superimposed. In

tenors hastened to adopt this dangerous procedure. Panofka, the celebrated Russian teacher of singing, expressed himself in the matter as follows: 'Duprez sang the part of Arnoldo with a tenacity and energy worthy of a better cause; and who can deny that afterwards most tenors set themselves the task of imitating Duprez's mistakes, seeking nothing but the brutal force of the high C? Who can deny that, from that day of inauguration by Duprez, the rôles of Arnoldo, Raul, and Eleazaro were not sung as *tenori di forza* instead of *di grazia*, for which latter the parts were originally scored? Who can deny that such tenors had to engage in an athletic contest with their voices, a struggle from which the voice came out second best? Who can deny that the sopranos, in order to compete with the "tenori di forza", were obliged to force their voices beyond the normal?'

"If Duprez had been content to secure his *forte* with purely natural means, he would not have lost his voice so early in life. Of which fact he made confession when he wrote to Rubini, famous tenor 'di grazia' of the old School, 'I who am comparatively young have lost my voice; how do you, who are getting on in years, manage to keep yours intact?' To which Rubini blandly replied: 'You lost your voice because you sung *on capital*; I, on the contrary, have always sung on interest.' "

[It is stated above that "Duprez sang without producing one single note of falsetto". The writer, an impresario of note in the nineteenth century, evidently meant pharyngeal-falsetto to distinguish it from the so-called "chest" voice. Again, in the last paragraph above, he suggests that Duprez should have secured his *forte* with "purely natural means"; it is clear, therefore, that he considered the employment solely of the "chest" or normal voice up to the highest notes as unnatural, or, in other words, forced; and the employment of the pharyngeal-falsetto as natural. All of which reflects the technical usage of his day, and the general opinion held. The modern student must, however, bear in mind that only church tenors employed just pharyngeal-falsetto without any basic mechanism or normal voice on the head notes, whereas the operatic tenors in the Rossini-Bellini-Donizetti period produced their head voice mainly with the pharyngeal-falsetto combination with, however, an added percentage of basic or real voice. Even though this percentage was small it gave *substance* to the tone. If their high C was mainly pharyngeal-falsetto, the C♯ and D were produced with pure pharyngeal and falsetto without any basic whatever. (Author's note.)]

the case of a fully developed vocal organism either naturally (which is very rare indeed) or as a result of study, the falsetto dovetails downwards into, and slightly overlaps, the top part of the pharyngeal, even as the pharyngeal dovetails downwards into, and slightly overlaps, the top part of the basic.

In Chapter XIV we explained how the attack must operate *mentally* in a downward direction, and that the physical reaction to this downward thought when attacking the tone is a correct adduction of the cords and altogether a firm, well-balanced muscular adjustment. Now the actual engaging of the three mechanisms is actuated in depth by the same downward trend of thought: first the falsetto, then the pharyngeal, and finally the basic can be engaged in downward succession. (In a sense the three mechanisms may well be compared to three superimposed inter-locking gears.)

The downward thought can be controlled to a nicety; it can be arrested at will so that a degree of falsetto and, say, only half of the pharyngeal are engaged together; or the entire pharyngeal layer may be engaged in depth while retaining a small percentage of falsetto. In both cases a mixed tone of agreeable quality is produced. If this *downward*-gearing thought is pursued, the basic gradually engages in depth as required by the singer, where-upon a mixed tone of richer quality is produced. At the will and discretion of the singer, percentages of all three layer-mechanisms can be engaged to function simultaneously, producing a mixed tone of excellent quality.

Being the correct principle of attack, the downward thought (the *touch* of which must always be delicate, light, but firm) is a valuable device when it is desired to engage the basic mechanism directly without reference to either the pharyngeal or the falsetto. The mental message can engage at will the basic mechanism (normal voice) directly, going right through the falsetto and pharyngeal layers, ignoring them completely, so to speak.

Expressed in this way, a much magnified picture of the operation is given, for actually the downward thought has very little travel even though it goes "right through" the first two layers in this case. Switch the message to either of the other two mechanisms and we get a direct gearing-in of one or the other. That is the extraordinary part of the three-in-one vibrating unit, and such is the possibility of thought educated on these particular lines.

When the tenor produces, say, a high A with adequately eliminated vibrator, a certain percentage of pharyngeal comes into play *automatically;* but the singer can, however, introduce, at will, a greater percentage, whereupon the note acquires that extra tinge which marks the difference between cold normality and magnetic personality. That which scintillates with life and buoyancy must ever appeal to the listener's æsthetic instinct. A goodly tinge of pharyngeal injected into the basic makes the tone sparkle and adds considerably to its carrying power.

The tenor student should note that the pharyngeal tones are by nature well "placed"; this is particularly true when its mechanism is well developed and properly moulded, whereupon it acts as an infallible "pointer" to the basic voice. Furthermore, the knowledge that *a well developed pharyngeal mechanism acts as an infallible guide to the normal voice,* absolutely removes all fear of the high notes. The majority of singers, men in particular, are "scared stiff" of high notes; which fear clearly reveals that lack of confidence in self and in the voice which is a direct outcome of technical ignorance and shortcomings. In every field of physical action lack of knowledge breeds fear, sometimes in paralysing form.

Although the pharyngeal layer looms large in the above theoretical diagram, it is actually of little depth; so the exaggerated depth in the drawing is meant to illustrate merely its importance in the vibrator network. As a matter of fact, the singer, when producing the pharyngeal, feels quite distinctly that he is employing the surface and seemingly only the surface of the thread-like upper edges of the cords—a surface having little depth, paradoxically speaking.

The pharyngeal mechanism comes effectively into its own only when at a given pitch the cords are of certain (decreased) thickness, and of certain (decreased) length.

We come now to a curious phenomenon: In the tenor voice (and in the light baritone possessing it) the pharyngeal mechanism does not come into *effective* operation until *after* the first octave and a half, viz. F, fifth line; consequently, being essentially a surface mechanism, it is built into the *front half* of the vocal cords and therefore is interested only in the last eight notes of the tenor's normal compass, and in the last four or five of the light baritone's. This tenor F, as we know, although written on the fifth line for convenience sake, is *acoustically* an octave lower, i.e. F, first space.

And it is precisely this pitch on which the first effective note of the pharyngeal mechanism is produced in women's voices. Consequently, in all female voices the pharyngeal mechanism is built into the *back half* of the vocal cords, and is therefore only interested in the medium notes from this F to D, fourth line, a matter of ten notes.

So we see that the pharyngeal operates effectively in both male and female voices as from the same *pitch* (F, first space) and for the same series of notes, acoustically. Which series of notes (and here lies the phenomenon we mentioned above) represents the tenor's and baritone's head notes, and the soprano's, mezzo's and contralto's lower medium notes. A truly wonderful phenomenon worthy of investigation by the acoustician and aerodynamical expert.*

In all these vocal categories the pharyngeal can be extended, in certain cases, below the said F, and sometimes down to C, an extra five notes; but it is neither effective nor particularly useful as it rapidly tapers to extinction.

In every case the singer must lift up and lighten the tone in order to engage the pharyngeal which must be *willed in* every time, otherwise it might be by-passed.

Never can the pharyngeal be engaged by thrust of breath, but by a combination of lightness and tension of the vibrator, by a *willed* nervous-mental energy translating itself into muscular action.

There are individual exceptions, of course, but we must point out that it is by no means easy to make perfectly graduated *decrescendos* on high notes when employing only the basic voice; and even so, they are obtained at the cost of much wondering anxiety and will lack therefore that sense of buoyant freedom which expresses ease of execution. But why all the preoccupation when the pharyngeal is only too willing, and competent, to co-operate and finish the job with a minimum of effort? How many tenors today can execute a perfect *messa di voce*, how many can taper their high notes down to a perfect *pianissimo*, sustain them and build them up again with a perfectly graduated *crescendo?*

Sometimes in a tenor voice, and without any particular study, all three mechanisms are perfectly integrated by nature; that is to

* Even as the tenor's pharyngeal-falsetto tonal mixture has much in common with the tones of a contralto or mezzo, so these two categories sound like tenors at times, particularly when they consciously, or unconsciously, employ a mixture of basic and pharyngeal on the said series of notes.

say, the singer is able to pass from falsetto to the pharyngeal and then on to the basic smoothly without a tonal break, hitch, or hold-up, and, in the same breath, back again through the pharyngeal to the falsetto with the same oil-smooth action. In these particular cases nature has, through recondite circumstances, *completed* her work—as sometimes she thinks fit to do, to show us one and all what a *completely natural* voice is, and how it operates, and what tonal effects it produces. On the other hand, she is generally very remiss in this sense and apparently is content to leave things in an unfinished state, albeit with full mechanical potentialities, under the assumption that man will exert himself to complete the work. Indeed it is far better so, for such industry, such striving, is creative of both art and the artist.

More often than not, however, there is discontinuity of mechanism reflected in discontinuity of tone, a "gap", therefore, between one mechanism and the next, a tonal break in a downward direction followed by a slithering up-sweep; this peculiarity is generally more pronounced between the pharyngeal and the basic. In every case the so-called "gap" is due to lack of muscular development of, and within, the pharyngeal layer, and the obvious remedy is the systematic exercise and development of the mechanism by itself. Whereupon the bottom part of the pharyngeal will develop downwards, so to speak, and finally dovetail into the upper part of the basic, assuring thereby the required *muscular continuity*.

If there is a "gap" between the falsetto and the pharyngeal, then both mechanisms must be exercised separately in order to secure the full muscular development that finally spells continuity. The bottom part of the falsetto layer will then be felt to dovetail into the upper edge of the pharyngeal.

Most female voices can produce falsetto tone, particularly on the high pitches. For *p* and *pp* effects, sopranos in particular can produce a flute-like tone on the high notes with just the falsetto mechanism, and then make a *crescendo* into the basic voice with perfect continuity (women have no pharyngeal on their head notes); generally there is no "gap" or break during the process. As a matter of fact, the light soprano and coloratura can effectively employ the falsetto as a "pointer" or guide for the ensuing basic tone, for it is practically infallible as regards tone "placing" or tuning—or what the Italians call *impostazione della voce*.

In some of the bigger calibre sopranos, however, the dovetailing from falsetto to the real voice seems to be physically impossible without a tonal "break". Gentle persuasion will often solve the problem where violence invariably fails.

N.B.—These and other considerations have given and still give rise to much speculation anent the falsetto voice and the mechanism producing it: Some investigators (who ought to know better) have attributed it to the so-called false cords, which are merely the edges of two small pockets suspended, so to speak, above the true cords. To discount this idea we may add that they are not even built for the function of vibrator: they have no power of adjustment (save that of lateral approximation during phonation), no shortening process, no thinning process, no vertical tensioning mechanism; in short, nothing appertaining to a vibrator that must be adjusted to suit variations in pitch. Furthermore, there is an actual gap separating the false and the true cords, a gap that never can be closed by muscular or any other development. Against all such guesswork one threefold factor stands out in disproof, positive and unassailable, viz. (1) there is absolutely no muscular continuity; (2) no contiguity of mechanism; (3) no vibratory connection. In fact, vocal vibrations do not possess the acrobatic tendencies of the electric spark, and cannot therefore jump a gap to engage a lower mechanism. It is obvious that there can be no tonal continuity where there is no muscular continuity of mechanism. It is extraordinary how certain investigators and writers on voice production should have ignored such self-evident truths.

Sensations of vocal tone, when resulting from *correct* mechanical adjustments, are all-revealing as regards the processes involved.* Any singer, particularly a tenor, who, naturally or through

---

* After all, it was precisely *correct* sensations of vocal tone accruing from the constantly accurate mechanical adjustments of the *completely natural* voice—carefully examined and analysed in considerable number over a period of time by a number of enthusiastic exponents of the divine art—which constituted the concrete foundations of the old Italian School, ultimately raising an edifice to a peak of technical and executive perfection. The conclusions drawn from a process of induction (based on such correct tonal sensations) revealed the mechanical processes involved, the whole being synthetized into what ultimately was called vocal technique, in which anatomical considerations hardly came into the picture, if at all. The *completely* natural voice is a typically Italian product. A great artist is not produced by voice alone, however, no matter its technical perfection and quality of tone. How could such a school of singing have been built up except on Nature's own perfect model? (See footnotes, pp. 32, 202.)

training, has the three mechanisms well amalgamated, will tell you: (1) that according to well-defined sensations the three voices or mechanisms—falsetto, pharyngeal, and basic—form part of one perfectly homogeneous vibrating whole; or, in other words, he actually *feels* they are embedded in *one* operational unit; (2) that the sensation of *tonal continuity*, when passing from one mechanism or voice to the next, informs him in no mistakable terms how the three mechanism-voices are *physically contiguous*, and that they dovetail or merge one into the other, forming one vibrating network; (3) that each of the three is separable at will for creating its own individual, characteristic tone, and that they can also be made to merge and mix at will as one continuous vibrating unit for producing characteristic mixed tones; (4) that mechanical and therefore tonal development (falsetto-pharyngeal-basic) obtains in a *downward* direction with an oil-smooth action; equally, the return excursion: basic, pharyngeal, falsetto, is smooth in action. Only the singer himself can have perceptive knowledge of the three mechanisms; the laryngoscope never.

In the return upward excursion: basic-pharyngeal-falsetto, some voices, naturally or untrained in this particular art, encounter a "gap", or slithering of the tone with or without an actual break, particularly during the transition from the basic to the pharyngeal. And sometimes on attempting to enter the falsetto from the pharyngeal there is also a slight (or pronounced) slithering tendency of the tone before the falsetto gets properly engaged. We call it a slithering break, for want of a better term. The feeling is that one loses control of the tone. And it is only after the moaning slither and possible break characterizing this loss of tonal control that the required mechanism gears in. More often than not the return upward excursion is more difficult of accomplishment than the downward one.

And because of the greater difficulty encountered on the return journey from basic to pharyngeal, it is absolutely necessary to *support* the tone—which really means supporting the actual laryngeal machinery as a whole with the underlying breath. Note that we say support, and *not* upward drive, even as a buttress, a prop, a pillar, *supports* but has no active upward drive or thrust. It is precisely when the tone is being tapered down in order to effect the entry into the pharyngeal that this breath support is more than ever necessary. Which support, however, must be "girded" by a sufficiently intense mental-nervous energy (bordering on a state of excitement), which is as intangible as it is effective in this and in many other respects. This support is not felt to be so much physical as "ethereally" substantial.

An important point to remember about the pharyngeal is, that as it is part and parcel of the vocal cord mechanism, it is naturally also subject to the process of gradual elimination of its "mass" in both length and depth even though, as a mechanism, it has very little mass, little depth, and is of limited length, seeing that by the time it comes into effective operation at F, fifth line, in tenors, the mass of the vocal cords themselves will have undergone considerable "elimination" (when production is correct); furthermore, *the pharyngeal is subject of course to vowel modification in relation to pitch.* The student must bear in mind the fact of this modification when exercising the pharyngeal by itself, whatever the vowel employed; for is it not part of the cord mechanism?

During the period of *isolated* pharyngeal development with the special exercises given below, it will be necessary at first to use a very flat, closed *eh* vowel sound, as explained above, in order the better to seek out, engage, and isolate the mechanism itself. The student must literally *feel his way* to it carefully, delicately but firmly. But once it has been discovered and well developed as a separate unit (separate in the sense that when employed it apparently lives, moves, and has its being in a world of its own), it will readily respond to any and all vowels.

The pharyngeal is eminently a producer of resonance. Provided there be a small percentage of basic on which to *found* it, the mixed quality of the tonal product will invariably have body and brilliance, and fine carrying power. High notes are easily produced in this way and sustained, without the fantastic drive and general all-out effort to which we are now more or less accustomed and which is reflected in the singer's frowning anxiety.

And now a word of warning: During the first period of study, say a fortnight, the pharyngeal itself should not be worked for more than about ten or fifteen minutes at a time, once a day. It is inclined to be rather fatiguing at first. Let not this deter, however, for any such (athletic) fatigue will be temporary and salutary. Like the entire vibrating network, the pharyngeal mechanism has extraordinary powers of recuperation and gaily accepts, and quickly settles down to, the new work required of it.

Work the pharyngeal by itself systematically every day, allowing no falsetto and no basic whatever to creep in and mix with it. After the above first period of work add five minutes to the daily work every week so that at the end of about three months one hour's pharyngeal practice per day is reached. Don't be afraid: it will stand up to the work, for, in the last analysis, it is the "toughest" part of the vibrating network, and the gradual build-up in these three months' exercise develops its natural powers of resistance to fatigue, in no small degree. If you cannot possibly spare so much time just for the pharyngeal, try and devote at least a good half hour daily. Above all, *rest* a few seconds (15 to 30, or more) after each exercise. The rest factor is highly important, and more so than most singers realize; it applies to all vocal study and work. The vocal organs need short periods of rest during work.

The tenor student, during his work on the unmixed pharyngeal mechanism, must be prepared to produce tones which are the reverse of beautiful (his sense of self-importance may well experience a shock), because it is admittedly a crude affair on its own and produces most ungrateful sounds (even as salt, vinegar, lemon juice, etc. are harsh by themselves when unmixed with softeners), which, however, acquire quality when harnessed to either the falsetto or the basic. This crude sound of the pharyngeal used to be known as "the old woman's cackle" by exponents of the old School. On the other hand, the utility of this mechanism is prodigious, for it supplies the key to every refinement of *mezzavoce* singing, and is a begetter of tonal intensity.

Once the pharyngeal itself is adequately developed (this may take anything from six to sixteen months, according to the individual voice) percentages of basic should be introduced, small at first and then in increasing degree. Firstly the student will readily feel the splendid isolation as the pharyngeal is developing on its own, and then the dual sensation of the two mechanisms working simultaneously. By fully developing first the pharyngeal on its own it will be easy to dovetail it into the basic without a tonal slither or break. The *messa di voce* (*pp-p-mp-mf-f-mf-mp-p-pp*) should be attempted, and practised at length, and worked and worked until perfection of tonal graduation is attained. Whereupon small percentages of falsetto can be introduced (by "lifting up" slightly and *willing* the falsetto in).

Even as the pharyngeal voice by itself is unpleasing to the ear, so the falsetto by itself is useless because its tone is spineless; but judiciously mixed with the now developed pharyngeal it acquires substance for itself and imparts to the pharyngeal its own carpeting softness. As the old School used to say, *the falsetto is the pile of the pharyngeal carpet.* The pharyngeal puts life, lustre and intensity into both the falsetto and the basic; this is particularly true of the tenor's high notes. Falsetto is the velvet cloak for the steely pharyngeal, and the latter provides a solid base for the falsetto.

As the falsetto is produced by the thin upper edges of the vocal cords *only* when they are slightly ovaliform during phonation, and as the pharyngeal is produced with the same edges, with the cords no longer ovaliform but closely approximated (linear) during phonation, it is obvious that in order to introduce a percentage of falsetto into the pharyngeal it will be necessary (apart from "lifting up" and *willing* it in, as stated above) to ease somewhat the tension of the pharyngeal. The more the tension of the pharyngeal is eased the more the edges separate towards the ovaliform, and the degree of release is compensated by the introduction of falsetto in equal degree.

To abandon any such falsetto percentage in order to return to the pure unmixed pharyngeal, all we have to do is to exert a *slight* downward pressure, the effect of which is to approximate the cords to the linear again and restore their tension.

It is well to exercise the voice also with the mixed tone of falsetto-pharyngeal, abandoning the falsetto at times (while sustaining the note on one breath) to produce pure pharyngeal and then renewing the mixture; which interplay should be thoroughly mastered also in the case of the mixed pharyngeal-basic tone.

Be it noted that the aforesaid downward tonal pressing must be exercised with great care (and delicacy, in a sense); it is mainly mental, so there must be no actual deliberate physical pressing at any time, anywhere. The reaction to this downward thought is sufficient. Will the student please bear this in mind?

The same downward-engaging thought operates also when it is desired to gear the pharyngeal into the basic. When the downward engaging from pharyngeal to basic is pressed to the maximum, the former will be eliminated and cease to function; the basic only remains to continue the tone. It is a matter of *touch;* and, as we all know, touch is capable of being educated to extreme sensitiveness.

The pharyngeal, as a mechanism, is resiliently firm even though its cordal layer is extremely shallow, and is airtight in the sense that no breath (i.e. pressure-air) escapes past the vibrant cords, whereas the falsetto mechanism offers little resistance and permits a considerable leakage of breath, not usefully employed in producing sound, and therefore causing a certain degree of tonal attenuation.

When the pharyngeal is mixed, as above, it cannot prevent a certain escape of breath through the falsetto and consequent attenuation of the tone because the falsetto is a breath waster.

As the singer passes in a downward direction from falsetto to pharyngeal he gets the feeling of "standing", vocally speaking, on a slightly lower plank; and the same sensation obtains as he passes from the pharyngeal to the basic, the latter feeling being more substantial than the former.

When produced on the same pitch and with the same vowel, all three voices have one and the same focal point, or point of impingement; the transition from one mechanism to another, either way, does *not* alter the actual location of the tonal focus. The tonal focus is therefore *one* for all three voices (on the same pitch and with same vowel). We have purposely repeated this fact. But if the vowel be changed on that same pitch, or the pitch changed while retaining the same vowel, or if both pitch and vowel are changed, then naturally in every case there will be a change of location of the three-voice focus.

All these things added will give to the singer that measure of confidence both in himself and in his instrument which casts out all fear of high notes—the bugbear of all singers whose technical knowledge is poor, or non-existent.

The development of the pharyngeal mechanism is of considerable assistance in correcting that atrocious universal complaint known as the "wobble", for, when adequately strengthened, it acts as a "girder" and irons out the wavering wrinkles. The author has corrected the tremolo in many voices, male and female, with the aid of the pharyngeal combined with the correctives advocated in *The Science and Sensations of Vocal Tone.*

Hereunder are a few exercises suitable for developing the pharyngeal. The student himself can make up many others on the same line. It is not so much what, but *how* he sings them.

z

1. eh ——————————————————————

2. eh ——————————————————————

3. eh ——————————————————————

4. eh ——————————————————————

5. eh ir eh ir eh ir etc.

6. eh   eh   eh   eh   eh   ir   ir   ir

N.B.—*Women should start these exercises an octave lower, then transpose up a semitone at a time.*

CHAPTER XXIII

THE HIGH LARYNX DISABILITY

ONE OF THE MOST DISTRESSING IMPERFECTIONS is that of the high larynx. It is encountered particularly in English-speaking countries; and it is therefore reasonable to suggest that it is due, in part, to the slovenly manner of speech habituated from infancy rather than to the character of the language itself. But it is also due undoubtedly to slight and sometimes pronounced anomalies of structure of the internal mouth, tongue, chin, teeth, neck muscles, and angle at which head rests on the neck. In most cases it is mainly a congenital weakness of the depressor muscles.

The number of students afflicted with this physical disability is much greater than one would suppose; and to judge by the number that has sought the author's advice, few teachers seem to be familiar with the symptoms, let alone the correctives, that accompany the high-larynx abnormity.

Place the tip of your finger on the larynx (the protuberance popularly known as Adam's apple or the voice-box) and open your mouth in the ordinary way. You will find that its position remains unchanged; but if, still retaining your fingertip on the larynx, you yawn, you will feel how it assumes a much lower position in the throat; the lowering is due to the action of the depressor muscles. If you now close your mouth the larynx will be felt to rise, assuming its original or normal position of rest. Now swallow, and it will be felt to rise considerably. This raising is performed by the elevator muscles. The high larynx in singing results from a greater strength of the elevators overcoming the depressors; it may be that the development of the former is abnormal and that of the latter subnormal. In most cases, however, it is mainly a question of strengthening weakish depressor muscles.

For the purposes of singing, the larynx should assume a normal position in the throat, normal to the above-cited extremes of depression and elevation: That is, not too high or too low. This normal we call "floating level". Should the larynx, during the act

355

of singing, assume a higher position than the normal or floating level, it is evidence of weakness in the depressor muscles.

It is easy to detect the disability if one proceeds as follows: Sing slowly up the scale from the lowest note first on AH. Particularly from the medium pitches upwards it will be noted that the tone gradually becomes more open or "white", while on the head notes it may be so open that it "bleats"—if it has not been choked off completely before reaching them. Now sing up the scale first on EH, then on EE (the latter being the best test of all because for their production the tongue arches and pulls the larynx up in greater degree than it does for the other vowels); and as the elevator muscles are so much stronger than the depressors, the upward pull is excessive. On reaching the upper medium pitches the tone begins to choke off and is completely strangled to extinction on the head notes which simply are not forthcoming. Another marked symptom is a pronounced general stiffening of the neck and jaw, while the chin juts out rigidly, trembling visibly. The all-round strain is obvious, and the singer himself has a distinctly uncomfortable feeling.

The remedy for the high larynx weakness lies in exercising the larynx itself in such a way as will gradually increase the strength of the depressor muscles to the point of equalizing that of the elevator muscles. This corrective exercising embraces a range of *gradually darkening* vowel colours, i.e. AH², AH³, AW, OH, OO and U (as in *put*). To produce these darker vowel sounds the larynx is *obliged* (by the gentle persuasion exercised by the very fact of the vowel-rounding) to descend in degree and take with it the tongue, while the soft palate rises in equal degree. It is this lowering work that will strengthen the depressors. There must be no attempt to physically lower the larynx; that does no good at all and only imposes a further strain. The depressor muscles cannot be strengthened directly, but indirectly through the action of the shaping of the mouth-pharynx cavity for producing the afore-mentioned dark vowel sounds.

It is best, at the outset, to confine the corrective work to, say, about the first octave or little more, then add a note or two as progress is made. Slow sustained exercises are best. The EH and EE should be left alone for the time being, then gradually introduced. Considerations of space will not permit the development of this subject as we would have liked.

CHAPTER XXIV

CONCLUDING

ALL VOICES have within them a principle of growth that under the influence of time and well-directed study can be carried to that fullness which alone a ripe experience can give. As in the embryo there is fine promise of adolescent completeness through gradual development, as in the gradual flowering from bud to blossom, as from caterpillar to butterfly, so in the mechanically incomplete and undeveloped voice (as most voices are in varying degree) there is the promise of completion.

Both in this and in the parent work the keen student will find clear and satisfying answers to most if not all the questions of technique that may be troubling him. In both works the text, illustrated by numerous diagrams, lays bare the mechanical processes obtaining within the larynx proper, and the resultant tonal effects (sensations of vocal tone) within the whole resonating system consisting of mouth, pharynx, and head cavities. It elaborates in extraordinary detail the behaviour of the sound-beams accruing from the different vowel-cum-vibrator settings from the lowest to the highest pitches, demonstrating withal how tonal "placing" or focusing relative to every vowel and pitch is secured on a *natural* basis. The average student who is prepared to *study* the contents will be enabled to check up on his own production. He must bear in mind, however, the fact of slight variations in the behaviour of the sound-beam and in the tonal sensations which assuredly are encountered in the individual voice. For no two things are exactly alike in the world; there are infinite variations in shape: marked, minute, microscopical. And so no two heads are exactly alike in shape, externally and internally.

It may be that, in the opinion of some, both works are rather too elaborate. Detail, however, should not deter but inspire and stimulate one to work with greater emphasis and determination. Essential details, especially when magnified, must surely attract the true lover of this art of arts for its own sake. Is it not detail enlarged under the microscope that both thrills and enlightens the scientist, be he physicist, physiologist, biologist or metallurgist?

Again, a certain type of student may feel that the writer is navigating in a tonal sea uncharted and forbidding; but this first impression is due solely to unfamiliarity with a subject presented on novel lines. There is nothing extraordinary about this or the parent work: they merely represent the accumulated experience of very many years of devoted study and practice. But they do require unremitting study.

The study of vocal technique can never be a study of surfaces, however highly polished.

We feel that the technical exposition in the two works is well suited to the needs of the present generation which looks to Science as the corroborator and justifier of all claims to a knowledge of the truth. In this connection I desire to acknowledge above all my indebtedness to that eminent acoustician, the Rev. Noel Bonavia-Hunt, M.A., who has devoted as much study and experiment to the acoustical and aerodynamical properties and behaviour of vocal tone as anybody living; the Scientific Notes he has contributed to this treatise will be found highly instructive.

It is extraordinary how as a result of striving, of repeated trial and error, flashes of intuition pierce suddenly the dark chambers of thought; small at first, these rays of illumination grow in brilliance and duration. As each aspect of technique is revealed it should be embodied in the mounting fabric. To strive is to expect. Expectancy generates impulsion. Thought multiplies itself. Once the cycle of ideas is set in motion there is seemingly no end to their sequence.

Desire must be strong, determined, unfaltering on a high plane of thought that will carry forward effort upon effort, overcoming with equal persistance every obstacle and setback. The beacon ignited by momentary failure should reveal where the student's knowledge is incomplete. What is this striving on the part of the really keen student primarily for technical perfection but the pursuit of beauty and its ultimate manifestation through individual effort. In such desire there is quality.

Those who wish to travel the whole road must disburden themselves of impatience from the outset. "We have to make our way among pitfalls and obstacles," wrote Sir Oliver Lodge (*Evolution and Creation*), "to make progress and with difficulty, and gradually to learn what is true by finding out what is false." This, from one of the world's greatest scientists. And Huxley, another great man, wrote: "Clear knowledge of what one does not know is just as important as knowing what one does know."

The student should not be discouraged if he fails at first to apprehend the full meaning of every detail of technique as it arises; understanding on such a subject can come only gradually, obscurely even at first. Once detail upon detail is mastered, synthesis is both easy and rapid. Whereas analysis resolves a thing into its constituent parts (splits it up in detail), synthesis composes or puts together the details to form a working whole. And this actually is what the master-singer's mind is doing all the time he is in action. In fact, a characteristic of the truly great singer is that almost careless ease which masks precise accuracy; all the necessary details of technique being gathered up and compounded into a focused tonal point—on every pitch and with every vowel.

Obstacles to apprehension of the truth lie in the student's own mental approach, particularly when imbued with prepossessions as to what constitutes and what does not constitute vocal technique. So many seem unable to give free rein to the intuitive faculty. And so many fail to recognize the truth instinctively when they meet it; a kind of mental cussedness leads rather to the acceptance of fancy for fact. Error noisily rattles the door of the external ear, whereas truth reaches the inner ear in gentle whispers. The noise of erroneous methods has a great appeal to many.

Even as the rose unfolds in the sunlight while its roots seek the depth and darkness of the soil, so the resonance, the tonal product, emerges into the outer space while the vibrator (vocal cords) basically responsible for it, is rooted in the dark recess of the laryngeal chamber. The vibrator and resonator units are inseparable halves of the same thing: they are soul-mates, male and female.

Beauty of vocal tone, enhanced by emotion, expression and accent, can *only* obtain through a mechanical medium that is perfectly adjusted and "tuned" for every pitch and with all vowels. A sensitively responsive mechanism rests upon accurate, well-tuned adjustment in strict obedience to certain known laws. And what is a law? Science observes how a particular part of nature behaves in certain circumstances and calls an unfailing repetition of that function a law. Laws are therefore known as "memoria technica". Without them we could not theorize nor accumulate knowledge.

The repetition of the same vocal sensation as experienced by the singer provides a *fact*, when the sensation is a correct one in relation to pitch and vowel. (And by sensation we mean the same vowel sung repeatedly on the same pitch with *exactly* the same all-round adjustment of the vibrator and resonator systems, the same sensation of sound-beam and size of focal point.) And what is a correct sensation but a right thought or idea translated into concrete actuality. Physically speaking, it is the grosser manifestation of vocal cord undulation transformed, aye, transfigured, into the finer substance of focused resonance. It is *thought* resolved into *thing:* The Voice of the Mind, a correct thing rising from a correct thought.

If the mastery of vocal technique in its every detail is felt to be a challenge to the student intellectually and physically, as it indeed should be, let him go right ahead and he will find that through mastery it becomes a comfort. Vocal technique must call out the best in the student before he can find the best in it. After intelligently striving, experimenting and practising, the student will feel unexpected forces closing round him, as it were, rallying always to his aid. It is an axiom in all progress that the more we conquer the more easily we conquer. Let him bear in mind that every achievement has left behind a trail of innumerable failures.

That which antagonises is actually a helpmeet; and so the student will find his skill sharpening against the difficulties that technique may present. Every battle with a difficulty tempers endeavour to a finer degree; every successful encounter quickens the student's power of execution through a keener understanding of precept and practice.

Failure on the student's part to externalize through appropriate vocal tone such physiological, acoustic and aerodynamical laws as apply to and govern vocal mechanism and tone, is no proof that such laws do not exist; it merely indicates his inability to understand and apply them.

Let the student beware of the modern guesswork, conjectural methods and of the idiotic ideas of which they are mainly composed, for once accepted by him they first make a clown of reason and then put it to flight; they are a denial of rationality, and have no basis in *fact*. It matters not one whit the legend that such and such a great singer taught, in retirement, one or the other method. But if true, as in some cases it was, then the once great artist descended to a low plane to dispense evil compounds, obviously at a loss to pass on his knowledge and experience to others, lacking the art of explanation. But good or bad teacher, students will always flock to worship at the shrine of fame. "How sharp the point of this remembrance" (*The Tempest*).

* * *

EPILOGUE

Art is akin to the sublime eagle whose flight is bounded only by Heaven. Of all art, singing is nearer to expressing the Divinity. In music, as in all art, there is a part accessible to our endeavours: the thousand and one artificialities of musical science and grammar which serve to manifest the primitive idea. But the sublime part, the essence of the art, is either possessed in the natural state of development, or is lying dormant and unexercised in the depths of soul.

Melody is the soul of music; harmony, counterpoint, tonality, rhythmic combinations, and instrumentation are its body.

Voice is the true vehicle for expressing the soul of music, and the soul of man.

There is a force, a great fount of good and power behind the voice of a good singer. Every effort to redeem and restore to present and future generations the traditions of a glorious past, every attempt to advance the frontiers of knowledge, assuredly would be worthy of the divine art of singing.

Oh! The little More,
And how much it is!
And the little less,
And what worlds away.
Browning

APPENDIX

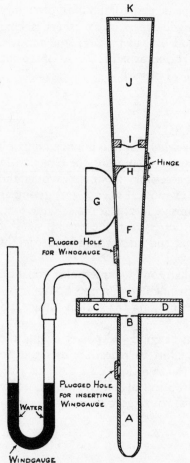

BONAVIA-HUNT EXPERIMENTAL VOICE-PIPE

EXPOSITION OF THE FIGURE

K   Top lid (circular) with circular hole admitting outside air (cf. *nasal cavities*).

J, H   Removable top section of resonator (cf. *head cavities*).

I   Paper diaphragm (8 mils) set in sympathetic vibration by sound-beam from E (cf. *soft palate*).

G   Output to atmosphere (cf. *mouth*).

F   Coupling of resonator (cf. *throat and pharynx*).

E   Aperture at which vortices strike inside edges and convert lateral air-waves into sound-waves which reinforce the sound-waves from the reeds (cf. *false vocal cords*).

C, D   Intermediate air chamber in which the jet from B is just sufficient to maintain the vortex system which produces air-waves in this chamber. The pressure is so reduced that no reading is shown at the wind-gauge (cf. *ventricles*).

B   Pair of thin, tightly stretched elastic para-rubber membranes acting as reeds (cf. *true cords*).

A   Air pressure channel from bellows (cf. *trachea*). (Pressure registered in windgauge, 8 inches of water displacement.)

NOTES. (1) With resonator (E K) removed, a *thin* reedy note is produced; pitch varying with pressure at A. Harmonics from 1st to 8th well developed.

(2) With resonator F H only, the note is less reedy and gains in power and *fullness;* pitch slightly lowered; 5th, 6th and 7th harmonics considerably reduced.

(3) With top portion H J added, the note is *richer* and louder still, with lowered pitch; certain harmonics above the 8th slightly stronger.

N.B. (a) No attempt is made to reproduce the actual materials, etc., of the original human mechanism, which would be impossible.

(b) Object of pipe is to illustrate the basic *aerodynamic* conditions and functions of the human vocal mechanism and apparatus.

INDEX